William Jarman

U.S.A. Uncle Sam's Abscess

Hell Upon Earth for U.S. Uncle Sam

William Jarman

U.S.A. Uncle Sam's Abscess
Hell Upon Earth for U.S. Uncle Sam

ISBN/EAN: 9783743419452

Manufactured in Europe, USA, Canada, Australia, Japa

Cover: Foto ©Suzi / pixelio.de

Manufactured and distributed by brebook publishing software (www.brebook.com)

William Jarman

U.S.A. Uncle Sam's Abscess

U.S.A.

UNCLE SAM'S ABSCESS,

OR

HELL UPON EARTH

FOR

US.

UNCLE SAM.

W. JARMAN, ESQ., K.G.L., T.C.K.,

Knight of the Grand Legion of North America,

WHO SUFFERED TWELVE YEARS IN

THE MORMON HELL ON EARTH,

AS ONE OF THE

"VIRGINS WITHOUT GUILE,"

AND

A PRIEST AFTER THE ORDER OF MELCHIZEDEK:

WHERE

POLYGAMY, INCEST, AND MURDER

ARE TAUGHT AND PRACTISED AS RELIGION UNDER THE

"ALL SEEING EYE,"

AND THE SIGN

"HOLINESS UNTO THE LORD."

Copyright secured in both Hemispheres.

EXETER: ENGLAND, 1884.

PRINTED AT H. LEDUC'S STEAM PRINTING WORKS, EXETER, ENGLAND.

AMERICAN PREFACE.

It's an inveterate fact—" Uncle Sam " is afflicted. Thorns in the flesh—messengers of Satan buffet him. I portray the malady, and prescribe its remedy. A Morbid Ulcerous Cancer afflicts the body-politic of America. I name it "U.S.A."—Uncle Sam's Abscess, or Hell upon Earth for U.S—Uncle Sam." The Abscess first appeared at the Top of the Head (of New York State.) Shifting its position it infected the vital parts (of Ohio, Missouri, and Illinois), and finally settled in the Heart (of the American Continent). There it swells so alarmingly as to shock the whole system (All true Citizens). The administration of Anti-Polygamy Act Physic of 1862, the Poland and other Pills (Bills) prove abortive; each dose fails to act—(the Acts are inoperative.) Quacks and timid Doctors lack skill or *fear to lance*. (I saw no regiments of Lancers there.) It needs Surgeons skilled in the use of scientific instruments, (Armstrong, Gatling, and Eighty-one ton Guns.) "The aid of Foreign Skill was sought." (Secretary Evart's Letter to the Foreign Powers).

Foreign Surgeons not understanding the case are ineffective. Unfortunately, (or fortunately, as the case may prove) circumstances forced me to a dire *inside study of the matter*, which made me familiar with both Disorder and Patient. It's a stubborn case, requiring prompt decisive action, and solid practical treatment. First, United States Bayonets must pierce and open it; then purge with Powders and Pills (both Ball and Shell from Cannon and Mortars of American Artillery), together with an injection of Grape, Canister, and Shrapnell. This will eradicate every taint of *the foul blot*, and restore the body-politic to robust health, and pristine vigor. Then will the Great Republic enjoy Life, Liberty, and Happiness; while mighty millions will rejoice that the power which Abolished Slavery also Emancipated Religion from the curse of Polygamy, Incest, Murder, and Crime. But, permit its continuance, then America's Noble Institutions—its true pride—will totter and fall; and Tyranny, Anarchy, and Oppression triumphantly reign. For the Utah Evil contains the seed of a most corrupt, cruel, and wicked Despotism. Though none can deny the existing Abscess, some may question my Remedy. Hence I suggest the milder, but less potent treatment, *Disfranchisment*, thereby cutting from the body-politic, every particle of this Foul Ulcer. For *out it must come*, or farewell to free Republican Institutions.

But Americans seem hard to arouse: they are "wide awake Yankees" in some respects, but not in all. Meandering near 20 years through America's Great Republic, and viewing with good eyesight the vast dominion of my dear Uncle Sam, I saw a thing or two, "you bet." I saw Uncle's Liberty Pole, but it had a *night cap* on. It's been *fast asleep* since the *Blacks* were freed. Utah's WHITE SLAVES pitifully cry, "Wake up and free us!" America *talks in her sleep*, and answers: "N-o! W-h-i-t-e T-r-a-s-h a-i-n-t s-o i-m-p-o-r-t-a-n-t a-s N-i-g-g-e-r-s." Actions speak louder than words.

Oh! Americans, chop your Liberty Poles into kindling wood! or wake up and free your WHITE SLAVES IN THE WEST, held *now* in a slavery of body and soul, worse than ever existed in the South, and *far more filthy*. Burn that *dear* old Cap, declare to the World you no longer love liberty, decency, law, and order: that America is the filthiest, most lawless, and slavish country in the World, unless you *at once* clean out THE NASTY FILTH existing and growing in your midst, and which ruins the bodies and souls of hundreds of thousands. I saw the Proud American Eagle with its wings clipped, chained in the Great Basin of the Rocky Mountains. I saw what was once a grand and noble thing "THE STAR SPANGLED BANNER," *trailed and trampled in the dust at Salt Lake City*. I saw "my Uncle's Executive"-- my eyes being *in loco*, I saw some "hang out their shingle, TO BE SOLD OR LET." This put me in mind of the Poet :—"When infamous venality grown bold; writes on its bosom To Be Let or Sold." I saw my Uncle's Free Love Oneida Community, his Shaker Dancing Dervishes, his Celebate Harmonist crowd of Old Maids and Batchelors, and his Great Filthy Harem at Utah. This is a perfect HELL ON EARTH, inhabited by greater, meaner, and more dispicable Devils than the fiends of the Bottomless Pit. *I challenge Earth or Hell to produce as mean Devils as Utah can*; I have heard Brigham Young throw out the same challenge from the pulpit. The Devil himself wont accept the challenge: he knows the Devils in the Great Bottomless Brimstone Basin are not half as bad as the fiends in the Great Basin of the Rocky Mountains. The challenge remains unaccepted.

In my Uncle's Harem and Purgatory these "Meanest Devils" introduced me to Lucifer, the Boss of the other Hell. He seemed perfectly intimate and on the best of terms with the Boss of the UNITED STATES HELL, Utah. This is no opposition hell—it's CO-OPERATIVE in every sense. Both Boss Devils tried their bluff game on me; said "I'd make a BOSS DEVIL;" and anointed me with their unholy fat. I had a good basting so as to roast well and be *tender*, but I *hardened*, resisted the Devils and said, "You git," but it was no go: "nary a peg" would they budge. I was "*delivered over to the Buffetings of Satan*" FOR 1,000 YEARS. I asked Brigham to curtail the sentence, and call it 20 years, or for life; but no, he said, "not a day less, not even 999 years and 364 days, but 1,000 years." Think of it! The time will soon expire, or death relieve all "Lifers and Long Sentence" Criminals in Convict Prisons; whereas *I*, having served 15 years, have 985 *years more* to put in— *Death wont relieve me:* it transfers me to the other co-operative concern yonder.

Out of *pure love* they wished to open my wind pipe, lest I should tell what I knew about Devils. The Anti-Lancet, Zoist, and modern Physicians, oppose bleeding, but Devils " go in for it." Thinking my British blood had too much " Johnny Bull Grit " in it, and fearing it would *boil over and scald the Devils,* they sought to lance my jugular vein, and let out this vile Anglo-Saxon blood *to atone for my sins.* I objected and said, "Not for Joe, oh, dear No !" or words to that effect. However they made it so *hot* for me, my blood boiled, and what little corpulance I possessed, diminished without the aid of Anti-Fat Remedies. The Devils then took a notion that if I longer remained above ground, the worms would be swindled out of their rations; so out of kindness to the worms they dug my grave and prepared to feed them. When *I looked into my grave* and saw the worms "out of grub," crawling in the bottom, poking their heads out at its sides and ends, and whetting their appetites, as it were, for a feast off my ribs, tenderloin, and prime cuts, somehow my boy-trick got the best of me—I placed the tip of my thumb on the end of my nose, and with fingers extended, exclaimed, " Don't you wish you may get it ?"

This bleeding and killing was to spiritualize me, " For a Spirit hath not flesh and bones as ye see me have." Besides, I was so wicked in resisting Devils, they said (Devils always quote Scripture), " Thou shalt not live out half thy days." I was yet under 35, or half the allotted days of man. Do not think, dear people, I lecture and write to make money ; I have all I care for now, and can live the balance of my days without making another cent. But over a new made *grave, dug for my body,* I swore, if spared to escape from that Sodom, I would do all in my power to expose its evils, as I know them to exist. This is why I lecture, and why I write this book, and if my humble efforts help root out and destroy the abominable evil, I HAVE NOT LIVED IN VAIN.

I take this opportunity to publicly thank the Rev. Dr. Talmage, Dr. Fulton, Dr. Newman, Rev. H. L. Morehouse, D.D., Rev. Walter M. Barrows, and the many other rev. gentlemen who gave me so much valuable aid in New York. In New England, and other parts of the United States, I am indebted, amongst many others, to the Rev. J. W. Hamilton, Rev. J. J. Lewis. Rev. J. M. Webster, Rev. W. A. Lamb, Rev. J. Noyes, Rev. G. W. Martin, Rev. A. Noon, Rev. G. S. Shaw, Rev. J. A. Corey, and Rev. E. H. Tuniclift, whose hearty co-operation made it easy for me to expose the great Utah evil in America. THE AUTHOR.

ENGLISH PREFACE.

This history of American Polygamy and Crime reviews Mormon Doctrine and Practice from the time Joseph Smith died and Brigham Young became its Notorious Leader, up to date. I deal with "Uncle Sam's Abscess" as it exists in the present age: for its inception, rise and progress years ago, has been amply dealt with by others, and did it but trouble Uncle Sam, this child of care would never impose this book upon long-suffering Britishers. But knowing it takes British blood, bone, and sinew to nourish it, and increase its growth: and having myself been drawn into the vortex of this filthy corruption—this Hell upon Earth, and narrowly escaped, it becomes my duty to warn my fellow citizens, and try to prevent them being allured into the *Great Basin* of crime, misery and woe. For after all that has been said and written about this AMERICAN HELL, *the half has never been told*. To-day the world knows but little of the goings on in THE YANKEE SODOM. I know it all, and so far as these pages allow, tell what I know of the Utah Latter-day Devils; who preach and practice as religion all the crime of the Decalogue. Their Missionaries come here with an open Bible, and seduce Good Christian People by tens of thousands, and drag them to a far worse Sodom than existed anciently. These Devilish Wolves come in the very best Sheep's Clothing, and appear as the Devil himself often does, "As an Angel of Light."

When the Devil's abroad the Devil a Saint will be,
When the Devil's at home, the Devil a Saint is he.
(*Hudibras slightly altered.*)

They come prepared "to deceive the very Elect," and are quite successful. The Sacred Garb they assume cover their nefarious schemes, and hellish aims, and not until we arrive in America's "Sodom," are we aware of their filthy and awfully wicked practices. There the Bible is cast aside to give place to other books, and even *newspapers*. Christ is Blasphemed; they say "He was a jolly good fellow, had lots of wives, and squalling brats." It shocks one trained a Christian to hear them Blaspheme Jehovah, Christ, and all sacred subjects. In Great Britain, Mormon Missionaries, to seduce Christians, preach Christianity far better than its own Ministers can. For Mormons belong to the

Devil, serve him, and get his aid: Mormons and Devils know Scripture well, can quote it to suit exactly, and beat any Christian D. D. who is in opposition to the Devil. Marvel not then, that I a Church member was entrapped. I wonder they do not catch every Christian by their glib talk. They nab scarce any but Christians, quite nine-tenths of their converts are from the Churches of Christendom. My object in giving this to the world, is to arouse Pastor and People, and warn them against those shrewd Yankee tricksters, who know how to use "soft soap." I am ashamed to think the Government allows her people to be "religiously" swindled under false pretences, and not pass laws to prevent it. I am also pained to find so much spent on the Clergy and Ministers of all denominations, while they allow their flocks to be taken by these Mormon Wolves, without even a word of caution. I would give anything to have been cautioned by my Minister and spared this curse of my life. It's no use crying over spilt milk; having been drawn into the evil, good may result by my telling what I know of it. In this work I give the true character of Utah's Abominations, whose Missionaries compass Sea and Land to make one proselyte. I aim to guard the innocent, and show the licentious and wicked their Paradise—where a life of Sin and Shame is Sanctified and Relished. All determined to lead a vicious life should leave their country for their country's good, and Emigrate at once to Utah. There they honor you, and you get the best positions for what you'd get put in jail for here! So don't stay here, pack up your duds, take the first steamer and be off to this Hell upon Earth. We can well spare you, and much rather have your room than your company. In Utah you will be a "Hail fellow well met," and have a jolly time. If you have a craving for Drink, Lust, or Murder, go to Utah! your keenest appetite will there be fully satisfied, and your valuable services command a premium. A word to the wise is sufficient—to Christians I say, Beware! Beware! Beware!

The Ministers, and the Ladies and Gentlemen who have helped in my work since my return from America, will be gratified to learn, that through their own and my efforts, all Mormon Missionaries have been driven from Devon and Cornwall, the only Counties I have as yet visited. I am preparing for a tour through *all* the English, Scotch, and Welsh Counties; and if similar aid and success follow me, truly the days of Mormon Missionaries in Great Britain are numbered. These Mormon vermin will meet the fate of the venomous reptiles of Ireland in the days of Saint Patrick, and every one of them will be driven from the shores of our dear old Native Land. To this end I labour, and may I not ask and expect the earnest aid and co-operation of every Christian Minister, every faithful Christian, and Philanthropist of this, our beloved Country.

As I say things hard to believe, and unless supported by indisputable evidence, would seem overdrawn, I copiously extract from Authentic Mormon Publications—"Journal of Discourses," "Millennial Star," "The Seer," "Deseret News," &c. Sold at the Mormon Book Depôts, 42, Islington, Liverpool; 19, Southerland Street, Pimlico, London, in England; and "Deseret News" Office, Salt Lake City, America. Also "The Salt Lake Tribune" and "Anti-Polygamy Standard," both published in Salt Lake City. Form Clubs, address Editor "Salt Lake Tribune," Salt Lake City, America, for terms of both; their perusal will well repay. All who can afford it should get "The Rocky Mountain Saints," by a Mormon High Priest Journalist. Price £1. Address—Appleton & Co., New York; or for 12s. get of Bryan, Brand & Co., St. Louis, U.S., "The Life and Confession of John D. Lee," A Mormon Bishop, who sat in Utah's "House of Lord's Spiritual;" and helped Murder 120 men, women and children by Mormon Authority; and was Executed by United States Authority. I give all I can from these, and other publications, and though I cram this 200 pages with small print, equal to 500 of larger type, yet I have to curtail the quotations very much, I wish all my readers who can to read up the whole of it. Booksellers can get them for you. Those out of print I so name. I give a brief account of my chequered life in the first chapter, which may interest some readers. Then I portray "Uncle Sam's Abscess," and I have no doubt by the time the reader gets through, he will say with me, "It is a perfect "Hell upon Earth." I have only to add just this:—

> There is on Earth a Hell, I know, for I've been there,
> But I got out, the tale to tell, and warn you of the snare.
> Wolves in sheeps' clothes, cry "Heaven Below!"
> List not to these your foes, or else, too late, you'll sure to know
>   Sorrow, and crime, and woes.
>
> It's in A-mer-i-ca, this Hell on Earth is found,
> The situation's quite O. K., but Liberty is bound,
> Its Bosses prate, "Break every law!   [of jaw,
> "Take more than one dear mate!" This brings a vast amount
>   More than I can relate.
>
> Suffice to say, just here, 'tis Hell on Earth to all,
> Who for more wives than one doth care, or list to Mormon call—
> "Lo Christ is there!" What downright lying!
> Its but a fearful snare. For Lust and Murder there they're plying,
>   Beware! Beware! Beware!

Done at Ye Ancient and Ye Honourable Citie of Exeter on this Ye First Day of April, Anno Domini, 1884, and between Ye 47th and Ye 48th Year of Ye Reign on this sad vale of tears of Ye trulie unfortunate,

WILLIAM JARMAN.

58, Parr Street, Exeter, Devon, England.

CHAPTER I.

The Author's Noble Birth—His Checkered Life—The Middle and Both Ends of it—Some Hard Facts.

Fate and misfortune conspiring against me, I was born in the Haymarket, London, instead of St. James' Palace. "So near and yet so far." To add insult to injury, and make me appear a natural born idiot, the truly sad event occurred on "All Fools Day," Anno Domini 1837. This cruel outrage upon an innocent babe and unsuspecting victim is not all; I often get "particular fits." Why is this thus? I had no fall out with Fate, and though I never loved Miss Fortune, I tried to bear with her, never shirked her, but "let her rip."* Yet behold this man-child with blood as Royal as any, and made fit to dwell in any "Court," dumped in The Old Haymarket. I feel worse now than at the time, for though stranded near the Royal Court a perfect wreck, I was reckless; but when in pensive thought I reflect, I feel "put out." I shall not put in, or attempt to establish a claim to the Throne lest I miss the Royal seat, and get a seat in jail with Sir Roger Tichborne: Between these two stools I come to the ground, and take the ground that "God made of One Blood all Nations of Men." That liberty is sweet, cry "sour grapes," and say "uneasy lays the head that wears a crown."

After all, my birth was not so bad as it may have been. I might have been born at the Agapemone, or in the Oneida Community: in either case I should have been a natural-born Orphan. I was supplied with a couple of parents—one more than most unfortunates get. My parents were of opposite sexes: I am a Middlesex man.† Like myself, my parents were of Noble Birth, having been born like anybody else. They were both Britons, that's a consolation; suppose they had been Hottentots, and I born to "bow down to gods of wood and stone?" Then again:

"I was not born a little slave to labor in the sun,
And wish I were but in my grave and all my labor done."

Oh, no! I was born in a Christian land, in the parish of a "Saint," where people get tired of life, and neither wish nor wait, but simply shuffle off this mortal coil by aid of a rope, a jump in the Thames, or by poison, razors, revolvers, and such like. Do not ask what time I was born—the rushlight burnt dim, and my eyes were so suffused with tears, I failed to see the clock. My mother (now eighty-five, and may be expected to tell the truth) says: "The first thing he did was to kick up a jolly row." She ought to know for she was there, and I cannot prove an *alibi*, but to speak thus of the first noble act of my life is just like her. Suppose I did kick up a row, effect follows cause, and show me a baby who would not kick up under such circumstances; then I will show you one that will fail to make *a mark* in the world. I made mine, and a very pretty mark it is when you come to look at it. If I remember correctly I expressed myself on that interesting occasion, woke my neighbours and informed them of my arrival on this "Terrestrial Bawl." They came at once to see *the stranger* and "wet" him. The benighted people of

---

* A Yankee phrase, which means let her do her best, or worst. R.I P., has another meaning, but wait 'til we get to Brigham Young's funeral.

† The Haymarket is in the County of Middlesex. My Mother belongs to the Female sex, my Father belonged to the Male sex, and I belong to Middlesex.

those dark ages used to wet babies at birth, christening, confirmation, and even at burial. In those days, Births, Deaths, and Marriages to be strictly legal must be "wetted." Profane History fails to record these ancient customs, and that posterity may learn of the cruel barbarities of their ancestors' "Sacred Rites," I here insert how it was done. The few friends present put themselves outside a bottle of Gin: a larger company managed to get outside of two or three bottles. This Gin being made of oil of vitriol, *acqua fortis* and alcohol, would burn like blazes, raise fury, and make the best friends fight. It often caused men to kill their wives and babies. Some got raving mad, and were straight jacketed in lunatic asylums, others cut their throats and otherwise mutilated themselves. Many disfigured themselves for life by shooting in at the ear a ball of lead, which would penetrate the brain, and rush out at the top of the head, and in various ways shoot, stab, and kill. Men, women, and children, lost what little sense they had, and became totally insensible. I have actually known people under its influence do penance by making their bed in a mud gutter, in the pouring rain, and as they made their bed so they lay in it. But then this was away back in the dark nineteenth century when the miserly people expected Archbishops to eke out a miserable existence on £15,000 a year, and other of the then "lights of the world" had to live on a similar ridiculously low scale of wages. Can we then wonder at the worse than Egyptian darkness of that day? Certainly not! I was not born a total abstainer, "London Gin" had helped me on the road. A Cockney once said to me, "It aint true that I was born in Sin, and in Sin did my mother conceive me." I replied "that all are born in Sin." He answered "No, in my case put G in the place of S, and say I was born in Gin, and in Gin did my mother conceive me, then you will speak the truth." How many can truthfully say the same?

The wetting was duly attended to, I yelling all the time. My mother, nurse, and neighbours considered my trouble "wind on the stomach;" they further considered gin a good thing for the wind. Does gin raise the wind? Many raise the wind to get gin. I have known gin "raise the Devil—the Prince and Power of the Air." In this sense it may raise the wind. It was decided I must have some gin and wet myself. I sucked it in and became insensible, or to use a Police Court phrase, "Drunk and Incapable."

* * * * *

I told the printer to put in these stars to note the blank that now intervened. I may have slept and snored like people do when drunk, but I am not going to tell what transpired while I slept. If the Roman Guards were bribed to say "His disciples came by night and stole him away while we slept" it is no reason why I should follow suit. Between my Birth and Christening the wind in my stomach increased, so did the yelling, and the all powerful gin remedy was applied in larger and more frequent doses, to settle the wind, knock me over, and keep me quiet.

This continued till four days after the Queen's eighteenth birthday, when my friends and neighbours all thought I was about to kick the bucket. Mind you, I never told them what I intended to do. I kept my own counsel; some babies would just kick the thing and get out of it; in fact, more than half the babies do, and a good job too, for a baby who wont put up with a few little inconveniences at the start, is not fit to "Battle with life." This chap was of different metal: when the doctors all said I was going, I said nothing, so they did not know that my mind was made up and that I was bound to stay and fight it out, but so far as all these short sighted creatures knew, I was dying, and awful, to relate, had not yet been christened. This was terrible: to die without it I could not enter Heaven, and as only two places appear on record as our future home, I must weep and wail and gnash my t——(by Gum, I forgot, I had no teeth), IN HELL FOR EVER, whereas a drop of water on the tip of the finger dropped on my forehead, would save me from that awful place, and land me safe in glory. My parents being Christians, were anxious their baby should be saved. So the Christening was duly attended to and likewise another wetting. (Christians were not all teetotalers in them days: this was before the Blue Ribbon, or Salvation Army invention). To compensate for the unfortunate circumstance of birth, I was given the ROYAL name of WILLIAM, and if Gin drinking could do it, the tremendous "success to our Royal William," so heartily drank only 23 days before Victoria began to reign, I should have been enthroned as WILLIAM THE FIFTH, and Britons saved from being under petticoat Government. Do not think I hate Petticoat Government, I rather like it, and it suits me; I began with it, have so far been subject to it, and am willing it should continue, "Long may she wave,"*

* My mother, sisters, and all my wives wore petticoats, the latter often tried to wear the breeches also.

Astrologers say I was born heir to more ills of life than most babies, ; be that as it may, I have had them. To cut a long story short, I devoted the first three years of my life to feeding doctors: poor things, they must live you know. Do not think that during this time I neglected my dear parents, I stuck close to mother: she was the best friend I had in this world up to a certain time, to be mentioned hereafter. Father was busy day-times. I could only bestow my affection on him at nights; I loved him so I could not afford to have him miss the golden opportunity it was in my power to make him enjoy, and also wishing to endear myself to him, I made him walk the room at nights in his shirt and sing "by baby by" while I sang in my own peculiar fashion. I kept up this game three long years and gained my point (Father learnt to say "My dear boy.")

After my third birthday wetting I began to "run away," and ran into all kinds of mischief and accident. Shoulder bone and nose broke, teeth knocked out; besides the vaccination was not proper: it never is. I have cause to curse vaccination and all who uphold it, and will say right here I have eight children, and no filthy virus has been inoculated into them, I would smash the right arm of any man who would dare poison the blood of my child. Let every man take that stand and vaccination will be considered unhealthy. Remember doctors say it prevents disease, and they ask us to believe they are anxious to prevent it and thus spoil their trade. You can believe it if you wish: I do not. My children passed through the small pox O. K.†; it did them good, and they will compare more than favourably with your scrawny vaccinated victims. [Query— Are we created imperfect? If so, can Doctors perfect the imperfect work of the Creator? Has it taken the Creator near six thousand years to discover that man—His noblest work—requires to be inoculated with disease to perfect him?]

My parents removed to Devonshire, their native place. The land of cream and cider was now my home, for my parents' board and lodgings suiting me I continued with them, though they left the Haymarket. The fact is, I could not pay my board bill, and did not like to leave, though I afterwards left them I found it impossible to settle up, and its not paid yet; I fear they made a bad debt, and were I pressed for payment I must become bankrupt. I am not the only one in debt, big men and big nations are sometimes in debt; I have heard that even wealthy England owes a trifle. I must not gossip about outside affairs. I am now in lovely Devon; to get out of the City of Gin did me no harm. Here I was put to a school kept by a maiden lady of 60. My schoolmates and I led the old lady a nice time of it; we learnt more mischief than Algebra. I was removed and placed with a good Irish schoolmaster. He fancied I had been wrongly trained, and began to untrain

†O. K. In Yankee common parlance means All Correct, First Rate, Real Good, Tip Top, &c.

me. I felt cool toward him, but he warmed me so with his heating apparatus, the cane, that I soon regarded him. My regard for the Irish is peculiar: my little education was beat into me by Irish hands. Circumstances forced me to board and lodge in Ireland at one time for 14 months, and in America I was thrown into Irish society very frequently, hence I know as much about the Irish as many who say more about them than I do. I speak of a man as I find him. I found many good men and true among them. In reading the history of England's wars I find the Irish were full of loyalty and valor, and but for the Irish, Scotch and Welsh, where would England's greatness be? Have the Irish been wronged? So have the Scotch, Welsh and even English, and while I deprecate the dynamite fillibustering of Irish Americans, I admit Ireland is justified in asking for her rights; so we all are, but let us prefer the ballot to the bullet; and when Ireland, Scotland, Wales or England rightly use the powerful ballot, they will not only ask, but have, that their joy may be full.

When 11 years old I left school to try earning a living by travelling with Tea. This canvassing from house to house gave me an insight of life. I found others far worse situated than I was.

"Whene'er I take my walks abroad, how many poor I see."

I determined to make the best of life, and travelling in the rural districts of Devon dealing out Tea, brought me in contact with many old women from whom I could glean the hard facts in regard to life and what it really is. I loved to gossip with them, but though gaining information, I lost in a financial point of view; I stored my mind and emptied my pocket. At the age of 18 being hard up, I entered the Queen's Red Coat Service. Here I got into the wrong trade again. I was not cut out for a Human Butcher, and the happiest and best of it was when Sergeant Jarman, after serving 5 years and 40 days received his discharge with the part often cut off, containing "Very Good."*

*Military men understand it, but "civilians" wont, hence I am compelled to say I earned a very good character.

I was glad to be free, but was soon bound again. Somehow there got into my head an old fashioned idea, very much in vogue when Noah entered the Ark, and not quite extinct yet—I got Married. I should not have done it, only that a Devonshire Farmer had a daughter he regarded less than I did. He offered to give her away so I took her better for worse. Mighty risky business: he had known her 24 years, I but little over 24 days. And he so willing to give, mark you, give her to me, and not so much as ask me to work on the farm seven years for her. Yet a better bargain was never struck. We had no big fuss on our wedding day: I do not believe in it, and a man that gets married pretty often cannot afford it. After we had jogged along together ten months WILLIAM THE SIXTH was born. This was the best baby in the world (many first-borns are so considered.) It was *the very picture of Pa.* Joy reigned in our home at that hour. But, Alas! Alas! how short my joy. A taste, as it were to an hungry soul; and then gone! For the event that gave me the title of Father, made me a Widower. I prefer to pass over the sad event. The babe when two years old seemed to require a Mamma; failing to find one for him I procured the next best, a stepmother. At best this is a poor substitute for any child, but what could I do? My wounded heart was healed, and yearned for some one to love besides a baby. My widower friends, you know how it is yourself. I trust the Married may never know it. As this second partner of my sorrows (never mind the joys; they are insignificant) figures in her proper place (She is now in Utah a fast Mormon) you will hear of her soon.

Once I got on the Spree; from what I have said it may be easily inferred that I rather like Gin, though its my enemy: I have to continually guard against it. Once when not on Guard I got on a tare, and Gin made me crazy. It was at a wedding "wet." I managed to get outside of a lot of Gin.

Possession is nine points of the law; the one inside gets the best of it. So in this case, Gin was inside, and Gin was Boss, "when the liquor's in the wit's out." Gin made me go home and smash up things. The wife and neighbours thought it a case of insanity, for when they interfered, Gin made me take a poker and assert my rights. The doctor certified to what wife and neighbours said, and I was placed in a lunatic asylum. But it was only a case of *Temporary Insanity*. The next morning I awoke not knowing where I was. My keeper kindly informed me. The Doctor consoled me, saying, *I was as sane as he was*; he thought it was only a case of intoxication but was compelled to admit me on the Certificate sent with me. He was glad to see me all right, said I must make myself at home for a month, as they are bound to keep all their *patients* one month at least; it was a law framed like that of the Medes and Persians, and could not be altered, even in my case. This Patient's patience would not suffer him to patiently wait one month. I scaled the wall in my Lunatic Garb, ran off and defied them to catch me. They tried hard to do so.

When they came to the house that secreted me, with ropes to secure me, I got out at the garret window and made my escape over the house tops. I kept on the quiet, and kept gin on the outside; thus I soon convinced people that there is no insanity in our family. This was over twenty years ago, and to-day everybody and myself are perfectly satisfied that my Upper Story is all right so long as I do not allow Gin to take up lodgings there. Gin always gets possession of the Upper Story when entering this house of clay. Its many a year since intoxicating drink got into this Temple of mine, I find *to be safe I must not rent my Upper Story to King Alcohol*. I am determined to have a better tenant, or keep the apartments *empty*. Who blames me? Do you? If so, ta-ta, no more at present on this point.

A word about my trade at that time. It was my business to feed vanity, and tempt the ladies by selling drapery on tick. Wives often took up things unknown to the hubby—that is to say, behind the husband's back or when his back was turned, and then turn their backs on me, and tell the child to say "Mother aint home," or lock the door, and often when I peeped through the key hole I saw them. A very trying business to a Christian—I was a Packman. The rude called me "Johnny Fortnight" because I allowed them to pay for their finery in 1/- a fortnight. For this base ingratitude, I made them pay one "bob" a week (when I could catch it.) This has grown into a usual custom now. Some think it impossible to be a Christian Packman; this is not so. I admit to peep through key holes and keep from swearing is no joke, and when I say my sins of commission and omission were many, try to believe it, for the "Tally Trade" is apt to make one worldly-minded. I can truly say "we have left undone those things we ought to have done, and have done those things we ought not to have done," and would readily confess my faults, if they were not so many and would cram the book too much. In this work I must give my history a "lick and a promise." I promise to give my very remarkable history in full, if I ever scrape up money enough to publish it, without mortgaging my property. The Packman part of it would fill this book, hence I drop it to yarn about Emigration.

I was not led to emigrate by flaming advertisements of interested Shipowners and Railway Companies. I did not believe that in other countries, Pigs ran around with knives forks and plates in their mouths, crying "who'll eat me?" or that nicely prepared farms awaited those willing to cross the ocean and take them without labor, money or price. Such worldly inducements, even if true, would never induce me to cross any ocean. But when the Mormon Missionary came with "Thus saith the Lord," and from the Bible convinced me that the world was wrong side up, and they were turning it upside down as the ancient Apostles started in to do, I concluded to lend a hand.

Besides "the Christian Churches were all wrong. The Catholic Church was the Great Mother of Harlots. The Established Church, and all dissenting Churches having sprung from her, were her daughters, and all living in filth and Sin. Their Ministers were blind and leading the blind. All were going headlong to hell. God was about to overthrow these religions, and was now crying through his servants, the Mormons, Come out of her my people that ye be not partakers of her sins, and that ye receive not of her plagues," and God was calling one of a family and two of a city and bringing them to Zion. These Mormons come with an open Bible and lead Christian people into their net. They catch but few others. NINE-TENTHS OF THEIR CONVERTS ARE FROM THE VARIOUS CHURCHES OF CHRISTENDOM. What are the Christian Ministers about? Why do they not warn their flocks? These Mormons come as WOLVES IN SHEEPS' CLOTHING, take the sheep from the fold, and drag them to the Mountains and high hills of Utah. How true is the word of the Lord to Ezekiel " MY SHEEP WANDERED THROUGH ALL THE MOUNTAINS, AND UPON EVERY HIGH HILL: YEA, MY FLOCK WAS SCATTERED AND NONE DID SEARCH OR SEEK AFTER THEM." Oh! why did not my pastor warn me? I knew nothing of Mormonism; and would to God I had been warned, then I should not have wandered to the Mountains of Utah or had such bitter experience. Oh! what would I not give to have been saved from it? To day thousands in Utah cry the same, and these were once members of England's Christian Churches. I trust every Christian will help expose the awful wickedness revealed in this book, and that Ministers will warn the people. For these wolves are among the sheep now, worse than ever, and are leading unwary dupes to the Sodom of the 19th century, which they brazenly call the "Zion of God."

Fate detained me two years in New York which is half way to Zion. Here I became somewhat Yankeeized, and unfitted for the Kingdom. America well suited me, but Utah did not. In America I was a Royal Man and a Boss:*
  *Boss. means "Guv'ner, Master, or Higheockaloram" in English.
there, everybody is, or will be, when Women's Rights are patented. What if they are all bosses? I was a boss among bosses, I could jog along first rate. The first real, downright Yankee I met on landing was a brick. I asked. "Are you governed here by a Queen or King?" "How?" he replied. Yankees answer that way first; we repeat the question, when they answer by asking another. I repeated my question. He then answered, "May I ax if you arn't a blarsted Britisher?" I said "I am a British subject." "Do tell; I want to know," he replied, though I had told him and he knew. Extending his hand, palm up, he added "Put it there." Prompted by instinct, having nought else to guide me in this foreign land, and not understanding the language, I placed my hand in his. It was like taking the handle of an electric battery, when the full force is on. He gave me such a hearty welcome, said how glad he always was to see his relations; I was his cousin; John Bull and Uncle Sam were brothers. Then answering my question he said, " I guess the King and Queen biz, is kinder played out in these diggings; we don't need such trash around here—No s-i-r-e-e horse and buggy—you hear me—Not much we don't—not if I knows myself. I'm on it you bet, and that's what's the matter! Take, don't you?" Of course I took; took to him, to his ideas, to his country, and was glad I had come. He requested me to make myself " ta hum " (at home), for there was plenty of room, grub, work, pay, and above all, plenty of liberty. All men were " Ekal, and do as they darned please, subject only to the constitution of the United States." All this was said in language hard for the uninitiated to understand. When, in answer to his question, " you savvey?" I replied " you bet," he exclaimed " Bully for you! your'e old pie, jist my stile, you hear this Rooster !†

† Yankees call males under 18 Young Roosters, from 18 to 60, "Roosters": up to 100 and over "Old Roosters." A Rooster is the male fowl, which the English Call "A Cock."

Much could be said of this trait of character in real Americans. They very heartily welcome all good emigrants, especially their "Mother Country Cousins." Like most good things this is abused, for the scamps of the world find shelter there; those who leave their country for their country's good go to America; while Mormon scamps who rule Utah, do all they can to increase their rascally power by decieving the very Elect. The unsuspecting Christians of England, Scotland and Wales, are decieved by this YANKEE TRICK. Mormonism is but a cunning Yankee Trick; Yankees schemed, planned, devised and still carry on the whole business, and they find it easier to swindle and dupe the English, Scotch and Welsh than any other nationality. The Irish are not entrapped by it; I found but three Irishmen in Utah, two of them came from Australia, and first rate chaps they are, both regretted coming and would gladly get away but cannot; the other is a complete Jesuit; but tries to be a good Mormon, because of his *particular fondness for many wives*. Mormon Missionaries fail to draw the Irish into their net, and why? Is it because they have more sense? I admit Irish wit, but that's not it. We find it otherwise: here's the rub, "Mormon Priests come as angels of light" and present their RELIGION OF HELL as the A. 1. Simon pure Religion. Members of the Church of England, Methodists, Baptists, Presbyterians, and such, sometimes change faith and jump from one sect to another. Catholics do not. The Irish, who are Catholics, are satisfied with Catholic Priests, hence Mormon Priests fail to convert them.

I meandered through Sodom and Gomorrah, Utah's *Hell upon Earth*, twelve years, married muchly, had plenty of Mother-in-laws, but somehow they were different to my Mother. I was a Priest after the order of Melchizedek, and A VIRGIN WITHOUT GUILE ('ticklers bye and by.) Becoming disgusted I withdrew from the CHURCH OF HELL, when bitter persecution followed. I was thrust into dungeons. My grave was dug three times. They tried to kill me, and I narrowly escaped. My Wives, Children and Property were all stolen and I reduced to beggery and want. As I describe all this further on, I will merely say I finally escaped, got back to New York, and started my little tongue wagging against the Mormons. It will continue so to wag until silenced in death or Mormonism pegs out.

I found another difficulty now. My tongue, so long accustomed to wag in the Mother tongue, refused to alter. They have no King's English in America, you know; they use Republican English. King's English is O.K in the Kingdom of Utah, but in the United States they actually snicker at good plain English. When I introduced myself to various Ministers for the purpose of obtaining their Churches to lecture in I said; "Hi 'ave the 'onor hof being ha free born Hinglishman, but 'ere hi ham without 'ouse hor 'ome, 'avin lost hall, heven my Childring hin the Salt Lake 'Ell.' Believe me these sedate men laughed, and said "Excuse me smiling, the land of thy nativity is patent the moment you open your mouth." Says I "Good for the Nativity! Good for the Patent!" To keep my mouth shut after I got out of Hell was not my little game. In Sodom, *Mums the word*. In Utah Sabbath Schools they learn to keep their mouth shut by opening it, and singing to the tune of

Rorey-o-More, or Captain Jinks, as follows:—

"Keep your mouth shut, and breathe through your nose,
Is the counsel which wisdom on mortals bestows;
And, one thing is certain, 'twill be for your gain,
And save you quite often from trouble and pain.
When cold winds are blowing, and Jack Frost doth nip,
Don't open your mouth—keep a stiff upper lip;
When others provoke you, and fearfully scold,

Place a guard on your mouth, and your lips tightly fold.
When asleep, if the nightmare you'd always avoid,
Your slumbers will seldom by dreams be annoyed;
If this rule you'll observe, and the habit maintain,
You'll in health and in happiness constantly gain. *

Mountain Warbler, p. 100. "Dedicated to the service of our Heavenly Fathers cause on earth ; and to Superintendants, Teachers and Pupils of the Sabbath Schools." Printed at the Mormon "Desert News" office Salt Lake City 1872.

This I failed to learn. I was not born tongue-tied, but to let loose oft in the stilly night to arouse slumbering Haymarketers, and in School, Street, Court, Alley or Lane, it was my prerogative to holler as loud as any boy. To swop such a noble birthright for a mess of pottage was impossible! I must be heard even in Hell! and when old Brigham or his Apostolic scoundrels would "fearfully scold and provoke me *my* upper lip *failed* to keep stiff ; *these lips refused* to tightly fold," consequently I got "Trouble and Pain quite often," nightmare, daymare and various mares and scares: besides the "old hoss, old boots, Danites and sich" were after me. Instead of a gain in health and happiness both went to profit and loss account, especially the loss. But to resume.

I was glad my story was so far credited ; if they so readily believed the balance it would be O.K. Beecher refused to let me Air Polygamy in his Church; it was not to let for Anti-polygamy purposes. Come to think of the impropriety of it after the Beecher-Tilton rumpus, I don't blame him. Just think! "Ungodly Newspapers" would re-hash all the Beecher-Tilton Business ; dish up nice morsels again, and spread it like wild-fire that "Crock called Kettle smutty." Plymouth Church may well say "I pray thee have me excused." I 'scuse 'em. I found a good whole-soul man even in Brooklyn not mixed up in the Brooklyn Scandal. He had just let loose on the Utah Harem. "Puck," (the Yankee Punch,) caricatured Dr. Talmage, Brooklyn Tabernacle, John Taylor and Salt Lake Tabernacle in a wrangle. Thinking Brookling Tabernacle a good fort to commence my attack from, I secured it. Dr. Talmage held the fort, but capitulated to me. I began to hold the Fort, and hold forth at 8 p.m., November 19th, 1880. The Tabernacle was full "inside and out" as Paddy said. I opened fire with a volley, to use a Salvation Army term.

General Garfield was just elected President of the United States, and I felt safe. I had met him in Salt Lake and knew he was *down on Polygamy*. I have something to say about that good and great self-made man presently, for I loved him, so did Queen Victoria and every true Briton. I doubt if Americans regard him more than Britons do, I know my Yankee cousins feelings well, but so far as I have proved my brethren at home, it's "nip and tuck." The British seem to vie with Americans in their esteem for Garfield. The Yankees claim to beat the world, and the world says the Yankees beat everything: this is incorrect. A long experience with Americans learnt me to speak correctly of them, hence I say A YANKEE BEATS EVERYTHING BUT HIS WIFE. An Englishman *licks his wife.* Do not say I digress; it all fits in, and whatever cap may fit any particular reader he is welcome to it free of extra charge. But what I was actually driving at was the King's English.

At Brooklyn Tabernacle, "The New York Times," "World," "Sun," and such luminaries had reporters. The next morning they all came out with big head lines, and devoted long columns to your humble servant's lecture and views, said I had murdered the King's English, and they knew I was an Englishman by my talk, and so forth, etcetera. Some of the papers said I murdered the Queen's English. I am not a murderer; I have not the heart to kill a chicken, and cannot bear to see it done. I sometimes contemplate becoming a vegetarian. This charge of murdering the property of our beloved

Queen gave me the bile, riled my blood, which boiled. British blood comes to a boil on Yankee soil, especially on July the Fourth. For forthwith they bring forth the Fourth forcibly, and forerun the forepart of the forenoon in Guy Fawke's Day style. The forerunners forenamed forthissuing, foreshow and foresignify the forthcoming. At or before four a.m. on the Fourth, you are foredoomed to forego snoozing. If you have foreknowledge or forethought you forejudge what's up, and get up forespent, stick in your four false foreteeth, brush back the forelock of the foretop with the forefingers and sally forth forthright to forsee, and forstall, those without foresight to foreknow the Forefather's Fourth. I thus particularize the Fourth because it's America's Great Day of the Feast. Fourthly, British memory not being at long range point on those points, they make it a point to point pointedly to the pointingstock poignant date 1776. It appears from their yarn, the Yankees at or about that date, tried to make the Atlantic Ocean one nice old cup o' tea by steeping whole ship loads of big chests of tea in it. But the water was unfit for making good tea and spoiled the lot. The fish nibbled at the tea leaves, which made them nervous, as I found when fishing around Boston they won't bite at any bait. On the Fourth the Yankees are proud to tell of Washington, La Fayette, and others, but forget their most valuable man—Thomas Paine. I make bold to assert, what history proves, that, but for Paine, America would not have gained her Independence. How they glory in making the Redcoat tails fly. This was before Boers were invented. Up to 1776 the enemy seldom saw a British Soldier's coat tail. The Soudanese did, and but for Gen. Buller, it strikes me those Brigades would need Armor Plates in the seat of their trowsers, where Paddy put his. Intimating that all those things happened at a period long forgotten, a big fisted Yankee slapped his paw on my shoulder exclaiming, "And don't you forget it!" But to resume. The "New York World," from which I quote, says:—" After a brief introduction by Dr. Talmage, the lecturer (that's me) a slight young man (that's true, I never was corpulent or old and never wish to be), with a pronounced Cockney accent (what cheek these Yankees have, and how inconsiderate ; circumstances over which I had no control made me a Cockney; could I have had my way, knowing what I do now, I should have had myself born a Yankee, and made my way to the White House, being constitutionally fit for the Presidential Chair, but my constitution being wrecked in the Haymarket as aforesaid, I am constitutionally unfit even to claim squatter's rights and squat in the said P. C. But Americans have no time to consider: they go ahead). This one says I said "Hamerica, slumber on, hand you will 'ave a question on your 'ands far more difficult to settle than slavery—mark my words to night." They did "Mark my words" as you will see. I said "slumber on" because I found "live wideawake Yankees" fast asleep, with the Mormon question for a pillow, the heads of the nation (they are all heads and no tails in America) had on liberty night caps, big enough to cover said pillow. There's where the shoe pinched. I disturbed their nap, they were all knocked up (N.B.—If this book accidently falls into American hands, I don't mean the Yankee "knock up," but the English, which means tired out),* tussling with t'other twin relic of barbarism —Slavery—and did not hanker after a tussell with Polygamy 'till their nap was over. This Britisher coming forth to torment them before their time, riled them, even this "N. Y. World," generally harmless and quiet, could not "let up" without trying to injure my show, and wound up with "The lecture closed with a series of views in Hutah." I had the whole thing pictured; I was, as it were, holding up the "Brazen Serpent" that the bitten Yankees might see "whats up," but history again repeated itself; I stood there and held up the thing two hours, and tried to wake 'em up and take a look, but they only ridiculed it. See what the "New York times," the Yankee

In America "knocked up" means *enceinte*.

thunderer, said next morning, Nov. 20, 1880. Twig the big head lines:—

"ODD SIGHTS IN TALMAGE'S.
CROWDS IN THE TABERNACLE HEAR A FUNNY LECTURE.

TALKING ABOUT MORMONISM AND MURDERING THE QUEEN'S ENGLISH—PICTURES TO MAKE A HORSE LAUGH—THE SHOW TO GO ON—CASH NEEDED TO GET IN."

This shows these animals' animus: now see their cutting remarks:—

"A huge canvass screen, 25 feet square, stretched in front of the great organ in the Brooklyn Tabernacle, last evening, like the sail of a ship, made Dr. Talmage's house of worship look just about ready to put to sea. Every seat in the house was filled, and people were standing. When Dr. Talmage and the lecturer of the evening stepped upon the platform, the latter was carrying an armful of books, newspapers, bows, arrows and manuscripts. Dr. Talmage said that the lecturer's name was William Jarman.

"The lecturer stepped to the front and the Tabernacle was still. He murdered the Queen's English in the most shocking style for nearly two hours, and then gave an exhibition of pictures. Of all the surprises the Tabernacle has ever turned out, this was the greatest.

"The speaker gave a harrowing account of the Mountain Meadow massacre. Holding up one of his arrows, he asked, "What shall I say of the young girl, 16 years of age, from whose body this harrow was taken?" "'Ark!" he continued, " is that the voice of a Hindian?" Then began the stereoscopic exhibition, the lights were turned down, and pictures, representing the creation, were shown. The first scene showed the elements, looking like a snowstorm on a prairie. Then came the earth and the waters; then the making of the beasts, with a whole canvass full of impossible cats, dogs, crooked-legged tigers, broken-backed camels, and consumptive elephants. Then came man— a curly-haired Adam, sitting on a rock. Then Eve in a costume that made the audience say "Oh!" Then there came the tree of life, with Eve plucking the apple, and the Devil sitting under the tree smiling. Adam was meanwhile lying stretched on the ground, sickened by the loss of a rib. It was a rare gallery of art gone mad, and the lecturer catalogued the pictures somewhat in this order:—

"The Deseret Alphabet;" "A little Rogues' Gallery of Prominent Mormons;" "Salt Lake City;" "The Projected New Mormon Temple;" "The City 'All;" "A Salt Lake Whiskey Shop;" "Polygamy in Wealth;" "Polygamy in Poverty;" "A Mormon Woman;" "The Lord's Theatre;" "Emigrants Dragging them 'And-carts over the Plains;" "A Mormon Massacre;" "A Mormon Angel (with a pipe in his mouth);" "The Hindians;" "Two Little Girls going to the Spring, with Little Flags in their 'Ands;" "Mountain Meadow Massacre Scenes;" "More Massacre—Sculls, Wolves;" "Joe Smith;" "Brigham Young;" "Smith in the Woods (great deal of woods, by little Smith;)" "A Bedstead two Blocks (half a mile) Long, containing Brigham Young's Wives and Children." The last scene was the standard stereopticon view, entitled "The Rock of Ages."

"It was an exhibition that would have made most churches weep; but the Tabernacle stood it without a groan. The Tabernacle's Pastor even announced before the crowd went out, that Mr. Jarman had not yet told a quarter of what he knew about Mormonism, and that he would repeat the dose a week from next Tuesday evening, when a small admission fee would be charged."

This is how they saw things before they were properly awake. But I hung on with British bull-dog tenacity, and finally got their eyes open; then they saw very differently and the great American papers came out with splendid notices of my lecture and exhibition; I could fill a volume with them, all stating about the same, viz:—"The best Pictures ever shown—the best lecture ever given." The British bull-dog's barking woke them up and brought 'em too.

> And with his everlasting clack, set all men's ears upon the rack,
> Not by the force of carnal reason, but indefatigable teazing;
> With vollies of eternal babble, and clamour more unanswerable,
> As bones of Hectors, when they differ, the more they're cudgel'd grow the stiffer.—*Hudibras*.

At first they yawned and said "Guess we can wipe out Polygamy any day we're a mind to." This gave me a point. They had previously "guessed" to put down slavery before breakfast; finding their mistake out they hollered for help, just for three months in that time they could make a clean sweep, finish the job, bury the dead, wipe off their chin, pull down their vest and return to the bosom of their families. But they had to take breakfast on the gory field five years instead of one little pic-nic. If Yankee guessing is worth ought, and the before breakfast job lasted five years, what will the other guess of any day or one day spin out to? It strikes me, according to that reckoning, if they start at once they wont finish in this A.D. 19th century. At first the Press flattened me; now they flatter. Knowing they believed as I do in the power of the Press, I got them to put old Polygamy in the Press, now let them keep her there until flattened and annihilated. I kept busy pegging away in America until called home at my father's death to see after my aged mother; she wished me to stay with her while she lives. I swore to do so, and will not repent.

When I left the Mormon Church my British wife left me, and I am told married Brigham Young. (This is hearsay but in making this, my affidavit, I say that, from my experience in Mormondom, what I state from information, I verily believe to be true.) He having died, MY DEAR WIFE IS A WIDOW. That is more than most men can say of their wives, though they often say funny things about them. I deeply sympathize with all widows, *except my own*. How could a man sympathize with his widow? I ask the dear men— Could you? Men can tenderly regard other men's widows, and often act very uncautiously; I myself disregarded Sam Weller's advice to his Son," Samivel bevare of the Vidders." For after all my trouble with the tender (and tough) fair sex, I married the widow of an American Senator (out of regard for the Senator of course.) My left off wives had all got married again, (they nibble at second-hand wives in America,) so I thought "Faint heart never won Fair Lady, and if at first (or third) you don't succeed, Try, Try, again," so I tried again, as you see and won the widow. And the last state of this man was—Never mind the State—I am in the Kingdom of Great Britian now. Here the law says my British wife, or Widow, or whatever we may call her, is still mine until divorced by English Law; that I cannot marry again until divorced from her here. But I've been and gone and done it. My English Lawyers and Friends say the Senator's Widow is not my wife, I cannot marry again, but the trouble is I have done it. I am like the man in the Stocks whose friends said to him, "They can't put you in the Stocks for that," but, replies the man, "They have done it: here I am in the Stocks, now tell me how to get out." So say I. Here I am in a terrible fix: tell me how to get out. In America you can be divorced for going to bed with cold feet, (and not a bad idea either) or if Man and Wife look cross at each other and should happen accidently to have a few words, either party can go into Court and swear they cannot live together in the Marital relation in Peace and Union, and the Bond of Matrimony is dissolved. It's cheap too; only costs a few bobs; they can then marry any one they please. My Yankee wife (*i. e.*) could not bear to live in a country where she was not considered my wife. So she packed up her duds, cleared out, put the Atlantic Ocean between me and her, and says if—I want her I know where to find her. She's not dead yet. What a consolation! Just think of it for a moment. According to American Law I HAVE A DEAR WIFE ONLY 3,500 MILES OFF. Our English Law gives my Bosom, yet another Wife 7000 miles away, in Utah. Rather a Distant Relation, and its mighty galling to yearn 7000 miles at a stretch. Sometimes "Distance lends enchantment to the view;" but there is much in the Utah atmosphere I do not like, it ill suits my constitution, and would be more unhealthy for me now than ever, 'twould kill me. Besides where I to go there to claim her—

     I should find her Adored,
     By a Mor Man named Ford,
     Whose Bed and whose Board,
     She shares with Accord,
     And this Wife of My Bosom could never Afford,
     To receive this, her dear Legal Lord.

     She is there safely Moored,
     I am point blank Ignored.
     As I just wont be Floored,
     And have my blood Poured.
     Or in Salt Lake's big Grave Yard have this body Stored,
     I'll stay home, not go there to be Bored.

     (Peculiar Metre.)

  I started to make this SIXES AND SEVENS, but that's the metre of my Marital Relations, and I'd hate to see Poetry so badly mixed as that; besides tautology's bad, so is apology; though the latter seems needed here, it ain't: spose the poetry don't amount to much, that's not my fault. I was born too late to become a Poet; every time I hatch out (excuse me I mean incubate) a bit of poetry, and get in high glee over it, if I happen to take up a volume of Milton, Byron, Burns, or any of them chaps, I find they've used up all the big words in their effusions; and if I published mine the world would say it was "smouched." *(Shakespeare.)* I shall let that Long Range Wife R. I. P.

  At the 3,500 mile end Cross Roads, the way is clear, but 3,500 miles requires a stretch of imagination to fancy myself consoled by her tender sympathy. Think: every time I wish to speak to my dear wife I must spend ten days of relaxing sea sickness and lots of cash to get at her. True, I could use the Telegraph, but it is expensive and moreover would be public. To expose secrets to the vulger gaze, which only a wife should know would never do. Besides, domestic secrets and conjugal amenities, although often governed by magnetic influences, are not improved by mechanical electricity.

  And besides I cannot leave my Mother, and break my word; I promised to stay with her while she lives, and if either of my wives want me, they know where to find me. I cannot say fairer than that. In the case of my Yankee wife who could not bear the English (except one) or England, I will say with John Wesley, when his dear wife got her back up and left him:—" I did not tell her to go, and I am sure I shall not ask her to come back." (I treat of Marriage with DECEASED AND LIVING Wife's Sisters further on.)

  Father left sufficient to keep me and Mother out of the Workhouse, and quite independent of Parochial Relief, *i.e.* if I can boss the gin. Having done so for 20 years, I think I can manage to boss it another 20. If so, being now 47 years old, I shall be pretty well up toward the sear and yellow leaf by that time, and expect to be well able to still rub along without it. I am afraid of strong drink now. It would make me sell my property, and thrust me and Mother into the Union, I know it; I feel it; it has done the like over and over again. As a close observer of Men and Things I find Lunatic Asylums, Jails, and Workhouses are mainly filled through intoxicating drinks. Hence I have decided according, to my best judgment, to leave the drink alone. You who are stuck after the aforenamed places are at liberty to go it, and go in if you like: I wont. If this cap fits anybody, please wear it.

Arriving in England after near 20 years absence, I found Mormon Missionaries still here, and taking away Christians by Thousands. The Ministers all the while sweetly sleeping and allowing MORMON WOLVES to take away the Sheep and Lambs. This fires me anew. To think that my fellow countrymen are yet being swindled by these infernal scamps, and that our English Girls are dragged away to live a life of Sin and Shame in Utah's Harems. I cry, GREAT GOD! GIVE ME A ZEAL ACCORDING TO MY KNOWLEDGE! That I may be able to wake up both Pastor and People, and am determined to wrestle hard, Yea, even work myself into an early grave to drive away Mormon Missionaries from the Shores of Dear Old England. I am thankful to say I am not compelled from mercenary motives: I could stay home and lounge upon an easy sofa, the balance of my life, if I wished, but I cannot be easy while I know my fellow country-people are being deceived by the Monsters, and dragged away into misery and crime. Oh, what a disgrace that Christian England allows it! Why wont the Government stop it? The Idea of allowing her citizens to be lured into Slavery and robbed of Virtue, Liberty, Money, and all under false pretences. The Government knows all this or should. The late Government did if the present could be excused, but they cannot, there is no excuse for either. Secretary Evarts, the American Secretary of State wrote to the British Government pointing out these things, and asked them to stop it. But No! What does our Christian Government care, though all England's daughters be seduced into lives of Ill Fame, and every true born Briton robbed of Life, Liberty and Happiness? What care they? Everlasting Shame to England's Cabinet! SHAME TO ENGLAND'S HOUSE OF LORDS, SPIRITUAL ESPECIALLY, and to the Commons House of Parliament. For the letter of Secretary Evarts is Pigeon-holed. I have asked my servants, the Officers of State, for a copy, but it cannot be found. Fie upon you Great Britian! Go humble thyself in the dust and dont send any letters to the American Government asking them to stop Fenianism in America, since they have asked you to stop Mormonism in England, and you wont. Find that letter, act upon it at once, drive every vile fellow calling himself a Mormon from our Shores and bid them never set foot upon it again; then you can expect America to attend to your request and every Dynamite Fenian will be expelled from America, and not till then. Mark my word! Look at Noble Germany; the Mormons played the same tricks with her people, but when Secretary Evarts wrote to that Power as he did to England, God bless Germany! her Government at once passed Laws to protect her citizens, and drove Mormon Missionaries from their land. That gives a few hundred more to England, who to day are busy in this country wrecking the peace, happiness, and liberty of thousands of her citizens. England, let me speak! I must Speak! I ask: Art thou become a Second Rate Christian Nation? Are you diminishing in the Scale of Christian Morality? If so, call home thy Missionaries from every Land; shut up thy Bible and Tract Societies; turn every Church and Chapel into Theatres and Dance Houses; and make every habitation in Great Britain a place of Ill Fame. Let us all do as the Mormons do in these respects. For if Mormonism is so good that so many of England's worthy citizens are to be crammed with it, let us have it at home and not go 7,000 miles away for it. With these few remarks in regard to my life and career, together with a few of my ideas on matters and things, I leave this, (shall I say Biography) at present, in order to more fully pitch into the great curse of my Life, and that of tens of thousands of others—Mormonism.

CHAPTER II.

The Abscess formed—Devils on the Wing—Sodom Located—The Utah Hell and Uncle Sam at Loggerheads—Infernal Sermons.

When the Mormon Prophet, Joseph Smith, died, there was a perfect higgledy-piggledy scramble for the vacancy. Sidney Rigdon, who with Joseph and Hyrum Smith, had constituted the "First Presidency" or ruling power of the "Kingdom," now that Joseph and Hyrum were dead, sought to establish himself as the only surviving President and "Boss" of the whole concern. One Strang also came boldly forward with "Divine Revelations Hieroglyphic Plates," and such like trash, from which he translated the "Will of the Lord" in the matter; while Gladden Bishop, Hendrick, Brewster, and other "Apostles and Elders" revelled in Revelations which completely muddled the "Divine Will." Among these aspiring tricksters was that inhuman Arch Fiend, the crafty, shrewd, and cynical misanthrope, Brigham Young. Most Authors first introduce their noted characters' birth; I start further back. In embryo Brigham existed in Massachusetts; but his "Ma," said to be now "full of the Devil," emigrated to Vermont, six months ere Brigham migrated to this mundane sphere; *id est* before the "little devil" was born. Fortunate Massachussetts! Favoured Boston—"Hub of the Universe!" thy lucky fate saves thee from bellowing—"Woe is me that has borne me a man of strife and a man of contention to the whole world!" (Jer. 15—10.) Vermont, proverbial for its native keen "Down East Yankees," gave birth to Joseph Smith and many leading Mormons: and as if to prove Brigham's belswagger, belluine, bamboozle, balderdash "Kingdom," a real "Yankee Trick" hatched that infernal monster also. *

* Good Dictionaries define "Belswagger, Belluine, Bamboozle, Balderdash," thus:— Lecherous, Beastly, Brutal, Deceptive, Nonsense.

Brigham soon taught his co-aspirants that Rome lacks elbow-room for two Cæsars. Rigdon was "cut off and delivered over to the buffetings of Satan," for seeking to "rule or ruin the Church." All Prophetic aspirants were served about ditto, which caused "a high old time," and a jolly hierarchial high-flying skimble-skamble. Rigdon, Strang, and others, started "Kingdoms on their own hook." These high-flown Monarchies are said to have "gone up higher than a kite, busted, and vanished;" while the exultant Brigham ejaculated—"How's that for high!" Anent this hurley-burley, many, disowning Brigham and all pretenders, and preferring the predicted son of the Prophet, formed "The True Latter-day Saints Church," and are commonly called "Josephites," in contrast to the False "Latter-day Devil Brighamites" of Utah fame. †

† Joseph Smith "The Seer" saw, and said—"Brigham will play the devil with the Church and lead it to Hell." "Fallen Saints," who trust in man, now board and lodge "in a salt land." (Jer. 17. 5—6 v.) The whole land thereof is Brimstone and Salt, and burning like Sodom and Gomorrah. (Deut. 29—23.)

These "Josephites" repudiate the Polygamy, Incest, Murder, and crime of the Brighamite gang of infernal curs; and though I unsparingly dissect the Abscess, lay bare Utah devilism, and drub the lawless banditti severely, I faithfully portray the Brighamites only—whose creed and practice defy law and order, and spare the Josephites, who conform with law, are good citizens and well worthy of respect. ‡

‡ Could Josephite Missionaries disseminate their principles among the Utah fanatics it would do more than anything else possibly can do toward the overthrow of this Hell upon Earth. (see my chapter on "The Remedy").

In a hurry-skurry, Brigham, *a la* Moses, led his rabble of knaves and trollops on a kingdom-hunting wild-goosechase into the "Wilderness;" and kept them on a helter-skelter dog-trot jog, slap bang to the "Promised Land." This "Modern Israel" regarded "Uncle Sam" (The American Government) as "their Pharoah;" the United States—"the Land of Egypt;" the Capital—"The House of Bondage." Across the Missouri lay the "Wilderness" and Rocky Mountains, beyond was "The Land of Canaan." The Rocky Mountain, Salt Lake, and California Region then belonged to Mexico. Brigand Brigham and his banditti craved an asylum far beyond "Uncle Sam's" control. Brigham could play a tripartite rooly-pooly game of Moses, Aaron, and Joshua: Moses to lead the sorry crowd; Aaron to work Golden Calf affairs; and as, the Modern Yankee, Joshua, plunder Mexico, whip the "Greasers," and "Possess the Land." As a blind to cover Brigham's Kingdom speculation, "The Kingdom of God" was "set up." His dupes believing him "God's Prophet and vicegerent on Earth," God's Kingdom and Brigham's could easily unite, and co-operate swimmingly as one and the same thing. This united Co-operative Kingdom, they say, is the one Daniel saw in vision, "Set up in the last days and given to the Saints." (Of course these are the last days and the ungodly Brighamites are the Saints; understand that, or you wont catch "the hang of it.") Say what they may, it is Mahommedanism Yankicized—"Elohim of Kolob" is God, and Brigham His Prophet. Through this Prophet, the Kingdom was established; and through the Prophet the dupes maintain, and "roll forth the Kingdom" at all hazards. The keys to bind on Earth, and in Heaven, are held by the Prophet, and he is "Boss:" Boss of the United States; Boss of the whole Earth; Boss of Heaven, and Boss of Hell. The Prophet's voice is God's voice; he makes known God's will and commands; to disobey, or fail to comply is death. God reveals His will to His Prophet, and so far as the Prophet "let the cat out of the bag" and revealed the Revelations, we learn that Brigham's God is far worse than "Allah" ("by a darned site" as the Yankees say.) He is almighty huffy, and down on "Uncle Sam;" hates him, intends to "play smash" with him, give him fits, measels, small pox, gripes, and subject him to all sorts of unpleasant sensations: then starve him, make it hot, roast him without basting fat, and finally "use him up." Some think and ask, "Would it not be merciful to kill him at once and have done with it?" Such thoughts and questions show how little the "ungodly" know and understand Brigham's God. "His ways are not as our ways or his thoughts as our thoughts." He is determined that pestilence, famine, fire, and sword shall bother and destroy our poor dear "Uncle," and all who fail to take refuge in his big Seraglio. The Utah Harem is the only place of safety, not only for America, but for all the World!

I hear they intend to roof in the "Great Basin" from the Rocky Mountains to the Sierra Nevada, and make it one Great Brothel: wont it be jolly? The sublime idea must have been "Revealed." I have not seen the Revelation; this is hearsay. I expect Lawyers will "object," and "move to strike it out" as inadmissable testimony; Judges so rule, so take your rule, move to strike out, by wiping the rule, see its straight, then scratch the pen neatly across the sentence: do not blur and spoil the book, but strike it out. I have 10,000 pages more than I can possibly jam in here, of what I saw and heard, all good evidence, admissable in any court, that none can reject. So what I have seen and heard declare I unto you.

Brigham had many strings to his bow, but mostly harped upon one that took immensely—"The Martyrdom of the Prophet." I admit the killing of Joseph Smith by an infuriated mob was unlawful, and it certainly was most unfortunate, for the Blood of the Prophets is the seed of the Church. But to blame the Government and all the People for the acts of a few is decidedly wrong: yet every time I went to Mormon worship a perfect tirade of abuse was hurled at the American Government and People. They had murdered the Prophet, and rejected the Gospel. The President, Government Officers and People were all (that is bad)—were going headlong to hell without any possible chance of salvation. We were all taught to hate and despise everything American with an especial hatred. This is readily done by most, who are principally Foreigners and Aliens to Republicanism, and being always accustomed to kingly rule and authority: the Kingdom is in their line, and they can easily hate and despise a Republic that dared oppose a Kingdom. We also learnt that although America actually killed Smith, and must expect "Hail Columbia" the whole world are in for it, having consented to his death, and "rejected the Gospel." If, as the Brighamites claim, they hold a Heavenly Patent, and exclusive monoply of the Gospel I will risk my eternal peace and safety without it, and advise everybody to do the same. We were "gathered home to the valleys of the mountains while the indignation of the Lord and His Great Anger vexed the nations, and all made to drink the wine of the Wrath of His Fury poured out without mixture." To clear the road, and save all he did not wish to hurt, "Divinely appointed Apostles," as hunters and fishers of men—and women—(those from 15 to 25 years old being specially angled for,) hunt and fish out "The Elect," gathering them "from the uttermost parts of the earth" and pushing them into the great Utah Brothel. When the Elect are all in this "Modern Ark of Safety;" the door locked, "sealed up," and the key shoved under the door, it's no use a knocking at the door, for the "Saints" inside commence "Divine Worship" by singing the original old time Sacred Hymn:—

"Who's dat knocking?" You can't come in for you are too late;
Yer eyes dont shine, and yer hair's too straight;
Tis no use knocking, stop dat knocking; get away a knocking at the door."

Its rough on the poor creatures the wrong side of the door, for Brigham's God now turns himself loose and "wires in" on all outside the Bagnio. The Devil also is let loose, and if this Lucifer is looser than now, I sincerely pity the poor human beings then alive, for with Brigham's God and the Devil "hard at 'em,"

["The ungodly" aver that Brigham's God and the Devil are one and the same, a sort of Twinity in Unity. What "Spiritual blindness." See "Dialogues of Devils," p. 79.]

better they had never been born, or that a necklace with millstone drop pendants adorned their ungodly necks, and they dangling at sea bottom, ready to be chawed up, and transmogrified into chile by the gastric juice of Sea-monsters' stomachs, and thus become Monarchs of the Ocean. †

†This is not exactly the true rendering of King James' or the revised Edition, but this is what it means and as near the naked truth as I can fetch it.

In locating "The Kingdom," "The Lord and Brigham" made a big blunder: they ignored suitable Timbuctoo, The Cannibal Islands, Egypt *proper*, and even the Soudan where False Prophets are fashionable; and hooked on to Squatters' Rights, drove stakes, hung out their shingle and stuck right in the midst of "Uncle Sam's Almighty and Everlasting Free Republic;" the last place on earth fit to set up a Kingdom in. Real good free Republican Soil is poor stuff to fix kingdoms on, and its a mistake to try to set up a Kingdom claim, by jumping a Republic.‡ The Kingdom thus set up must "get up and git;" Yankee Prophets to the contrary *notwithstanding*: "'twont stand no-how any way you kin fix it; its worse nor humpty dumpty after he tumbled off the wall. All the doctors in the land cant make this humpty dumpty stand."

It has a slippery footing, and a mighty shaky foundation. Whereunto shall I liken it? It may be likened unto a house built upon the sand: let the torrents from the President, Cabinet and Congress of the Republic descend;

‡In America, certain conditions must be complied with to secure title to lands and mining claims; failing to comply within a given time, another takes possession, which is called "Jumping."

and let the floods come from Pulpit and Press, and let the winds of Public Sentiment blow and beat upon it; and down she comes dead sure, "you bet." You may bet your bottom dollar on it; go the whole pile and go in and win; you hear me! The Brigamite will snicker at this and say, "I teach as one having authority and not as a scribe." Though the Scribe may not be up to much, I give the *naked truth,* and the word *with the bark on :* and ere I write finis at the tail end, the Authority will be found "O. K." It will also be discovered that this Rooster has received ample Authority, having graduated in "the School of the Prophets;" "The Devil's Acadamy;" yea and also "The Mormon Academy of Music;" where 2500 "Ishmaelite" Brats yell "Sally Come up," and invite seven Salls to "take hold of one man," and then burlesque "John Brown's wife got a baby," simply because such a fuss was raised over one baby: followed with "'Tis nice to be a father," revised to date, showing that to be a real "dad" one must have a gross of "Home Manufactures" on hand, with a dozen or so on the stocks. (I am not joking: I naturally burlesque, yet I deal with facts not fantasy.) One of their Sabbath. School Hymns on "Home Manufactures" runs thus :—

"TUNE—*Sprig of Shillaleh.*'

The first on the list of our wants I will mention,
Are the boys and the girls that most claim our attention,
For building up Zion in these the last days;
And these must be raised on the old fashioned plan
Which Abraham and Isaac and Jacob pursued,
To give many women to every good man,
And raise up a host from our own mountain brood." *

There are seven verses this size and style, but you and I must be content with one, to catch a bit of another sacred Sabbath school ditty which goes to the

"TUNE—*King of the Cannibal Islands.*"

"These Mormons marry many wives, and every man among them strives,
To raise the greatest crowd of boys, to thrash the wicked Gentiles."†

Sorry I have not room for all this "Sacred" Carol. Mormon Hymns are double long metre, 12 lines 16, and very peculiar metres. I give a "wee" bit from another.

"TUNE—*Female Auctioneer.*"

"The best of all the plans to swell the emigration here,
Are arrivals from behind the Vail,‡ when the babies do appear."

As these urchins of "Modern Hagers" are mainly fed on Crab Apples and Sourkrout; then crammed with tartaric acid and brimstone to purify their polygamic blood, the music in this academy has a sour-grape, teeth-on-edge twang, and is Sulphuric Acid concentrated. I am before my story, got into Polygamy too soon; let me "back out," for we are all going into it shortly, then you and I will have spasms: I understand them, and expect to get through all right: you may expect fits and spasms when I drag you into the Harem-Scarem Polygamy business. "The blooming thing" is a violent spasmodic dynamite affair anyhow: the "blow ups" of Polygamy shake things worse than Modern Fenian Explodes, and old Vesuvius "on a bender" is peace and security compared with it. I have been through the blooming mill you know; but you have not. To be exempt from damages I caution you, that

* Page 24, "Mountain Warbler"   + Ibid Page 50.
‡Ibid Page 38.—"Behind the Vail" means, in embryo. For a more correct idea of these precious "Sabbath School Hymns, see Appendix B.

the exciting episodes convulse: some laugh, others roar, few cry, while many burst. Ladies must have someone to love and hold on by, rejecting tight fits and pull-backs to be safe. Gents can take care of themselves if their buttons are O. K. The Masher will find Polygamy a Smasher. But ere we enter Polygamy, *revenons à nos moutons*.

Brigham's Kingdom and the American Republic could not co-exist and jog along together amicably. "The Gospel according to Saint Brigham" tells how the wind blew; and to feed hungry souls I cram in extracts of nicely cooked up, and highly flavoured Sermons from the "Journal of Discourses."*

It will be much more interesting if you read Appendix A before proceeding to read these "sacred" Discourses. The reporters tried to make these sermons read decent; they are not near so rough as really delivered. The "Leading Shepherds" growl because the printers "left out the spice" and took the wind out of their sails."

Says Brigham:—"Do you suppose that I'm going to crouch down and suffer this people to bow down to the rod of corruption? No! I tell you we are at the defiance of all hell. Are the officers of the (American) Government, the judges of our religion? It's none of their business whether it is true or false.

> For we'll have our own way, be't wrong or right,
> And say by strength of faith the crow is white.—*Hudibras.*

He adds—So help me God, I will use them up. (All the congregation said 'Amen'). So help me God we will slay them. If they had any respect for their own welfare, they would come forth and say, whether Joseph Smith was a Prophet or not, 'We shed his blood, and now let us atone for it.' And they would be willing to have their heads chopped off, that their blood might run upon the ground, and the smoke of it rise before the Lord as an incense for their sins. I love them that much. At present they have the lead and say, 'Now you poor Mormons, are you not afraid that we can muster our thousands and destroy you?' 'Go to hell,' say I, 'and be damned; for you will go there, and you are damned already.' Again they say, 'We are afraid you saints are becoming aliens to the United States; we are afraid your hearts are weaned.' Dont talk about weaning now, for we were weaned long ago. We are determined not to rest until we revolutionize the United States, and the whole world; and gather out the honest 'till there is hardly enough left to elect a President, even among the Know-Nothings. If you let us alone we will do it more leisurely; but if you persecute us we'll do it quicker, and sit up nights to preach the Gospel. We will bear off the Kingdom, and you may pile on State after State, Kingdom after Kingdom, and all hell on top and we will roll on the Kingdom, build the Cities and Temples of Zion, and I establish the Kingdom to bear rule over all the earth. If ever a man should lay his hands on me, I would send that man to hell across lots, I am always prepared for such an emergency. If any miserable scoundrels come here, cut their throats! (All the people said 'Amen') May God bless you, Amen." Thus endeth the first reading of the Gospel according to "St. Brigham."‡

‡There is plenty more of Brigham's high-flown sentiments, worse and more of it, to follow further on. The above is culled from Vol. 2, Page 186-7. See also pages 182, 255, 311, 312, 317, 320, and 322.

"Apostle" Kimble, the Prophet's chief cook and bottlewasher, played second fiddle to "God's mouthpiece," Brigham, and chimes in thus:— "The thread is cut between the United States and us, and we will never gybe again —no never, worlds without end (voices, Amen!) The day of our separation has come, we have declared our independence, we are a free and independent people. This Kingdom, this people, Our Governor (Brigham) will stand, and we never shall be ruled over by any of them again Never, no never; I am glad, and can shout Hallelujah! and let all Israel say Amen! (the assembly responded Amen!). I'll not talk as I think; if I did, I would knock this pulpit head over heels. Get out of my way you poor stinking curses. Your leaders all say, Uncle Sam has got to ground arms from this time henceforth. But we have shouldered arms, and it's present arms; and do you not see that the next thing is to take aim? Brigham said his sword should never be sheathed again. I will back him in it, and so will every officer in the Kingdom of God."—

"We're free of every spiritual order,
To preach, and fight, and pray and murder."—*Hudibras.*

"What do you say my dear brethren, will we go it? If so raise your right hands and say Aye. (One loud 'Aye' ran through the congregation). But let me tell you, gentlemen we will take it just as God dictates: and if he says rough and tumble, let us take it rough and tumble, and pitch them headlong where they belong. We shall prescribe a course for the United States to take after this. The President of the United States and his coadjutors shall never rest again, for they shall go to hell. The United States will be cut off from being a nation, and her star of empire set, and set in blood. Well this is just as brother Brigham has said here hundreds of times." This "Latter-day Apostle" proceeds to vilify Senator Douglas in language disgusting to Ladies and Gentlemen, hence I omit it. He winds up by saying "I will burn my property, and fly to the mountains with my family in rags, sheepskins and goatskins, rather than succumb to such an ungodly, pussillanimous President, with his coadjutors, as those that govern this nation."*

*" Journal of Discourses" Vol. 6. Page 37-8. See also pages 33, 34, 35, 48, 67, and 68.

Other "Leading Shepherds" deal out similar fodder to the wild flock. "Apostle" Hyde, says:—"The fearless Prophet and Seer commands you to stand up, and assert your rights, the sword of the Lord and of Brigham will back you up, and fight your battles. Trust in Brigham; be valiant, fear not, and the Kingdom is yours." And adds:—Do I believe the United States will be divided? Yes, I do; the prayers of all the saints throughout the world should be to that effect. However strongly it may be urged that the Government's intentions are good towards us, this singular people will not believe a word of it. Brigham Young, or his duly chosen successor can alone govern the Mormons; the man chosen of God, armed with the power of revelation and the visions of heaven, is the man to lead the Latter-day Saints. No less will satisfy them. To the rule of no other will they submit. We never can, we never shall yield to the powers of this world, world without end. Remember Joseph in Egypt! The anger of the Almighty will wax hot against the United States, causing them to drink the cup of bitterness and division, and the very dregs stirred up by Foreign Powers: and cause famine and pestilence in all the world, who will come bending to Joseph in Utah to buy corn. Politicians oppose our gathering together, but have plenty of wheat, pork and beef on hand, all hell cannot stop them from coming here. Look out for the old man and all the boys to come bending unto you, and I'll venture they will not quarrel with you about Church and State, at least not until they have had their breakfast. If the United States will not make Brigham Young Governor, wheat will. Joseph's brethren never voted to make him Governor over them: but he was elected to that office by a joint ballot of wheat and corn. There is more Salvation and Security in wheat, than in all the political schemes of the world, and more power in it than in all the contending armies of the nations. Raise wheat and lay it up until it will bring a good price: not dollars and cents, but Kingdoms. Countries, Peoples, Tribes and Tongues. They have sold themselves for nought, and must be redeemed without money. It will take wheat to redeem them!"†

†" Journal of Discourses" Vol. 2, page 206-7. See also Vol. 6, page 12 to 15 & 360.

"Bishop" L. D. Young, brother of Brigham, says :—" I could jump up and cry ' Hallelujah!' and ' Glory!' like a Methodist, because the Kingdom of God is set up and given to the Saints of the Most High. The yoke of oppression is broken off, and independence is given to us, that the Kingdom of God may advance on the earth. Well here we are a free people. We are at liberty to go out in the defence of Zion. The stone that is cut out of the mountain without hands (Mormonism), has begun to roll, and it will fall on the feet, toes and legs of the image, and crush Great Babylon (all Christian Churches) to pieces: by its power the nations will be broken. I have long prayed that the Lord Almighty would destroy the nation that gave me birth. Yes, I pray that it may be broken to pieces and become like an old vessel that is broken and thrown out to rot."*

" President " Joseph Young, another of Brigham's brothers, says :—" Our enemies (the Government and people of America) are not sane. They are no more sane after they have set their hands against this people. The administrators of the Government are just as insane as they can be. They do not comprehend that those men (whose sermons I quote from), who stand at our head, hold the keys of Salvation ; but I do believe they desire to extirpate the last vestige of hope that is on the earth. (The Mormon Church). This is the folly and meanness of man, to destroy those who hold the power and keys of salvation to the inhabitants of the whole earth."† He then prates about their "Independence," and the imbecility of their enemies (the Americans,) which I must omit.

One more " Gem of inspiration " from " The Prophet," which runs thus :— " I turn the key that opens the heavens to restrain you no longer from this time forth. You are at liberty to let loose to blood and thunder. But be cool, be deliberate, be wise, act with almighty power, and when you pull do it effectually— make a sweepstakes. *I will spill the last drop of blood in my veins and will see all my enemies IN HELL.* To bear longer would be a Sin. Shall we bear it any longer? (One universal ' No '! ran through all the vast assembly like a peal of thunder.) Some say they will mob us ; let them mob and be damned! and let them go to hell and be damned! If mobs come dung your gardens with them. We don't want any excitement, but we will rise up Washington-like, and break off the hellish yoke that oppresses us. I swear in the name of Almighty God, and with uplifted hands to heaven, I will spill my hearts' blood in our defence. I will turn up the world - I will make war, and will fight with guns, sword, cannon, whirlwind and thunder, until they are used up like Kilkenny Cats. Will you help me? If so raise the right hand. (There was a unanimous response, a perfect sea of hands being elevated.) Here is truly a committee of the whole. If the authorities on the earth will not sustain us in our rights, we will claim them from a higher power,—from Heaven,—Yea, from God Almighty. May the blessings of Heaven rest upon you, Amen." Thus saith the Prophet.‡

The Probate Judge, and " High Priest," Elias Smith, says :— I have been with the Saints in all the scenes they have passed through, and I have striven to do all I could for the cause, have endeavoured to do what I was told by those over me; and that will be the case with me to-day; and then after I have spoken to you, I shall go and do something else. If we obey the counsel and advice of those set over us, nothing will molest us. The United States may send all the Armies they please—I have that faith and confidence in the work of the Lord that I feel assured, if we carry out those principles and the advice of those set to lead us (The Prophets, Apostles, and Bishops, just quoted), all will be well with us, and our enemies (The Government and people of the United States) will have no power over us whatever. But as to their

*Journal of Discourses, Vol 6, p 224-5. †p 207. ‡Vol 2, p. 164-5. also p. 166 7 8 & 9.

conduct awing us into subjection, I feel as though it never would be done. (Voices: Amen!) I am aware the prophecies are fulfilling, and we shall soon have scenes of war and commotion, and may be brought into collision with the United States; but as to their having power to destroy our leaders as they wish, I do not believe they ever will." [This old Rooster crows considerably over poor old "Uncle Sam," as he calls the American Government. He is going to capture Jackson County, Missouri, and says, "I expect to go there and see Israel (The Mormons) victorious over all her enemies, and that the measure they have sought to measure out to us we shall have the privilege of measuring to them." To this Brigham shouted "God Grant it!" and the people said, Amen. *]

From what I have quoted from these "Sermons" we see that Brigham's "Kingdom," and "Uncle Sam's" Republic can never be friends. To exist on the same soil means constant collision, and the further Mormons get from "Uncle Sam" the better for both parties. Pioneers sent to "spie out the land," at the time of the "Mormon Exodus" from Egypt (United States) to the "Promised Land" (Mexico) reported glowingly, and when Brigham & Co., after a tedious 1100 mile journey got a glimpse of Salt Lake Valley, they exclaimed—"The Land of Promise! The Land of Promise!—held in reserve for the Saints!" The "Saintly Devils" had designed to settle in California. John Taylor, who left the Church of England and is now "Boss Prophet," or "Chief Cock of the Dunghill" composed for the occasion the following:—

"In upper California, Oh that's the land for me!
It lies between the Mountains and Great Pacific Sea:
The Saints can be supported there, and taste the sweets of liberty
In Upper California,—Oh that's the land for me. Oh, that's &c.

We'll burst off all our fetters, and break the Gentile yoke,
For long it has beset us, but now it shall be broke:
No more shall Jacob bow his neck; henceforth he shall be great and free
In Upper California—Oh—that's the land for me! Oh, that's &c.

Then join with me my brethren, and let us hasten there;
We'll lift our glorious standard and raise our house of prayer.
We'll call on all the nations round to join our standard and be free
In Upper California—Oh, that's the land for me! Oh, that's &c. †

There is more of this "Sacred" doggrel but my space is too valuable. "British Saints" caught the "Yankee Doodle Saints" California fever. "A Johnny Bull Elder" gives his ditty thus:—

"On Zion's land there will be rest, for all the saints that's *here oppressed*;
On Zion's Mount we shall be free, and *there* we'll have our Jubilee.

CHORUS—To California's land we'll go, where from the mountains, wine
  doth flow;
A land of peace and liberty, to California! Go with me.
No Tyrant shall annoy us there, we'll serve our KING without a fear;
In California's beauty plains, we'll meet to learn celestial strains.
               To California's &c.

The everlasting hills we'll view, and to England bid adieu;
To sing and shout on Zion's hill, where sighs nor sorrows never thrill
               To California's &c." ‡

There are twelve verses of this stuff, but "Enough's as good as a feast," I guess all hands can feast on what I give.

* Journal of Discourses, Vol. 6. p. 218-19.   †Mormon Hymn Book. Hymn 299.

‡ "Millenial Star" Vol. 11 p. 47. Published by "Apostle" Pratt, 42, Islington, Liverpool. Where Mormon works are sold at "A Devil of a Price."

Brigham and his gang reached Salt Lake Valley, July 24, 1847, and found it naturally adapted for settlement, and for the furtherance of his nefarious schemes. Here, isolated, a thousand miles from Christian and Civilized influence; in the heart of the American Continent, this "Foul Blot" was destined to grow and flourish. This is when the loathsome cancer should have been cut out, and destroyed while their numbers were few. It is not as the world supposes, that Brigham led all the Mormons to Salt Lake- not by a long odds. It may be news though a fact; only the odious scum, olid dregs and offal of the Church took chances in Brigham's buccaneer guerrilla enterprise, sworn to "git up and get" out of "Egypt," bounce Mexico, grab "the good and large land flowing with milk and honey" and build up the kingdom, *Vi et armis, vide* Exodus 3-8. Brigham could only nab his own kin, the paucity of which can be seen by tracing the facts. "Apostle" Snow said, "Since its rise (1830, in ten years, to 1840) this (Mormon) Church has gathered 100,000 Souls."† Authentic Statistics show 150,000 at Smith's death when Brigham "made havock of the church" and led to the Salt Lake Sodom all he could hoodwink and "lead by the nose," as their ragamuffin brats when inside their Sunday duds yell:—

"Though many, we're one and are easily led."

"The Mountain Warbler." Page 121— See Appendix B. for these Choice Rhymes

"Apostle Pratts Epistle to the Saints in Great Britain," dated "Great Salt Lake City, Sept. 5, 1848," 14 months after its settlement says:- -"Our population amounts to between 4000 and 5000 Whites, besides several tribes of Indians who have come to live with us.**   The FIRST GENERAL EPISTLE FROM GREAT SALT LAKE VALLEY, TO THE SAINTS SCATTERED THROUGHOUT THE EARTH—GREETING," says:—"We number about 5000 Souls."* This "Epistle" we are told is "Indicted by the Holy Spirit" and being signed by Brigham Young and the "First Presidency" two years after filching their Salt Lake "inheritance" must be correct, and clearly proves that, "The Lion of the Lord," Brigham, snatched and gobbled less than 5000 Rams, Ewes, and Lambs from a flock of 150,000. The United States should have then destroyed the Vile Ulcer ere the nasty thing grew. "The Lion of the Lord" was allowed to roar and grow in the Mountains of Israel."

"Brigham, Lion of the Lord, here brings forth *his* holy word."‡
Another of the "Songs of Zion" has a chorus.

"Brigham Young is the Lion of the Lord,
And the world soon shall tremble at his word."

I had not intended introducing the Devil until I came to the "Endowment House" where I met him alive and well, and had a good chat with him. But as the Devil is a Poet, and one of his dittys fit in here, I give a line or two from the very Devil himself.

" Lo the Lion's left his thicket : up ye watchmen, be in haste ;
The destroyer of the Gentiles goes to lay their cities waste.

Chorus.—We're the true born sons of Zion, who with us that can compare?
We're the royal branch of Joseph, the bright and glorious morning Star."

"Sacred Spiritual Songs" 12th. Edition p. 332 Hymn 257. I give more of the 1 evils Hymns, the Devils Sayings and the Devils Doings, as they fit in.

A better place than the Great Salt Lake Basin in the Rocky Mountains could not be found for Br'gham's purposes. Here, surrounded by snow capped mountains, "the everlasting hills," "Zion" could be firmly established. As the mountains were round about Jerusalem, so mountains far more impervious

†"The Gospel Reflector" P. 22. Published at Philadelphia U. S. 1841, by "Elder' Winchester. (Out of Print.)
°*"Millennial Star", Vol. 11. p. 22.   Ibid. 1849. Vol 11. p. 228.   ‡Mountain Warbler p 7.

guarded this "New Jerusalem." Corresponding with Palestine's Dead Sea was the great Salt Lake. The river running northward between two lakes corresponded with ancient Jordan, and was at once named "The River Jordan." Besides, Scripture says "O Zion, get thee up into the *high* mountains." Utah Mountains are 10,000 feet above sea level; plenty high enough to fill the bill. Again it says, "And it shall come to pass in that day (Brigham's day of course), that the Lord shall set up an ensign for the nations, and assemble the outcasts of Israel and gather the dispersed of Judah: and bring my sons from far, and my daughters from the ends of the earth; let them shout from the tops of the Mountains." A poor standpoint to shout from: I found it very difficult to fetch breath in Utah altitudes, we puff and blow with plenty of wind all around on the outside; but the lungs refuse to inhale sufficient for shouting purposes. I am satisfied, that Scripture cannot refer to the Rocky Mountains, besides, what good is it to shout to the wind in a volcanic region? Geologists find it was once literally what it now is figuratively —"Hell upon Earth"—apt to burst forth again any time and set things in a blaze; and there is brimstone enough around there to start another "bottomless pit." No one cares to shout in such a region. To return to prophecy, Brigham had read: "In that day seven women shall take hold of one man, saying we will eat our own bread and wear our own apparel: only let us be called by thy name." Here was the very place to successfully carry out that part of it. It is in Utah that 7, and 7 times 7: yea, 70 times 7 women *take hold of one man*: and so literally is this prophecy fulfilled, that the Polygamic trollops of that "Hell on Earth" have to find their own "grub and duds" or go without. Again, Brigamites claim that the following refers to Brigham Young, "Behold my servant whom I uphold. He shall bring forth Judgment to the Gentiles." Hence Brigham was "The Lord's Anointed One." Now John Taylor is the only "Lord's Anointed" on the earth. This old Prophet Rooster found his way to Utah truthfully singing:

"I'm all the way from Manchester, and want no work to do."

This lying old Polygamist claims that by "Divine Right" he has to "Boss the Yankees," "Whip John Bull" and then "Govern the whole Earth." I shall take you into the "Endowment House" presently and show how we take the most binding oaths under the penalty of the throat being cut from ear to ear and the tongue torn from the mouth, that we will "never speak against the Lord's Anointed Prophet." I have "done gone and done it," as the Darkies say, and any Mormon would feel perfectly justified in opening my windpipe just under the chin, and "shut off my wind" as they term it, and then make sure my little tongue stops wagging by jerking it out like a dentist does a tooth, simply for speaking as I do against these "anointed" vagabonds.

To continue. Under this prophetic leadership the "Saints" must "lay judgment to the line, and righteousness to the plummet." To them, "All Nations are as a drop of the bucket, and all the inhabitants thereof as grasshoppers." I have had some experience with grasshoppers, and from what I know of their peculiar characteristics I say "Go it ye drop of the bucket grasshoppers, pounce upon and eat up these rank weeds: lay bare and clean the earth of all the 'Anointed' vagabond scamps that infest it." Again, they are to "chase, thrash, and tread down their enemies:" (all non-Mormons are enemies). "One Mormon shall chase a thousand, and two put ten thousand to flight. Their enemies, confounded at all their might, will lick the dust."

The Saints believe that Brigham firmly established "THE KINGDOM" which the Prophet Daniel foretold should be "set up" in the last days, which shall never be destroyed: but it shall break in pieces and consume all other Kingdoms and Governments, and Stand for Ever. Here was the very place to carry on the game of kingdom building, kingdom smashing, and so forth.

Here in Mexico, while the Mexicans laboured under serious difficulties, Brigham grabbed a vast portion of their land, and staked out the "Kingdom of God."

With the following boundaries, to wit: commencing at the 33° of north latitude, where it crosses the 108° of longitude, west of Greenwich; thence running south and west to the boundary of Mexico; thence west to and down the main channel of the Gila River (or the northern line of Mexico), and on the northern boundary of lower California to the Pacific Ocean; thence along the coast north westerly to the 118° 30 of west longitude; thence north to where said line intersects the dividing ridge of the Sierra Nevada mountains; thence north along the summit of the Sierra Nevada mountains to the dividing range of mountains that separate the waters flowing into the Columbia River from the waters running into the Great Basin; thence easterly along the dividing range of mountains that separate said waters flowing into the Columbia River on the north, from the waters flowing into the Great Basin on the south, to the summit of the Wind River chain of mountains; thence south east and south by the dividing range of mountains that separate the waters flowing into the Gulf of Mexico from the waters flowing into the Gulf of California, to the place of beginning. (I give Mexico's present boundary).

This embraces most of the States and territories between the Missouri and Pacific Ocean, and the present Northern boundary of Mexico, to the British possessions: within which, the Monarchies of Europe could find plenty of elbow-room. Here then "Uncle Sam's Abscess" has swollen and grown until it holds the balance of power in nearly all the States and Territories embraced in this area; has gathered to its fold the great tribes of Indians; and are now busy, gathering the once whipped but dissatisfied and rebel South. In this they are remarkably successful; and why? Ah! echo answers Why!

"They who have been vanquished bear silence—but not submission. In his lair

Fix'd passion holds his breath, until the hour which shall alone forbear— none need despair."

Look out Uncle Sam! watch well the intrigue of Mormons with the South, and do not for a moment imagine that Southerners have forgiven, or ever can forget your taking away their darling, Slavery. (More anon on this).

The land was Mexico's in 1847, when Brigham gobbled it; but the Hidalgo Treaty of 1848 ceded it to the United States, and although the "Saints" had taken such trouble to get away from "Uncle Sam," they were by the Treaty with Mexico, brought again under the dominion of the hated American Republic. This not suiting the "Saintly Devils," they established "A Free and Independent Government," made Brigham Young their KING, and filled all state offices with Apostles, Priests, and Bishops, and this they had the bare-faced impudence to call "Zion." "The new Jerusalem" "The Kingdom of God;" in fact calling it everything but its right name. For after 12 years careful scrutiny of the whole business, living and travelling in and out among them, I can only call it "Hell upon Earth."

I said Brigham was made king, and I mean it; I am bound to state facts as I know them to exist. We have noticed the British "Saints" fired with zeal, exclaiming "We'll serve our King without a fear" when they have "bid adieu to England," and "Sing and shout on Zion's hill among the everlasting hills," in Utah. This is no mere fantasy; it is well understood by British Mormons that the Prophet is "King over all the earth" in *this* day. I was unmistakeably told that the Prophet of Utah is "King," and the only King reigning upon the earth by "Divine authority;" that I must obey him in preference to any king, ruler or potentate on earth. Startle not, my American cousins that you have ruling in you midst "a divine king," and "a god almighty," in the person of the Mormon Prophet, and according to Mormon doctrine, you will soon realize that fact. If you attempt to put them down, they at once cry "persecution," and tell you "if persecuted, they will sit up nights" to carry on their game. What are you going to do about it? I would advise that you study well my remedy, and act immediately.

The children in Sabbath Schools delight to sing the following—

"TUNE—*King of the Cannibal Islands.*"

"These poor deluded people say, o'er all the world they'll soon bear sway,
And sweep the Gentiles all away, and send them to hell across lots.
For none but Mormons there can stay, I'm sure there'll be the devil to pay,
Unless there's something quickly done to put these saucy Mormons down.

Chorus:—And Brigham Young he is their KING, to him they tithes and offerings bring
And he controls in everything, in the midst of these awful Mormons.
And men and women all agree, to Brigham they'll obedient be,
And at his little finger's crook, they'll bring outsiders all to book.
And Brigham Young he is their king, &c.

"Mountain Warbler" page 49. See Appendix B. for these "Sacred Cantatas."

Another of their Sunday Schools Hymns, not yet adopted by the American Sunday School Union, runs thus:—

"Tune—*Old Potomac Shore.*"

There's a song that all are singing in this merry land of ours,
On the mountains, in the meadows all around,
It sings on the hills and echoes in the vales
While angels catch the sound,
And bearing it on high, re-echo back the cry,
By myriad voices sung, God bless our Prophet, Priest and King,
Our leader, Brigham Young.

Chorus:— Hail to Brigham Young, hail to Brigham Young,
Praise him every tongue; and sing,
God bless our Prophet, Priest and King, our Leader
Brigham Young.

Mountain Warbler, page 91. Sabbath School teachers, and superintendents, see Appendix B.

I quote hymns often because I believe in them; show me your hymn book and I will tell you your faith and practice. If I go into a strange place of worship, and know not what creed is taught therein, I get their hymn book and find out. Again, poetry fires the heart, and has a more lasting impression, and again, Savages know the value of war songs. Americans admit that "Yankee Doodle" fired the hearts of the revolutionary fathers and helped them on to victory, and who doubts but that "Rule Britannia" and similar songs, raises British enthusiasm. So with the Mormons, they understand the value of poetical effussions, and as they sing in that last song "All are singing it on the mountains, in the meadows all around," and you hear in Utah "God bless our Prophet, Priest and King, our Leader, Brigham Young," as much as "Pop goes the Weasel" or any favourite ditty was ever heard in England.

When Young Brigham, "Chip of the old block," who is a perfect representation of King Henry the Eighth, came here to swindle the poor British dupes, he claimed Royalty, and set himself up as " Prince of Utah"—Eldest Son of the King of Utah. John D. Lee, in his dying confession, from which I quote all I can in this work, says:—"The Son of the Prophet Brigham, while on a mission to England, concluded to measure arms with Queen Victoria and the Prince of Wales, by driving as many horses as she did to her carriage. This was violation of law. The Queen very soon gave Prince Briggy to understand that she was ruler of that kingdom ; that if his father could measure arms with the President of the United States, his son could not do so with her. Prince Brig was shut up in jail. I have been told that 26000 dol. (£5,500.) were paid for his release." * British Saints have no need to be "told."

"Life and Confessions of J. D. Lee," p. 163, Bryan Brand and Co, St. Louis, U.S. 1879.

they know, and have cause to well remember this little episode, for the money wrung from their hard earnings liberated the " Royal Impostor " from " Quad " or in plain " Yankee English," the Jug, which means a cage made for jugglars who juggle juggingly, (See Walker's Dict.) More anon of " Prince Brig and his Royal Pa, King Brigham."

"The Kingdom" began to grow when planted in the Great Basin. Wild weeds grow rapidly and even Polygamy is no very great drawback to the growth of a community. Besides they were a " peculiar people " in a peculiar land. To quote from American Newspapers, "The Mormons have the most remarkable spot in America—Since the children of Israel wandered through the wilderness, or the Crusaders rushed on Palestine, there has been nothing so historically singular as the emigration and recent settlement of the Mormons. Thousands of them came from the Manchesters and Sheffields of England, to join other thousands congregated from New York and New England—boasted decendants of the Pilgrim Fathers—together to follow after a New Jerusalem in the West. 7000 are now settled on the Plateau Summit of the North American Continent. Thousands more are about to join them from Iowa, and thousands more are coming from Wales." * This published after the " First General Epistle " which gave the number as 5000, shows that the " Saints " had begun to increase, and obey the command " Be fruitful and Multiply." The " New York Herald " says :—" The Mormon Saints, have, at last found a New Jerusalem, or Holy Land, in the Great Salt Lake Valley between the Rocky Mountains and the Sierra Nevada. This is one of the most remarkable regions on the face of the globe. Certainly they have a vast country before them, one of their fields contains 8000 acres, and none of their corn patches number less than 1000 acres. It seems to be a sort of Holy Land on a large scale, it has the Salt Sea in it, much larger than that of Palestine ; and it has also a Jordon, a Mount Horeb, and almost all the great features of the ancient Holy Land, but on a tremendously large scale. Brigham Young seems to be the Moses of the whole concern. This expedition of the Mormons has some analogy to that of the exodus of the Israelites from Egypt. Illinois, and Missouri, and Iowa have been to the Mormons the land of bondage from which they have escaped. Now they promise to become a free, powerful, and prosperous people. They have a great deal of religion, and a great deal of cant. But cant is a very necessary thing in a cold climate. It keeps them warm." I quote this from leading American papers to show what they thought of it at the time. Now they no longer " promise to become a free, powerful and prosperous people," but *have* thus become, and if Mormon prophecies are verified this Hell on Earth will subdue the Great Republic of America; the Mexican Republic; those of Central and South America; and the British Possessions. For the whole of North and South America by " Divine Right " (they claim) belongs to " Zion " and is the modern " Land of Promise " The Prophet Brigham said :—" The Land of Joseph is the land of Zion and it takes North and South America to make the land of Joseph. The New Jerusalem is built upon this continent (America) which is the land of Zion."

Journal of Discourses, Vol. 6. p. 296 and 345.

"Elder" Winchester, gives 345 buckets of hodgepodge hogwash, then adds :—" These predictions must apply to America, and the reader will dis-

* Cincinatti Atlas, A paper published in Cincinatti, U.S.A.

cover that the land of America is a promised land to the Mormons, as much so as Canaan to the House of Israel." *

* The Gospel Reflector, p. 113. out of print.

In the preface of this out of print volume, the "Elder solicits the prayers of the Saints that he may help to roll on the stone cut out of the Mountains without hands; which will roll till it fills the earth." As this "Gospel Reflector" contains "Apostle" Cowdery's letters to the Devil, and other interesting matter I shall refer to it again. Though it is gone out of print, I snatched a copy before it went. I was twelve years in Utah gathering these out of print works, and to satisfy my readers will cram in all I can of them.

It may be news to most people to learn that America is the Old World and not the New. False Tradition led us to believe that the Garden of Eden was in Asia. That Cain killed Abel just outside that garden. That Enoch walked with God, and Noah built the first boat on the Eastern Hemisphere, etc. No my friends, No! I must preach "Mormon Gospel" (good news) to you, and say, "It is all an Error."

Eden, where Eve listened to the Devil, and fell, was in the United States. The Devil after being cast out of Heaven, Immigrated to America thousands of years before Columbus discovered it. The Fall, the Flood, and so forth and so on, all transpired in the same land where Sodom and Gomorrah reigns triumphant to-day, (viz.), in the glorious land of America. Though I often heard this proclaimed from the "Jack in the box" pulpits of America's "Zion," matters of such "deep import," call for more than my bare word; hence I give "Words of Inspiration,"—real "Modern Apostolic Theology" by a "Live Yankee Apostle," published at the Seat of Government, Washington, D.C., U.S.A, under the very nose of the President, Cabinet, Senate, and House of Representatives of the Great Model Republic, in this enlightened 19th century of the Christian Era. If this fails to satisfy your cravings, then a far worse case than that of Oliver Twist exists, if the public "asks for more from Mr. Bumble." Before introducing this "Grand, Divine, and truly wonderful Yankee Apostolic flummery," it must be understood that all Mormon publications, even Newspapers, are the "Word of God:" far more so than the Bible. The latter is merely God's word to guide Ancient Israel, which the Mormons call "Dead Revelations:" while the former are "God's living revelations through his living servants to govern all who live on the earth in these last days."

> "They a bold pow'r o'er sacred scriptures take,,
> Blot out some clauses, and some new ones make."
> (Cowley's Puritan and Papist.)

I could, if space permitted in this book, give a vast amount of such "sacred" trash, with chapter and verse, but it would fill a volume no library shelf could hold, and would be anything but a "Sea-Side library," or Railway Traveller's Pocket Companion. Even Britons, who carry more baggage than Americans, would not care to pack it around. While I indulge incredulity on weighty matters, I claim credulity on the less important— *ab uno disce omnes.* I am compelled to omit a vast amount for want of space, and not from the inadequacy of the many Mormon publications in my possession. To omit to give "The Sacred Word," given through "An Apostle" at the very Seat of Government at Washington would be a sin, and to prove that Eden, &c., was in America: "The Mormon Holy Bible "—" The Seer," page 262, says :—"From what God has revealed concerning this great Continent of America, this is the very land where the righteous were in the days of Enoch, and this is the very land where once flourished the Garden of Eden. From American soil was formed the first man, beast, fowl, and creeping thing. Here Satan introduced sin, misery, and death. Here holy messengers guarded with flaming sword the tree of life. Here Cain killed Abel. Here was built an ark of safety, wherein seed of all flesh was preserved to repeople a world cleansed from wickedness by baptism in the mighty flood. America, then, may be considered the Old World—the cradle of the human race—the theatre of events pertaining to the Antediluvian age." Thus endeth the present reading of the Scriptures "inspired" at Washington. This sacred volume, No. 1, p. 1, opens with the "Masonic All-Seeing Eye," in the centre of a heart surrounded with refulgent rays, and the words "THE SEER" in large fancy letters. This is followed with, "ALL YE INHABITANTS OF THE WORLD, AND DWELLERS ON THE EARTH, SEE YE, WHEN HE LIFTETH UP AN ENSIGN ON THE MOUNTAINS.—*Isaiah xviii.*, 3.

PROSPECTUS OF 'THE SEER.'

"THE SEER is a title assumed for this Periodical in commemoration of JOSEPH SMITH, the great SEER of the last days, who, as an instrument in the hands of the Lord, laid the foundation of the Kingdom of God, preparatory to the second coming of the Messiah to reign with universal dominion over all the Earth.

"The pages of the SEER will be mostly occupied with original matter, illucidating the doctrines of the Church of Jesus Christ of Latter Day Saints, as revealed in both ancient and modern Revelations. The doctrine of *Celestial Marriage, or Marriage for all eternity*, as believed and practised by the Saints in Utah Territory, will be clearly explained. The views of the Saints in regard to the *ancient Patriarchal Order of Matrimony, or Plurality of Wives*, as developed in a Revelation, given through JOSEPH, the SEER, will be fully published. The Celestial origin and pre-existence of the spirits of men—their first estate or probation in a previous world—the great benefits, derived by descending from Heaven, and entering fleshly tabernacles; and keeping the laws of their second estate, and their final redemption and exaltation, as God's in their future state—are subjects which will, more or less, occupy the pages of the SEER.

"It is hoped that the President elect, the Hon. Members of Congress, the Heads of the various Departments of the National Government, the high-minded Governors and Legislative Assemblies of the several States and Territories, the Ministers of every Religious denomination, and all the inhabitants of this great Republic, will patronize this Periodical, that through the medium of our own writings they may be more correctly and fully informed in regard to the peculiar doctrines, views, practices, and expectations of the Saints who now flourish in the Mountain Territory, and who will eventually flourish over the whole Earth. And we say to all nations, subscribe for the SEER, and we promise you a True and Faithful description of all the principal features, characterizing this great and last "dispensation of the fulness of times."

ORSON PRATT, *Editor, Washington City, D. C.*

"DECEMBER 21, 1852.

"The Seer," is a rich, rare, and racy book, hence I give all I possibly can in Appendix C. I have given plenty to show where "Zion" is and of what it consists. In the following chapters I will tell how British Christians are drawn into it; and what I saw, heard, and felt in this "Hell upon Earth."

N.B.—The italics and capitals are theirs. Why I quote so much from Mormon Periodicals and Sermons is because I wish to deal fairly with the question from a Mormon standpoint as much as possible, Mormons, of course, will not object to a wide circulation of their views.

NOTE.—The incorrect spelling, such as illucidating for elucidating, &c., occurs in the Mormon print from which I copy.

CHAPTER III.

How British Christians are "Sucked in"—Led into Sodom I got "Roped in"—What I Saw and Heard in Hell.

Mormon Missionaries sneak around Great Britain like Three Card tricksters and gamblers do, seeking to entrap unwary Christians, and all whom they may devour. Trained by the Devil ere they land at Liverpool, they are up to every trick and know all the moves on the board. Their Yankee Tricks nab the English, Scotch, and Welsh Christians by thousands upon thousands. Mormon Baptisms attract the Baptists and make them easy prey. Universal Salvation and "The final perseverance of the Saints" as preached by Mormons, catch the Methodists; Calvinists get in ecstasy over the beautiful gathering of the "Mormon Elect;" while Scotch and English Presbyterians, Established Church members, Congregationalists, Brethren, Quakers, Bible Christians, and all classes of Christians, but Catholics lay hold on the hope set before them in the "Mormon Gospel:" simply because forsooth the Devil trains the Missionary how to set the bait to suit any particular creed or dogma. He becomes "All things to all men," especially to Girls from 10 to 15, and young women between 15 and 35 years old; the younger, the more tender the sympathy. "He Mormons" have a particular fondness for the fair sex provided they are not old: "The younger widows refuse," is not in the Mormon Bible. They regard old maids as lacking in spiritual efficiency, ladies over the age of 35 and unmarried, seldom embrace Mormonism in any shape or form. If married they are considered as being "up to snuff;" and the Mormon Priest has a peculiar way of reaching them: they "creep into houses" when the husband is not at home and "lead captive silly women laden with sins, led away with divers lusts, for of this sort are they." Each has concubines 7000 miles away, but too far for fellow sympathy here, and though their brothels are "crowded like an omnibus there's room for more," and they come here for the very purpose of securing prostitutes for their hellish dens of infamy in Utah. So they creep in as aforesaid, do their "level best" to seduce other men's wives and daughters, lead them away to their Seraglios, or swop them off for others with some Apostle or Bishop who prefers a change.

These Libertines, and habitual Lechers, are thrown upon the British public for three years, and we are expected to believe that during that time they live a life of Celibacy. You can believe it if you like; I don't; nor shall I, until fish live without water. Mormon fish are not long out of water in England, if at all: there is so much water around our little Island.

A "Good Saint"—that is a man who can marry and whip a lot of wives—being ordered on a Mission to England, I knowing his proclivities so well, said to him, "You will take a few of your wives along won't you, as you cannot well get on without them?" He replied, "I'm no such d——fool as to carry coal to Newcastle, I can get all I want in England: there's plenty there!" Knowing his extra-ordinary wants in that direction I pitied the poor victims he might happen to come across. As I have a special chapter dealing with Missionaries and their nice goings on, I say no more here on that point.

The Mormon Elder is equal to every emergency. If a girl's parents object to her going to Utah, she is quietly put on board ship and sent off to Utah's Brothels to become a Prostitute. Does the kind Husband and Father object to have his wife made a "Saintess"? He comes home some night, finds that his bosom's partner has ransacked the house, stolen the valuables, gone off with the children together with the old lecherous Priest to Utah, there to become his fifth tenth, or fiftieth wife while at the same time the Stepfather also becomes the husband of all her daughters over twelve years, and of the others when they attain that age. Should the "Dear Husband" embrace Mormonism, and the wife refuse to embrace it, or him, unless he renounces the vile thing, the Mormon Devil to encourage the deluded victim quotes this Scripture to him, "Every one that forsaketh father, or mother, OR WIFE, or children, for the Gospel's sake, shall receive AN HUNDRED-FOLD *now in this time*, and shall inherit everlasting life." Now says the Mormon Priest, "If you believe the Bible you *must* leave wife and children for the Gospel's sake: no wife should hinder a man's salvation; sell out, leave wife and children (males) on the Parish, and go to Zion: and I promise you in the name of Israel's God, an hundred-fold of wives and children in this life, and in the world to come, life everlasting. You shall enjoy the blessings of Abraham, Isaac, David and Solomon, for God who changeth not hath given Apostles, Prophets, Evangelists, Pastors, and some Teachers the right to enter Polygamy as anciently; to raise up a righteous seed, for the work of the ministry and the perfecting of the saints. If thou art faithful in a few things, and will forsake thy wife and little ones as God commands, he will make thee ruler over many things (many wives), if He sees thee worthy, as was David and Solomon, his son. Take up thy Cross, follow Christ, and all will be well with thee for time and in Eternity."

A decent man who scruples to become prostituted is tenderly informed that "God is faithful, and He will not suffer *him* to be tempted above what he is able to bear. Polygamy is very rarely practiced; it's only occasionally, when the Lord finds a worthy Solomon that the thing is permitted at all." In short, God is at the helm, and, according to Mormon teaching, steering all the Utah filthy business.

I have seen hundreds of thousands who have thus left the various Churches of Christendom, and gone to Utah's Hell; the Catholic Church only being exempt. Catholics are perfectly satisfied with their Priests; view Mormonism as an Opposition Priesthood, and resist its (Mormon) Priests. Hence Mormon Missionaries fail to convert the Irish. ["True 'tis a pity, pity, 'tis, 'tis true;"] I must tell the truth, and in my bungling way put it in the best shape I can. I travelled over a thousand miles of Mormon Territory; spent twelve years in their Cities, Towns, and Settlements, and found but three Irish; two from Australia, the other a renegade Jesuit, who, had he remained in his Native Country, would have kept as many mistresses as he now does concubines in Utah. He likes it, has a jolly time, does the thing "quite up to Dick," *

* "Up to Dick," is English, Yankees say "quite toney" or "smart,"

says, "the work in which he is engaged is true, and the Kingdom is the O. K. thing." But oh! I saw thousands of Christians from English, Scotch, and Welsh Churches, bitterly lamenting the sorrow and crime of that Hell upon Earth; but before relating it I must tell further how Mormon Missionaries work, and how I got into the trap.

Though they single out victims and depend much on fireside chat, yet their unholy zeal fires 'em up at times to come out boldly, and try to take a town by storm. London is even now being flooded with hand bills in which these devils "cheek it out," and call themselves "The Church of Jesus Christ of Latter-Day Saints:" here is a *verbatim et literatim* copy, but recently sent me :—

"WHICH IS RIGHT?

There is ONE Body (Church), ONE Spirit, ONE Lord, ONE Faith, ONE Baptism."—Eph. iv., 4-6

THEREFORE OF THE 666 DIFFERENT RELIGIONS OF THE DAY 665 ARE WRONG AND BUT ONE IS RIGHT.

WHICH IS RIGHT?

That Church which corresponds in all respects to the Church established by Christ and His Apostles, teaching FAITH, REPENTANCE, BAPTISM by immersion for the remission of sins, THE LAYING ON OF HANDS for the gift of the HOLY GHOST with signs following the believer; and which has for its officers, APOSTLES, PROPHETS, EVANGELISTS, PASTORS, TEACHERS, aids, governments, &c., all of whom are CALLED and AUTHORIZED of God, as were these officers in the early primitive Church.

THE CHURCH OF JESUS CHRIST OF LATTER-DAY SAINTS is the only Church which corresponds to this perfect pattern, and consequently is the only ONE by which mankind can BE SAVED IN THE KINGDOM OF GOD. Jesus says—John v. 39—"Search the Scriptures, for in them ye think ye have eternal life. Therefore we earnestly request all lovers of truth to examine the following passages:—

FAITH—Heb. xi. 6 and 1; James ii. 14 to 26.
REPENTANCE—Luke xiii., 3 and 5; Eze. xviii., 30; Acts xvii., 30.
BAPTISM BY IMMERSION—Matt iii.; Mark xvi., beg. 15; Acts ii., 37 to 41; John iii., 5 and 23; Rom. vi., beg. 3.
HOLY GHOST, HOW CONFERRED, &C.—Acts viii., 17; 1 Cor. xii.; Acts xix.; Matt. iii., 11; 1 Cor. xvi., 26; Acts ii., 3, 4, and 17.
OFFICERS—Eph. iii., 5; ii., 20; iv., 11, 12, and 13; Luke vi., beg. 13.
AUTHORITY—Rom. x., 14 and 15; John xiii., 20; John xvii., 18; Heb. v., 4; Ex. iv., beg. 15; 1 Sam. xiv., beg. 8; 2 Chron. xxvi., beg. 16; Acts xiii, beg. 2; *John vii.*, 17; *Gal, i.*, 8.

OUR MEETINGS ARE HELD AS FOLLOWS:—

NORTH LONDON BRANCH.—42, Penton Street, Pentonville, on Sunday at 2.30 and 6.30 p.m., and on Thursday at 8 p.m.
WHITECHAPEL BRANCH at Orson's Assembly Rooms, 23, New Road, Commercial Road, on Sunday at 2.30 and 6.30 p.m.
LAMBETH BRANCH at Kennington Hall, Upper Kennington Lane (near Licensed Victuallers' School), on Sunday at 2.30 and 6.30 p.m.
Also at 59, Berthon Street, Church Street, Deptford, at 8 p.m., every Tuesday.

THE PUBLIC ARE CORDIALLY INVITED. ALL SEATS FREE.

JOSEPH A. WEST,
President London Conference,
143, *Albany Street, Regent's Park, London, N.W."*

[Thanks for the cordial invite, I shall attend when I visit my native city.]

This is followed with another showing *but a few* of their very many doctrines. You will notice that Polygamy, their great fundamental doctrine is left out in the cold in both. I give the hand bill as it is:—

"ARTICLES OF FAITH,
OF THE
CHURCH OF JESUS CHRIST OF LATTER-DAY SAINTS.

1. We believe in God, the Eternal Father, and His Son, Jesus Christ, and in the Holy Ghost.
PERSONALITY OF GOD.—Gen. i., 26, 27; v. 1; ix., 6. Ps. c, 3 Eccl. vii., 29. Matt. xii., 50. John xv., 15, 16. Gen. xviii.; Gen. xxxii., 24-32. John xx., 17, &c.
PERSONALITY OF CHRIST.—Matt. iii., 17. Ps. ii., 7. Isa. vii., 14; ix., 6. Mark xv., 39. John xv., xvi., xvii. Heb. i, &c.
HOLY GHOST.—Matt. iii., 16. Is. xi., 2; lxi., 1. Mark i., 10. Luke iii., 22. John i., 32, 33. Acts i., 5; ii., 4, &c.

2. We believe that men will be punished for their own sins, and not for Adam's transgression.

MAN PUNISHED FOR ACTUAL SINS.—Acts xvii., 32. Rev. xx., 12-15. Jer. xvii., 10; xxxii., 19. Matt. xvi. 27.

3. We believe that through the atonement of Christ, all mankind may be saved, by obedience to the laws and ordinances of the Gospel.
ATONEMENT OF CHRIST.—1. Cor. xv., 20-23. Romans v., 12-19. 1 John i., 7-10 Mark xvi., 15, 16. Isa. liii.

4. We believe that these ordinances are: First, Faith in the Lord Jesus Christ; second, Repentance; third, Baptism by immersion for the remission of sins; fourth, Laying on of hands for the gift of the Holy Ghost.
FAITH, REPENTANCE, BAPTISM, AND LAYING ON HANDS.—Heb. xi. 6. Rom. i., 16, 17. Rom. x., 14, 15. James ii. Mark xvi., 15, 16 Acts ii., 38, 39. John iii., 5. Acts viii., 14-17. Acts xix., 1-6. Heb. vi., 1-6.
LORD'S SUPPER.—Matt. xxvi., 26-29. Acts ii., 46. 1 Cor. xi., 23-30.

5. We believe that a man must be called of God, by "prophecy and by the laying on of hands," by those who are in authority, to preach the Gospel and administer in the ordinances thereof.
CALLED OF GOD.—Heb. v., 4-10. Romans x., 14, 15. Gal. i., 8-16. Mark iii., 14. John xv., 16. Acts xiii., 1-3. Acts xiv., 23. 1 Tim. ii., 7. 1 Tim. iv., 14. 2 Tim. i., 6. John xvii., 18. 1 Peter, ii., 5-9. Heb. iii., 1. Rev. i., 6. Rev. v., 9, 10. Rev. xx., 6. Mal. iii., 1-4.

6. We believe in the same organization that existed in the primitive Church, viz.: apostles, prophets, pastors, teachers, evangelists, &c.
ORGANIZATION.— 1 Cor. xii. Eph. iv. Eph. ii., 19-22.

7. We believe in the gift of tongues, prophecy, revelation, visions healing, interpretation of tongues, &c.
SPIRITUAL GIFTS.—Mark xvi., 15-20. 1 Cor. xii. James v., 13-15. 1 Thes. v., 19, 20. John xiv., 12. Acts ii., 17.

8. We believe the Bible to be the Word of God as far as it is translated correctly; *we also believe the Book of Mormon to be the Word of God.*

(These italics are my own, their copy has the same words in Roman.)
BOOK OF MORMON.—John xxi., 25. Acts xvii., 26-27. Psalms lxxxv., 8-12. John x., 16. Hos. viii., 11, 12. Ezek. xxxvii., 15-28. Isa xxix., 9-24.

9. We believe all that God has revealed, all that he does now reveal, and we believe that He will yet reveal many great and important things pertaining to the Kingdom of God.
LATTER-DAY REVELATIONS.—Isa. xxviii., 10-13. Acts ii., 17, 18. Mal. iii., 1-4. Mal. iv. Isa. xi. Ezek. xx., 33-38. Matt. xxiv., 31. Rev. xiv. 6. Joel ii., 28-32. Hab. i., 5. Zech. xiv.

10. We believe in the literal gathering of Israel and in the restoration of the Ten Tribes. That Zion will be built upon this continent (America). That Christ will reign personally upon the earth, and that the earth will be renewed and receive its paradisiac glory.
GATHERING.—Jer. xxx. Isa. xliii., 5-9. Jer. xxxi. Jer. xxxii., 37-44. Jer. xvi., 14-16. Ezek. xx., 33-38. Ezek. xxxvii., 19-23. Isa. xlix., 22-26. Isa. xi., 10-16. Zech. x., 6-12. Zech. xiv., Jer. xxiii., 3-8. Ezek. xxxviii. Ezek. xxxix.

11. We claim the privilege of worshipping Almighty God according to the dictates of our conscience, and allow all men the same privilege, let them worship how, where or what they may.

12. We believe in being subject to kings, presidents, rulers, and magistrates, in obeying, honouring, and sustaining the law.

13. We believe in being honest, true, chaste, benevolent, virtuous, and in doing good to *all men*; indeed, we may say that we follow the admonition of Paul, "We believe all things, we hope all things," we have endured many things, and hope to be able to endure all things. If there is anything virtuous lovely, or of good report, or praiseworthy, we seek after these things.—JOSEPH SMITH."

[The beforegoing handbill was being circulated in Plymouth also, before my recent visit there, and mark—there is nothing said about Polygamy! the pivot upon which the whole thing turns].

They sell a dwarf pamphlet for one penny, the size of circulars usually given away by travelling shows. On the front is printed in type exactly like this:—

"THE LATTER-DAY SAINTS' MILLENNIAL STAR'

BUT WE DESIRE TO HEAR OF THEE WHAT THOU THINKEST: FOR AS CONCERNING THIS SECT, WE KNOW THAT IT IS EVERYWHERE SPOKEN AGAINST.—*Acts xxviii.*, 22.

How beautiful upon the mountains are the feet of him that bringeth good tidings, that publisheth peace: that bringeth good tidings of good, that publisheth salvation; that saith unto Zion, " Thy God reigneth !—ISAIAH LII, 7.

LIVERPOOL:

EDITED & PUBLISHED BY JOHN HENRY SMITH, 42, ISLINGTON.

LONDON:

FOR SALE AT THE LATTER-DAY SAINTS' BOOK DEPOT, 19, SOUTHERLAND STREET, PIMLICO, S.W."

This "Bright and Morning Star," given me recently by a Devonport Mormon, thus devotes its "valuable space." "We have heard a number of times lately of a vile fellow by the name of William Jarman, who has been about the South of England lecturing against the Mormons, and visiting the Saints wherever he could learn of any living in that region for the purpose of poisoning their minds against THE PRINCIPLES they had EMBRACED." Then follows a perfect tirade of abuse to which I shall devote my valuable space, and VERY KIND REGARDS in a special chapter, when I have more fully shown "THE PRINCIPLES EMBRACED." Though I must not picture all that a Mormon Embraces, I will do justice to it so far as the law allows. I just notice the scurrilous article to prove by Mormon Authority that what I say in the preface is true. I've hurt 'em, "let the galled jade wince." So long as they remain here, and the breath of life remains in me, they will hear still more and more of this " vile fellow."

The Mormons would feel indebted to me for freely advertising this small fraction of 'their creed, did I but stop at that. But having sworn to tell the truth, the whole truth, and nothing but the truth, I must tell it all. Why do they not preach it *all* in England as they do in Utah? Echo answers why? There they proclaim that a man *must* have from *two* up to 500 *wives* according to his several abilities and his several—well call it "Etcetras," or he cannot be saved, and exalted among the gods; that any one who leaves the Mormon Church MUST HAVE HIS THROAT CUT or he will be everlastingly damned; that Christ is one of their class—a full fledged Polygamist; that he married Mary Magdalen, Martha and Mary, and a host of women over around Judea when he was there, and begat a crowd of children that eclipse many of the big Utah families—as an old Mormon Priest once, when speaking of Jesus, said :—" He was on it you bet, he was as fond of the women as any——son of a——here, and lor' did'nt he have a——lot of——squalling, ragged——brats calling him Dad! Of course he did, or how by——could he '*See his Seed*,' and prolong his days and the pleasure of the Lord prosper in his hands?"

I heard preached in Utah Tabernacle that Jehovah keeps a far bigger Harem than Solomon did: he had only 1000 wives and concubines, whereas

Jehovah has Millions. Adam, they preach, is the God of this Planet, and the reigning Mormon Prophet is the God of this generation. To disobey him, or fail to carry out his edict, is punishable by death. These and similar doctrines, I heard preached in Utah. Now if Mormon Elders would preach like that in Great Britain, I could trust the British Christian Public, for I know they would gain but few converts, if any, from among us. But here they do not so preach. In England, Scotland, and Wales, they preach what they call "The sincere milk of the word—first principles," and it certainly is cooked up to suit the palate of the most fastidious Christian.

When the "Elder" first came to my house at Exeter, he quietly closed the door, raised both his hands, then with an expression of countenance such as we expect to see only on the Saviour himself, with *Angelic* voice exclaimed, "Peace be to this house!" This astonished me, my wife, and another Christian then present. (This was shortly after my asylum episode, when I had determined, as far as I could, to lead a godly, sober, and religious life.) When we expressed our astonishment, he said, "I presume you are Christians, and understand this book," taking from his pocket a nicely bound Bible. Replying in the affirmative, he at once said, "Then I will read the words of our blessed Lord and Saviour Jesus Christ. 'Behold I send you forth as lambs among wolves. (He should have transposed the last three words, and read, 'wolves among lambs.') Carry neither purse nor scrip, and into whatsoever house Ye enter, first say 'Peace be 'to this house.' If the son of peace be there, your peace shall rest upon it, if not, it shall turn to you again. And in the same house remain, eating and drinking such things as they give; for the labourer is worthy of his hire. Go not from house to house. Luke, 10th chapter, 3rd, 4th, 5th, 6th, and 7th verses." He closed the Book, sat down, and seemed to feel at home. Dinner was ready, and fancying he rather emphasised the words, "If the son of peace be there, in the same house remain, eating and drinking such things as they give;" and being anxious to know if the son of peace was in my house, for if not this chap was not going to stop, I rang the bell for dinner, and said "My Friend, you will stay and take dinner with us." But how can I describe my feelings when this man of God (the Devil) replied, "I have meat to eat the world knows not of; my meat is to do the will of him that sent me." Oh! how I had inwardly to chide myself for being so wicked as to fancy that emphasis was "put on." I knew it was my duty "to entertain strangers; for thereby some have entertained angels unawares," and thought, am I in an angel's presence? does my house now shelter an angel and I not know it? I looked at the man—he had on good Sheeps wool, dyed in the wool, real West of England Wool dyed Black Broadcloth, like that made formerly in Devonshire.

I could not penetrate his sheep's clothing or I should have seen that inwardly he was double dyed in sin, as I afterwards found his sins were not only "scarlet and crimson," but as black as a blind Ethiopian in a dark cellar at midnight, just before new moon, looking for a coal-black colour-blind tom cat. If any one can give a better definition of real blackness, and will forward it to W. Jarman, 58, Parr Street, Exeter, Devon, England, he will gladly pay for it to insert in future editions. Please send the bill with it. Draw it mild, don't stick it on; remember I give a lot for a little money.

In brief, things went on all right, for the "Elder" did nothing but quote Scripture, till in answer to my question he said, "He (the Elder) was a Latter-Day Saint:" my wife, who knew a little of the Mormons, charged him with believing in and practising Polygamy as part of their religion. Seeing she knew something about it he did not deny it, but said "Polygamy is very rarely followed; the Prophet Brigham, and *one or two* others practise it because God revealed to them that they must do so. But Mrs. Jarman it is not essential to salvation, as you seem to think, that men must become Polygamists. It is very different. Even supposing the Lord revealed to the Prophet that Bro. Jarman should take another wife. Before he can do so, you must be consulted and give your consent. If you refuse to consent that ends the matter, and your husband cannot become a Polygamist. It could not be otherwise, dear sister, or else see what sorrow and trouble would result." This settled the affair with my wife, as she said "I should never be such a fool as to consent to my husband marrying another wife so long as I live, so there will never be any Polygamy in our family." "That's so, of course there won't, if you object Sister Jarman," replied the Mormon Missionary. "And I certainly should object," said Mrs. J. "And you certainly can," answered the Mormon wolf, and added, "It's no use talking upon that point for that's settled."

Polygamy, the only objection then known, having been thus disposed of, the way was clear. This Mormon Missionary baptized us into the Mormon Church, and in two weeks thereafter we were on board the steamer on our way to Zion, only just in time to save our bacon ; for " God was about to pour out his judgments on Great Britain, and was gathering out his Elect." They spin the same yarn to-day : God is always just about to do it, but somehow He fails to verify the Mormon Missionaries' predictions. Again, the Mormon Missionary pictured the beauties of Zion where God was gathering His people. There everyone we met was a brother (or a sister) and a friend. There only "one Lord, one faith, one baptism, one God and Father of us all" prevailed. All worshipped together in one big Tabernacle. Said the "Elder," "Only fancy, suppose all the people of Exeter were Christians, and all of one faith, and every man you met here was a brother and a friend ?" Dear Reader, please suppose the same of your own City, Town, or Village, and you will think as I did—it must be like a Heaven below. Besides, silks which I was foolishly selling here at 2s. per yard would fetch 12s. 6d. a yard in Salt Lake City, and all my drapery goods would be similarly enhanced in value if transported to Utah. Again I could have 160 acres of land for nothing, and another 160 acres at 5s. per acre, and have three years in which to pay for it ; thus my 320 acres of land would only cost on the average 2s. 6d. per acre, and that not to be paid for until the expiration of three years, so as to give me time to raise enough off my farm to pay for the land. With such inducements, coupled with the religious part of this programme, is it any wonder that Mormon Missionaries entrap the unwary ? Is it any wonder that so many, especially of the poorer classes of British people are caught, and begin to sing—

> "To the West, to the west, to the land of the free,
> Where the mighty Missouri rolls down to the sea,
> Where a man is a man if he's willing to toil,
> And the poorest may reap of the fruits of the soil."

And are not satisfied until they get there. Thousands are being thus caught to-day.

We sailed from England in the summer of 1866. Arriving in New York we found the Indians were causing great trouble out West ; it was unsafe to cross the plains. We accordingly had to stop over until the next summer. Large companies of "saints" were then expected to gather to "Zion." I accepted a situation in Whitney and Myers' Dry Good Store (Drapery Establishment), Albany, New York. The Indians were so troublesome the following summer there was no emigration of British Saints to Utah ; consequently I remained with the same firm until July, 1868, when the first company from England crossed the plains. It was then I left my good situation, and with my family and the British saints set out on the weary pilgrimage to Zion.

To describe that journey is impossible here ; but, in passing, I must say, the Missionaries, who had been three years in England, seemed to have special regard for the Female Lambs of the flock, and were I to tell what I saw during that six weeks' journey over the plains, camping out as we had to, night after night, and sleeping in waggons, under waggons, under trees, bushes, or any shelter we could find: I say, were I to tell all I then saw and heard this book could not be sent by mail, while I myself would be sent to jail. If I protested in any way I was kindly informed that I had better mind my own business, or I should be put where the dogs could not bite me. Afterwards at a Bishop's meeting one of the Missionaries publicly said, "I should have been murdered on the plains but for him, that I found fault with everything, and the "Saints" wanted to kill me there and then. I told them the reason I found fault with everything was because everything demanded it. But I must not dwell on this.

We arrived in the Mormon capital, Salt Lake City, Aug. 21st, 1868, having travelled the last 500 miles over arid plains and rocky mountains by waggon. Here I was in "Zion, the perfection of beauty," beautiful for situation on the sides of the north. I certainly must say I found Salt Lake City a beautiful place "where every prospect pleases and only man is vile."

I had thought to have found these so-called saints approaching something near perfection, but alas, found that human nature is human nature even in Zion. The first thing that attracted my attention on arrival was two "saints" drunk—the one trying to help the other home, and both swearing outrageously. On going up to them to ascertain if they were really saints, the answer I got was "Why, certainly." I also found on enquiry that the Church manufactured a villanous sort of whisky, which the saints called "Valley Tan," a little of which will go a long way toward making a man drunk; this whisky is sold in stores over which is a sign, having thereon the "All seeing eye" and the words, "Holiness unto the Lord." On going further up the street I found a crowd of men discussing the suicide of a saint, which had that day taken place. I was as much surprised to find that a saint had committed suicide as that saints could get drunk. I asked what had caused him to commit this rash act, and was informed that he had married two sisters in addition to the wife he already had, and that notwithstanding as sisters they had got along all right, yet as wives to the same man they were not a success. They used to fight as Polygamic wives will, and pull each other's hair, and made things generally very uncomfortable for the affectionate husband, which preyed upon his mind, and finally led him to commit suicide. Poor fellow! in sympathising with another I always put myself in his place. I thought if I had married three wives who fought and cut up as they did, I should be tempted to commit suicide also.

I was introduced to the Prophet, Brigham Young, a man about 70 years of age, a tolerably fine-looking thick set man, possessing an indomitable will, very austere, and well calculated to govern the dupes that surrounded him. Brigham Young was married. He looked every inch a married man; in fact I found him muchly married, the most married man I ever saw.

That Brigham Young was married, no one can dispute; that he was a father is clear to most minds. He, more than any man, could sing "'Tis' nice to be a Father." If asked how many children Brigham had, I treat it as a conundrum, and give it up; who can count the "chips of the old block," which lay scattered all over the territory of Utah. The illustrious parent himself seems to have forgotten (if he ever knew) the vastness of his progeny. One time when some boys were fighting in the street, Brigham undertook to chastise them. One young urchin bawled out, "say old man my dad will fix you for hitting me." Brigham demanded to know who his father was. The boy replied "Brigham Young's my dad, and ee'd go for you." The boy ran off and reported the circumstances to his mother, describing the old villain, and urged his mother to persuade dad to have his revenge out of the old cuss.

When relating this circumstance to a Mormon Elder, I asked if it were possible that there should be men in Utah that did not know their own children? the Elder assured me that he himself had children he should not know were he to meet them. At this juncture, a little girl, whose hoop had trundled into the stream from which she could not recover it, stood crying. The Elder took no notice of the little one, being, as I supposed, too much used to children's screams; having secured her hoop and wiped away the tears, I asked the child its name. To our surprise she gave the name of the Elder I was with, and in reply to a question from the Elder, said her mother's name was "Liz, you Bet," and pointed to the house where she resided, thus the father and child were made known to each other. It is a wise father in Utah that knows his own child. Brigham's children are mostly girls, and now that they have grown into womanhood and married, Brigham declares the Devil owed him a grudge, and paid him off in son-in-law's. In regard to Brigham's children they are in a very tangled condition, and to cut a long story short, I will merely say they are too numerous to mention. But what is home without a family. Some have asserted that the wives of Brigham Young were more numerous than his children. One thing is certain the name of his wife is Legion. In this Brigham has loved not wisely but to many well. The bosom of his family is somewhat extended, and one would fancy that with so many gentle loving wives to minister to his comforts and soothe his oft distracted mind, his life would be a heaven below; but with the heart-burnings, hair-pullings, and jealousies of polygamy, such is not the case; for instance, when he has a few unpleasant words with Amelia, and that fair creature sends the sewing machine crashing over the stairs after him, the feelings engendered are anything but lovely; and again when Ann Eliza sues for a divorce and alimony and shows the old man up in his true color and loosens his purse strings, it is anything but pleasant. His wives are expensive; they always want something. In one of his sermons Brigham said "I have not a wife but would see me in hell rather than she should not have what she wanted," and in the same sermon he threatens them all with a divorce, and says, "I will go into heaven alone, rather than have them scratching and fighting around me." His wives fight and scratch so among themselves, that when they get into a row he allows them to fight it out according to Hoyle, or any other style that suits them, and after the melée one may gather enough hair to stuff a mattress. The cares of married life weighed heavily on the Prophet, and he oftimes wished he had remained single. It has been estimated that if Brigham were to undertake to kiss his wives the operation would take just six weeks to perform. I once ventured to ask the Prophet if he considered he had secured all his lost ribs, or was he yet a rib short? "Well," said Young, "my heart is like a crowded omnibus, there is still room for another."

I saw his mother-in-law while I was there, I can't exactly tell how many there is of her, but it is a good deal. It strikes me that one mother-in-law is enough in one family, unless a man is over fond of excitement. One is often unbearable; imagine vast numbers afflicting one poor unfortunate man. I was once introduced to a Bishop who had married six sisters; when I asked his reason for doing so, he replied "don't you see by marrying these six sisters there is only one mother-in-law to the batch, whereas had I married six from different families, I should have had half a dozen mother-in-laws, by this transaction I escape five rascally mother-in-laws." [More anon on this.]

No trouble can arise on the deceased wife's sister question, in Utah; they simply marry all the wife's sisters at once and have done with it. Said one Mormon "What ridiculous nonsense to make the gals wait for their dead sisters' shoes, I'll marry the whole lot of any mother's daughters; they are dragged up together under one parental roof, I'll take the batch and let 'em jog along together under my roof. One dad is enough for the lot and so is one hubby. I think any gal who wants a whole man all to herself is almighty selfish and ought to go to hell." If the mother happens to be a widow, the Mormon will marry mother and daughters, and thus become "Husband to the Widow and to the fatherless " and keep the family together, as it were. In England a man is prohibited from marrying his wife's sister whether the wife is living or dead : he is actually prevented from marrying his grandmother; yet we call this a land of Liberty, nice Liberty that : for no matter how badly a man wants to marry his grandmother, he is not allowed to do it. There are no such "ungodly" restrictions in Utah

I never ventured into the sleeping apartments of the Harem, but I have seen a blanket that would cover the inmates of a good sized female reformatory; this was said to be Brigham's blanket. I have also seen a picture of a bedstead about 500 feet long, described as the bed of the Prophet, but latterly Brigham took to sleeping alone in a little chamber behind his office for quiet and safety. I don't blame him, poor man, he must have been bewildered. We sometimes sympathise with Poor Caudle, but then there was but *one* Mrs. Caudle ; imagine hundreds of Mrs. C's lecturing one poor fellow, and you will readily perceive the wisdom of the master mind of Brigham in preferring to sleep alone; it is a wonder that with such a confused state of affairs he could sleep anywhere. Brigham Young has departed; I don't blame him ; I think if I were in the position he was, I should want to depart. But his widow survives.

When I think of the Widow Young and compare her with the Young Widow surely "Comparisons are odious." She who manifested such selfishness as to become the sole and only partner of his joys and sorrows, finds herself solitary and alone at the grave with no one to share her grief. Whereas the one who could share her husband's affections with scores of other women, as in a sort of Joint Stock Company, finds herself only a shareholder in the grief of the concern, according to the stock held by her in this limited liability association. It was remarked at Brigham's funeral that no tears were shed ; how could there be ? Take for instance the tears of the average lone widow, and divide them among the widows of this arch polygamist, it would not amount to a tear each, and in the dry climate of Utah, should a tear have struggled to come to the front it would have evaporated ere it crossed the eyelid. I have stood at the grave of many Mormon Polygamists when the numerous widows paid their last respects to THEIR dear departed ONE, and judging from the expression of their countenances, their feelings, if uttered would be "Our husband is gone ; he is taken from a world of care and excitement, happy release, what he suffered at our hands, and tongues cannot be described. Let him RIP. (Rest In Peace.) Peace to his ashes," and after taking a last look they move off in search of another victim. Weller had no idea of the widows of Utah or his loathing of "vidders" would have been greatly intensified, The Utah widow emboldened by the doctrines of the Church becomes brazen and seldom "lets up" until she is united to some old polygamist. The faithful elders are admonished to take these widows and perform the kinsman's part to their dead brother, thus—A. takes the widows of B. to wife, while the issue resulting from the Union belongs to and is called by the name of B. The Great Fundamental Principle of Mormonism being to "Increase and Multiply" widows past a certain peroid of life are "turned out to grass," and not allowed the happy privilege of "roping in " another "Saint."

The Prophet was interred in the private grounds of his estate, but his grave is sadly neglected, no monument or headstone marks his last resting place. This results from leaving too many afflicted widows—what is everybody's business is nobody's business. When the condition of her late husband's grave is mentioned to Mrs. Young No. 10, she replies, "well if he wants a tombstone let that proud, stuck up Susannah Young get him one, its as much her business as it is mine," and when the subject is brought to the attention of the said Susannah who is Widow Young No. 48, she retorts, "Let Margaret Ann Young attend to it; she has known him longer than I." And it looks as if he would never get a tombstone.

I am often asked how the practice of Polygamy works among the "Latter-day Saints." Briefly I reply that Polygamy is about the same to-day as when Sarah cried "Cast out the Bondwoman and her Son." All first wives feel like casting out the Hagars and their offspring. To assert that a true woman can share her husband with another is a gross libel upon her nature. I visited their Polygamic harems, but failed to find a happy one. At one place I found a little girl gathering up hair that had been made to fly during a recent fight among the affectionate wives of the harem. I asked the child what she was gathering the hair for? She replied, "to make my doll a mattress." I invariably found that when Polygamy came in at the door, joy and peace flew out at the window. If my readers imagine they know anything about jealousy, let me remind them that none but Solomon with his 700 wives and 300 concubines could inform the world that "Jealousy is cruel as the grave." Outside Polygamy Jealousy is a mere phantom. You, dear readers, are ignorant of jealousy, and "Where ignorance is bliss 'tis folly to be wise." To find jealousy in its zenith go into the Mormon harems where every word and action, every crevice and key hole are avenues of that most vehement flame spoken of by the said Solomon. Polygamy is Slavery—men barter, sell, or exchange wives with impunity. I witnessed a mule trade where a man threw in a wife and five dollars to boot, and got the mule. I find most men inquisitive to know how so many wives are supported: that they have enough to do to support one. Why not ask how slaveholders support so many slaves? The fact is, the wives are slaves; these work in the fields, the very affectionate husband sits on the fence with a whip—if they lag, he whips them like a refractory mule, in fact, he holds a mule in higher estimation than a woman for if he beats his mule to death it costs money to replace it, whereas he can get another wife without money or price at anytime, or so soon as a new batch of emigrants arrive from Europe. One man I know well, who has twelve loving wives—fancy thirteen souls with but a single thought, thirteen hearts that beat as one. He takes contracts for sheep shearing, and loading up his dozen wives in a waggon, each armed with a pair of sheep shears, he drives them to the field of operation—there, like a nigger driver, he sees that they perform their work faithfully. When sheep shearing is over the haying time has come, then follows the grain harvest, and when out-door labour is over, the spinning jenny and loom are kept busy by the same wives.

One man has a ranch and dairy, which the wives attend to while he sits in the shade in summer, and toasts his shins by the fire in winter—the wives, of course, hauling in the wood—and woe to the wife who dares sell a pound of butter, a chicken, or egg. His first wife, a poor old cripple, fancied a cup of tea—a luxury denied the women of Utah. It would never do to have all these women tea-drinking. It would ruin any man, it costs too much: water is cheaper. This poor old wife, when her lord was absent, exchanged a few eggs for the wherewith to make the coveted beverage. Her hubby found it out; by the way they find out everything, the reigning favourite wife watches the other wives, and is a perfect tell tale. When he found that his first wife had committed the enormous crime of drinking tea, he dragged her to the stream, plunged her under water, and kept ducking her till she promised never to repeat the offence. I could enumerate scenes of this kind, but there are other features of Polygamy.

A Bishop married a young girl while his first wife was on her death-bed. One blunt old lady remarked, "it is rather out of place." The kind-hearted husband replied, "It's rather rough on Jane that she can't join us, but we could not have a spree right after a funeral, so we thought we'd have the wedding before Jane died." What a festive occasion: one wife dying, another being duly installed. The poor first wife died in agony, crying "An eternity of happiness cannot recompense me for this torture," but the husband of her youth and father of her children was not present either at the death or burial—he was off with his young bride. One grief-stricken wife, finding her husband determined to take another wife, implored him not to, saying: "we have been so happy together; I shall die if you take another." Hear the response of the affectionate husband: "Die then! hundreds of better women than you are in their graves, who died from the same cause." Accursed Polygamy, when the sorrows of a woman become too great to bear, she is roughly told to join hundreds of others who have died from its blighting and withering effects.

I will now give another feature of Polygamy. One woman had several sons before her husband took another wife; these are all good young men, but the one born after his father took a second wife was a desperado, whose hands were fearfully stained with blood, and was finally lynched for a most diabolical murder. When the poor mother heard the fate of her son, she exclaimed "Poor boy, it's not his fault, its the accursed Polygamy; for months before that boy was born I wanted to kill his father's second wife. Murder, and nothing but murder was in my heart all the time; that poor boy has paid the penalty of his father's crime and mother's sorrow." Then raising her withered and trembling hand she cursed Polygamy as only an injured wife and bereft mother could. The anathemas, as I have heard them in Utah's harem's, make one shudder; not only do the women curse it, but the offspring, as they verge into maturity, curse the system which made them what they really are, illegitimates; and yet the system continues.

In 1876, while Americans celebrated the glorious achievements of one hundred years of liberty and progress, one thousand polygamic marriages took place in Utah. America should at once put a stop to this degrading evil of Polygamy, or cease boasting of her advancement and civilization.

Though the foregoing incidents are personally known to me, I will not allow the public to take my bare word. They have all been published before and to increase your faith I give a few extracts from "The Anti-Polygamy Standard," published in Salt Lake City. Vol. I, No. 2, says:—

"THE BEAUTIES OF POLYGAMY.

"(Under the above title we shall relate a variety of authentic incidents, illustrating the loveliness of the so-called "celestial" marriage system. These incidents have all been furnished us either by the participants or eye witnesses of the scenes they describe. We leave our readers to judge for themselves as to the holiness of this "divine ordinance." Eds.)

"In Sugarhouse Ward, two miles south of Salt Lake City, lives a good Saint who of course lives his religion and has several wives. It was the duty of one of the plural women to work on the farm and take care of the cattle and the mules. When not engaged in other saintly avocations it was the husband's custom to sit on the fence, holding a horsewhip in his hand like a slave driver, and oversee the woman when she was at labor in the field. If she failed to perform the work according to his idea and instructions, he used to lash her like a refractory horse or mule; in fact, he often whipped her more severely than he would his animals, for he held a mule in far higher estimation than he did a woman. He could get another wife any time, but it cost money to get a mule. Occasionally, when there was not enough to keep her busy on the farm, he hired her out as a house servant, and always collected her wages himself, asking quite a high price for her services. She happened to be hired to a neighbour of mine, and one day when he came for her wages he demanded an extra dollar a week because he had to hire a man to do her chores in the field. This Saint believed in polygamy, because when one woman wore out or outlived her usefulness as a labourer, he could easily replace her with a fresh one.

"A few miles further from my house, in what is called Mill Creek, lives another saintly polygamist whose three wives are held to the strictest account for every pound of butter, every chicken and egg on the place, and woe to thee adventurous one who dares dispose of either without the consent of her lord and master. The first wife who is old and crippled with rhumatism once longed for a cup of tea, a luxury forbidden to the women, although the husband frequently indulged in that and other material comforts. She watched an opportunity when he was absent and traded a few eggs for the wherewithal to make the coveted beverage which she enjoyed, as she thought, in secret The husband, however, found it out—a man in polygamy has no lack of tale bearers—and he dragged the poor old woman to the creek, plunged her under the water and held her there until he thought her sufficiently punished for her sin of meddling with his eggs, and until she promised never to repeat the offence. I have suppressed the names in both of the above cases, although I could have given them, because I understand it is the policy of the STANDARD, not to show up individuals, but to expose the workings, and the debasing effects of the system. The first incident shows in what estimation the majority of the men hold the women, and to what depths of degradation the system can reduce a woman who allows herself to be placed in such a position. But more anon of the Beauties of Polygamy."

In Vol. 1, No. 5., is the following:—

"A good Saint in this very city who had three wives already and sixteen children, felt duty urging him to live his religion to a still greater extent, and he began to pay his addresses to a young companion of one of his daughters. One day, while endeavouring to gain her consent, and speaking of the advantages of the divine ordinance, she met him with the question, "Brother M. you are not a rich man, you can scarcely provide for the families you have already, how do you expect to support any more?" "Oh," was the reply, "I have taken care of the old ones long enough, they must now do like the chickens turn out and scratch for themselves." "Then I suppose I should have to do the same thing after a while," said the girl, "so I prefer to scratch for myself now." The words of this saint are characteristic of Mormon polygamy, when a man wants new wives he will turn the old ones out to "scratch for themselves."

Vol. 1, No. 6, contains:—

"THE EFFECTS OF POLYGAMY.

"The first wife of a certain prominent Mormon had several sons, the youngest of whom evinced a most cruel, vindictive, and bloodthirsty disposition almost from his very birth. From his earliest childhood he seemed to take the greatest delight in torturing and then killing animals or birds, and as he grew older, he became a perfect terror in the neighbourhood where his parents lived. When people came to his mother to complain, or to demand satisfaction for some new depredatory act, she would shake her head sorrowfully and say, "poor boy, it is not his fault, it is only his misfortune." When asked for an explanation of her words, she declined to give it, but would repeat them over and over again, much to the disgust of her friends who pronounced him to be "without exception the worst child they had ever seen or heard of." Neither the tears and prayers of his mother, or the punishments inflicted by his father made any impression upon him, and as the years went on, he steadily grew worse. When he was about 16 years old he went away from home, and for some time nothing was heard of him, until at last it was discovered that he was living with a band of desperadoes, who were both robbers and murderers. More than once were his hands stained with the blood of a fellow mortal before he met his own death, being lynched by an infuriated mob for a peculiarly unprovoked and outrageous murder. When his mother heard of his dreadful end, she shook her grey head sorrowfully, as she had done of old, and repeated the same words, "poor boy it was not his fault, only his misfortune, I knew it would end just as it has." Shortly afterward, some friends came to condole with the heart broken mother, among whom was a person high in authority in the Church. An eye witness told the writer that she will not forget the scene until her dying day. After a few sympathetic words had been said, the poor, half-crazed creature rose, and looking the elder straight in the face, said, in thrilling tones : "You are responsible for the fate of my poor boy, you, and the infernal doctrine of Polygamy. It was *you* who persuaded my husband to take another wife, to live up to his privileges, as you term it. We had lived happily until that time, but Polygamy made our home like the abode of Satan. For months before the birth of that boy, I felt as if I wanted to kill his father's second wife, the woman who had robbed me of my husband's love, and destroyed the peace of our home. Murder, and nothing but murder was in my heart all the time, I never looked on her but I wanted to kill her. There were times when I would willingly have yielded up my own life if I could have had the satisfaction of seeing her dead first. That poor, unfortunate boy has only paid the penalty of his father's crime, and his mother's sorrow." Then raising her withered hand on high, she continued, "I pray God that the curse of an injured wife, and a bereaved mother may follow you all the days of your life, for it was *you* who lead my husband into Polygamy."

[We would like to have all our exchanges copy this article, so as to give it all possible publicity. Let the people of the United States learn some of the effects of the abominable system of Polygamy. If any person is in doubt as to the truthfulness of the above incident, our informant is willing to make affidavit in regard to the facts.—EDS. STANDARD."

There are other features very amusing, which show that the dear men often get in for it, but as I give a chapter on "He and She Devils"—Raising the Devil," &c., further on, just to show what you may expect I give one wee bit here from a paper published in Salt Lake City—"The Salt Lake Tribune.—"One of the Saints who took unto himself recently a second wife has been brought to law by the first. On the morning after the nuptials had been celebrated, the newly married couple were rather late rising. Wife No. 1, went up about 10 o'clock, and finding the couple still in bed took a rope and larruped the two soundly, with the remark to her lord and master, "I'll learn you to stay in bed until after 10 o'clock when you have business to attend to."

"'Tis not restraint or liberty that makes men Prisoners or Free.—*Hudibras.*

[Get these "Tribunes" and "Standards." See English Preface, page 10.]

Nature has not provided for polygamy in the United States. The census report for 1880 shows that there are a million males in excess of females in that country. If the "Revelation" that one man should marry 20 or 100 wives is to be adhered to, where are the women to come from ? As it is for every 25 men, one is left out in the cold, with "no one to love, none to caress," doomed to be an old bachelor. Polygamy could not be kept up, were it not that Mormon Missionaries drag so many girls to Utah from the manufacturing towns of England, Scotland, and Wales, and the British Government should arrest these scamps who come here to make white slaves of our English girls, and to procure inmates for their filthy harems. I shall give a chapter of horrors in regard to the brutal and murderous practices of polygamy further on, here I pass over tragedy, and merely relate one case. To show this in a proper light, I will introduce a paragraph of Apostle Kimball's sermon preached at Salt Lake. " What power has any one of my wives to act independently; she has not a particle of power. She must act in connection with me as the limb acts in connection with the tree from which it springs. If not she is a dead limb; will they ever come to life again after they are dead? No! *They must be cut off and thrown back into the earth to return to their mother element.*" [Journal of Discourses, vol. 6, p. 67]. The case I give is that of a Mormon who had ten wives, one of them disobeyed him, or in the words of the sermon quoted, " acted independently of him." Her lord and master sharpened his razor, then taking this wife upon his knee he lovingly kissed her, and then cut her throat from ear to ear, and held her till she expired. He afterwards dug a grave in his garden, and consigned her to mother earth " to return to her mother element." This man still lives in Utah, with his other nine wives, and no law reaches him. On page 469 of " The Rocky Mountain Saints " is the following:—

"KISSED HER AND CUT HER THROAT."

"One of the wives of a Polygamist was unfaithful during his absence when he was on a mission. On his return, the " Reformation " was in full blast, and the unhappy wife believed that, from this *faux pas* she was doomed to lose her claim to motherhood over the children which she had already borne; that she would be cast aside in eternity as well as in time, by her husband; that, in fact, she would only ' be an angel, and with the angels stand;' and that she could not reach the circle of the gods and goddesses unless her blood was shed. She consented to meet the penalty of her error, and while her heart was gushing with affection for her husband and her children, and her mind absorbed with faith in the doctrine of human sacrifice, she seated herself upon her husband's knee, and after the warmest and most endearing embrace she had ever known—it was to be her last—when the warmth of his lips still lingered about her glowing cheek, with his own right hand he calmly cut her throat and sent her spirit to the keeping of the gods. That kind and loving husband still lives near Salt Lake City, and preaches occasionally with great zeal. He seems happy enough." [See Chapter of Horrors for more.]

Polygamy produces curious consanquinity. A man married a widow and two of her daughters. Shortly after he married another of his wife's daughters, who had also been left a widow with three girls, and when these girls grew up he married these three stepdaughters also, so as to keep them in the family. This man was, therefore, the husband of grandmother, mother, daughter, grandaughters, and step daughters; in addition to this he married two of his nieces, and to cap the climax, married his half sister, and they all bear him children. Now what relation do these children bear to each other? and what is the relative position of the father in this case? Figure it up, and you will find that this man is his own uncle and step son, and if you trace further you will discover that this very individual is his own grandfather.

The creed and practice of the ' Saints " in Utah differs vastly from the Mormon Missionaries' statements in England. There were about 3,000 dupes gathered there at the time I was. It must not be said that I was the only fool in Great Britain, or the only one here who could possibly be duped and " roped in " by these Mormon Missionary scamps; I wish it were so, but the facts show otherwise. On the Sunday we, 3,000 " Greenhorns " as they term fresh arrivals from Europe, went to the Tabernacle. " Apostle " Pratt preached for our edification as follows:—" I want to talk to the new comers, and let me tell you plainly, you have come from Babylon—the churches of Christendom—but you might as well remained in your Baptist, Methodist, and other Churches, unless you fulfil the whole counsel of God and go into Polygamy. No man can be saved unless he has at least two wives. You can't get into Heaven lop-sided like a crab, with one woman pulling you down at one arm; you must be evenly balanced with a wife on each arm, then you can

get into Heaven but not else. If you have a dozen or so hanging on to your coat tails, all the better: the more wives the more glory you will have, but if you stick to the one wife and refuse to take others, I tell you every one of you will be damned, and any woman who refuses to give her husband another wife will be eternally damned. Utah 'expects every man this day to do his duty,' and take all the wives possible; any wife found raising objections to this shall be destroyed, for thus saith the Lord in his Revelation commanding Polygamy." This was the kind of preaching we all had to listen to. To more fully show what they preach in Utah I give extracts from Authentic Mormon Publications. The following is from "Journal of Discourses," vol. 1, pp. 58, 63, 64:—" The Lord ordained marriage between male and female as a law through which spirits should come here and enter into the second state of existence." * *
" Then is it not reasonable and consistent that the Lord should say unto His faithful and chosen servants, that had proved themselves before Him all the day long; that had been ready and willing to do whatsoever His will required them to perform—take unto yourselves more wives, like unto the patriarchs, Abraham, Isaac, and Jacob, of old—like those who lived in ancient times, who walked in my footsteps, and kept my commands?" * * * * *

" What will become of those individuals who have this law (of Polygamy) taught unto them in plainness, if they reject it? [A voice in the stand, 'They will be damned.'] I will tell you : THEY WILL BE DAMNED, *saith the Lord God Almighty.*" " The woman who marries out of this Polygamy marries for hell."

" We are created for the express purpose of increase."—*J. of D.*, vol. 1, p. 93.

" Suppose that I had the privilege of having only one wife, I should have had only three sons, for those are all that my first wife bore; whereas I now have buried five sons, and have thirteen living. It is obvious that I could not have been blessed with such a family if I had been restricted to one wife; but by the introduction of this law I can be the instrument in preparing tabernacles for those spirits which have to come in this dispensation."—*Brigham Young, J. of D.,* vol. iii., p. 264. This was thirty years ago, he has married muchly since. But he never tells how many daughters he has. Like the Ancient Jews they consider daughters not worth reckoning. In fact, Mormonism seeks to despise and crush woman.

" The fleshly body of Jesus required a Mother as well as a Father. Therefore the Father and Mother of Jesus, according to the flesh, must have been associated together in the capacity of Husband and Wife; hence the Virgin Mary must have been, for the time being, the *lawful* Wife of God the Father: we use the term *lawful* Wife, because it would be blasphemous in the highest degree to say that He overshadowed her or begat the Saviour unlawfully. * * It was also lawful in Him, after having thus dealt with Mary, to give her to Joseph her espoused husband. Whether God the Father gave Mary to Joseph for time only, or for time and eternity, we are not informed. Inasmuch as God was the first Husband to her, it may be that He only gave her to be the wife of Joseph while in this mortal state, and that He intended after the resurrection to again take her as one of His own wives to raise up immortal spirits in eternity."

" One thing is certain, that there were several holy women that greatly loved Jesus—such as Mary, and Martha her sister, and Mary Magdalene. If all the acts of Jesus were written, we, no doubt should learn that these beloved women were his wives."—*The Seer,* p.p. 158-9.

" The grand reason of the burst of public sentiment in anathemas upon Christ and His disciples, causing His crucifixion, was evidently based upon Polygamy, according to the testimony of the philosophers who rose in that age. A belief in the doctrine of a plurality of wives caused the persecution

of Jesus and His followers. We might almost think they were 'Mormons.'"
—*Elder Jedediah M. Grant, Councillor to Brigham Young, J. of D.*, vol. i. p. 346.

"Jesus was the bridegroom at the marriage of Cana of Galilee." "Now there was actually a marriage; and if Jesus was not the bridegroom on that occasion, please tell who was." "We say it was Jesus Christ who was married, to be brought into the relation whereby he could 'see His seed' before He was crucified." I shall say here, that before the Saviour died, He looked upon His own natural children, as we look upon ours; he saw His seed, and immediately after that He was cut off from the earth."—*Hyde, President of the Apostles, J. of D.* vol. ii. p. 82.

"I see that some of the Eastern papers represent me as a Great Blasphemer, because I said that Jesus Christ was married, that Mary, Martha, and others were His wives, and that He begat children. All I say in reply, is, they worship a Saviour who is too pure and holy to fulfil the commands of His Father. I worship one that is just pure and holy enough 'to fulfil all righteousness;' not only the righteous law of baptism, but the still more righteous and important law, 'to multiply and replenish the earth.' Startle not at this! for even the Father Himself honoured that law by coming down to Mary, without a natural body, and begetting a Son; and if Jesus begat children, He only did that which He had seen His father do."—*Orson Hyde, J. of D.*, vol. ii. p. 210.

Speaking of the Mormon Prophet "Apostle" Grant said:—"He holds the keys of life and salvation upon the earth; and you may strive as much as you please, but *not one of you will ever go through the straight gate into the Kingdom of God, except those that go through by that man and his brethren,* for they will be the persons whose inspection you must pass."—*Deseret News*, December, 1856.

"Apostle" Kimble preached thus:—"I have often said that *the word of our leader and Prophet is the Word of God to this people.* We cannot see God, we cannot hold converse with Him, but He has given us a man that we can talk to, and *thereby know His will, just as well as if God himself were present with us.* I am no more afraid to risk my salvation in the hands of this man, than *I am to trust myself in the hands of the Almighty.* He will lead me right if *I do as he says* in every particular and circumstance." †

† "Deseret News," October 1, 1856.

"Apostle" Grant, in the Salt Lake Bowery, September, 1856, uttered the following:

"We have women here who like anything but the Celestial Law of God, and if they could break asunder the cable of the Church of Christ, (Polygamy) *their is scarcely a mother in Israel but would do it this day.* And they talk it to their husbands, to their daughters, and to their neighbours, and they say *they have not seen a week's happiness since they became acquainted with that law, or since their husbands took a second wife.*"

In the *Deseret News*, October 1st, 1856, is Brigham Young's sermon:—

"Men will say—'My wife, though a most excellent woman, *has not seen a happy day since I took my second wife.*' 'No, not a happy day for a year,' says one; and another has not seen a happy day for five years."

"This hardly comports with the Apostle Pratt's picture of a family, "where *peace* and salvation reign," and it is not a little amusing to read of the promises from his pen of "this glorious era," when the women were to "rejoice" because of the high honours and privileges conferred upon them; "the glorious prospects" which were opening before them, and the "freedom" in the dales of Utah. Polygamy in Utah is the martyrdom of civilized, Christian womanhood, and the enslavement of every noble instinct in man." [A Lady's Life in Polygamy, p. 221.]

CHAPTER IV.

"A John Bull Yankee," Boss Devil of "Hell upon Earth."

At Brigham Young's death, seven years ago, the World said, "Mormonism will fall to pieces," but to-day it is stronger than ever. The fact is people know very little about it. A greater than Brigham exists. John Taylor, the present Prophet, a Church of England man from Manchester, understands Church and State and kingdom affairs, much better than Brigham did. Americans admit that English, or "John Bull Yankees," as they call them, beat the Natives. The Prophet Taylor knows well how to instruct his Missionaries in the art of seducing Britishers; and having himself been a missionary and lied like the Devil, he makes a first-class Boss Devil in this "Hell upon Earth." In France, at a public debate, he denied Polygamy, although at the same time he had five wives at home. On page 8 of "Three Nights public discussion at Boulogne-sur-mer," published in Liverpool by the same John Taylor, I find the following :—

"We are accused here of polygamy and actions the most indelicate, obscene, and disgusting, such as none but a corrupt and depraved heart could have contrived. These things were too outrageous to admit of belief; therefore leaving the sisters of the 'white veil,' the 'black veil,' and all the other 'veils' with those gentlemen to dispose of, together with their authors, as they think best, I shall content myself with reading *Our views of chastity and marriage*, from a work published by us containing some of our articles of faith, 'Doctrine and Covenants,' page 330." Inasmuch as this Church of Jesus Christ has been reproached with the crime of fornication and polygamy, we declare that we believe that one man should have but one wife, and one woman but one husband, except in case of death, when either is at liberty to marry again."

The "High Priest" Journalist, on page 195 of "The Rocky Mountain Saints," says:—"At the very time that 'Brother Taylor' read these pages in Boulogne-sur-mer, *he had himself, living in Salt Lake City, five wives;* one of his two companions who likewise testified during the discussion, had also *two wives* there; and the other companion had likewise *two wives in the persons of a mother and her own daughter!*

Taylor also read:—"We believe that it is not right to prohibit members of this Church from marrying out of the Church." To show that Taylor preached one thing and practised another, "I quote from "Fifteen Years among the Mormons," by Mrs. Mary Ettie V. Smith :—

"When Col. Steptoes' regiment halted a short time in Salt Lake City on its way to California, she says:—"One of the officers formed an acquaintance with a daughter of John Taylor—Mary Ann. She was a very interesting girl; and the intimacy ripened into a mutual attachment. Her father is one of the Twelve Apostles (now Prophet), and a man of great influence in the Church, and at the time edited a paper in New York known as the 'Mormon.' She succeeded in getting married. This was a termination more fortunate than she could have expected had the father been at home. For when he heard of it, he wrote to the Prophet blaming him very severely for not preventing the marriage by the sacrifice of her life. He wrote that he should always feel dissatisfied because the blood of his daughter had not been shed to atone for the sin of marrying out of the Church." This work is published by Belknap and Bliss Hartford, Con., U.S., 1870. If you want the nightmare, or your hair to stand on end, get Mrs. Smith's book, price 8s. I give her affiadavit and what else I can in future chapters, but my quotations must be brief.

I have often heard this Prophet, when playing parson in the pulpit, swear what he is going to do, but as many of his sermons are published and sold in Liverpool and London I will first extract from them; then you will be more apt to believe what I tell you I heard, which is not in print, and to more completely show that there actually exists to-day in the Heart of America's Republic a Kingdom with a Prophet King, to whose mandates all Mormons are constrained to yield implicit obedience, and to show that the present "Prophet," John Taylor, is on a par with Brigham, if not more rampant, I quote from his sermon on

"THE KINGDOM OF GOD OR NOTHING."

"In the Second Epistle and last verse of the Gospel according to Saint Brigham will be found the following words:—'WE SAY IT IS THE KINGDOM OF GOD OR NOTHING.'—

The sayings of modern men of God are of as great importance as the sayings of ancient men of God, and a great deal more applicable to our condition.

In looking at the Epistle to Colonel Alexander, and considering the important things said in it, I was particularly struck with the last words, which compose my text—'The kingdom of God or nothing.'

We believe in living Priesthood—in present revelation—in the Church and kingdom of God as it now exists on the earth.

What is the kingdom of God? We need not go into the nonsense of sectarianism: we will let it go entirely, hook and line; for we know enough about it to care nothing about it, nor about the absurd ideas entertained by sectarians of the kingdom of God.

We, as a people, are determined to be free; for with us it is—'The kingdom of God or nothing.'

When we talk about kingdoms, we talk about governments, rule, authority, power. The kingdoms of this world have their powers, authorities, rule, regulations, law-givers, &c., according to the kind of government they adopt. Hitherto we, as a people, have been amalgamated to a great extent with other nations. It is true we have had a Church government, Church laws, Church discipline, and by the holy Priesthood associated with this Church we have governed the people. Still we have been subject to another government, power, and authority, to Gentile rule, Gentile dominion, Gentile laws, to Gentile usages and customs, to which we have been willingly subject, so far as they were righteous; and it was told us by the Lord, that if we observed the laws of God, we need not break the laws of the land.

What law have we transgressed? I have tried to find out. We have examined the Constitution of the United States and the laws pertaining to these matters; and if anybody here or elsewhere can point out any law that we have transgressed as American citizens, they know more about it than I have been able to learn; and I should like such a person to put me in possession of that information.

What next? Why, on the back of this, after lying about us, slandering, abusing, and imposing upon us, trampling upon our rights, and sending the meanest curses among us that ever disgraced the footstool of God—men they are ashamed of themselves, they have now sent an armed force contrary to law and right and to the principles that ought to prevail in the United States. They have no more right to do this than I have to cut any of your throats.

Shall we lie down and let those scoundrels cut our throats? Shall we untie our neckcloths and tell them to come on and cut and carve away as they please, and knock down, drag out, and introduce their abominations among us—their cursed Christian institutions—to prostitute our women and lay low our best men? Shall we suffer it, I say?

If they have a mind to cut each other's throats, we have no objections. We say, Success to both parties. But when they come to cut ours, without ceremony, we say, Hands off, gentlemen. We are not so religious as to sit down meekly and tamely submit to these things. We understand something of the difference between what some call treason, or treasonable acts, and base submission to the will of a tyrant, who would seek to bring us into servile chains—into perfect submission to his sway.

'This is pretty plain talk,' say you. I meant to talk plain: I do not wish to be misunderstood.

We will not submit to such a state of things for ever. If you, our enemies, are determined to invade our rights, trample upon our liberties, snatch from us the rich boon we have inherited from our fathers, to make us bow in vile subservience to your will, we will resist you: we will not submit to it. We will say, Stand back, and give us our rights. We will act the part of freemen, and we say it shall be 'The kingdom of God or nothing.'

Why is it that we are persecuted? It is because we believe in the establishment of the kingdom of God upon the earth—because we say and know that God has established his kingdom.

What is the cause, then, of the evil planned against us? It is because we are the Church and kingdom of God.

I speak, if you please, as a politician. On this ground I ask what right any people or number of people have to come and interfere with us? There is no such right in the catalogue, gentlemen.

They, however, do interfere with us; and what is the cause of it? It is because of the kingdom of God—because of the truth of God—because of the Spirit of God and certain principles that exist among this people. And what are they? It is polygamy that they are so incensed against. They need not draw down such a long face about that, for they themselves do a thousand times worse than that, were it even as heinous a crime as they say it is.

I am not going to find fault with God or the Devil. I suppose the Devil is as necessary as any other being, or he would not have been.

The righteous have been trampled under foot, but it is well with them. It was not their day. The time for them to reign and have dominion was not come. While wrapt in prophetic vision, they could view the events that were to transpire in the last days, and prophesied of a kingdom that should be set up and stand for ever. They looked with joyful anticipation to this day.

In relation to the kingdom of God, what is it? Is it a spiritual kingdom? Yes. Is it a temporal kingdom? Yes. Does it relate to the spiritual affairs of men? Yes. Does it relate to the temporal of men? Yes.

Was the kingdom that the Prophets talked about, that should be set up in the latter times, going to be a Church? Yes. And a State? Yes, it was going to be both Church and State, to rule both temporarily and spiritually.

Who sets up the kings, the emperors, and potentates that rule and govern the universe? The Lord.

And who is there that acknowledges his hand? Where is the nation, the people, the church even, or other power that does it? You may wander east, west, north, and south, and you cannot find it in any church or government on the earth, except this Church of Jesus Christ of Latter-day Saints.

Why is it that thrones will be cast down, empires dissolved, nations destroyed, and confusion and distress cover all people, as the Prophets have spoken? Because the Spirit of the Lord will be withdrawn from the nations in consequence of their wickedness, and they will be left to their own folly.

What? are Christians ignorant? Yes, as ignorant of the things of God as the brute beast.

The time was to come, *and is now*, that God *has* set up his kingdom upon the earth, and he is determined that men shall be in subjection to his laws.

Can the Lord go to any other people but this and declare his will? He cannot. There is not a nation, kingdom, power, or people,—there is not a political, moral, social, philosophical, or religious society in the world that would receive the word of God, except this people.

If there cannot be a people anywhere found that will listen to the word of God and receive instructions from him, how can his kingdom ever be established? It is impossible? What is the first thing necessary to the establishment of his kingdom? It is to raise up a Prophet and have him declare the will of God; the next is to have people yield obedience to the word of the Lord through that Prophet. If you cannot have these, you can never establish the Kingdom of God upon the earth.

What is the kingdom of God? It is God's government upon the earth and in heaven.

What is his Priesthood? It is the rule, authority, administration, if you please, of the government of God on the earth or in the heavens; for the same Priesthood that exists upon the earth exists in the heavens, and that Priesthood holds the keys of the mysteries of the revelations of God; and the legitimate head of that Priesthood, who has communion with God, is the Prophet, Seer, and Revelator to his Church and people on the earth.

Are we here in these mountains, surrounded, as a people, by the barriers of the everlasting hills, brought out from our enemies to inherit these valleys? We acknowledge the hand of God in it. Does an army come to make war on us? We acknowledge the hand of God in it. We feel that we are in his hands, and say, "It is the Lord; let him do what seemeth good unto him, and we will seek to do what is right on our part. Have we to go to war? We will acknowledge the hand of God in it.

In peace and prosperity, war and adversity, we will lean on the hand of God, and acknowledge it, and say, "Hallelujah! the Lord God Omnipotent reigneth."

What does it matter whether we are farming, building, planting, fighting, or anything else, if we are doing as we are told? Who cares? I do not.

And now, having been forced from the United States, after having been driven time and time again from our homes by our murderous enemies—having fulfilled all the requirements that God or man would require of us, and kept every law necessary for us to observe,—after all this, and more, I say, shall we suffer those poor, miserable, damned, infernal scoundrels to come here and infringe upon our sacred rights?

['NO!' resounded throughout the Tabernacle, making the walls of the building tremble.]

NO! It shall be 'The kingdom of God or nothing' with us. That is my text, I believe; and we will stick to it—we will maintain it; and, in the name of Israel's God, the kingdom of God shall roll on, and all the powers of earth and hell cannot stop its progress. It is onward, ONWARD, ONWARD, from this time henceforth, to all eternity. [Voices of 'Amen.']

'Are you not afraid of being killed?' you may ask me. No. Great conscience! who cares about being killed? They cannot kill you. They may shoot a ball into you, and your body may fall; but you will live. Who cares about dying? We are associated with eternal principles: they are within us as a well springing up to eternal life. We have begun to live for ever.

Who would be afraid of a poor, miserable soldier—a man that gets eight dollars a month for killing people, and a miserable butcher at that—one of the poorest curses in creation? Mean as the Americans are, they will not, many of them, hire for soldiers. But the Government must hire foreigners for eight dollars a month to come out here to kill us! Who is afraid of them? Let them come on or stay and wiggle, it's all right.

We are the Saints of God; we have the kingdom of God, and the devils in hell and all the wicked men on the earth cannot take it from us. *We shall rule and have dominion in the earth,* and they cannot help themselves. They can take their own course. They may fight against us, if they like, or they can back out and leave us; but the kingdom will go on. They may take what course they please: the kingdom is ours. *(Journal of Discourses. vol. 6, p. 18 to 27.)*

As this is the voice of *the present* lewd and licentious "Prophet of this Last Dispensation," of the 19th century's "Inspired Yankee Tricks." I devote extra space to the chief buccaneer's Brazen harangue and continue to extract from another of John Taylor's sermons from the same volume, pp. 111.

"If we were now in Egypt, we could not say we were eating the leeks and onions, for we are now eating them. Our enemies are on the outside.

How do we know but they will come in here and swallow us completely up? Brother Brigham says 'We shall have to be greased first.'

I feel, notwithstanding our inexperience, and the many blunders we make, and the various evils many of us fall into, that we are the best people under the face of the heavens.

Let the devil send up one thousand, ten thousand, or five hundred thousand men against us, all right. I was going to say, who the devil cares? We are in the hands of God. He is going to build up his kingdom, and all kingdoms, powers and dominions will be brought into subjection to the kingdom of our God.

If we, who profess to be Latter-day Saints—we, who have taken upon us the name of Christ—we who have been baptised in his name for the remission of sins and had the laying on of hands for the gift of the Holy Ghost—who have received our washings, and anointings, and teachings from the mouthpiece of Jehovah,—we who live under the sunshine of the light and intelligence that flow from the mouth of God—if we try, each one of us, so to live, act, move, and obey, and so to fulfil the laws, commandments, and ordinances of God, in every position we occupy, we shall move along like a well-organized piece of machinery.

Suppose Uncle Sam should rise up in his red hot wrath, and send 50,000 men here—[President Brigham Young says his own fire would burn him out] —you see the position we are placed in that we are dependant on the Lord and on his counsel, and all that we can do or say will be according to that from this time henceforth and for ever. Zion begins to rise, her light being come. The glory of the Lord is rising upon us.

It needs a guiding hand—a man filled with the Spirit of God, and not only that, but the Lord to communicate with, that he may comprehend the designs of God and lead forth Israel in the paths they should go.

What shall we do then? Shall we begin to fret, and whine and grunt, and groan about this and that, and because we think things are in a very bad fix? We ought to feel that we are in the Church and kingdom of God, and that God is at the helm, and that all is right and will continue to be. I feel as easy as an old shoe.

What, if we should be driven to the mountains? Let us be driven. What if we have to burn our houses? why set fire to them with a good grace, and dance a jig round them while they are burning. What do I care about these things? we are in the hands of God, and all his right. Brother Brigham says we are used to it, and we shall not feel it hard.

Brethren, we are eternal beings and are associated with eternal principles: we are in the Church and kingdom of God upon the earth, and that kingdom is an eternal kingdom, and we are bound by and associated with eternal principles: we are beginning to live for ever, and are acting not only for time but for eternity. And if we should have a war and a few things like this, never mind: who cares? Just grin and bear it.

My opinion is, that, far from these things that now surround us being an injury to us and the kingdom of God, they will give it one of the greatest hoists that it has ever had yet; and all is right and all will be right, 'whatever is is right,' God will control all things for our best good and the interest of his Church and kingdom on the earth."

Worse and more of it. On page 162 of the same Volume, "God's Mouthpiece" chitchats in juggle jingle style the following:—

"I feel that we are all of us in the hands of God, that we are all associated with this kingdom, and that if any people under the face of the heavens can be properly called 'the Saints of the Most High,' we are that people.

When we reflect upon the myriads of human beings that crowd the earth in every nation, country and clime, and then consider that we are the only people that do really acknowledge the hand of God in all things; that we are the only people that God has chosen and selected to place his name among; that we are the only people that can emphatically be called the servants and handmaidens of the Lord; that we are the only people that have a right and claim upon the promises of God; that we are the only people that entertain correct ideas pertaining to our present position and our future destiny; that we are the only people that can stretch back to ages that are past, and look forward to those that are to come, and that can act understandingly in relation to our worship and the ordinances of the house of God, having a knowledge of the past, the present and the future; that we are the only people under the heavens that have a legitimate right to the promises and blessings of God, whether they relate to this world or that which is to come; that we are the only people that understand anything about the present position or the cause of the organization of the world and of man, and that understand anything correctly about a preparation for a future state; that we are the only people who know how to save our progenitors, how to save ourselves, and how to save our posterity in the celestial kingdom of God; that we are the people that God has chosen by whom to establish his kingdom and introduce correct principles into the world; and that we in fact are the saviours of the world, if they ever are saved;—when we reflect upon these things, there is something connected with them that is calculated to make our hearts swell with gratitude and thrill with joy; and when we feel the consoling influence of the Spirit of the Most High God resting upon us and round about us, and the visions and glories of the future that we are destined to enjoy are open to our minds, if we are faithful, and the great events that are about to transpire in the last days are manifested to our minds, there is something in them that is calculated to sing, Hosanna!—hosanna to the Lord God of Hosts!

If we look abroad in the world, what are their enjoyments and hopes? They corrupt their bodies, debase their minds, and they are not fit receptacles for the Spirit of the living God; nor have they any among them that are capable of teaching them anything about that Spirit; but they are in the dark.

When we reflect upon these things, have we not something to be thankful for? I think, if any people are blessed under the heavens, we are that people, we may exclaim, as the ancient Israelites used to, 'Happy is that people whose God is the Lord.'

It certainly is a lamentable thing, when we come to reflect upon it, to see so many of the human family ignorant and careless, knowing nothing about God—knowing nothing of their origin or destiny. What has the Lord done for us? He has opened the heavens, and has revealed the principles of truth. He has sent his holy angels to communicate unto the children of men the things calculated to promote their peace and happniess in time and throughout all eternity. He has given unto us, his people, the holy Priesthood after the order of Melchisedec, which "holds the keys of the mysteries of the revelations of God," which draws back the curtains of the invisible world, and enables him to penetrate beyond the vail, and discloses the great purposes of Jehovah pertaining to himself and to this world, as they shall roll forth in the accomplishment of his purposes.

What a contrast between this and the religion of the world! This shows man imperfectly at the present, it is true; but it will show him perfectly how to become a saviour—how to redeem this world, which has been overrun with anarchy, destruction, misery, folly, and evils of every kind—how to redeem this world from the curse under which it labours and groans: it will show him how to teach the human family, that they may understand correct principles and be saved in the kingdom of God.

The germs of this peace are with us; the intelligence concerning these matters has begun to be developed, and there is a communication opened between the heavens and the earth—an unction that dwells with the Gods, an intelligence that governs all worlds and controls all nature, a particle—a spark of Deity straight from the eternal blaze of Jehovah, opening, unfolding, enlightening, and teaching. It emanates from him to the authorities of this Church, and flows through all the ramifications of the Priesthood. That spark from the bosom of Jehovah enabled them to commence that reformation that will redeem a world from the ruins of the fall.

This kingdom and this organization will save all that are governed by its principles, and is destined by its influence and workings in the world to spread and increase until every knee shall be made to bow and every tongue confess to the glory of the Father.

These principles have begun to be developed among us; whisperings of the Spirit of the Lord pours intelligence into our bosoms, broods over us, causing peace and joy to be with us, we have then, more or less, a faint glimpse of those things that are laid up for the faithful; and it is then we feel as though we and all that we have are in the hands of the Lord, and that we are ready to offer ourselves a sacrifice for the accomplishment of his purposes upon the earth. These are our feelings, and we feel proud of our associations with the Church and kingdom of God.

Most of us have come out of and been mixed up with the world; we have been associated with, and have received our education and ideas in the midst of corruptions of every kind, and we have sucked it in as with our mother's milk. Even our religion has been corrupt, and our ideas of morality have been wrong; our politics, laws, and philosophy have all been wrenched, twisted and perverted; our customs, habits, and associations have been wrong; and all that we have come out from is vanity, evil, corrupting, and damnable in its nature.

Is it surprising, then, that we should find it difficult to live according to the light and intelligence that dwells in the bosom of God and that is manifested partially unto us, his people? Is it surprising that, surrounded as we have been, and wallowing in corruption all the day long, that we should have partaken more or less of these things, and that they should still cling to us?

When Joseph Smith had anything from God to communicate to the children of Men or to the Church, what was it he had to fight against all the day long? It was the prejudices of the people; and, in many instances, he could not and dared not reveal the word of God to the people, for fear they would rise up and reject it. Hence he had to treat them like children, and feed them upon milk, and unfold principles gradually, just as they could receive them.

How is it now, under the administration of President Young? Much the same, in this respect. He has often found it very difficult to make the people understand things as the Lord has revealed them unto him.

We ourselves have not got rid of our evils. We have so much professed righteousness and foolish tradition within us, that we feel indignant many times at righteous principles, when God reveals them. Have you not felt so, brethren and sisters? I know you have, and you know you have.

We are all aiming at celestial glory. Don't you know we are? We are talking about it, and we talk about being kings and priests unto the Lord; we talk about being enthroned in the kingdoms of our God; we talk about being queens and priestesses; and we talk, when we get on our high-heeled shoes, about possessing thrones, principalities, powers, and dominions, when at the same time many of us do not know how to conduct ourselves any better than a donkey does.

The world has been apostate for generations past: it has been under the dominion of the prince and power of the air, even the god of this world, who rules in the hearts of the children of disobedience. As I have stated before, they have been wrong in their national affairs, they have been wrong in political affairs, they have been wrong in their religion, and they have been wrong in everything.

What is God going to do, to set the world right? We are the people who are called to do his work; We are a little nucleus, a mere handful, that he has selected from among the nations, to put his name among. Yes, we are that people, with all our faults, our foibles, and vanities. We do acknowledge the hand of God; we do acknowledge the Prophet of God and the teachings of the Most High, and we do feel willing to be governed by those teachings.

We are here in the tops of the mountains, just as the Prophet said we should be.

There is no nation now that acknowledges the hand of God; there is not a king, potentate, nor ruler that acknowledges his jurisdiction. We talk about Christianity, but it is a perfect pack of nonsense. Men talk about civilization, but I do not want to say much about that, for I have seen enough of it. It is a sounding brass and a tinkling symbol; it is as corrupt as hell; and the devil could not invent a better engine to spread his work than the Christianity of the nineteenth century.

How are the nations going to be redeemed? How is the kingdom of God going to be planted upon the earth? Will it be by preaching, or by power? Will it be by the natural course of events, or by moral suasion? Will it be by the outpouring of the judgments of God on the nations? Will it be by kingdoms being overthrown and empires crumbling to ruins? How is it going to be done? I answer, These things will be accomplished by the guidance of the Lord through his Prophets who are in our midst. Don't you see this, brethren? For 'surely the Lord will do nothing, but he revealeth his secrets to his servants the Prophets.' Then it is for us to believe what the Prophets say.

Sectarians profess to believe in the Bible, but they will not let the Lord have any Prophets. If the Lord will tell us what to do, we will do it, whether it is to fight armies or do anything else.

The servants of God will teach and instruct us in the things of God; and we shall grow up in virtue, intelligence, holiness, and purity, and learn to understand correct laws; and our rulers will be from among ourselves, and our Governor will be one of us—one of the Lord's appointing—not of the Devil's. The kings and princes of the earth will come, in order that they may get information and teach the same to their people. They will come as they came to learn the wisdom of Solomon.

We have intelligence and ingenuity among us to do all that is required, and we have got to set to work; and, as the Lord gives us wisdom and revelation from time to time, we will carry out his purposes and his designs."

I jump to page 258 and catch the same high-flyer "going it." The Apostle George A. Smith had just proclaimed the necessity of sending hordes of Missionaries to convert the world to Mormonism, said he:—"You may suppose we are sending out but a few Elders—probably not more than 150; but we intend to continue the work, and send out Elders enough to set the world on fire." When he subsided, John Taylor preached as follows:—

"Brother George was talking about setting the world on fire. I think, when the Elders have travelled through the world as far as some of us have, and seen the rottenness and weakness of their institutions—the folly and corruption that everywhere prevail, they will find that it is pretty near time, as the Prophets have said, for it to be burned up, and all its works.

"But I suppose it is necessary, before the world is burned up, that the good wheat should be saved and gathered into the garner, and prepare to take a fresh start in peopling the earth and placing affairs upon a proper foundation. They are living without God in the world—without hope, and they are dying without hope ; consequently, they are careless, profligate, and reckless.

"The Lord has shone upon us ; he has lit up a candle of intelligence in our souls—has imparted to us the principles of eternal truth, opened the heavens, and sent his holy angel to put us in possession of principles that will exalt us in the scale of intelligence among men, and raise us up to be associates of the Gods in the eternal worlds.

"Then shall we, who have thus been blessed with the visions of eternity—with light and intelligence—we, who are filled with the Spirit of God burning in our hearts, who have gazed upon the hidden things of eternity, and contemplated the purposes of God in their majesty and glory—I say, shall we shrink from the task of going forth to snatch these fallen sons of men from everlasting burning ?

"Those who have to go out have to put their noses to the grindstone, and keep them there, and let them grind at it, and not murmur a word ; and then, before they are healed, put them there again, and bear it all the time, and go along without saying anything ; for you know it is a sin in the religious world to get angry. You cannot go and convert the world all at once ; for it is too far sunken in folly and vice. You need not think of going abroad into the world, and going as the Methodists sing ' on flowery beds of ease.'

"This is the difference between us and the world. They meet with difficulties, and they quash down under them, while we ride over them and become victorious. This is the reason why there are so many institutions among the Gentiles that come to naught. They meet with difficulties, and fall before them : we meet with the same, but we have a God at the helm, and we triumph over them. I won't occupy your time further. May God bless you, Amen."

I have heard the "Prophet" Taylor declare thus :—" I will send missionaries enough to convert the Church of England, and all the honest in heart among the so-called Christians of Great Britain to Mormonism. That no one, not even a Saint, can receive any blessing from God, but though the Mormon Prophet (Journal of Discourses, vol. 6, p. 107). On page 109, he says, " It needs a great controlling, directing influence, to sustain, govern, direct, enlighten, and dictate." I could fill volumes with sermons to show that the people must be guided and directed in all things by the Mormon Prophet ; that no woman can rightly set up a stocking, or do the chores of the house, without his immaculate dictation, but I fear too many sermons will make the book so dry, you would have to "wet" it. In his book, "The Government of God" Taylor, after showing how God set up the ancient kings, says :—" Thus, then, these men, delegated and appointed of God, acted as his representatives on the earth. They received their kingdoms from him. They were anointed by prophets of God." After showing that Queen Victoria and other Royal personages are not in their proper place (they should all be in Utah). In speaking of the Emperor of Russia, he says :—" Although he is not delegated to establish the kingdom of God, he may nevertheless be appointed as Cæsar, Nebuchadnezzar, and others as a scourge to the nations, and thus fulfil his destiny, for as we are on the eve of great events, and a fearful doom awaits the nations, some powerful means must be made use of to bring these things about. God regulates his own affairs ; and while the world is in a state of idolatry, apostacy, and rebellion, he, by his providence overrules the affairs of the nation, as Daniel says, 'to the intent that the living may know that the Most High ruleth in the kingdom of men, and giveth it to whomsoever he will, and setteth up over it the basest of men,' It is very evident from what has been shown, that there is no proper government nor rule upon the face of the earth; that there are no kings who are anointed, or legally appointed of God (except the Mormon Prophet) and that, however much disposed any of them may feel to benefit the world, it is out of their power, it exceeds the limits of their jurisdiction, it requires a power, spirit and intelligence which they do not possess." As we have seen the Mormon Prophet is the only king now reigning upon the earth by real Divine authority. Taylor continues, "This earth is the rightful inheritance of the (Mormon) Saints. The greatness of the kingdom under the whole heaven shall be given to the (Mormon) Saints. This earth is man's eternal inheritance. If people suppose that they will inhabit a heaven not on the earth they are mistaken. The Saints of God will inherit the earth for ever, in time, and in eternity." He goes on to say that "the world is ignorant of God and his laws, not having had any communication with him for 1,800 years. The (Mormon) kingdom of God on the earth has been small, weak, unpopular, trampled under foot of men; and none but men of noble minds, firm hopes, and daring resolution (the Mormons) have advocated its principles. There is no more similarity between Christianity as it now exists, with all its superstitions, corruptions, jargons, contentions, divisions, weakness, and imbecility, and this KINGDOM OF GOD (the Mormon Kingdom) than there is between light and darkness. The nations having lost the spirit of God, will assemble to fight against the Lord's people (the Mormons) being full of the spirit of unrighteousness, and opposed to the rule and government of God." He asks " Where has God ever had a people, but they have been persecuted? The testimony of God has always been rejected, and his people trodden under foot." But let the Mormons have their way, and let them overrun the earth with their filthy creed and practice, then says Taylor "God's worship will be known, and the religion of the Lord will lose its forbidding aspect; and God, and his religion be popular among the nations of the earth. In one of his Sermons, on page 260, vol. 6, " Journal of Discourses," he gives an account of his missionary work and says:—" Another Elder and myself staid in an hotel in a small town for about a week, the landlord of which was an infidel. After we had been there two or three days I told the Landlord I was a religious man. He replied, "Oh, you are religious, are you? Religion is a pack of nonsense! I told him I cared as little about the religion of Christendom as he did; but the one I believed in, I told him would benefit both body and soul in time and in eternity. I told him about the success and prosperity that attended our works; and finally he said, 'I dont know but I will sell out and go to America; you have got the right religion; and had I found this, I should have been a religious man." There is much in that sermon showing that Taylor well knows how to become "All things to All men," but I must omit it.

Taylor carries in his flesh a bullet received in Carthage Jail when Smith was shot. In the " Priesthood meetings " where outsiders can never enter, or ever know what there transpires (except through such as me), I have heard Taylor swear, that he " will make the D—d—infernal Yankees eat that bullet," and language that would soil even " Hell upon Earth."

And curl'd with a thousand adders venomous, He lolled forth his bloody-flaming tongue :

At them he 'gan to rear his bristles strong, And felly gnare.—*Fairy Queen*.

And showed the effect that bullet will yet have upon " Uncle Sam." If Americans consider the Mormon Prophet a loyal American citizen, the sooner they undeceive themselves the better: for I know he is working with Southern rebels, savage Indians, and alien foreigners, who care nought for the Republic but to cause trouble, and if possible, dissolution; or to use his own words, " Bust up, Uncle Sam " and set up his own filthy Polygamic, Tyrannical and Despotic Government in its place. Taylor is a Poet, and his ditties are considered very sacred by the Mormons, I can only give part of one here from " Sacred Hymns and Spiritual Songs," p. 349, hymn 297,

> " A Church without a Prophet is not the Church for me ;
> It has no head to lead it ; in it I would not be ;
> But I've a Church not made by man,
> Cut from the mountain without hand ;
> A Church with gifts and blessings—Oh, that's the Church for me.
> Oh, that's &c.
>
> A Church without Apostles is not the Church for me ;
> 'Tis like a ship dismasted, afloat upon the sea :
> But I've a Church that's always led
> With the Twelve Stars around her head ;
> A Church with good foundation—Oh, that's the Church for me.
> Oh, that's, &c."

The following is from the Salt Lake Tribune :—" John Taylor, the present head of the Mormon Church, when in the Utah Legislature, 1876, introduced a bill to limit the time of bringing prosecutions for murder where Mormons were concerned as defendants, to three years. He refused to extend this privilege to non-Mormons, and advocated the passage of the bill in a speech full of abuse of the Federal courts."

"John Taylor not only broke the laws of Illinois, but in 1857 married a young lady named Maggie Young, in New York, in wilful defiance of the law of that State. Some years previous he brought the two Whitaker sisters from England to Utah, and if he did not marry them there, he should have done, so manifest was the disgusting playfulness of their intimacy. Dare any one deny these facts ? "

This was published in Salt Lake City years ago and not denied yet. I know he married the two Whitaker girls. I shall have occasion to refer to this " Prophet " Taylor again. The " Tribune " has plenty such, and were it not published under the protection of American Guns and Bayonets—look out, as it is their men sometimes get " Hail Columbia."

I think this sufficient to show what the " John Bull Yankee " Taylor is, and that he is just the man to " boss this Hell upon Earth." Another John Taylor, " The Water-Poet, Motto works, 1630," must have been a Prophet ; for he seems to represent his namesake, the present boss of Utah's Hell as possessing—

" The knowledge of the thriving art, A holy outside and a hollow heart."

He also said that—
> " They have a gin, that wond'rous quick and well
> Sends unbelievers headlong into Hell."

And after prophetically viewing his namesake the Mormon Prophet and his rascally transactions, the Water Poet, John Taylor adds :—

> "——— I hope, Thou wilt conclude thy roguery in a rope ;
> Three trees, two rampant and the other crossant, One halter-pendant.
> And a ladder passant :
> In a field asure, clouded like the sky, Because twixt earth and air I hope thou'lt die."

To which I say, Amen ! ! and add :—
" Be ready gods, with all your thunderbolts ; Dash him to pieces ! "
Shakespeare's Julius Cæsar.

CHAPTER V.

The "Endowment House," its Secrets and Freemasonry—
The Devils' Pinafore—Weddings in Hell.

Having heard so much about the "Endowment House" I had a great desire to go through and see what it really was. Mormon leaders will not allow converts to enter that "Holy" place until tried and found faithful, which sometimes take years. I managed to get my necessary papers, which are required to gain admission, four months after I arrived at Salt Lake. Here I was to see Gods, Angels, the Devil, Gabriel, Michael, Peter, James, and John, and learn from them my whole duty as a man and a brother. It may be termed the Secret Lodge of Mormonism, where candidates for future glory are initiated into the "Mysteries of the Kingdom." The Saints in England are assured that in this House they will meet Jehovah and "learn the ways of the Lord more perfectly." It is held up to us as "a very sacred place." They disclose no more than Free Masons, and other kindred societies before initiating a candidate; it is all mystery till we get in, and then it's too late to get out with clean hands and a pure heart. No man or woman can possibly go through that sink-hole of iniquity without becoming totally oiled and very much soiled. I will tell all that I can with decency, and as this book will not be sold in a sealed envelope, or be given to the public as obscene literature, I am compelled to omit very much that I would like to have an opportunity to whisper in men's ears. Those gentlemen who have heard my private lecture to men only, are better posted in the things transpiring in that "sacred" place. To give a faint idea of what it is like, I quote from a work written by a lady who passed through it. On page 50 of "Fifteen years among the Mormons," Mrs. Smith says:—

"Now in conclusion of my disclosures upon this 'Endowment' subject, associated as it is with hateful memories of that peculiar kind, most distasteful to the recollection of a pure woman, I deem it my duty in compensation for what I have felt compelled to omit, especially of that never-to-be-forgotten scene in the 'Garden of Eden,' to state that the '*moral*' and *object* of the whole is, socially to unsex the sexes; * * * * * * * and when I call the attention of the reader to the fact that while I have described the *dress* of all the parties to this inhuman display and ocular demonstration, I have *not* mentioned the dress of '*Adam* and *Eve*,' nor the nature of the 'FRUIT' by which each was in turn tempted; I think, he will admit, that while I have said *enough* I have also left more unsaid than the imagination, held with the loosest possible rein, would be likely to picture; and I have only to add, that the reality *is too monstrous for human belief*." See Mrs. Smith's affidavit, &c., Appendix D.

I coincide with her publisher, who adds this foot-note:—"It would seem to be a misfortune that a false estimate of propriety should be allowed to interpose a barrier against the exposure of these Mormon debaucheries."

Mormon Leaders defy Apostates to tell it, and well they may. The indecencies, oaths, and penalties effectually bar its exposure in most instances; many have attempted it and checked themselves suddenly, just where they should go ahead. Not that I blame them. Life is dear to most people, and these attempts at exposure were made in America, within reach of Mormon "Destroying Angels." General Beadel, in his work "Life in Utah," page

500, says:—" Apostates universally have a horror or fear of speaking about it, and never do until they are safe beyond the power of the Church." I am 7,000 miles away, and can snap my finger at all the Mormon infernal devils, so fond of cutting throats and sending people "to Hell across lots." Moral decency and a great desire to have this book pass through the Post, is all that checks me from giving a complete exposure, and every word used in that Hell within a Hell. I give all that anyone can possibly give in public, and much more than has ever before been given. Men can learn more at my private lectures.

"H. Jenson, the Apostate Mormon who was threatened with blood atonement for revealing the Endowment House Oaths, died on Sunday at Brigham City, Utah."—*Salt Lake Tribune.*

The secret place of initiation into Mormon mysteries is called the "Endowment House," where we are said to receive our "Endowments." This endowment affair originated in a drunken revel. The heads of the Church met together to plan a scheme to more effectually bind the followers in absolute subjection; to aid them in their arduous duties a keg of liquor was supplied; this the "saints" emptied, and thus became full of the spirit, or in the words of one who was there "Gloriously Drunk." As drunkenness and debauchery, are so closely allied, can we wonder at the licentious and villainous scenes enacted in the endowment ceremonies, scenes which can only be characterised as filthy, obscene and disgusting. I will describe what I can.

The *Dramatis Personæ* is as follows:—

ELOHIM, OR HEAD GOD—JEHOVAH—MESSIAH, OR CHRIST.
[The Prophet and his two Counsellors represent the above.]
MICHAEL—GABRIEL—ADAM—SATAN—APOSTLE'S PETER—JAMES—AND JOHN—THE GREAT HIGH PRIEST—EVE—PROPHETESS—PRIESTESS.
Clerk, Washers, Attendants, Sectarians, Chorus, and Endowees.

This Drama, if such we may term it, has been smuggled chiefly from "Milton's Paradise Lost and Regained—The Mysteries, or Holy Dramas of the Middle Ages—The Eleusinian Mysteries of Ancient Greece, and Morgan's Free Masonry Exposé."

It takes nine hours to go through all the rites and ceremonies, grips, signs, oaths, covenants, obligations, and filthiness. We enter the Endowment House at 7 a.m., taking with us a well-filled lunch basket, and a bottle or more of olive oil. If a man is to take one wife, two bottles of oil are sufficient, but should he be matrimonially inclined, and is about to take unto himself two wives at the same time, he must have three bottles of oil, and so on, adding another bottle for each additional wife. It takes a pint of the best oil to slide each individual through these ceremonies. At the time I went through and received my "Endowments" there accompanied me some forty men and sixty women who were fellow candidates for the same "Blessing." Each person, in addition to the lunch and oil, has also a little bundle; the man's bundle contains a clean white shirt, a pair of white socks, the "Holy Endowment" or "Wedding Garment," a white linen robe, or loose gown—somewhat after the style of the ancient eastern costume, and a linen sash, a turban or cap, also of white linen, and the "fig leaf apron;" this is made of a square of green silk, upon which is worked with brown floss nine fig leaves. These articles, together with a pair of white linen moccassins form the contents of each man's bundle. Pardon me for peeping into the woman's "little bundle," but being of a curious and sort of "Paul Pry" disposition, I must take the consequence. The "Daughters of Zion" not only slide into the kingdom *a la* olive oil, but a certain paraphernalia of dress is also requisite to complete the *modus operandi*. In the female's bundle we find such interesting articles as a chemise, purely white and clean, a snow white bed gown, a pair of white stockings, garters with the motto " Honi soit qui mal y pense " omitted, a sort of night cap (white of course) with a huge veil; this veil is used but once to cover the face, although it is very badly needed for that purpose during the disgusting ceremonies. There is also a large flowing linen robe, a sash, a pair of white linen moccassins, the "fig leaf apron" of the same material and description as the men's, and likewise the "Endowment," or "Wedding Garment." Much importance is attached to this article of apparel, and we are here reminded of the man who got into the feast without the Wedding Garment; and we are given to understand by the Priests that should any of us happen to get in without this garment, we shall be "kicked out." I cannot better describe this garment than by saying it is under shirt and drawers in one. If my readers wish to possess a "Wedding Garment" just take a pair of drawers and a vest or undershirt; stitch them together making one garment of the twain and you have it, only be sure to cut off the buttons and sew up the button holes and put tape strings in their places for tying instead of buttoning, for buttons and button holes are patterning after the "Gentiles" and considered very worldly: there's nothing "Heavenly" about buttons and button holes. We are cautioned never to be found outside of this "Holy Garment." It must ever after be worn next to the skin, for with this garment on we are told it's impossible for the Devil to enter one's body, if we are in a building on fire without means of escape, this Garment will keep us from burning, we shall pass through the fire like Shadrach, Meshec, and Abednego, with our hair unsinged and no smell of fire upon us; so you see it's a complete fire escape. Then again if shipwrecked and no lifeboat handy this Garment becomes a swimming apparatus which beats Paul Boyton's: we cannot sink. It is a wonder to me that no "Yankee" has yet patented the thing; think of it; here we have a Garment warranted Devil-proof, fireproof, waterproof, and what not, and the patent not applied for yet, what a chance for some enterprising Yankee. So careful are the "Saints" never to be without this garment, that when changing the soiled for a clean one, they first pull off a sleeve of the dirty one and immediately slip the arm (bare but an instant) into the sleeve of the clean garment; then the corresponding leg is slipped off and replaced at once within the leg of the clean, and so on, till finally the whole garment is changed.

Having thus described the contents of the "little bundles," I will merely say in passing, the lunch we take with us is for the "Priests" that minister before the "Lord" in that "Holy Place." We get none of this, we get meat to eat the world knows not of, strong meat at that. What we get in the "Endowment House" can in no way be termed "milk for babes," Oh no! we are supposed to have grown by this time to the stature of full men and full women in the Lord; in fact before entering we obtain from the Bishop a Certificate that we are strong enough in the faith to endure the scorchings and searchings, the fire and awful grandeur of this sublime place. This Certificate also states that the holder thereof is in good standing in the "Church of Jesus Christ of Latter-day-Saints"—has paid up his tithing and is in every particular worthy to receive his or her "Endowments." If a man intends to marry two or more wives at this particular time the certificate states that he is worthy and recommends that he be allowed the "privilege."

On entering the "Endowment House" we present the Certificate to the officiating Priest, who examines it and, if found correct, enters the same in a book kept for that purpose; the name, place and date of birth, and the Parents' name of the person presenting the certificate are also entered; we hand over to the Priest the lunch and the olive oil, keeping the little bundle ourselves. When all the Certificates and names are duly registered and the house is full, we are ushered into another room called the bath room and ordered to disrobe; 40 men and 60 women had now to get rid of their vast sins by means of a bath. A Mormon "Order of the Bath." I saw at a glance that the first in the tub would get the cleanest bath, for many of my brethren showed unmistakable signs of having neglected their ablutions for a very long time past, hence I preferred to take my bath *before*, rather than *after* them, and being quick at undressing I was the first to spring into the bath tub. Here the High Priest stood ready to manipulate. He began by scratching into the roots of my hair like a barber shampooing a man, and as he kept scratching away he said Bro. J.—by this process I now wash away all the unholy thoughts that have previously occupied your mind, at the same time passing his hands over my forehead. He then washed my eyes thoroughly saying, "I now wash away all that you have ever beheld of iniquity." My mouth received a cleansing and was rinsed out with cold water, The Priest said "I now cleanse you from all the evil you have ever said," thus all the naughty words I had uttered, and all the little and big lies I had told up to this time were washed away. My ears next received attention, and all the evil and sin I had heard was cleansed. My hands received a complete washing, so that if I had helped myself to anything that did not belong to me, or had given anyone a blackened eye, or any and every sin my hands had committed was also washed away. My arms, breast, in short away down through the whole body every part was carefully attended to right down to the soles of the feet, so that if my feet had been swift to do evil those sins were also removed; in fact I was pronounced "clean every whit."

Having been thus cleansed from all my sins I was shoved over to another Priest, the Priest who had washed me bawled out "Next" as he gave me a push, and another victim took my place at the same bath tub, and in the same water that contained all my sin. The Priest I was so unceremoniously pushed toward was the "Aaronic Priest Called of God as was Aaron." It was this individual's prerogative to attend to the "Anointing" business; he took my bottle of olive oil and poured the whole pint into an old cow's horn, called the "Holy Horn of Anointing." First of all he poured Oil on my head "that ran down upon the beard, even down to the skirts of"—here the quotation fails for we had no garments on; however it ran down to the toe nails, then the Priest vigorously scratched the oil into the roots of my hair like a barber when he uses bay rum after a good shampoo. Now says the Priest "I anoint your head so that for the future nothing but holy thoughts shall occupy your mind, your eyes that you may turn them away from beholding of vanity or evil, your mouth that you may always speak the words of truth and righteousness," and so he kept on rubbing in the oil at every part, and mumbling nonsense right down to the tips of the toes and soles of the feet. I was thoroughly greased, oiled all over. I felt just then that I certainly was a Slippery Customer; this oil is supposed to remain upon the person as—"The Holy Oil of the Anointing," but its stay on me was of short duration "you bet," for I found no rest until a hot bath removed all that "Holy" or rather oily stuff. Talking with a good Mormon "Saint" whose presence I did not like, especially in hot weather, he told me that he was oil'd 25 years ago and the consecrated stuff was still on him, for he had not taken a bath since. My Apostacy was attributed to the fact that I had washed off the consecrated oil, so that the sacred influence refused to *stick* to me. In addition to the sin of divesting myself of all oily substances, I also found the "Wedding Garment" most uncomfortable to wear, and having to sleep with the thing on, my rest was so much disturbed, I concluded to leave it off. Thus the Devil got possession of my body again and entered in, "And the last state of this man was worse than the first," at least, so say the Mormons. After being oiled, I had to put on the "Wedding Garment," but how to get into it was a caution, I suppose I never should have got the thing outside of me had not the Priest very materially assisted in the operation; having got the sacred rags on (for I had split the concern in making the rash attempt) the Priest whispered in my ear the "New name, which no man knoweth, saving he that receiveth it." He first ascertained that my Christian name was William, and then gave me the name of "James." All the names are either John, Peter, James, David, Solomon, Abraham, or such like; there are no surnames given in the "Endowment House." This new name must never be divulged only to St. Peter. (Dear reader, don't tell him I told you or I shall "catch it." It's between you and I, you know).

At this juncture I was introduced to the "Angel Gabriel." I shook hands cordially with his Angelic Majesty, but being unaccustomed to meeting angels I was somewhat embarrassed, and knew not what to say; however, I summoned up courage to remark, "happy to meet you Mr. Gabriel, its a fine day ai'nt it," forgetting that angels usually live so far above the clouds that they are unaffected by atmospheric influences. I also ventured to say that I had expected to have heard him blow his trumpet before having the pleasure of his acquaintance. He smiled, and this relieved me, for I had expected to find angels very grave and solemn, but here was an angel that could actually laugh. I began to feel at home with him, and thinking that he knew something about future and eternal affairs, I proceeded "to draw him out," and gained considerable information in regard to the resurrection and other matters, for at this point of the proceedings we, who had been washed and oiled, had to wait while the rest of the men and women received similar treatment, for be it remembered that all sin must be washed away from the candidates in the manner described, and the Holy Oil must be applied to each person before we are considered fit to associate with the "Angels" and the "Gods," to whom we are introduced afterward. The women undergo the same process as the men, only that it takes a little extra effort to extract sin from a woman, she being so full of the Devil; and possessed of very many devils, it takes some scrubbing and washing to thoroughly cleanse a woman, judging from the splashing and splurging—the giggling and chattering—it seemed the women were highly delighted at the way and manner in which they were getting rid of their sins. Women also receive a new name. Sarah being a pet name, whose daughters they are so long as they consent to give their lords a concubine, and obey their Abrahams as Sarah of old did. The women's new names are taken from those of the women of Scripture. This difference is observed in regard to the new name of the man and that of the woman—while the former reveals his name to no one but Peter, the latter must reveal hers to her husband. I asked the "Angel Gabriel" why this difference? and received from him this choice piece of theology. "You see" said the "Angel," "Adam was not deceived, but the woman being deceived was in the transgression; she gave way to the Devil in Eden when she had no business to, and then she coaxed and wheedled around her old man Adam, until he yielded to her. He did not yield to Satan only inasmuch as the Devil was in Eve. Now the woman having given way to Satan, it will never do to entrust her with Salvation, for she would give it over to the Devil in five minutes; the husband holds the wife's Salvation, and has power to raise her up at the resurrection." Interrupting, I asked what became of the spinsters and old maids? "Gabriel" laughed heartily this time, and said, "When they die their spirits are shoved into prison with the spirits of all the old bachelors, and that's hell enough for both parties; there the Gospel of Matrimony is preached unto them; and if they get over their prejudice and join in wedlock, they are let out of jail and go straight into glory." Here the "Angel" paused, then said "let me see we had got so far as the resurrection; now don't you see that it is very important that a man should have the power to resurrect his own wives. It will not be as you have supposed, that I shall toot my horn and wake 'em up, oh no! it's not my business to wake up the women. At the resurrection I shall only call forth the men; for instance, take your own case, supposing you marry forty wives, perhaps several of them will have perplexed or bothered you so much in this life that you won't want to be troubled by them in the next world; no one would know better than yourself who to resurrect out of the lot. It will be my duty to call you up, there you will stand at the graves of your forty wives, and you will then call forth those you wish, the remainder will sleep on in their graves, and never see the light of eternity. Not one woman's name is found in the Book of Life."

So far as I could learn from this celebrated "Angel," I should stand at the graves of my forty wives, provided I had so many, and should soliloquize thus: There's Jane, she was a first-rate wife, and very faithful, I'll have her up, hence I would bawl out, Jane come forth! and up she'd come. Well, there's Maria, she was a vixen, I had enough of her during this life, I don't want any more Maria in mine, she lies there and don't come up. I then turn to the grave of lovely Susan, she was a darling. Susan arise! Up she comes, bright as a daisy, and so on, with Alice and Angelina, Lucy, Betsy, Bertha, and Bridget, Dora, Dina and Dorothy, Caroline and Catherine, Louisa, Martha, Matilda, Miriam, and Elizabeth; Pauline, Jemima, Priscilla, Rachel and Rebecca; Mabel, Agnes, and Abigal; Isabel, Rosabell, and all the other bells, be they many or few. Thus I their lord and master, resurrect those wives that have been faithful and obedient to me, while the disobedient and unfaithful are doomed to everlasting oblivion. "You see," said the "Angel," continuing his strange theology, "This doctrine makes the women obey their husbands when nothing else will." Polygamy is a peculiar affair, and it requires strong doctrine to regulate the domestic concerns of plurality; hence we teach that the husband is the only Lord and God the wife will ever know or be answerable to, and that her Salvation depends entirely upon her husband, he alone can damn or save her. Even this don't keep Polygamic wives from fighting, scratching and hairpulling, and oftimes when they continue in a disobedient course, the husband has to resort to the means which Bro. Kimball preached, viz :—To cut them off, and send them back to their mother earth. Just like brother Andrews cut off that unfaithful wife of his by cutting her throat, and by such measures being adopted, we can often regulate the family affairs when all other efforts fail." With a cunning wink Gabriel tapped me on the shoulder and said, "I tell you what it is brother," (fancy singing "I want to be an Angel, and with the Angels stand," here I was an Angel's brother.) "This doctrine of Polygamy is a queer thing to get along with anyhow." I confessed that the *Singularity of Plurality* was a matter I could never understand, to which the Angel replied, "practice makes all things perfect, even in Polygamy. You must practice plurality, young man, before you can understand its singularities." I thought the most fitting prayer for the occasion was "I pray thee have me excused." But to return to the matter the "Angel" wished to convey when he cast that knowing wink, he said, "sometimes the terrible consequences of polygamy will drive a man into Apostacy, then it becomes the duty of the "Destroying Angels" to attend to him as you will learn furthur on; but sometimes they evade the grasp of our blood atoners, and get away. Now then, this theology of ours teaches that the man being the only Lord and Saviour of the woman, when he leaves our church, the wives must leave him and marry some faithful brother that can save them. Hence you will find women in this territory who have been married to ten or a dozen different men." I knew a woman that claimed 13 fathers for her three children, but then this is only a small part of the singularities of plurality. It's a queer thing when you come to go into it. Having received such soul stirring and refreshing doctrine from an "Angel," and anticipating more information such as I could not get, in any of your worldly, sensual, and devilish schools, I was somewhat sorry to find, that all the 40 men and 60 women had by this time got rid of all their sin in the bath tub, and stood before me looking very slick, having each received a coating of oil and the "Wedding Garment." The women had also put themselves inside their chemise, and we men to match them had to don our shirts; in this condition we were all ushered into a dark room and made to squat higgledy-piggledy upon the bare floor; we were now supposed to represent the Sons of God which sang together at the Creation. I did not sing, who could sing in the dark and not see what they were singing about? I failed to *see* the point. Presently there was a sound as of a mighty rushing wind that filled the place; in the dark we could hear considerable mumbling and jumbling; this we were given to understand was the "Gods" in conversation. I thought if they had anything to say they might as well speak out. Shortly a voice which we were told was that of "Elohim" rang out "Michael go down and gather the elements together and prepare to make a world." "Aye! aye"! responded Michael, "behold it shall be done according to thy word." Then the sound of footsteps tramp, tramp, tramp, convinced us that Michael was on the march to fulfil the command of "Elohim."

After fumbling about in the dark awhile, the same footstep was again heard, conveying the idea that Michael having performed the task assigned him was returning from whence he came. When he got back he called out, "All right Elohim, behold all things are done as thou hast commanded." Michael is thus sent to and fro by Elohim on several errands in connexion with the Creation now supposed to be taking place, and finally when the command is given "Let there be light," and when " there was light," we the unfortunate candidates were in a curious predicament, here we were squatting around looking worse than a group of " Digger Indians," and right before us stood the "Gods" and "Holy Angels." Here was "Elohim the boss God," impersonated by Brigham Young. "Jehovah" was represented in the person of a Murderer, who ought at that time to have been dangling at the end of a rope. The "Messiah" or "Christ" was impersonated by a man with a Glass Eye. "Michael" being represented by a thorough "Masher and Smasher" that could captivate and thrash wives to perfection. There were "Gods many" and "Lords many,"—"Angels" and "bright personages" too numerous to mention; I shall describe some of them further on. Now being in the light we could see as well as hear all that was going on, but I must necessarily omit a great deal of what transpires in this "Holy place." I pass on to where we find ourselves after the world is completely organized and made ready for the habitation of man. Now "Elohim," "Jehovah" and "Christ" say. "Let us make man in our own image, after our likeness, and let him have dominion over all these our works." Then up jumps "Adam," a fine looking specimen of humanity: he was a stranger to me at the time, but I afterwards found he was as good a man as ever cut a throat or scuttled a ship. Poor Adam looked kind of lonely and forsaken standing there alone, which drew out the sympathy of the "Gods" who noticed his forlorn condition. The result was the "Gods" came to the conclusion that it was "not good for man to be alone," and they decided there and then to make a "help meet for him," but for some reason we were not permitted to see how the thing was done. Adam was mesmerised on the spot, then we were all told to go to sleep, and being obedient, we stretched ourselves on the floor and began to snore. As we are not supposed to know what takes place during our sleep (though at this particular time I slept with one eye open) my readers must be content to know that we were aroused from our slumber, and on arising we beheld "Mother Eve" in all her beauty—Venus like, courting her Adonis, or rather Adam, and persuading him to get married, not that she feared a rival or had other choice, but Eve seemed to be on the marry, and looked determined to give Adam no rest until she obtained her "marriage lines." While Adam and Eve were making such a confounded fuss over each other, we, the candidates for "future glory," were ushered into another room called the "Garden of Eden." The walls of this room were painted to imitate shrubbery and trees, the ceiling was frescoed with numerous stars, while sky and clouds were roughly outlined; there was also large pots containing bushes and shrubs of various sorts to give the place the appearance of a garden; this was "Eden." Here "Adam and Eve" were married, but the "Gods" having made but one woman there was no plurality of wives for Adam. I could not help thinking that surely this was the time and place for Polygamy, if such was necessary at all during any portion of the world's history, why it was excluded from Eden I have yet to learn. Mormonism is a jumble of blasphemy, tragedy, and burlesque; although I treat some of the subjects in a bantering style, they are nevertheless true. Let the Reader, however, here pause for a solemn consideration of the fact that Adam was only furnished with one wife notwithstanding the command, "Be fruitful and multiply." Aye, and at the Flood only *four* women went into the Ark—*one* mate for each male. According to Mormonism, man, who has degenerated, and cannot be said to possess the pristine vigour of primitive times, is now (after thousands of years), and contrary moreover to philosophy, physiology, and psychology to have wives *ad libitum*. Let the dupes of the "religious" libertine consider this, and, however some parts of Scripture may be perverted, use only their commonsense. [To continue the Endowment House story]—

"Adam" and "Eve" being now man and wife, the "Gods" strictly charge them to be fruitful, and multiply and replenish the earth: after showing the consequence of disobedience, the Gods leave the garden. Adam having got over his honeymoon starts out for a walk by himself, like many a married man in this our day, leaving his dear wife to look after the garden and herself at the same time. No sooner is Eve left alone among the shrubs, when the Devil appears. Yes, dear reader, I have seen the Devil. This being the first time I ever saw his Satanic Majesty, I must describe what he is like.

To select a man to impersonate Satan requires something more than ordinary shrewdness. It is not every man one meets with who is adapted to make a first-class devil. Here we see the craftiness of Brigham Young in choosing Judge Phelps; could any one imagine a more fit and proper person to represent the Devil than a Lawyer,—a sombre Judge. Brigham always despised the legal fraternity, and would often brand, and define them as a set of devils. I suppose this to be one reason why a Lawyer was selected to play the part of Satan in this Endowment drama. This devil of a Lawyer, or Lawyer-Devil, stands about five foot two and a button-hole—a withered shrivelled up old fogy. I had always felt a dread of meeting the Devil; there seemed to be so much sulphur, brimstone, and pitchforks connected with him and his trade; and as he was supposed to be carrying on a roasting concern, or a sort of old-fashioned bake-oven on a large scale, I must confess that my thoughts and ideas of the Devil were anything but refreshing. You may imagine how relieved I felt when standing before that small "wee bit" of a Satan—there he stood—all there was of him. How ridiculous the thought of being afraid of him; any man present could have snapped the life out of him at one pop. But he was of such a very pleasing disposition that no one could entertain the thought of doing him any harm. When I was introduced to him I shook the old chap's paw heartily: I wasn't afraid; no, not I. Why should I? He smiled a sort of Satanic grin: this was performed very poorly; I could have done it better myself; however, I thought it best to make friends with his Devilship in case I may need a situation in his establishment in the future, and as the goodwill of a dog is better than its ill-will; I thought surely the goodwill of the Devil was far preferable to his ill-will; besides I concluded that it was more than possible I may be able to learn a trick or two from him; hence I sought to be on friendly terms with the Devil. As we "Sir" everybody in America, except women, and this particular Devil being of the masculine gender, I smiled and said, "Good morning, sir, happy to meet you, for I presume you are an American Citizen!" "You bet yer boots that's jist what I am" he replied. "Do you exercise the franchise, and vote at elections?" I ventured to ask. "Why certainly, and so does all my better haffs," he answered. "What! Are you married?" I asked. Oh yes! and a daddy! said the Devil. I ventured to remark pleasantly that I had heard him spoken of as "the Father of Lies," but that there should be a Mother of Lies had never entered my mind till now. He asked, "How can there be a father unless there is a mother?" To get at what I started in to know I said, "Pray tell me, did Apostle Pratt give a true account of the Fall, &c., in his curious book called "The Seer." "Oh dear, Yes!" says the Devil, " Pratt is right, and the Bible and all the God forsaken Ministers are wrong. I can't help grinning to think how the blind lead the blind. The Garden of Eden was in Jackson County Missouri where Eve "fell flat," as they call it, and showed her wisdom, by being convinced the forbidden tree was good and pleasant, and a tree to be desired to make one wise and become as Gods. You will see presently how she became convinced, and took of the fruit thereof, so you need ask no more on that point. I'll guarantee to make it all plain to every God forsaken child of man present before you get out of here."

The Queen of Sheba's remark to Solomon, "The half has never been told," was given to me with "New Light," too dazzling for these pages. Furthermore Great Salt Lake was fresh water before "Old Mother Lot suicided by steeping herself in it; she was a briny old cuss and made the water devilish salty. That's why it is called 'The Great Salt Lake' to this day. Remember Lot's wife."

I asked "Are there infants in Hell a span long, or any unfortunate babies whose parents failed to have them Christened? "Look you here my friend," said the Devil (fancy I was now the friend of Satan.) "There is no Hell! except what we get upon earth." "But we read of a bottomless pit," I replied. "Git out," says "Satan." "How can there be a pit without a bottom: besides it also says, it's full of fire and brimstone, how can a bottomless pit ever get full? Where can you get the brimstone to keep the thing agoing? Brimstone burns out rapidly, and there ain't enough in the universe to keep the thing running night and day for a month on the stretch, and yet they say 'the fire is never quenched.' If the fire is always burning how can it be a place of darkness as they say. Its all humbug, you hear me! Don't you believe such nonsense my friend." Then Satan enquired "How many wives are you going to marry to-day?" I answered "Only two." Says the Devil "If you don't get Hell enough out of that two, you can eat me, boots and all." I said "Are we not commanded to take more wives than one?" "Yes," replied the Devil, "but the hell of it is you are a darned sight too miserly over the thing, take my advice young man and marry at least a dozen, or you'll have Hell upon Earth with them two. Two is always bound to fight and kick up nell, the one is jealous of 'tother all the time, and you wont have a minute's peace: but if you marry a dozen and mind your P's and Q's it'll be a darned sight better for you, and—" I was vexed to have this interview cut short, I wanted to ask more about these Lucifer Matches as they are namesakes of his, and various other matters, but this chat occurring " behind the scenes, between the acts," the time was up, and the Devil had to proceed to business.

To describe him more fully—he was clothed in a suit of black velvet; on his head he wore a sort of scull cap of the same material; this cap had two large ears which made him look somewhat Devilish, he also wore an apron made of a square of white satin on which was worked in with dark silk floss two large pillars representing the pillars of Solomon's Temple, and a lot of serpents. He was a tricky customer, and oh, how he could lie! It is no wonder he is termed the "Father of lies": and as the Mormons have been well trained by the Devil, it is no marvel that they are the greatest liars upon the face of the earth. The Devil is also a great deceiver, and the fact that Mormon Missionaries are well trained by the Devil in Utah is the reason why they manage to deceive so many people in England and other places when they come in search of dupes.

With this description of the Devil I will now describe the part taken by this "Lucifer" in the ceremonies which follow. Of course, Eve so pure, so beautiful has to fall, and "no devil no fall," hence the Devil has a very important part to play in this hellish drama.

Satan, who had been in close proximity peeping through the bushes when "Jehovah" commanded Adam and Eve " to be fruitful and multiply, and replenish the earth," now finding Eve alone seeks to instruct her in regard to this very important command; for this purpose he steps forward and shaking hands says, " Good morning, Eve, it's a fine morning, and what a beautiful place you have here!" Looking all around he adds, " what beautiful fruit!" and going straight to the tree containing the forbidden fruit Satan plucks some, tastes it, pronounces it very good, and offers some to Eve. She, of course, very politely refuses, and gives the reason— it is forbidden. Eve assumes a very maiden-like and innocent touch-me-not attitude.

Then the Devil, with much adroitness, convinces Eve that in order to fulfil the command "Be fruitful," she must partake of a particular fruit. I cannot here explain what takes place between Eve and the Devil, these matters are not intended for the "unregenerate," they are to be " spiritually discerned." If you cannot discern I can only help you a little by referring to "The Seer," vol. 1, page 85, par 69 :—" That our first parents would have had no mortal children if they had not partaken of the forbidden fruit, is not only reasonable, but it is clearly revealed in the Book of Mormon. The Prophet Lehi says, If Adam had not transgressed, he would not have fallen. AND THEY WOULD HAVE HAD NO CHILDREN ; wherefore they would have remained in a state of innocence, having no joy, for they knew no misery; doing no good, for they knew no sin. Adam fell that men might be; and men are that they may have joy " (2 Book of Nephi, 1st chap., page 58.)

" And in that day the Holy Ghost fell upon Adam, and Adam blessed God and was filled, and began to prophesy concerning all the families of the earth : blessed be the name of God for my transgression, for in this life I shall have joy, and again in the flesh shall I see God.

" And Eve, his wife, heard all these things and was glad, saying, were it not for our transgression, WE SHOULD NEVER HAVE HAD SEED [The capitals in these quotations are as in the book], and should never have known good and evil. And Adam and Eve blessed the name of God, and they made all things known unto their sons and daughters."

This is why the sons and daughters of Adam know so much now-a-days. It has been handed down, and the Devil has had a hand in it also, as we learn in the same paragraph from which I have quoted, thus:—"BECAUSE THAT ADAM FELL WE ARE: and by his fall came death, and we are made partakers of misery and woe. Behold Satan hath come among the children of men, and tempteth them to worship him: and men have become carnal, sensual, and devilish, and are shut out from the presence of God." It appears from this book also that we have cause to be truly thankful that Eve fell and then managed to seduce Adam, for the prophet Lehi continues; " Therefore I lift up my heart in praise and thanksgiving before the Lord ; yea, I bless God with all my soul, that our first parents did transgress; for, because of this transgression my spirit has been permitted to come from Heaven and enter a tabernacle of flesh and bones—because of this transgression, I am permitted to know, in this life, good and evil, joy and misery, justice and mercy, love and hatred—because of this transgression, I learn by experience things which I never could have learned in any other way: and but for this transgression the great family of spirits in Heaven would have been disappointed in their anxious longing expectations to receive bodies." "The Seer," p. 88, see Appendix C. for more of the Seer.

I have conversed with thousands who have been through these ceremonies and from what I learned from them it is very evident that some parts of the performances are varied at times, so that should we attempt to expose them there would be conflicting statements. At one time Satan himself consummates the fall of Eve; at another time Satan only explains matters to Eve, and Adam accomplishes the fall. Sometimes men and women are huddled together entirely nude; at other times partly dressed. Mormon leaders are very tricky, and I have no doubt the ceremonies are varied occasionally. I can only give the facts as I saw and heard them. While they vary in regard to some particulars, they all agree as to the washing and oiling part of it.

"It is quite probable the ceremony is frequently changed,"—"Beadel's Life in Utah," p. 492.

It is a matter of surprise among decent people that a woman could be found in this our day and generation to take the character of Eve in such a place, and the question naturally arises, who is she? To answer briefly. She styles herself "*Miss* Eliza R. Snow." That you may form a correct idea of this Miss I will state that I have heard her say in public that when the "Revelation on Polygamy" was first given she immediately married Joseph Smith, while his wife, Mrs. Emma Smith, was still living with her affectionate husband. In fact, this Miss Snow constantly boasts that she was the first to obey the Revelation and to enter into Polygamy. When Smith died, Miss Snow married the "Prophet" Brigham Young, and since the demise of this worthy I understand our Miss has united herself in holy Wedlock to the present "Prophet" John Taylor. I have no doubt this latter is correct for she seemed wonderfully "stuck after Prophets." She is termed by the "unwashed" of Salt Lake the procuress of the Church, as she spends most of the time when not engaged performing "Eve," in seeking to induce young girls to marry the lecherous old scamps who are ever seeking fresh victims for their filthy Polygamic harems. Mrs. Smith, on page 45, "Fifteen Years among the Mormons" says:—"Eliza Snow performed the part of Eve more than any other woman. Now at fifty years of age she is even yet very beautiful, and she may be said to perform infamously well." Having said this much in regard to Eve, we will again turn to the scenes in "Eden." The Devil having thoroughly instructed Eve concerning the forbidden fruit and other details concerning the fall, proceeds to show how it is to be accomplished, and having finally adjusted matters the Devil goes off and hides behind a tree to await further developments. At this juncture Adam, who has taken a stroll alone, now returns when Eve plays well the part consigned to her by the Devil. Here, then, we have before us the sad picture of the first fallen woman, who, being created as the "help meet" of the man, helps him to his downfall. and we are informed that "Adam is the first, but not the last man thus drawn aside from the path of virtue by a woman."

Some think that Adam should have remained firm and not have yielded to Eve. Had they stood with me and witnessed what I did, they would never blame him. Many men fall by "Temptation," less than Adam's. I can assure you Adam deserves credit; he stood out like a man, and it seemed doubtful if Eve would succeed in her undertaking so proof was he against all her subtleness. But finally human nature, even in Adam gave way and he fell.

The first chance I got between the acts (for all this is similar to a theatrical drama) I said to "Adam"—"How is it that you, so pure, and before the fall, could allow a poor fallen man like Joseph, to beat you in purity and virtue?" "Look you here," says Adam, "If you read that yarn about Joseph carefully, you'll find he had a coat on at the time of his temptation, which makes a darned sight of difference: 'twas his coat saved him. But, say!" continued Adam, thinking I was chiding him. "You fetch your Josephs' in here, and strip 'em, and let old Mother Eve git a hold on 'em I'll bet six bits,* she'll hold 'em, they won't slip away from her."

Eve fell first, then Adam fell, and just as the fall was completed, we, the candidates for initiation, were supposed to realise the condition of our first parents, when "they knew that they were naked," and being aroused to our true condition with much shamefacedness (for our eyes were now opened, they were supposed to have been shut up to this time), we dive into our little bundles and get out the "Fig-leaf Apron" wherewith to cover our nakedness. Then there is a fearful commotion in the garden. A loud noise of tramping, and thump, thump, is heard, which is supposed to be the approach of "Jehovah." Adam and Eve the fallen, are hid in the bushes. The Devil who has been watching all the proceedings from behind a tree, continues his devilish grins; while "Jehovah" appears, and loudly calls "Adam where art thou?" Adam comes sneaking out from the bushes looking very criminal; Eve follows looking awful sheepish and very pale. Poor Eve, I really felt sympathy for her, she looked like a mother of twins on her way to be churched. Satan comes forth from his hiding place and the remarkable trio stand confronted by "Jehovah." Adam was the first to break the silence that ensued; speaking to Jehovah, he said, "I heard thy voice in the garden, and I was afraid, because I wast naked, and I hid myself." Then Jehovah replied, "Who told thee thou wast naked? Hast thou partaken of the forbidden fruit?" Adam pushing the blame on his wife as men are apt to do now-a-days, answered, "The woman whom thou gavest to be with me, she got the best of me and I had to give in, it's no use talking."

At this, Jehovah turns to the woman and snappishly enquires, "What is this that thou hast done?" Eve, like her daughters of the present day, was not minus an excuse, she threw the blame on the Devil who had beguiled her. Then "Jehovah's" wrath was kindled, and I saw the Devil quiver as he received the cursing. Up to this point Satan had stood erect as a man, but when the words were uttered by "Jehovah," "Upon thy belly thou shalt go," the Devil stooped, placing his hands upon the floor, and ran around the place on his hands and feet, like we sometimes see boys when playing monkeys. Satan stopped occasionally to taste his new victuals, the "dust" but he did not seem to like it, and cast many a glance at the fruit on the tree with a nod and a wink, which was interpreted to mean that he'd have some when the way was clear. The woman also came in for a share of "divine" vengeance. "In sorrow shalt thou bring forth children," now rang in her ears; and not only was she to have sorrow where she anticipated so much joy, but the multiplication table was to be lavishly used in her case, "I will greatly multiply thy sorrow and thy conception," were the words now used for her edification. Hitherto she had held the upper hand: she was indeed "the better half." She could make Adam conform to her ideas and desires, but now her desire was subject to her husband, and she was dismissed with the consoling words: "And he shall rule over thee." It is this that gives Utah husbands the power they so freely exercise to rule their wives as with a rod of iron. Adam was let off pretty easily,—he was merely turned into a farm labourer. He had tried his hand at tailoring, but at this he was not a success, his fig leaf apron was a poor specimen of workmanship, besides tailors were in poor demand, for the woollen manufactories had not yet started—in fact there had been no sheep-shearing. The first requirements were husbandmen, especially as there was to be now some weeding to attend to besides the cultivation of the soil. We now file out of the garden, clothed with our fig leaf aprons, and in this "light

* 75 cents, or 3/. I can but think if these Mormons were to write a commentary on the Bible, what a precious work it would be.

marching order" costume, we are thrust out of Eden into the cold, cold world. Now we are in a bitter cold room without fire in the depths of winter, the thermometer registering ten degrees below zero. I found there was not much warmth in fig leaves. My apron was of little service, either as a non-conductor of heat, or to keep out the cold. The mercury of our enthusiasm drop'd below zero also.

I had a chat with the "Archangel Michael," and was surprised to learn from him that he was also Adam our Father and God; that after the war in Heaven, having beaten the Devil he came upon this earth as Adam. He was the first spirit to enter a fleshly tabernacle. The earth had been formed just prior to this "Holy War" and as there is no hell, the Devil and his Angels, when thrust out of Heaven made a bee-line for America, and landed in Missouri where the Garden of Eden was situated. He said get "The Seer" and read page 50 and 51, that will give the straight of it. I did so and straightway got the "straight of it" thus. "In the revelations which God gave through Joseph Smith the Prophet, we are informed that Adam was Michael, that the war in Heaven had ended before Michael left Heaven, and entered a body of flesh and bones under the name of Adam."

The glass-eyed "Messiah" came to me picking his teeth, and said that He, Elohim and Jehovah had just been having a nice snack off the cold chicken and ham in my lunch basket, and told me where to find the empty basket. I tried to draw him out on matters spiritual, but he was too worldly minded. He had heard that I possessed some cash, and as he owned some saw mills, he wanted to strike up a partnership. But having heard of him as "the one-eyed pirate" I was on the look out, and though he was playing "Messiah" I was up to his trick and no bargain was struck. This was between the acts of the expulsion from the garden, after *the fall*, and the next act where we are "clothed upon with our holy garments," or in plain English before we donned our togs, I should think about one o'clock, but my watch was in my vest pocket, and I had not seen my clothes since I stripped six hours before, and of course there were no clocks or watches in "Eden."

Just as we were concluding that we had better freeze to death and thus wind up the ceremony, "Jehovah" appeared, seemingly in a much better mood than when we last saw him in the garden. He had been out helping himself to the cold chicken and ham in my lunch basket, and having refreshed himself, felt better. He deeply sympathised with us in our shivering condition and in the new rolle of tailor, dressmaker and outfitter, promised to make "coats of skins" for every man and woman in the place. We were now ordered to untie our bundles, the Priest who gave the orders sublimely saying, "Fetch out yer duds;" this was the signal to don our "Endowment Robes." There was considerable fumbling in the operation, the sash being purposely put on wrong to necessitate a change again at another part of the ceremony. We were now cautioned that if any of us ever attempted to reveal what we saw and heard in the "House" our memories would be blighted, and we should *be everlastingly damned*, for these "Holy" matters must not be mentioned after leaving the "Sacred Place." Hence, I suppose my damnation is secure, but how far my memory has been blighted my readers can judge for themselves.

I must not forget to notice the emblems one finds connected with this matter; my blighted memory shall only fail me in matters too indecent to publish—these I *must* forget. On the right breast of the "Wedding Garment" we have the "Square," and on the left the "Compass." There is also a small hole in the centre, and on the knee a large hole called the "stone." I once took this "garment" to a Chinaman to ascertain what that heathen would think of it. John carefully scrutinized it all over, especially in the middle, where he thought I had joined drawers and vest together to cheat him of one piece in the wash bill; then pointing to the "square," the Chinaman said, "You no good mason, you try cheat me one. No go. Shirt and drawers all-e-same two pieces." I failed to convince the heathen that it was but one garment, the pattern of which had been revealed from Heaven. He made me pay for two pieces. I have been asked, "is the Devil a Freemason?" I give it up, don't know; he said he was, but he lies so who can believe him? But this I know, I have seen the Devil wear an apron similar to that worn by freemasons. It contained the pillars of Solomon's Temple, which are used so much in Masonic emblems, but as we are coming to the grips, signs, etc., the fraternity will discover much that is "emblematic" as we proceed.

The first Mormon Prophet was a "Mason," so was Brigham Young. General Beadel, in his "Life in Utah," p. 499, says :—"The Mormons all became Masons. Joseph Smith out-masoned Solomon himself, and declared that God had revealed to him a great key-word which had been lost, and that he would lead Masonry to far higher degrees, and not long after their Charter was revoked by the Grand Lodge. How much of Masonry proper has survived in the Endowment, the writer will not pretend to say; but the Mormons are pleased to have the outside world connect the two, and convey the impression that this is 'Celestial Masonry.'"

Knowing this I was not much surprised to find Masonic emblems in the room, such as "The Compass, Square, Level, and Plumb-bob." To convince the Masonic Fraternity of the truth of this, I quote from page 48 of "Fifteen years among the Mormons," by Mrs. Mary E. V. Smith, where she says:— "Certain marks were cut with a small pair of scissors, besides others, the Masonic square and compass, upon the right and left breast of our garments, and upon the right knee, a gash, deep enough to make a scar, by which we were to be recognized as Mormons. It was a noticeable feature that the outside show of some of the regalia and furniture connected with these "Endowments" were made to conform with those of Masonry; and Mormons are anxious to have the 'Gentiles' associate all they know of these beastly 'Endowments' with Masonry, or as being a modified form of it, made eligible to women, as a blind to cover the real objects of this 'Institution.'"

I must now describe further how we are "made meet to be partakers of an inheritance with the saints in light;" or rather, how we are made "citizens of the Kingdom of God." A month prior to this I had been made a citizen of the United States, as I thought. Now I had to change my Nationality again, and I watched the "new departure" with considerable interest.

The Priests gave us "The first grip of the Aaronic, or lesser Priesthood," which consists in placing the thumb on the knuckle of the index finger, and clasping the hands around. We were then made to swear "to never speak against the Lord's Anointed Prophet (the Mormon Prophet), but to obey him and the laws of the Mormon Church, and all they enjoin, in preference to the laws of any kingdom or nationality, and more especially those of the United States." The penalty for refusing to obey, or revealing this oath and grip is, "that we will have our throats cut from ear to ear, and the tongue torn from the mouth :" the sign of the penalty is drawing the hand with the thumb pointing towards the throat sharply across, and bringing the arm to the level of the square, and with the hand upraised to heaven, we swear to abide the same.

There was a small altar on one side, at which there now appeared three rough-looking specimens of humanity. These, we were informed, were "Peter, James and John." Peter had two big keys which were "the keys of Death and Hell." He had been in the wet and got the keys awfully rusty, they seemed to have been out of use lately for "the used key is always bright." It struck me forcibly that no one could unlock either Death or Hell with them keys. So unless they get new keys I feel safe enough, for I know of none but Mormons who wish me dead and in Hell; of course, every good Mormon has that kind wish toward me. "Peter," with his rusty keys, stood between "James and John." At this juncture different men came in one by one, each making an effort to represent their various religious sects, presented their different dogmas and professed to be very anxious to save us fallen children of Adam. Each of these celebrated preachers coarsely satirized the various Christian sects. The one proclaiming Methodism ridiculed Calvinism, and repudiated the idea of infants a span long being in Hell, and dwelt most emphatically upon "The final perseverance of the Saints." The Calvinist, in turn, abused the Methodist, and assured us that "The Elect once saved was saved for ever; he cannot fall from grace and be lost." The Baptist was surprised to find there were people presuming to teach and believe "That mankind could get to heaven without rinsing. To think of being saved without immersion or even wetting the feet was preposterous."

We had to listen to harangues from the Ana-Baptist and the Pedo Baptist, the Quaker and the Shaker; in fact, from most of the well-known sects of Christendom. But the great wind up came when "Peter" preached unto us "The Mormon Gospel." Peter being an old hand at it, could dish it up in high style—

"He could deep mysteries unriddle, As easily as thread a needle."—*Hudibras.*

At one time during his Sermon when he arrived at his highest pitch of eloquence, a country girl that stood by my side gave me a poke in the ribs and whispered "How's that for high?" I answered "It's high you bet." She smiled and seemed disposed to carry on a flirtation. Peter twig'd it, and fearing a reprimand we "shut up" and did not flirt. Peter reviewed the gibberish of the "Christian Parsons," as he called the previous preachers, and said "these Gospel sharps are running various Gospel mills on their own hook. Here's these miserable one wife scoundrels among the Baptists, Methodists, Independents, and the various sects trying to get into heaven, all of a flippety flop, humpety hump, dot and carry one; with a solitary wife jagging 'em down at one arm "—(great laughter). "It's no go," cried Peter. "No man can get into celestial glory that way. I hold the keys, and no man can pass in unless EVENLY BALANCED with a wife on each arm; and he should have a score or two more hanging on to his coat tails, otherwise his glory in heaven will be no great shakes."

This great "Apostle of the Gentiles" assured us that "All the sects were wrong." The Catholic Church he described as the Great Mother of Harlots." The Church of England having sprung from this "Mother Church," was nothing more or less than "a daughter of the Great Whore." The Methodists, Congregationalists, Baptists, Independents, and every other body of so-called Christians of whatever name were stigmatized as of "Bastards;" whose existence was shown to be the result of a vast amount of "Religious harlotry." Peter admonished us that as we had drunk of the wine of her fornication we had committed fornication with her, and now the word of the Lord which he called upon us to obey was:—"Come out of her my people, that ye be not partakers of her sins, and that ye receive not of her plagues." Another command was loudly vociferated by the "Apostle," "Come out from among them, and be ye separate saith the Lord, and touch not the unclean thing; and I will receive you and will be a father unto you, and ye shall be my sons and daughters, saith the Lord Almighty."

"Peter" spun a long yarn, sailor like, of course, and in a manner becoming a fisherman. He could spin it out with great rapidity, and in a style peculiar to fish fags, including the choicest Billingsgate. Mixed up with the vast amount of his balderdash we gathered that, "All the Christian Churches of our day were fearfully corrupt, and groping in worse than Egyptian darkness." The World was in darkness, and had been for eighteen centuries until God appeared to Joseph Smith, a few years ago. That the only light in the world at the present time was in the Mormon Church. "The Church of Jesus Christ of Latter-day Saints" was the only true Church of God upon the Earth; this was established with Prophets, Apostles, &c., as in days of yore, and all would be damned who rejected the Gospel as proclaimed by this latter-day Church.

When Peter finished his wrangle: the Devil who had loitered around and assisted the "Divines" (all except Peter), came bustling up to the Altar, and offered to shake a paw with Peter. This "Apostle" tried to be polite, and giving him a hearty grip said to him "Hallo, Mr. Devil, why how do you do? It's a fine day, aint it, what are you doing around here: are you seeking whom you may devour?" "Oh dear no!" replied the devil: "When the sons of God come together, Satan comes also among them you know: and from what I can discover, these friends here (pointing around at us) don't seem to take to any of these religions: why don't you quit hankering after Christianity and have a jolly time like I do." Here Satan danced, and skipped about as merry as a cricket; and just in the midst of a jolly good "sailor's horn pipe." Peter pointed to the devil, caught his eye, and cried with a loud voice "You git! hurry up!" Satan gave a regular "break down" jump, stood looking at Peter a second then bounced out of the room singing "The girl I left behind me." The last of the refrain he sang as he stood just outside the door was:—

"Let the night be ever so dark, or ever so wet and windy,
I must and I will return again to the girl I left behind me."

The Devil is not only a Poet, but a very fair ballad singer, and would do well for a "penny gaff," or low pot house of a Saturday night. Many a publican would like to engage him for a Saturday night's "free and easy." but I must not digress.

When the Devil "shut up" and went off; Peter said "Resist the Devil and he will flee from you." He then gave us the second grip of the Aaronic or lesser Priesthood. To give this grip, the thumb is placed between the knuckles of the index and second fingers, and the hand tightly clasped around them. The penalty for revealing this is to be sawn asunder and our members cast into the sea. The sign of the penalty is given by drawing the hand sharply across the middle of the body.

The men then took the oath of chastity, and the women likewise. This as may be supposed is very chaste—very indeed! The man swears to be true to his numerous wives, together with his spiritual wives and proxy wives—his wives for time, and his wives for eternity. He swears to "cleave unto them, *and none else.*" Imagine the concomitant, conjugal conjugation that must inevitably follow when a man attempts to "cleave unto" a lot of women. I have seen it tried, and tried a little of it myself: it don't work worth a cent. Men and brethren, hearken unto me! if you dont believe it, you just try to conjoin a dozen or so of wives to yourself, and I'll guarantee you will speedily find that the word "cleave" means "cleft," and if you come out of the *fracas* with a sound mind in a sound body, consider yourself in luck.

The woman is made to swear that she will prove faithful to whatever part or parcel of her respective husband may be assigned to her, and to be fully and thoroughly satisfied with a tenth, fiftieth or hundredth part of a man—his attention, affection, &c., &c., &c. Except, that it is hereinafter provided. Should there be no issue from this fractional union, then the lady aforesaid shall select another man, drag him before the Prophet, and both get another oiling; after which they are made man and wife *pro tem* on the Q.T., and thus shall the sin of barrenness be removed far from Mormondom [See Par. 16. Revelation on Polygamy, Appendix E].

A married lady is informed that she is not yet tied to the man she thought she had married in England or elsewhere—"That all marriages performed outside the Mormon Church are illegal. No man but a Mormon Priest has any authority from God to bind on earth, hence God has not joined them together," and Mrs. Jones can leave Mr. Jones, Mrs. Smith and Mrs. Robinson, ditto, and they are at liberty then and there to marry Brigham Young or any "faithful brother" they choose; that all the little Joneses, Smiths and Robinsons are altogether illegitimate until adopted by some "true saint" and thus made "children of God and inheritors of the Kingdom." If Mrs. Jarman concludes to stick by Brother Jarman she must see to it that there are other Mrs. Jarmans united to her husband at once, for until that is done the said Jarman is not saved, his children are not heirs, and she herself will receive no resurrection. This is very trying to most wives and mothers, but then this is "The Cross" which they are called upon to take up, and "No Cross, No Crown!" I ask, what Greater Cross can a true woman be called upon to bear, than to share her husband with dozens, aye, scores of other women.

Having passed this "Fiery ordeal" a man rushed in hurriedly, and proclaimed the joyful news, that the Gospel which had lain dormant 1800 years was now restored to the earth. "The Holy Angel had appeared to Joseph Smith, and given him the keys of the kingdom and restored the blessings of the Ancient Gospel." This was called "The Latter-day Dispensation." The Priests pretended to accept this joyfully, and said it was the very thing they had been hunting for, nothing else having had the power to satisfy them. They then proceeded to give us the first grip of the "Melchizedek or higher Priesthood," which is said to be the same Christ held. The thumb is placed on the knuckle of the index finger, and the index finger is placed straight along the palm of the hand, while the lower part of the hand is clasped with the remaining fingers. We were then made to swear to avenge the blood of Joseph Smith and that of his brother Hyrum on the American Nation, and to teach our children and children's children eternal enmity toward the United States Government. The penalty for divulging this grip and oath is disembowelment, the sign of this penalty is to place the hand spread out on that part of the body, then clutch the hand as if grabbing a handful and then dashing the hand and opening it as if flinging its contents to the ground.

The next, being rather strong, and as I say so much that I myself could not believe had I not witnessed it, I give the next part from Beadels Life in Utah. On page 495, it says:—"The initiates are then ranged in order to listen to a lecture—

"*Peter.* Brethren and Sisters, light is now come into the world, and the way is open unto men; Satan hath desired to sift you as wheat, and great shall be his condemnation who rejects this light.—(The ceremony is explained up to this point.)—The holy priesthood is once more established upon earth, in the person of Joseph Smith and his successors. They alone have the power to seal. To this priesthood as unto Christ, all respect is due; obedience implicit, and yielded without a murmur. He who gave life has the right to take it. His representatives the same. You are then to obey all orders of the priesthood, temporal and spiritual, in matters of life or death. Submit yourselves to the higher powers, as a tallowed rag in the hands of God's priesthood. You are now ready to enter the kingdom of God. Look forth upon the void and tell me what you see." (Curtain is raised.)

"*Adam* and *Eve*. A human skeleton."

"*Peter.* Rightly have ye spoken. Behold all that remains of one unfaithful to these holy vows. The earth had no habitation for one so vile. The fowls of the air fed upon his accursed flesh, and the fierce elements consumed the joints and the marrow."

"*Michael.* Here all hearts are laid open, all desires revealed, and all traitors are made known. In council of the *gods* it hath been decreed that here the faithless shall die. Some enter here with evil intent; but none with evil intent go beyond this veil or return alive, if here they practice deceit. If one among you knows aught of treachery in his heart, we charge him now to speak, while yet he may and live. Brethren, an ordeal awaits you. Let the pure have no fear; the false-hearted quake. Each shall pass under the Searching Hand, and the Spirit of the Lord decide for his own."

"The initiates are placed one by one upon the altar, stretched upon the back, and the officiating priest passes an immense knife or keen-edged razor across their throats. It is understood that if any are false at heart, the Spirit will reveal it to their instant death."

In the "Argument of Judge Hemingrey before the House Sub-committee on Territories, he says:—The horrible scenes enacted in the 'Endowment house,' are graphically described in the book called 'Wife No. 19,' by Ann Eliza Young, Brigham's apostate wife. A portion of these ceremonies I now present from page 368 of that work:

"We raise our right hand heavenward, and take the oath of implicit obedience and inviolable secrecy. The women promised entire subjection to their husband's will; the men that they would take no woman as a wife without the expressed permission of the Priesthood. We all promised that we would never question the commands of our authorities in the church, but would grant them instant obedience; we swore also to entertain an everlasting enmity to the United States Government, and never to reveal the mysteries of the 'Endowment House.'

"The breaking of this latter oath was to be followed by the most horrible penalties; torture of the most excruciating kind was to be inflicted upon any one who should disregard this oath—his bowels should be torn from him while he was yet alive; his throat should then be cut from ear to ear; his heart and his tongue cut out; and in the world to come he should inherit eternal damnation. There should be, nor could be, no chance of salvation for him.

"These promised penalties are by no means mere forms of words, given merely to add impressiveness to the ceremony.

"The 'Blood Atonement' shows that they are carried out, and hundreds of cases could be cited in addition to those already given, to prove that the Endowment House penalties are by no means dead letters in the Mormon Church law.

"The cutting of every Gentile and Apostate throat, and the 'sending to hell across lots,' that have been so openly and emphatically urged from the stand by Brigham Young and others, is only a public expression of the mysteries of the Endowment Oaths."

Did I possess "Wife No. 19" I should extract profusely therefrom with pleasure, for as the Authoress was one of the numerous wives of Brigham Young, she certainly had opportunities of prying into secrets which I never had. I regret that I failed to secure such a valuable treasure as "Wife No. 19."

We are now marched into another room designated "The Prayer Circle Room." The sash and robes that had been put on wrong were now righted. Here we were made to take an oath of obedience to the Mormon Priesthood, which means "The Prophet, Apostles, Bishops, Priests, Elders, Teachers," and all in authority over us. Just like a private soldier has to obey everyone above him, from a Lance-Corporal to the Commander-in-Chief. We were to obey these "sacred" rascals "in all things." No matter whether we were ordered to cut a child's throat, or stick a pig, "WE MUST OBEY AND ASK NO QUESTIONS." All their sermons point to this "Blind Obedience." (I have hundreds of them, and if there is room will give some further on). Now the highest, or Grand Grip of the Melchizedek Priesthood was given. We clasped each other round the hand with the point of the index finger resting on the wrist, and little fingers firmly linked together. The place on the wrist where the index finger points is supposed to be the place where Christ was nailed to the cross, but they tore out and he had to be nailed again they say, and we then place the second finger beside the index on the wrist: it is called "The sure sign of the nail," and if the grip is properly given, it is very hard to pull apart. The penalty for revealing this oath and grip is to have the heart torn out, cut up in small pieces, and given to the fowl of the air.

We men now form a circle round the al'ar, link our arms straight across, and placing our hands on each others shoulders. The "High Priest" knelt at the altar, took hold of one of the mens hands with his left, raised his right hand heavenward, and prayed. He first prayed in an unknown tongue, and afterwards in English about as near as I can remember as follows, "Oh Lord, avenge now the blood of thy martyred prophet, Joseph Smith on these United States; hasten the day when they shall be United no more, grant that they may fight like Kilkenny Cats, and use each other up so that not one may be left to tell the tale; that thy kingdom established here in the mountains may roll forth and fill these States preparatory to filling the whole world: for thine is the kingdom, the power and the glory for ever Amen!" The Priest told us that the Electric current of prayer passed through that circle, and went straight to Heaven and "moved the arm that moves the world." Before he prayed in English he told us the nature of the prayer about to be uttered, and said we must all be united and "will strongly" every word uttered by him, adding if our wills were firmly united with his this unity of will penetrating the whole of us, and him, would pass as an Electric current right up to the throne in heaven. We are cautioned not to be alarmed at the idea of "Electric Prayer" that we live in an advanced age; Science produces wonders with Electricity and why not Electric Prayer. When anything important is required from above the electric current of prayer is set in motion, and they say this kind of prayer is always answered. This is the kind of prayer offered for President Lincoln, when, after he had abolished Slavery, he sought to extirpate Polygamy. The Endowment House rang with "Oh God curse Lincoln!" and in answer to this prayer we are told God smote Abraham Lincoln and the "Saints" rejoiced and gave glory to the God of Heaven for the assassination of that "stinking Abolitionist." They also had a big feast. The people came from all parts of the territory and there was a time of rejoicing such as was never before known there. When President Garfield was shot there was great rejoicing among "the Saints." And during that never-to-be-forgotten period, while Garfield lay between life and death, and while all Christendom prayed earnestly for his recovery, the Mormons put in motion their Electric Battery of Prayer, and prayed that the "puny man" Garfield, who had dared to oppose Polygamy might be cut off from the earth: and now they rejoice and boast that their prayer has been answered, that God does not listen to the false Christians of the world, but only to his true people the Mormons. Missionaries are making use of this as an argument right now, to convince their poor dupes that everything is O. K. in the Mormon kingdom, and this, it will be at once seen, is a powerful argument.

While the "Electric prayer" was going on the women stood outside the circle of men, with their veils covering their faces, the only time throughout the ceremonies that they did so. The prayer being over, we were all ordered up stairs. This was supposed to mean going up to heaven. On arriving at the top of the stairs we found ourselves in a very peculiar place. Here was a big room partitioned off with a large greasy dish rag or screen. This screen had once been white, but now filthy dirty. It was called "The Vail," and is said to be in imitation of the vail in Solomon's Temple. Some Mormons assert that it is the actual one, being preserved from the days of Solomon, and now in the possession of "God's peculiar people," the Mormons. On this vail are marks, like those on the "Wedding Garment," such as the square, compass, &c., together with various holes for putting the arms, and a hole at the top to speak through. It was also rent in twain. This rent was "the way opened up" whereby we could enter through the vail into "The Holy of Holies." The very holy place was inside of where we stood, and before going through to "t'other side o' Jordan," as the Priest expressed it, we received a general outline of instructions, similar to those received down stairs, "down in the kitchen," as the Mormon Bishop remarked. This over, the Priest took me straight up to one of the holes in the vail, where he knocked with a mallet. A voice (Peter's of course) from the other side, asked "Who's there?" The Priest answered for me by saying "Adam having been faithful desires to enter." It appears I was now transformed into "Adam." I was then led to where there was two holes in the vail. Here I had to poke both hands and arms through and "hug old St. Peter," who stood on the other side waiting for the embrace. While hugging this lecherous old humbug there was a strong smell of that Mormon "Heavenly" incense commonly called Whiskey. I had to whisper in Peter's ear my new name. To do this aright I had to put my head in at the hole; when I popped my head in the smell of whiskey was enough to knock anybody down. I stood my ground, however, for I was interested in the thing by this time, and was eager to see it through.

Having divulged my New Name to "Saint Peter," I was now considered ripe for Heavenly Glory, and was permitted to go through the vail into "Heaven." I now entered and took a good square look around; I must say I was very much disappointed. The bright notions I had hitherto entertained of Heavenly Glory, first flickered, then vanished; for anything more unlike Heaven I cannot conceive. It was a Hell within a Hell. What it lacked in purity was made up in filth. If I kept a pig and expected to eat the pork, I should not keep the animal in that place. Here I found the same *Dramatis Personæ* of "God's, Holy beings," &c., that I had seen below, minus "The Devil." Of course, he had been kicked out of this "Holy" assembly just before he visited Mrs. Eve, and I noticed it was a different "Peter" to what we had down stairs: I asked one of the Priests why that was, he said "we had to put a 'super' in Peter's place because his women where raising hell at home, and he had gone with a good stout rope to cast out devils."

Not wishing to enjoy this "Heavenly Glory" alone, I was informed that if my wife wished to marry me properly now was her chance. "Eve" was on the t'other side of Jordan (the vail) instructing her daughters in regard to this matter. My wife (or "missus" I spose up to this time) very prudently concluded to marry the father of her children. The chap who was playing the part of "Peter," while the real "Peter" was home larruping his wives, said to me, "How many women are you going to hitch on to?" I replied, "I have two outside the vail, which I brought for that purpose, if they have not changed their minds since they came into this house." "Come here and fetch 'em in, for here's where you get spliced for time and for eternity," says Peter's super. I said, "What! are we to be married in Heaven? I thought that in Heaven they neither marry nor are given in marriage!" "All a pack o nonsense," replied the "super," "that's yer old sectarian foolishness which you've fetched with you from wicked Babylon. You must drop all that stuff here. Come git yer women in," and added, "Tell Jehovah that you feel lonely and desire the companionship of a woman or two to help cheer your weary pilgrimage." I did so, when "Jehovah" answered, "It is not good for man to be alone, I will make help meets for him." Then I had to give the super my wife's worldly maiden name, for notwithstanding we had been married by the English Law—the best Marriage Laws in the World—she was not yet Mrs. Jarman. Besides this "mock Marriage" in England was only "till Death us do part." I should lose her at death and never have her again Death ends that contract, but now we were to be made one FOR EVER.

I was now taken to the holes where I had previously hugged the "Apostle," and stood just where he had stood. I then called for the woman I was about to marry, when she, I had hitherto erroneously called wife, stepped up to the holes, aforesaid, on the outside of the screen, to receive her hugging. Here we stood with the dirty screen between us, Eve was on the outside instructing my "missus," and Peter's super prompting me on the inside. Our knees were peculiarly placed, the feet also were properly adjusted, and with both arms around each other we were told to "squeeze tight." We managed to do a bit of tolerably good squeezing considering the circumstances. First she gave me her maiden name, and to make assurance doubly sure I heard "Eve" say, "Give him your New Name, and kiss him through the vail." This done, Eve told my wife to repeat after her a most disgusting formula or oath, which moral decency compels me to omit here.

The highest Melchizedek grip was again given, when we released our hold of each other. A "Priestess" or "Prophetess" then took my wife to the entrance through which I had been admitted, and rapped as the Priest had done in my case. "Peter" (or rather the super) for the real Peter had not yet returned. it takes time to wallop the devils out of eight wives. The super sang out, "Who's there?" The Priestess replied, "Eve having been faithful desires to enter." "Eve" was accordingly ushered into Heaven." I then had to go through the same rigmarole to "fetch in t'other woman," as they said, who was also to become a Mrs. Jarman. Having "gathered in" these two of my "lost ribs" I was directed to take them both to a table at which "The Gods," the heads of the Mormon Church were seated. Here I had to give first my own name, that of my parents, and place and date of birth. The two women I was about to marry did the same, and all was entered in a large book or marriage register. A copy of this register was then given me on a slip of paper, and I was directed to take that and the two women into the "Sealing Room," and give the piece of paper to the officiating priest, who would marry me to both those women according to the "Order of Heaven." I obeyed orders.

In this "Sealing Room" is the "Marriage Altar. Here we are married for "time and all eternity." Think of it! it's serious enough to be bound to a woman for time only, and how many wish they had married on probation. But what is that compared with marrying a wife for all eternity? It would scare most men. But every cloud has a silver lining somewhere, so also in this case. We can console ourselves with the thought that if the thing don't work right or is not exactly O.K: Smith, the Great High Priest, who is also the Probate Judge, and who prominently officiates in the tying up biz., will untie the knot and divorce us at any time; notwithstanding the fact that he married us for all time, and eternity into the bargain. Then again this fact is very consoling to the men—that at the Resurrection he need not raise up the bad with the good: he has his pick then, and can call up only those of his wives who have been very loving, very faithful, very quiet, &c., &c., &c.

I now come to a very important part of this "Endowment" business which I name "Weddings in Hell." I will state right here, that most, if not all the marriages solemnized in this place are Polygamic. A man may marry a first or lawful wife without going there, but no man can marry a second or plural wife unless he and his victim wade through all the filth of the "Endowment House" and he must be so married within its "Sacred" walls. When the various "Temples" now being erected are completed, Polygamic marriages are to be solemnized therein also. Up to the time I left "Zion," only the "Temple at St. George" was finished. There such marriages have taken place; and I am told by those who ought to know, that a far worse, and much more filthy ceremony is gone through within the "Temple" than within the "Endowment House." I know this much, "The Prophet" has often said that "There are degrees of glory and blessing which can only be obtained in a Temple consecrated to God for the purpose!" Knowing, therefore, what I do, I can readily believe there will be nice goings on in these temples when finished.

Before describing my wedding in this Hell, I will state that my English wife was not only willing, but desired that I should marry another. As our marriage according to the English Law was of no avail in the Mormon kingdom, and as we had to be married over again, she concluded that I had better marry two at once, and thus secure my eternal salvation, and the power to raise her up at the resurrection. This is only secured by Polygamy; hence the wife becomes anxious that her husband should take a second wife in order to secure the salvation of the man she loves, and her own eternal glory. Thus many of the first wives are lured into sanctioning the plural marriage. Another serious matter which the first wife has to consider, is found in what Mormons term "The Divine Revelation on Polygamy." In that precious document, first wives are instructed as follows:— "Verily. verily, I say unto you, if any man have a wife, and he teaches unto her the law of my priesthood as pertaining to these things, then shall she believe and administer unto him (*i.e.*, administer, or give unto him another wife), or she shall be destroyed, saith the Lord your God; for I will destroy her; for I will magnify my name upon all those who receive and abide in my law (of Polygamy). Therefore it shall be lawful in me if she receive not this law, for him to receive all things (any amount of women) whatsoever I, the Lord his God, will give unto him, because she did not believe and administer unto him, according to my word; and she then becomes the transgressor." See this Revelation given complete in Appendix E.

By this it will be perceived that the first wife has not only to choose between Damnation and Salvation, but she has to decide whether she will live out her allotted time on earth or be foully murdered. Again if she refuses to give her husband one extra wife, the Lord will give him a whole lot of wives. Another thing is also to be considered: if she cheerfully consents and helps her hubby to get another wife, she will be a Queen in Heaven, and thus by various strategems the first wife is generally induced to acquiesce, and not only so, but often becomes very anxious that the Polygamic marriage should take place, I have often known cases when the husband has been "backward in coming forward," and was inclined to shirk the responsibility of this "Heaven ordained Matrimony," the noble and self-sacrificing wife has boldly stepped to the front, gone out, looked up a second wife for her dilatory husband, and actually done the courting.

Yes dear reader, the same fanatisism that caused the Hindoo Mother to throw her child into the jaws of the "Sacred Crocodile" causes the Utah wife to throw another woman into the lap of her husband, marvel not at this, for what is there that a strange Religious Fanatisism will not do.

But it must seem strange to most people. Husbands fancy your devoted wife anxious for your spiritual and eternal welfare, out hunting another mate for you. Oh, how she will court and bill and coo for you! For having found one that would just suit you, and she knows what will exactly suit you in every particular, she will proceed to do the courting in a way and manner far better than you can yourself. In the first place she proceeds to give you a very good character, this is more than you could consistantly do yourself, as "self praise is no recommendation." Says she "Mine is a dear duck of a husband, he's immaculate, he's lovely, he's a darling, he has such a sweet amiable temper, and such a loving disposition, he is so kind, and so very affectionate! Having extolled your virtues in words too numerous to mention, she seeks to impress the fair creature she is wooing for you with the religious and divine aspect of the case; points out that a husband of such noble qualities is not only worthy of another wife here; but how wrong it would be on her part if she failed to do all in her power to ensure his future and eternal glory.

And then dear husbands think of it for a moment, with what tenderness of emotion your dear wife proceeds to offer YOUR hand and heart to the fair damsel she has picked out for you. She assures the dear maid, that she is not only willing, but very anxious to share her darling husband with her, and how nice it will be, when one wishes to go out for the other to remain at home to see to the domestic arrangements, so that the happy domicile need never be minus a wife at home. Then again, if one wife is taken ill, the other can so sweetly soothe the afflicted one in the absence of the affectionate husband, and still further, when becoming convalescent, how good to be able to take the arm of a dear husband on one side, and the arm of a partnership wife on the other, and thus walk out to survey and enjoy the beauties of nature: what a happy trio?

The first wife feels that can she but have the selection of the Polygamic wife, she will be sure to select one that will not only suit her husband, but herself also: she will pick out one that she can get along with, and foolishly imagines that can she but have her choice in the matter, all will be well. With such ideas, such arguments and courting as I have described, is it any wonder that the first wife so generally succeeds in obtaining the second wife, when once she makes up her mind to do so. I could fill this book with the numerous instances that have come under my own notice in Utah where wives have selected, courted, and insisted upon the second marriage in order to secure her husband's salvation and her own future exaltation.

As this will seem so strange to my readers, I feel I must give other testimony than my own. I could fill the remaining pages with quotations from those who have written on this particular matter and thus remove whatever doubt may arise in the reader's mind, but as I want to tell of other things I will only quote one, and will say do not doubt any thing I say in this book, for I have abundance of proof had I room to give it. Further let me assure you that no man or woman, in exposing Mormonism need vary one particle from the truth; for if they tell only the one hundredth part of what they can swear to upon their dying oath the World could not possibly believe it. I cannot, therefore, blame people for doubting such as I state. I judge from my own heart. Had I not witnessed those things I could not possibly believe it. But "seeing is believing," and though we must not tell all we see or know, I will try to make these matters as plain and convincing as possible.

Mrs. Mary E. V. Smith says on page 217, "Fifteen years among the Mormons":—"Wives are exhorted and instructed to use their influence to win, by every possible means, other wives to the home of their husbands; and this they often do, and for this reason as they say, that if their husbands must have more than one wife they have a choice, and they procure those most agreeable to them. The following is one of the 'Songs of Zion' used in their public worship; the teaching, of which like much of what is taught in their public meetings inculcates this doctrine.

"Now, sisters' list to what I say, with trials this world is rife,
You can't expect to miss them all, help husband get a wife!
Now this advice I freely give, if exalted you would be,
Remember that your husband must be blessed with more than thee.
Chorus.—Then, oh, let us say, God bless the wife that strives,
And aids her husband all she can to obtain a dozen wives."

This is all I can here give, for after describing my wedding in hell I shall have to show how the thing works afterward, and that though the dear wife may be ever so careful in selecting other wives for her Lord and Master, she always makes a mistake and chooses the wrong one, for they never agree after the Polygamic marriage is performed. It is then, and truly then, if not before, this Hell upon Earth is fully realized.

Now that everything is lovely, and my wife consenting to the plural marriage, I take her on my right arm and the bride-elect on the left, and walk them both into the "Sealing Room." Here I present the slip of paper containing my name, the name of my wife that was, or is to be, and that of the intended bride, to the Priest who sits at the Altar. He bids me and my two spouses to be seated, which we do, and await further developments. Having carefully examined the slip, or certificate, the Priest calls upon me the bridegroom, my wife, and bride to arise, which we do, fronting the Priest. I and my wife are now married for time and eternity, a very simple affair; its simply being married over again. Having been married to my legal wife she now stands on my left-hand side, while the bride-elect stands on her left. The Priest then put this question to my wife, " Are you willing to give this woman to your husband to be his lawful and wedded wife for time and for all eternity? If you are you will manifest it by placing her right hand within the right hand of your husband." This she willingly did, and this bridegroom and bride stood "hand-in-hand." My wife was now told to take my left arm as if in the attitude of walking: The Priest then asked me as follows:— "Do you, Brother Jarman, take sister (calling the bride-elect by her name), by the right hand, to receive her unto yourself, to be your lawful and wedded wife, and you to be her lawful and wedded husband, for time and for all eternity, with a covenant and promise, on your part, that you will fulfil all the laws, rites, and ordinances, pertaining to this holy matrimony, in the new and everlasting covenant, doing this in the presence of God and angels, of your own free will and choice?" I, of course, answered, "Yes."—The Priest then put this question to the bride:

"Do you, sister" (*calling her by name*), "take brother Jarman by the right hand, and give yourself to him, to be his lawful and wedded wife for time and for all eternity, with a covenant and promise on your part that you will fulfil all the laws, rites, and ordinances, pertaining to this holy matrimony, in the new and everlasting covenant, doing this in the presence of God and angels. The bride meekly answered "Yes." The Priest then said:

"In the name of the Lord Jesus Christ, and by the authority of the Holy Priesthood, I pronounce you legally and lawfully husband and wife for time and for all eternity: and I seal upon you the blessings of the holy resurrection, with power to come forth in the morning of the first resurrection, clothed with glory, immortality, and eternal lives; and I seal upon you, the blessings of thrones, and dominions, and principalities, and powers, and exaltations, together with the blessings of Abraham, Isaac, and Jacob; and say unto you, Be fruitful and multiply and replenish the earth, that you may have joy and rejoicing in your posterity in the day of the Lord Jesus. All these blessings, together with all other blessings pertaining to the new and everlasting covenant, I seal upon your heads, through your faithfulness unto the end, by the authority of the Holy Priesthood, in the name of the Father, and of the Son, and of the Holy Ghost. Amen."

The Priest then wrote on the slip of paper "O. K.," which signified the thing had been done "up to dick," that I was "done brown," and was now a thorough married man. This bachelor had hitherto been playing at marriage. Now it was a reality, and a fearful one at that, as you will presently see. The Priest opened the door and told me to hand the slip of paper to the Prophet, and watched me do it.. The Prophet looked at it, then gave it to the Scribe, who entered it on the general record. I saw him write my name, the maiden names of my two dear wives, and the place and date of this singular (I beg pardon) plural marriage in the big register. I asked for a certificate, but was politely told that such "nonsensical documents" were not required; that I had "the two women to show for it," and, says the Prophet, "If that ain't enough go out, look up a few more, fetch 'em here, and we'll splice you on to 'em mighty quick. You are all O. K., so take your women home and make the best of 'em."

A Mormon wife has no certificate to show marriage, and if occasion should so require and to shield their Polygamous brethren, the Mormon officials, will positively swear that they did not perform the marriage, while the big book can never be found, for that is safely hid.

The Great High Priest, Elias Smith, who is also Probate Judge, then confirmed me, and made me an "Elder and a Priest for ever after the order of Melchizedek." Moreover my "Patriarchal" documents show that I also held a wonderful position, viz.: "A virgin without guile." As these papers appear in full presently, I will merely say here that the "Endowment ceremonies" shook my faith in Mormonism, making a shipwreck of faith quite possible. I began to doubt the sincerity of its leaders, which is the first step to Apostacy. It seemed to me they were more like vile sinners than "Saints," and the words of *Sir John Birkenhead*:—

"If these be saints, 'tis vain indeed, To think there's good or evil;
The world will soon be of this creed, No God, no king, no devil."

came to my mind, remained uppermost, and I could not forget them.

At the wedding, please observe, I and my bride were asked "Are you doing this of your own free will and choice?" my wife was only asked "Are you willing." He should have asked "Are you subdued? Has the priesthood and this holy religion blunted every womanly feeling in your breast, and induced you to immolate yourself on the altar of Polygamy." The marriage ceremony being now concluded we are permitted to don our worldly clothing and leave the place, this being the conclusion of the "Endowment" ceremonies. We are cautioned to be sure and keep on the "Holy Garment" which covers the "Sacred Oil," and forms a complete coat of mail always proof against all the fiery darts of the Devil; all secular clothing must go on over this. Having put on my clothes as ordered, and being again fit to appear in decent society, I soon found my empty lunch basket and my way out. I left that building a wiser, sadder, and muchly married man: I could not help being wiser, but why should I be sad on this my TRUE AND REAL wedding day? Had not God commanded in the Mormon Revelation to take TWO wives, and had sworn to damn me if I failed to thus marry. Had I not obeyed and was now a saved man, and ought I not to be happy? But somehow I could not feel happy. There seemed to be a fearful dread of something terrible just about to happen, and it did happen as you will see, for my home was ever after "A perfect Hell upon Earth."

After giving such an exposé as I have of this infernal institution I must state, that though in England, and far removed from Mormon Assassins, Mormon vengeance would reach me if it could. I know how mad they will be, and further I know they have thousands of men who gladly do the bidding of their Prophet, Priests, and Bishops. Hence the people of England must not be surprised to hear that the writer of this book is villified, for Mormons will swear to anything, as I show presently; and would stop at nothing short of my death. They always defame the character of those who leave them, for as they cannot meet the serious charges which I or any other recusant Mormon can bring against them, if they can but get the public to believe me unworthy of credence and thus prevent my obtaining an audience, they would gain their point. The Author of "The Rocky Mountain Saints, on page 212, says:—"From the beginning of Mormonism, the ruling authorities have accepted defamation of character as the best weapon with which to assail the discontented or apostates." They also assure their British converts that all Apostates are full of the Devil, and very wicked, and strictly caution them never to listen to one, or credit a word they say. I find it hard work to get at those who have been converted to Mormonism in England; but am happy to state that I failed but in one instance to effect a recapture, and that one seemed to me more fit for a lunatic asylum than anything else. I have saved hundreds from going into bondage, crime and misery in Utah, and when I have saved the whole of Great Britian, and driven every Mormon scamp from our shores, I shall consider my work done, and not till then.

My Home a Perfect Hell.

In treating of my own domestic affairs I shall do so like a man, for no man would attempt to give the public all the peculiarities thereof, which the said public have no business to enquire into, while I shall give enough and trust that " Enough's as good as a feast."

I was now a married man in every sense of the word. My " Wives " having dressed themselves fit for decent society also, each made a grab for the left arm. Wife No. 1 (as I shall now call my " old stand-by " wife) managed to grab it successfully, while the bride *proper* awfully chagrined snatched at the right arm hugged it tight and looked daggers at No. 1. Whatever their respective thoughts may have been, and though awful fiery glances were exchanged between them, we left the house in solemn silence. I felt that a storm of more than ordinary portentions was brewing—I was downcast, though it was my wedding day and I had a DEAR wife on each arm, and was, of course, ripe for Heaven, yet I could not help feeling I was much nearer Hell. Both wives and myself as we jog along, look down, as if to find consolation on the earth. All I could read upon the ground, and it seemed printed in big letters, was HELL UPON EARTH. No. 1 hangs heavily on the left arm; The Bride drags sulkily though tightly upon my right arm. Behold this rose between two thorns, and if there is such a thing as sympathy in human nature, sympathize with this suffering trio. Men put yourselves in my place (metaphorically of course). Ladies put yourselves on my left or right arm whichever you please (figuratively) and find out our respective feelings on this very remarkable occasion. Must I, can I attempt to describe them? I will try.

This disconsolate hubby feels about " done up " and is ready to " pass in his checks," get up the " flume," " kick the bucket," or do anything to avoid what I feel sure is coming, and that without delay. I say to myself "I am in a nice fix, I've done a nice thing for myself and put my foot in it." Why was I born, why did I not commit suicide, or rob a bank, forge a cheque, or do something that would have transported me for life, then I should not have known this dreadful suspense. I glance, but for a moment, at wife No. 1, she that had so often shared my sorrow, but it's no use looking there for sympathy now; I see in her, a worse than Mary Magdalene, who knew nothing of Polygamy, and had but seven devils in her, whereas Mormon Polygamy makes the women complete Devils. It's useless looking to her—the pride of the morning, but now the bride of the hour—for sympathy for she also seems very much " put out " and anything but satisfied with the situation.

But how shall I describe the feelings of my better halves. Were I a devil, one of those accustomed to getting inside the women, I might be able to tell exactly how they felt, but I can only judge from external appearances, and what I afterwards found out. The most interesting person and the most interested, on wedding occasions should be the Bride. Therefore we will gauge her feelings. Though this is the first time she has been married; she is not satisfied. She feels that being the latest spouse and the only real bride of the occasion, she should have the place nearest her husband's heart. The left arm is hers, and she reasons thus—This is my first wedding day; that old wife of his has been married to him for years, it's no novelty to her; this is my honeymoon, not hers. She might yield a little to me on this occasion. I have as much right to my husband as she has, why should she seek to claim the best place in his affection? I have just married him, and I'll just let her know it—she wished me to marry him, or I am sure I should not. Now that I have I'll not go back on him, I'll stick to him through thick and thin, and show her I have as much right to him as she has. If she wanted to keep him all to herself, why did she wish me to share him with her; if she don't look out I'll make it so sweet for him that he will slight her considerably, and perhaps let her flicker solitary and alone. She must not trifle with my feelings just now or I'll make her rue it.

Wife No. 1 ruminates thus:—I never thought it would make such a difference. I and my husband *were* one, I could speak confidingly and pour out my soul to him in deep sympathy when I had him all to myself, but now I find the truth of the old adage "Two is company, but three is none." This interloper deprives me of my conjugal felicity, I'll teach HER to mind her own business, and not seek to mar the happiness of man and wife that have been so long wedded to each other. She evidently thinks she ought to have my husband's left arm; she will have to learn that his left arm is mine. She may consider that she, being the youthful bride has a perfect right to it, but I shall teach her that I am THE WIFE OF HIS YOUTH, and therefore have the greatest right to him. I shall not relinquish any of my rights for that stuck up thing.

Thus the mischief keeps fermenting, and not a word is spoken by either. What a wedding day? Did the All-wise God give that Revelation commanding such marriages? No Never! No, a thousand times, No! Its worse than Blasphemy to say it emanated from the All-wise Creator.

In the Endowment House the "new names" given to my wives were those of "Sarah" and "Rebecca," but amid the excitement I got them mixed, and when we came out I could not "tell t'other from which;" for the life of me I could not tell which was Rebecca or which was Sarah, both new names to them and me. What to do I knew not, for we must never reveal the one wife's name to the other, or speak of it at all; it is to remain a perfect secret between the husband and the particular wife. Yet I was anxious to know "which was which." Shortly we arrived at a small stream, over which there is no plank or bridge of any kind. Foot passengers jump over it. Now we newly-married trio, triune, triplets, tripartite party, or whatever we may be termed—do not get scared, we were merely three souls with but a thousand thoughts—three hearts that failed to beat as one. [Printer, please do not put inverted commas to this quotation, the whole thing is inverted quite sufficiently without it]. Now it is not to be expected that we three in one and one in three will try to jump the stream conjointly. Oh dear no, "It can't be did." We would have another washing if we tried to do so. The wives now release their hold of the husband's arms. Wife No. 1, in a vexatious moment, clears the stream with a bound. Now, thinks I, this is just my time to find out if that is Sarah or Rebecca that has just flopped over the stream. So I said to my bride, who was yet on this side of Jordan (the stream), "Let me see, your new name is Rebecca." She affectionately replied, "No, my dear, my new name is Sarah." "Rebecca," who stood just on the brink of the other side, heard the word "Rebecca" and very wickedly surmised, or at least the devils in her prompted her so, that I was confidentially telling the bride her new name. That was enough. "Hell hath no fury like a woman scorned," and to make a bad matter worse I jumped the stream and lovingly assisted the bride over. I and the bride would have got along O. K., if the other "dear charmer" had been a thousand miles away, but she was right there to pay particular attention to my left arm, &c., &c.

In helping my bride over the stream I had taken her right hand, and guided by a strong instinct, or else the Devil was prompting the batch of us to mischief, I did not release her hand until I had placed her right arm in my left. I not thinking of what I was doing, but the bride designedly, as she afterwards told me, for says she "I was determined to have my rights." Well she had them "right and left," so did I, and between the two I wished myself in Heaven out of it. My readers will not expect me to waste pen, ink, and paper and take up the valuable space in my book by describing the *fracas*, suffice to say the first round was won by Wife No. 1, time 5 minutes 57 seconds. My arm by this time was ready for a sling. The bride, overcome by the superior fighting qualities of No. 1, resolved to make good use of her weapon, the tongue, and give her "a good tongue lashing." In this she was successful, or at least equal to the emergency, and managed to get in "six to the half-dozen." As it often happens in a wrangle of words, something the bride said, aroused the ire of wife No. 1, and without calling "time!" round second was commenced with increased vigor.

On such interesting occasions wedding dresses, bonnets, ribbons, and such things are of small moment. Such trifles get scattered in fragments to the winds, while the dark glossy hair of the one and the golden locks of the other are handled most unmercifully, that is the hands of the dark-haired victim hitches to meddle with the golden locks and *vice versa*. And the one with the longest finger nails prides herself in doing the best scratching. Second round won by the bride, time 8 min. 32 seconds. With a brace of them, and both claiming the protection of their dear husband, what could I do. This "duck of a husband" was nonplussed, and now that No. 1 had witnessed defeat. She was surprised that her husband and protector failed to help her and give the bride a good thrashing, and demands that he shall protect her from the assaults of that "insolent hussy;" The bride insists that No. 1 shall not interfere with her marriage rights, demands the protection of her husband and is particular to state how the "deceitful old cat" lured her into marrying her husband. Finally we reached Ho——I was about to say home, the Poet says:—

"Home, home, sweet, sweet home, Be it ever so humble there is no
    place like home."

But the Polygamist can never sing that. If the author of those beautiful lines had married two wives and taken them to his home, he could have never composed the like. He might have given us something about a "Hell upon Earth," and depicted the fearful scenes of a Polygamic harem about as follows:—

It's here on this earth we do re-a-lize Hell,
Where women, as devils, do constantly dwell,
Because we here marry so many dear wives,
Who rage, vex, and pester us out of our lives.
    Hell, Hell, chief chief Hell,
Be it ever so wealthy, It is nothing but Hell.

My Home, in Utah, as well as every other Polygamic home, must hereafter be called "Hell upon Earth." We arrived in our "Hell at home" about 6 p.m., just in time to sit down to our wedding dinner, but my appetite was gone. In the Endowment House I had been crammed with so much of that "meat the world knows not of," and from what I have described I may be credited when I say all I now needed was peace and quiet and a good hot bath. I managed to get the latter but never the former two. I washed off the "Holy oil," during which time it seemed as if all hell was let loose, and ten thousand thunders, earthquakes, and dynamiters were busy tearing things. In the early morn when I left that "Home, Sweet Home," there hung on the walls such mottoes as "God bless our peaceful home." "There is no place like home," &c., while peace and plenty filled it. Now it seemed that all the Devils in existence had left the infernal regions, and gathered from the various parts of the earth where they had been going to and fro, and wandering up and down, and had now gathered together and made my house their rendezvous. I wept like a child, and why I was kept from committing suicide I am only beginning to learn—

"There is a Divinity that shapes our ends, rough hew them as we will."

A faint gleam of light seems to show that I had to go through all this Hell upon Earth business so that I might be enabled to expose the whole matter in such a way as to convince the world of its abominable evils and thus effectually bring about its speedy overthrow. If not, I ask, "Why was I lured into it and made to suffer so? And why when so often tempted to commit suicide was I frustrated?

I had been "counselled" to furnish a separate room for each wife, and devote one week to each alternately, the parlor, kitchen, and dining room to be used in common by the whole family. The wife that was to be a widow, as it were for the week, had to superintend the domestic arrangements, or in military parlance be "orderly for the week." In the conjugal bliss she would be exempt from domestic duty and the week widow become the "orderly," and so on one week about, But in my Domicile things went contrary—they do in all these Polygamic families, I would that mine were an exceptional case, but having travelled over Utah Territory, and boarded and lodged in the various Polygamic establishments there, I am compelled to speak the truth, and say, I found no happy Polygamic families through the length and breadth of the land. How could there be? The whole thing is so diametrically opposed to human nature. We find in the case of Polygamy, as in every other case where Nature is perverted or abused, Dame Nature comes back on us with severe penalties.

Within the first 24 hours of my "blessed Honeymoon," the furniture of my "Home Sweet Home," my "Hell upon Earth" appeared as if shaken and torn by a violent explosion, and to cut a long story short, I never experienced any of the bliss of this "week about" business. No. 1 at all times insisted upon bossing the household arrangements and would never allow the man— her dear husband—who had violated his British marriage oath and taken another wife to his bosom, to be on the same close relation as before, she being a wife only in name and nothing more, and there was therefore an end to all chances of any "pledges of affection." In vain did I endeavour to pursuade her to "live her religion" and try to "bear the cross," for every time I appealed to her I was met with torrents of abuse, while my bride was always mentioned in words not fit to appear here. I went to business mornings with a heavy heart and returned evenings with a far heavier one. A man after the toils of the day and worry of business seeks the quiet retreat of his peaceful home—his castle—removed as it were from the battles of life, to recuperate his strength and fortify himself for the morrow. Here the gentle sympathies of his help meet should soothe his oft distracted brow. Here he should find that comfort and consolation not to be found in the outside world which builds him up and fortifies him, enabling him the better to do battle with the stern realities of life. But now, it was no use for me to seek consolation, peace, quiet or rest in my house—my Hell—before reaching it of an evening wife No. 1 or 2 would be sure to meet me and prepare me somewhat for the big storm raging in my hell. If it was No. 1 who had so affectionately come to meet her tired lord, and lovingly cheer his few remaining steps homeward, she would wring her fist in his face and say "Now William I'm your lawful wife,

I married you in England"—I would try to break the sentence by saying, "Yes my dear, who says you ain't." Then I was treated with an outline of what had passed between "my wives" during the day, and if I tried to hurry along so as to get into hell and witness the worst of it as quickly as possible, she would pull me back—say she had come to meet me on purpose to let me know how things were, and like Sarah of old insisted that I must "Cast out the bondwoman." How vainly did I try to convince her that it was our "Holy Religion,"—that she should have thought of this before, and looked before she leaped, and consented to the union.

If it was wife No. 2 who met me, she would storm thus, "Now William, I married you according to our religion, by and with the willing consent of your other wife; had she refused her consent I would not have married you, yet the nasty old cat keeps calling me * * * * (this must be left blank) I think I have given enough to show how matters stood. It was useless for me to ask No. 2 to put herself in the place of No. 1 for a moment and consider had she been my wife for years and the mother of my children, and then have to submit to another, how very trying it must be, &c. The fact is Polygamy makes women perfect devils, and there is only one way to manage them, and that is the mode adopted by Nigger drivers in Slavery—The Horse Whip. That being out of my line I was not a successful Polygamist. There are other ways of managing these hells which I also refused to adopt.

It soon became known that "Brother Jarman was 'in for it,' and served him right, for a man in his position to be so niggardly and try to get along with TWO WIVES when he ought to have at least a dozen." One night on going home and neither wife having met me as usual my bosom thrilled with joy. Thinks I, now hostilities have ceased—the war is over—I shall yet have a Home on Earth. When I entered my house I soon found my mistake out. There were two men "Teachers" waiting to see me: They had heard the tremendous "rows" going on in that unfortunate domicile that day and had called to teach my "women" their "duty," and had remained to "teach" me in regard to my "duty" which was about thus:—As I had failed to learn the "Horsewhip Drill" I had better look out a half dozen good stout girls who would hang together—hold the balance of power in my household and bring these two viragos into subjection. Both men were strangers to me, so I said to the one who was " mouthpiece " " Excuse me Sir, but are you a Polygamist ? " " Oh yes," he replied. " How many wives have you ? " I asked, " Four " said he. May I ask " Can you keep peace in your family ? " He answered "I wish I could but it seems impossible." I said to the other "Teacher" "and pray Sir, how many wives have you?" "only three" was the modest reply. "Be kind enough dear Sir to tell me how matters stand in your home; can you keep your wives in subjection ?" he replied "I am sorry to say it is utterly impossible." I arose, opened the door, and said, "Gentlemen go home and learn how to rule your own households, and then come and teach me. At present you are not the teachers I require, I have no use for you. According to your own confessions, you are the wrong men in the wrong place, please withdraw, and when you can come and intelligently advise me what to do, I shall be very glad to see you, Good Night!" This was my first visible sign of Apostacy: I had refused to listen to those "In Authority."

Next morning early a brother " High Priest " called, said he wanted to chat with me, and as it was particular perhaps I would walk with him around the foot hills. So we took a morning walk. We had not proceeded far when he introduced his particular business thus:—" Brother Jarman, you made a mistake." I readily confessed I had. He continued, " I mean in marrying ONLY TWO: a man of your calibre should have married at least a dozen. Besides your two are strong-minded English women, and they'll always be fighting and scratching unless you do as I am about to tell you." Says I, "For God's sake—for my children's sake—for my wives' sake—do tell me, if you can, how to have peace in my home." Says he, "Will you do as I tell you?" "I said, "If I possibly can, I shall be only too glad to do whatever lays in my power to secure what I so ardently desire—peace in the family." Says he, "There are various ways of regulating these Polygamy affairs." [I knew he was a man of experience in that line, so I resolved to let him go a-head, and let me into the light of "the various ways" without interruption]. "In the first place you have two very excellent women, and you ought to think yourself in luck for having secured them." ("Ill" luck thinks I) "But you are a poor judge of human nature in women, and made this mistake. You married two only and each one is fit to be a boss; the one will never yield to the other. Had you picked out for a second some meek, quiet disposed girl, the first wife could have just whipped her into line, and made her do as she pleased: or had your first been of such a temperament that the second could have brow beaten her into subjection, all would have been well. Instead of that you have two natural born bosses. Now my advice to you is. There is a large importation of Danish girls to arrive in a day or two. You go down and pick out twelve, they are generally very quiet and harmless, and submit to anything; marry the dozen and take home the lot. Give six to one wife and six to the other, as servants like, to help them in their domestic affairs. You'll find they'll just whip those Danish girls around, and have their work cut out in bossing them, and you'll have a jolly time." Here I had to interpose a question. "But my dear brother, I don't know the Danish language, neither do my wives.?" "D——the difference," said the Priest. "We have Danish Priests that will tell those you "look out" to go with you and do as you tell them. You get a Danish Dictionary and you'll get along all right. Should any difficulty occur, just call for the Danish Priest, and he'll soon straighten things out, you bet." I thought surely here is a nice scheme, but it looked to me like "hopping out of the frying pan into the fire," but I did not say so. I was in the "pursuit of knowledge under difficulties." He further said, "There is still another way out of your trouble. If you don't like to marry so many, you just look out one real good vixen like woman, some regular virago, marry her and bring her on the scene, and if she don't regulate matters, nothing will. I tell you I tried that game, and it worked like a charm. This virago of mine has a daughter a regular 'chip of the old block.' She's only just turned fifteen, but lor she's a snorter. She's just a hitching and a dying to have a regular go in at it, and this brings me to my particular business with you this morning. This daughter (sweet fifteen in Utah), I'm speaking of has taken a fancy to you, and she deeply sympathises with you. Only last night when she heard of how your wives were a "cutting up," she says to me, 'Dad I feel for that dear man, he don't deserve such treatment as he gets. Why only last week when I called, there was roast, bake, and boil and plenty of everything. Yet that thousand dollars worth of furniture he bought when he married 'em was jist fit to light fires without much chopping.' Well Brother Jarman, I need not tell you all she said, but to the point, she is willing to help you out, and I promised her to see you and talk the matter over, and if you say the word come right along and take her through the Endowment House, marry her, take her home, and I'll guarantee she'll settle matters in short order. You're welcome to her my brother, and she wishes to become Mrs. Jarman. No. 3 right off, so say the word and the 'jig's up."

Now what could I do. Here was an extraordinary offer of marriage, how could I refuse, or be at all uncivil, especially to a brother Priest. So I said, "Then you are willing to give me your daughter, and that under such circumstances?" "Oh yes," he replied, "and she is perfectly willing to marry you at once, and I do actually believe she was born to help you out of your difficulty—she's cut out for the very purpose." I thanked him very kindly, said that "the proposition having come upon me so suddenly I must beg time to reflect upon it, and if I concluded to marry another, I certainly would give his daughter the first chance."

She never got that chance, I preferred to remain in the frying-pan and frizzle, that was hot enough for me, I also vowed if I could get forgiveness for marrying two wives at once, I would never do it again. Those who have read "The Infernal Conference, or Dialogues of Devils," by the Rev. John Macgowan, V. D. M., will see vast depths in every line I have written, which those who have not so read fail to see. Space prevents my introducing "Dialogues of Devils." Milner & Co., London, has a 1/- edition.

Time dragged heavily along, life was a weary burden. One terrible night when things were worse than ever I took my Colt's Navy Revolver and went up behind the grave yard, determined to put an end to this "Hell upon Earth" and try the other. I felt it could not be worse, and probably it might prove somewhat better than the Hell I was now in. I pulled the trigger three times with the muzzel in my right ear but without effect, it did not discharge. When placing it the fourth time, a feeling I cannot describe came over me, and the thought I had not kissed my dear little children "good bye," made me determined to go home kiss my innocent darlings for the last time—and make sure work of it. When I got home the sight of my own flesh and blood laying there sweetly sleeping, unconscious of their Father's or Mother's deep sorrow and trouble, deterred me from committing the rash act, though driven to desperation. Be it here understood that though I and my wife should have had better sense, I blame, not her, but the vile system, and all who uphold it. It was a trouble to her as well as to myself, although she has got bravely over it, as you will see, I have not, nor do I ever expect to.

On another occasion when my trials seemed too heavy for poor human nature to bear, I kissed my dear little ones "good bye," and this time determined not to be frustrated, took a razor, again went to the grave yard wall, a lonely place, fully resolved to launch myself into Eternity, I was so tired of Time, it dragged so slow, every day seemed years and that of wretchedness. Arriving on the spot I knelt and offered a short prayer that the Father of Mercies would have mercy upon me; and remember that my frame which was but dust, was too heavily burdened to proceed further on the journey of life that here I ended it, and trusted to Divine mercy for a better life hereafter. I felt perfectly resigned. Intending to cut my throat while upon my bended knees, I searched in my pocket for the razor, but it was not there. It had worked its way through a small hole in the pocket and was lost. I felt awfully dissappointed. I went home feeling very sad, but here one of my little ones having been taken ill, was crying for "Papa." The tears which now blot this manuscript, thank God, will not appear in print. When I think that my children have all been torn from me by the accursed system of Polygamy, and are now 7000 miles away and are being dragged up in that awful Sodom, I pray for the curse of the Almighty to rest upon America until she rids herself of that accursed Institution. And may England's Government wither and her Glory depart, and may England become a hiss and a by word among the nations so long as she allows Mormon Missionaries to pollute her soil and drag away so many victims to undergo the same as myself and thousands of Britishers have endured and are still suffering.

I suppose I am not the only father that possessed a PET child among his pets. This sick child was my pet and oh how earnestly I wished that sickness to prove fatal, that I might bury it and then speedily join it beyond. However it recovered and lives in Salt Lake City to day, a Mormon—a far greater trouble to me than if I had buried it.

As more of my hell and what I suffered appears in future Chapters, I will now show how things are in other families.

CHAPTER VI.

HE AND SHE DEVILS—WOMEN FULL OF THE DEVIL—MEN DITTO
70 TIMES 7 DEVILS IN ONE WOMAN—RAISING THE DEVIL—DRUNKEN
DEVILS—MEAN DEVILS, &C.

The reader will see by the following chapter, which is composed mostly of cuttings from Newspapers, &c., published in Utah, that my statements are fully borne out by others. From the " Salt Lake Daily Review " :—
"THE UTAH MONSTER."

"Behold, David and Solomon truly had many wives and concubines, which thing was abominable before me, saith the Lord. For behold I, the Lord, have seen the sorrow and heard the mourning of the daughters of my people, because of the wickedness and abominations of their husbands; and I will not suffer that the cries of the fair daughters of this people shall come up to me against the men of my people. For they shall not lead captive the daughters of my people because of their tenderness, save I shall visit them with a sore curse even unto destruction; for they shall not commit whoredoms like unto them of old, saith the Lord of Hosts. * * Behold, ye have done greater iniquities than the Lamanites, our brethren. Ye have broken the hearts of your tender wives, and lost the confidence of your children, because of your bad examples before them; and the sobbings of their hearts ascend up to God against you. And because of the strictness of the word of God, which cometh down against you, many hearts died, pierced with deep wounds.—*Book of Mormon, page* 118."

"Polygamy is truly a 'relic of barbarism.' Examined from any and every standpoint, it is repulsive to all pureminded men and women. On every hand the evils it has entailed are manifest. If those who have introduced it into our midst and sought to enforce its practice by pronouncing anathemas and the pangs of hell against those who did not obey it, are responsible for the wrecked happiness and blighted prospects of thousands who have experienced its mischief, then it were better they had not been born. There is no ground upon which it can be justified for an instant. The only point ever made to its credit, is that it is better than whoredom or desertion of monogamic wives. There is no emotional, spiritual, or intellectual culture in it. It vitiates the attributes of maritial affection; it severs the bonds that should make husband and wive dearer to each other than all other objects; it leads to a voluptuousness on the part of the wealthy that is destructive to the production of great men; it is practised for the momentary gratification of the sensual appetites; it leads to the debasement of womanhood, and deprives her of that natural companionship which Nature has designed for her, making her the mere instrument of administering to the physical pleasure of one not her own, finally leaving her in melancholy solitude, her mind clouded with an aimless and vague prospect in life, with nothing to stimulate or excite her ambition but to supplant her more favoured sisters and gain the supremacy of the household—seeking her happiness at the distraction of others. Its spirit is the disunion and division of families; it is a constant menace to pure enjoyment. Whatever is enjoyed, is done surreptitiously. We know the women of Utah are the most dispirited in the world. The fervid anticipations of youth are dissipated; life is not what the heart teaches. The object of life—happiness—has miscarried: and nowhere in Christendom is the life of women such a deteriorated blank. We have yet to meet the first woman who does not regret that its practice and trials are necessary to salvation hereafter. They bleed inwardly. Drop by drop the heart yields the happiness that God would give them, which the beasts of men have defrauded them of possessing. The young men and women of Utah are far behind other countries as regards refinement, civility, polite accomplishments and natural endowments. The majority of parents in polygamy have little conception and less care what trouble and mortification they are subjecting their own flesh and blood to. The man who, regardless of right, truth, decency and respect due to the welfare of others, persists in this practice, deserves the hottest place that the infernal one has prepared for the wicked."

Polygamy creates "He and She Devils," plenty of them. A few cases will show that I am not the only one who can truly say, "It is a perfect Hell upon Earth." It being so much cheaper to board and lodge all the wives under one roof, where one kitchen and parlor serves for the lot, it is considered the best way to manage the affair. But oftimes when wives are so terribly belligerent, separate houses are built, if the hubby can afford it. Even this separation does not always prevent "war." I know a man "blessed" with more than one wife, who built for his termagent wife a wooden hut in the foot hills, three miles off, and by removing her to this lonely spot, he expected to obtain peace. But alas!

"The best laid schemes of mice and men gang aft aglee,
And leave us nought but grief and pain for promised joy."

This virago would often rush down from her "Mountain Home," reinvigorated in mind and body, and make a vigorous onslaught upon the "Peaceful Home." She would come down through blinding snow storms, when least expected, just to have "a real good fight." It is impossible to have peace in Polygamy, no matter what they try.

I saw two wives of a merchant meet at the door of their husband's place of business. As the *Salt Lake Tribune* reporter saw the same, I give the account from that paper. It says:—"The elder of the two had made a wifely call at the Store, and on coming out met her younger rival, who was bent on the same errand. Her anger was aroused, and she went for that 'Nasty minx' in hot haste. Wife, No. 2, found herself divested of her head gear, and her back hair floating in the breeze before she knew there was anything the matter. She had come for connubial courtesies, and fell into dread Bellona's arms. It was a good place to get away from, and she made good time with her heels, leaving her scattered garments on the field as a trophy to the victor."

A next door neighbour of mine, also a merchant, took a second wife for the purpose of securing eternal glory, and, if possible, a son and heir to his worldly possessions. His first wife had "blessed" him with several daughters but no son. His fond hope was realized, for very soon the second wife gave birth to the heir. So soon as this new mother could mix with the family, she, in presence of the first wife, tauntingly addressed her babe thus, "You are papa's darling; you are papa's son and heir! He's papa's beautiful son! When she could take it out of doors, she would meet her husband at the gate on his return, place the babe in his arms, fondly embrace him saying, "Here's your darling son and heir, your pet baby!" while the first wife who had also come to the gate, stood looking on with feelings better imagined by the ladies than I can describe. This state of affairs grew worse, until finally it so preyed upon the mind of the first wife—a quiet, loving woman—she became a raving maniac. I could give the names in these cases but it would avail nothing, hence I omit them.

Just to show it is as bad since I left in 1880, I give a case from the *Salt Lake Tribune*, of May 12, 1881. Robbins is a merchant. A dollar is equal, all things considered, to one shilling in England.

"EDS. TRIBUNE: It seems that this people have made lies their refuge, and under falsehood have hid themselves. Another disgraceful affair happened here the other day, between the second and third wives of C. B. Robbins. A short time ago his first wife left him, and the second was about as sick of Polygamy as the first, consequently Mr. Robbins and his third wife, together with the priesthood, agreed that the second should be allowed 15 dollars per month for the maintenance of herself and family. It appears that when the second heard from her husband what her allowance was to be, she flew into a terrible passion, called her lord everything but a saviour, left the store, picked up a rock and went to the house of No. 3, rapped at the door, and as her antagonist opened it knocked her down, and with the spring of a tigress leaped upon her and tore the hair from off her head and the flesh from her face in a brutal manner. The hired girl ran for the husband, who came immediately, and with difficulty parted them.

"Such are the fruits of Polygamy; it has covered the Territory with blood and baptized it with tears; it has cast a shadow in the heart, in the sunlight, of every good and tender man and woman. I say let us rid the earth of this monster, and write upon every lintel in Utah, "Liberty and Law."

LOGAN, May 10th, 1881.   AMERICAN CITIZEN.

An old lady who was a close observer of the workings of this plural wifeism once remarked to me that the women in Polygamy were all either devils or melancholy fools.

During my difficulties at home, a fellow " Melchezidek Priest " called to see how I got along. In private conversation I told him that I seemed to possess two Mary Magdalenes, each of whom appeared to have 7 devils in her. He replied, "That's nothing, my women's chuck full of devils, I'll bet my last dollar that one of em, my wife Hanner, has 70 times 7 devils in her night and day. You're in luck my hearty, my best woman is never short of 7 times 7 devils, and I consider her my angel, I wish I cou'd find a woman or two that would only harbour 7 devils, I'd marry 'em this very minnit." He added "Cheer up, don't let your pecker go down." I answered that I could not cheer up, I could see no silver lining to my cloud. Says he " there's something wrong with you, take a little of this and it'll cheer yer up," taking from his pocket a bottle of whiskey. I said "no thank you, that would raise the devil worse than ever." "That's it " says he " Raise the devil, then devil wo'nt fight agin devil; when they see you're full of the devil they'll give in, that's how I fix 'em. I can't manage 'em till I get full of whiskey, and full of the devil myself: then I raise the devil you bet, and I'd like to see the devils that would stand agin me when I'm full. you hear me?" I remarked " *similia similibus curantur*" says he "what's that?" I said " Like things are cured by like." He replied " Ah! that's it." and took a good swig out of the bottle, was "vexed I wouldn't jine" him, and proceeded to tell how matters were "ta hum (at home). There's the devil to pay" he said, and he was "jist on it and gitting ready to fight it out with the she devils ta hum." Were I to tell what he said no one could possibly believe it of any man, much less one holding " The Melchizedek Priesthood." In addition to the task of subduing so many devils in his wives, he declared that his mother-in-laws possessed double the amount of devils. Reader, arithmetise the following: this man had 14 wives altogether (that is, wives, spiritual wives and proxy wives). One possessed 70 times 7 devils, the " Best " 7 times 7, and his mother-in-laws' double. He, when "full of Whiskey" professed to have devils enough in him to whip all the devils in his wives, question:—How many devils were there in that family. Please give the answer, my time is too precious, and this is beyond simple arithmetic which I am best posted in.

" Apostle " Kimble in one of his sermons said:—" Some women who think they know everything, go home and abuse their husbands and raise the devil in a man's family."—*Journal of Discourses*, vol. 6 p. 127.

"The devil is not dead yet; he is on hand to do his work, to perform his mission, which is to stir up the Saints to their duty." Brigham Young's Sermon—*Journal of Discourses*, vol. 2. p. 348.

"As this work progresses, so will the works of Satan increase."—"Apostle" Kimble, *Journal of Discourses* vol. 2, p. 150.

Now for another picture. A beautiful Kentucky girl eloped with and married a Mormon Elder, who soon became a bishop. As time rolled on, this once beautiful girl became the mother of ten children: when the time of her usefulness in this direction was over, her husband took a young wife to his bosom. This so worked upon the feelings of the hitherto amiable wife, as to transform her into a perfect vixen. She had sternly refused to consent to this plural marriage, and had sworn vengeance upon the incoming bride. The Bishop prepared for his concubine by adding a room to his dwelling. We will call it the "Bridechamber." This was situate on the ground floor, the window of which is easily reached from the garden. The wife also prepared to receive the bride with more than usual attention. For some days prior to the wedding, the contents of domestic utensils were saved for the momentous occasion. It was in the very hot weather, when the Bishop, who had hitherto been "blameless, the husband of one wife," married his second wife. He brought her from the "Endowment House" on this summer eve after dark when "all was quiet and his old wife and her children 'sweetly slumbering'" as he thought. He very quietly retired with his bride intent to pass the first night of his second honeymoon.

The first wife was not asleep as he supposed, but closely watching just outside the bridechamber window; and, as she anticipated, the heat of the room being so intense, the window had been opened to admit air. Underneath this window stood a row of buckets. The bridal couch stood close to the window, and when husband and bride were snugly ensconced, the wife gave them a different annointing to that which they received in the endowment house. The Bishop hastily dressed, assisted the bride to attire and took her to a lodging house, and soon provided a separate house for her.

For three years the wife was furious, made many rash attempts to murder her rival, and never permitted her husband to enter her house. The heart of the husband still clung a little to the wife of his youth, or she would have been "put out of the way and sent back to her mother earth." The Bishop often tried to become reconciled, and proposed to spend every alternate week with her, but she scorned the idea of being placed on a level with his concubine, and refused all overtures, unless he would discard the other woman. At length the Bishop fell sick, sent for his wife, and told her he was anxious to return to his family. She replied "You know the terms, you never return here or speak to this woman again." The Bishop humbly ejaculated "Hand me down my pants!" That ended the conflict: the pants were taken from the peg, and after three years of Polygamy, he gave it up and returned to his old home and family. If this Kentucky grit were infused into all Mormon women, the question of polygamy would soon be solved.

I once saw another Bishop lively chased down the street followed by a broom handle and a woman. As this was seen by reporters and appeared in Newspapers, I give it from the *Salt Lake Tribune*, which quotes from the *Philadelphia Times*:—

"The women of Mormondom evidently have it in their power to settle the Polygamy question. If they take it in hand as Mrs. Jones, of Salt Lake City, has done their work will supersede the necessity of further legislative or judicial action. Mrs Jones is the wife of Old Jones, and the only wife he has or is likely to have. Old Jones was contemplating additional matrimony, and like a dutiful Mormon, consulted the Bishop about it. The Bishop advised him to take two more wives, and Mrs. Jones happened to overhear the advice. Forthwith she determined to set her face against the project in a manner which could not be misunderstood. Procuring a large broom with a stout handle, she proceeded to discountenance old Jones. She chased him for a considerable distance along the street, inflicting, as opportunity offered, such whacks as were calculated to dissuade him from his cherished hopes of increasing the size of his family. After Jones had taken refuge under a friendly shed, she proceeded with what was left of the broom to discourage the Bishop from the giving of any more such advice. A crowd of Mormon boys followed the portly ecclesiastic down the street as he fled from the wrath and the broom of the demonstrative Mrs. Jones. As to marriages already made, most of them will have to stand. As to new marriages, the system adopted by sister Jones will blot out all probability of them. No man wants his wedding ceremonies thus turned into a mixture of circus and funeral. No woman will want to become a bride when the bride of former years threatens her and their joint spouse with broom exercise. Let Mrs. Jones be encouraged, and the doom of Polygamy is sealed."

The following articles are from the "*Salt Lake Tribune*":—Raliegh is a Bishop and Town Councillor.—DIVORCE SUITS.

"A Tribune reporter had a talk with Mrs. Elizabeth Raleigh. The latter is an intelligent, fine looking lady, whose hair is but just tinged with gray, the combined result of years of life and Mormon wedded bliss.

"Mrs. Raleigh's story is like that of a great many of the women who have married into the Church. She first went into Mr. Raleigh's family as nurse to his former wife, who was upon a bed of sickness from which she never rose. She declined to accept the proposals of marriage when first made, but in obedience to the mandate of Heber C. Kimball, then one of President Young's counsellors, and to whom disobedience was worse than contempt of court, she at length acceded. Her honeymoon was not a particularly bright one, but she took upon herself the care of her husband's children by his first wife, and was a mother to them during many years that followed. She was allowed to work all she pleased, and sometimes more, from the beginning, and as stated in the complaint aided in every way to build up the fortune of her lord and master. As a specimen of what was expected of her, one instance may be related alone. Shortly after the marriage one of the cows died, down in a pasture lot in the edge of town, it was supposed from having in some way become poisoned. She was sent with a Danish boy to skin the dead body, which they did, and Mrs. Raleigh carried the hide to the house over her shoulders, her husband, meantime, standing by with a linen duster on and walking cane in his hand, superintending the work.

"In the course of time new wives were added to the household, the number eventually reaching eight, and at one period six of them occupying one house, and working and eating together in one small room, which served as kitchen, dining-room, sitting-room and parlor. Each had a separate sleeping apartment. They were all expected to earn a living, and if they wanted anything special in the way of clothing, etc., they bought it themselves from money made at washing or otherwise. The head of the household bought his supplies by the quantity, and kept them under lock and key, dealing them out with a sparing hand. He was suspicious always that his wives were trying to rob him, and on one occasion, when he thought he missed a dress pattern off of a bolt of common heavy goods he searched the apartments of his wives, examining the bedticks, looking in small drawers that would not have contained the bulk of the dress, and when urged sarcastically by the plaintiff even peering into a pair of stockings which were hung up in the room. The plaintiff says the finest dress he ever gave her after their marriage was one of common material which would probably cost about a bit a yard now, ($12\frac{1}{2}$ cents or $6\frac{1}{4}$ d.

"As an evidence of the love felt for him by his children it is said that when he had been absent in England on a mission and was returning, they saw him, and one of the boys exclaimed 'there comes that old scoundrel,' whereupon they all hastened to conceal themselves. He was called by some less tender and respectful names at other times and all in all his life as a husband and father is not a happy one judging by the respect inspired in his family."

"ROUGH ON POLYGAMOUS WIVES AND CHILDREN."

"And the defendant further answering alleges, That at the town of Kirtland, in the State of Ohio, heretofore to wit, on the 10th day of January, 1834 this defendant being then and there an unmarried man, was duly and lawfully married to Mary Ann Angel, by a minister of the gospel who was then and there by the law of said State authorized to solemnize marriage, and that the said marriage was then and there fully consummated, and the said Mary Ann Angel, who is still living, then and there became, and ever since has been and still is, the lawful wife of this defendant.—*Extract from Brigham Young's amended answer in the Ann Eliza case.*

"At last we have something definite. The Prophet of the Lord has spoken; and says in unmistakable language, that Mormon 'plural women' are *not* legal wives—that 'Mary Ann Angel is his true and lawful wife,' and marriage with her a bar to any subsequent marriage. This Brigham Young has said and sworn to in his amended answer to Ann Eliza. Brigham admits himself to be a coward, and though his money is not in danger, his money is, and he coolly throws his religion and plural wives overboard to save his cash."

"A short time since a Saint was cut off from the Church, his offence consisting in setting aside a plural without procuring a divorce. 'Why should I pay 10 dollars for a divorce?' the thrifty Saint enquired of this writer. 'I wasn't legally married to the woman, and I could give her just as good a divorce as the President could.' His 'divorce' consisted in turning the unhappy creature out o' doors. But what is this but concubinage?

"When the peerless Ann Eliza sued Brigham Young for divorce, the disingenuous man of God set up for an answer that he was not married to her, his connubial relations with his first and legal wife being still undissolved. When Apostle Cannon was charged with polygamy before a committee of the House of Representatives, he solemnly declared that he was not offending against morality or living in violation of any law of God or man.

"These facts show that there is neither sacredness nor binding force in the celestial wifery of these lustful Saints, when the admission of such a relation stands in the way of profit or preferment."

"The wealthy head of the Mormon Church in Utah, has about as effective a way of ridding himself of obnoxious wives, as that of Henry the Eighth, of England, albeit it is not quite so summary. Starvation is Brigham's favorite mode of terminating his polygamous entanglements; the slow, agonizing, and certain method of murdering the poor slaves of whose faded charms he so readily tires. Thus there is one creature, the oldest, and only lawful wife of this monster, Mary Ann Angell, now in the seventy-fourth year of her age, whose vitality has withstood the tyranny of the harem for half a century, and she still lives, a reproach to the system which has degraded her condition to that of serf and drudge. This victim of oppression has recently been assigned a cold and cheerless shelter in the old school house behind the seraglio; one end of that dilapidated structure having been partitioned off like a stable, or a stall for a cow! Miserably furnished, and in no way a comfortable habitation for a person of any age, that dreary tenement is the abode of Brigham Young's lawful wife, the mother of three of his sons and two daughters. But this is the Kingdom of God, in which women are taught to bear their crosses of shame for the glory that is to come hereafter. The Prophet says so, whenever he leads a fresh victim to the closet of concupiscence. We make bold to suggest a visit to the venerable occupant of that dismal prison, from our kind hearted Executive. He will find there a scene to excite him to the deepest sympathy."

"The *Inter-Ocean* quotes the words of one of Brigham Young's daughters: 'My father, prophet, though you call him, broke many a woman's heart. If it required of me to break as many hearts and ruin as many women as my father did, I should go to perdition before I would go back into the Church. A religion which breaks women's hearts and ruins them is of the devil. That's what Mormonism does. Don't talk to me of my father,' and concludes that 'Honor thy father' does not seem to be in the creed of Mormonism, and does not wonder that it is not. Nobody does. The usages of the sect takes from young girls all purity of thought, and when that is accomplished what room is there for self-respect or respect for others? The inhabitants of Mohammedan countries manage affairs with much more care than they are managed in Utah. There is no such promiscuous living as abounds in the two-roomed harems of Utah, but even in those countries there is so little faith in the virtue of women that they are perpetually watched, and never permitted to appear unvailed in public. The customs of the Mormon Church tend directly to break down all a young girl's ideas of the sanctity of chastity." [All these quotations are from *The Salt Lake Tribune*, remember.]

"One day the Prophet said to the widow Baird, 'Now there is Brother Pierce; he wants a wife, and you want SOMEBODY TO SAVE AND EXALT YOU in the eternal worlds. Sister Susannah; I will speak to Brother Robert about it.' The result was, in the course of a few days, Elder Pierce, aged about seventy-five years, led the blushing widow to the altar, in the House of the Lord, where they were sealed up to life everlasting. Moved by the Spirit of his faith to chastise his better half occasionally, and not being content to make her labor in the harvest field like a man, he would heap insult upon injury by calling her a '—— old hell hound.' The elder would caress his wife with a hoe handle, as he did his cows, and on one occasion he knocked her teeth out and bloodied her nose. This conduct was continued until in July, 1875, when the elder punished her with a chair. Forbearance ceased to be a virtue, and MRS. PIERCE CALLED UPON HER PROPHET being full of the devil, to complain. After relating her story, interspersed with tears, Brigham feelingly said: 'Well, Sister Pierce, what did you come into the kingdom for? It is your duty to bear with your husband, you are his, and he has a right to do as he pleases with you.' But this was the kind of sympathy she was not looking for, and she told the Prophet so, whereupon he asked: 'How much property did you take to Brother Pierce?' She replied, 'I took some furniture; three chairs and—' 'You had three chairs, did you?' said Brigham cutting her off short; 'well, Sister Susannah, take your three chairs across the street and sit down in them until you are satisfied, and if you don't feel like obeying, do as you please, and you will GO TO HELL IN A SUN-BONNET.'

"She went home, which came the nearest to following out the last part of Brigham's instructions of any course she could pursue. Elder Pierce continued his abuse for another year, until finally, he drove her out of the house and forbade her ever to return."

"EDS. TRIBUNE. Another scandalous polygamic affair has happened in this city. The man has had five wives. His first wife died leaving several children. He then married again. This one left him. He took a third, who bore him more children. He then left her and she had to support her family as best she could. The poor woman worked and washed and almost went out of her mind, living in a log hut without care or comfort. Her husband then married a mother who had two young daughters. In a short time he began to tease the wife for the oldest child and she and her daughter had no peace until they both consented. When she attained the age of fourteen he took her through the sink hole, (Endowment House). It was not long before he began to cast loving winks at the other daughter and commenced to woo her. She had no more comfort day or night until she left her step-father and her brother-in-law, and married a young man. Her sister has lived a life of misery and wretchedness in a log cabin with her mother and the two families, their beds being in the same room and standing foot to foot. One night, after they had retired to bed, the old man talked to the mother, thinking the young wife asleep. Her faults were the subject of the conversation, the old man even calling her a prostitute. She heard the whole of the conversation. In the morning she wrote a note.

"JOHN ANDREWS: I am going to leave you and shall never again be your wife, nor any other man's concubine. It will be no use for you to follow after me, for I shall never return to be abused by you. My cup of sorrow is full."

"This she placed under her pillow and left the following morning. Her mother, the other wife, started in pursuit, but returned without finding the object of her search. The Mormons are trying to create the impression at home and abroad that the grease vats of Zion are no longer used and that polygamous marriages are no longer in fashion in the Kingdom of God on Earth. The smoothest liars are not to be trusted. The concubine factory is kept as busy as ever, and not a Thursday passes but numbers of these marriages are consummated.

"Last Thursday Bishop Davidson of the Third Ward in Logan, took a concubine in the person of Miss McNeil. The girl is nineteen years old, and has become the sealed mistress of the Mormon lecher in spite of the protests of the first and only wife. In the last three months in the Fifth Ward of the same place, four of these illegal alliances have taken place, and it is safe to say fifty have occurred in Logan within the last six months, and still our 'greatest Government in the world' does nothing to prevent them.

LOGAN, April 11th, 1881. AMERICAN CITIZEN."

"There is a Danish Saint at Spanish Fork, named John Hanson, who recently married two pretty Scandinavian girls who came over with the last cargo of immigrants that arrived in Utah, about two months since. This last addition to the Danish harem makes ten concubines that this old brute has, and, it is said, he works the whole gang in the fields while he goes around, like an overseer, well dressed, and well cared for. This old reprobate Hanson makes his ten wives work like beasts in the fields while he roams at large in high clover.

"Ten wives! And yet there are people who think the late cut in the *Police Gazette*, styled 'Mormonism Uncovered,' was an exaggeration; it was only too true."

[The Police Gazette reproduced W. Jarman's Illustrated Lectures for the information and amusement of its numerous readers.]

DWELLING TOGETHER IN UNITY.

"Among the 'infamous libels' charged against this godless sheet, is branding the issue of these illicit unions with illegitimacy. A short time since a knock down occured in a prominent Mormon store in town arising from two polygamous sons branding each other with bastardy.

"Those who know Mormonism best have predicted that the greatest enemies to polygamy will be its own offspring.

"William Jennings has boasted that as Mormons, his has been a happy household. His children, he says, live happily together, and all is lovely where once polygamy reigned. We do not doubt Brother Jennings' word; but if the rumour that reaches us be true, then his statement is incorrect. In the store on Monday evening, we are told that two of Brother Jennings' sons illustrated that unanimous spirit that invariably follows polygamy. Tom

Jennings, it seems, who is son of the first wife, called his half brother, Frank, a bastard. This was resented by a slap in the face, and the *happy* children went at it just like Gentile boys. The clerks separated them, and we presume happiness reigns in that home once more."

[This is the same Jennings mentioned in the chapter of what I suffered, &c.]

Correspondence, Tribune, November 1, 1880.

"Sunday the Bishop gave vent to the most reviling words, and the most violent abuse; standing in the pulpit as an inspired man of God, claiming to be directed by God in speaking, and then using language that could only have originated in the mouth of the lowest women at Billingsgate. That deepest thorn in their sides, the Apostate, received his special attention. 'They ought to be kicked out of here. You are too kind and forbearing toward the miserable whelps.'

"A comparison was drawn between the God of the Latter-Day Saints and that of other sects. 'Of what value,' said the Bishop 'is the God of the sectarian world? They have not seen him for 1,800 years; they receive no revelations from Him; He cannot assist them in any way. Let them keep their God; we do not want Him. Our God is one that we can talk to, and that can be seen. Joseph Smith talked face to face with God; he was as familiar with all the personages mentioned in the Bible, from Adam down, as we are with one another. He could tell you the color of their hair, the sound of their voice, their height, and every particular concerning them. The Apostle Paul was a small man, about five feet high, with a large Roman nose, bow-legged, cross-eyed, and talked through his nose in a wheezing and most disagreeable manner.'

"Two of our most respectable ladies had the boldness to enter the house of worship with the 'elect,' thereby defiling the house of the Mormon God with their presence. They were made the objects of the most scurrilous taunts, obscene and vulgar, too indecent to appear in print; language that would not be listened to except by a people who have sunk so low in licentiousness and depravity, as to have parted with all that is pure and chaste, and with all those fine feelings which tend to refine and elevate mankind above the level of common brutes!   BEAUMANN. '

Two Polygamic wives were induced to visit the President's wife at Washington. Of course the most steadfast in the faith were selected, and they pleaded hard for Polygamy. Polygamic wives, when on a mission, are peculiarly fascinating, and even American Members of Parliament have their sympathies, or the system would have been played out long ago. I have repeatedly heard Brigham Young preach from the pulpit that he could buy every member of Congress, from the President down, that each had his price, and he knew their figures. With this digression, I continue to quote from *Salt Lake Tribune:*

"When the two hens, who are representing Polygamy in Washington, were about to take their departure thither, the boss cackler, Eliza Snow, quietly instructed them to wear the plainest kind of home-spun clothes so as to appear to represent, even in dress, the Mormon women. This did not quite suit their ideas of the matter, and they consequently appealed to the greatest and smoothest liar of the Church for advice. He said Sister Eliza was wrong about it, and directed the two hens to put on their best bib and tucker, as a representation of the poverty of the Saints would not tally with the declarations they would have to make concerning the comforts and luxury which surround the inmates of the Mormon harems. Hence the two birds referred to took their flight attired in borrowed silks and 'sich.'"

These "Hens" are also called "Female Roosters."

"The convention of Female Roosters, called to protest against the passage of the Christiancy Bill, now pending in Congress, took place yesterday. The indignant females assembled from all parts, and when they all got together and commenced to cackle, the sight was one of the most ridiculous ever beheld. The idea is both laughable and absurd, and when over a hundred of these chanticleers, with feathers ruffled, crow in concert in opposition to the passage of a just law, which in the end will be beneficial to them, the spectacle becomes too ridiculous for description. This convention lasted about fifteen minutes, and as each female talked during the whole time in utter disregard of what her neighbor was saying, a vast amount of business was transacted."

Ann Eliza Young has written to Mrs. President Hayes. She says:—
'Emmeline Wells and Zina Williams came with pathetic pleadings to touch your heart with the picture of what would be the cruel condition of Mormon women and children if the law against polygamy shall be enforced. But these two women came to you with FALSEHOODS IN THEIR MOUTHS. For this Polygamy has no brightness such as they described, no excellencies such as they claimed. I could show you a picture out of the polygamous lives of these very women which would make you shudder and turn heartsick. I knew both of them intimately for years, and know that they both have experienced their share of the evils of polygamy, and the envy and jealousy and heartburning which are inseparable from the system. Your late visitors, and George Q. Cannon, the husband of SIX LIVING WIVES deceive you when they assert that there is entire harmony in polygamous families. The assertion is absolutely false. There is not a polygamous husband in all Utah who does not have a favourite among his wives, whom he favors far above all the rest. His time, means, and affection are expended upon her while the other poor souls are left in loneliness and usually in destitution. This fact alone furnishes one of the strongest arguments against the system.

Nor did these women speak the truth when they said polygamy gives all children fathers and all women husbands.

As a rule the men care only for the children of the favorite and those of the other wives look wistfully or jealously on seeing all favors and caresses bestowed upon the others. This partiality awakens most bitter and evil feeling in the hearts of the slighted mothers and children, and fosters a feeling of superiority and arrogance in those who are favored. Can it be a holy system which fosters such vile feelings as this system of polygamy does? If propriety permitted, tales could be told that would turn every pure-minded person sick with horror, and fill them with pain to think 150,000 people were so deluded and demoralized.

Has this system kept women from the insane asylum and the suicide's grave? Has it made women cheerful, happy, healthful wives and mothers, and kept despair and utter haplessness from creeping into their hearts and faces? To these questions I can say no, a thousand times, and know that what I say is true in God's sight. It has UTTERLY CRUSHED THE LIVES and happiness, and broken the hearts of thousands of women, as I can speak from personal knowledge, having barely escaped being one in the general ruin.

She concludes, polygamy desolates every home which it enters, and surely it will neither be improper nor unwise for you to exert your influence against that vast and increasing crime. It is opposed to all that you prize in domestic and social life; it makes the civilized Christian home impossible. Even if you can only do but little, though you can only speak words of sympathy, such words will speedily be wafted westward to thousands of aching hearts and will be refreshing as the dew of morning to many a weeping Hagar, wandering in worse than desert lands.

I am, dear madam, respectfully yours, MRS. ANN ELIZA YOUNG.
(19th wife of Brigham Young.")

Here I must give entire, as it appeared in the *Salt Lake Tribune* after I left Utah. "A FIRST WIFE'S STORY." "HEARTS BROKEN," AND YET LIVE ON.

"EDS. TRIBUNE, I should like to tell, through the columns of your paper, the sad story of my life, if you will permit me to do so without betraying my identity. I do not wish to do that because I am still a Mormon, at least I am bound to the Mormon Church by the innumerable ties of kindred and the friendships and associations of many years, and at my time of life I should find it hard to break them. As to my identity it does not much matter any way, for it may be merged in that of hundreds of other Mormon women in Utah whose history is perhaps more pitiable than mine.

"More than 25 years ago, when I was a bright-eyed, round-cheeked girl of eighteen, I gave my hand in marriage to the only man I ever loved. Ah! if I could only then have looked down the long vista of troubled years to the cruel ending. But I could not; what young girl can, as she stands upon the threshold of that awful mystery which marriage makes a reality. For more than 20 years I bore the burden of motherhood; the little ones came thick and fast, but with a patience which love makes possible I bore the oft repeated pangs of maternity, and as I laid each new-born baby in my husband's arms, and saw his smile of pleasure that 'another jewel had been added to his crown,' I thanked my God that I could thus give evidence of the love I bore him. From out the very depths of unearthly agony I gave his children being, and then through the long tedious nights for weeks and months that followed the birth of each new little life I lay with my baby at my breast, nursing away my health and strength, while my husband slept peacefully beside me, dreamlessly indifferent to my tired nights of broken slumber and weary unrest; or if he gave it one thought, it was to satisfy his conscience with the assurance that 'woman is formed for the burdens she is to bear.' Oh men! men! do you not know that in the next life, at the very judgment of God you must answer for the lives of the women you have murdered through your ungoverned lust, because physically, on the one hand, and some form of marriage, on the other, have made you the master? And does the reality in this world of a woman's life-long love and devotion weigh nothing against the expected joys of a possible Heaven hereafter? It seems not, in our creed at least, for like Henry the Eighth, the Mormon policy is 'Sacrifice the mothers if it must be, but give us children.' For more than 20 years I bore him children, watched over and tended them in infancy and illness, taught them to be pure and good, worked and toiled that house and little ones might be always bright and sweet for my husband's home-coming; struggled with a patient energy born of love, to make it the one spot on earth fairest and dearest to which my husband's and children's hearts might always turn with a thrill of pride and a feeling of sweet restfulness. Upon the altar of his desires I sacrificed my will. I saw myself grow worn and haggard and old before my time. I saw the roses fade from my cheeks and the gold of my hair turn gray, and if, as I watched these signs of approaching unloveliness, a fear crept into my heart I stifled it with the trust that they might only render me more dear to the man in whose service I had received them.

"At last the burden of maternity was lifted from my tired shoulders: the children were no longer little ones, but were fast approaching man's estate and blooming girlhood, and I felt I might now begin to enjoy that perfect rest and quiet which very many years of servitude and devotion had won me. At last, after the turbid turmoil, would come the sweet peace for which I had so often longed, and which would now be made doubly dear to me by my husband's love and tenderness. But alas for the security of Mormon wifehood! The dark shadow which forever clouds our life with an inspoken fear, may at any moment assume the tangible shape of a demon and shatter at once blow all our hopes of happiness. And it came to me. At last the fear was to become for me an awful living reality. It came to me one bright morning when I was so placidly happy—when my heart and life seemed in such accord with nature's sunshine and gladness. I was alone in my cosy sitting room; It was very quiet and very pleasant there. My hands had dropped the piece of sewing with which they had been busy and lay idly folded on my lap; an unspoken prayer of gratitude was in my heart. My trials were over—my toil was ended now, for the strong arms of my brave boys and sweet girls were busy even then lifting the burdens from mine.

"The door opened softly and my husband came in. Although always a good, kind husband, his manner upon this morning seemed full of unusual warmth and tenderness as he sat down beside me and taking my poor worn hand in both his own, essayed to talk with a degree of cheerfulness he evidently did not feel, for even as he smiled a troubled look was on his face. A look, perhaps, of pity for the victim about to be sacrificed upon the altar of an unmerciful faith. Then gently, ah, so gently, he dealt the blow which left in place of a heart the dull aching thing I have since carried in my bosom. I had been to him a good and faithful wife, and we had been very happy together he said, but I was no longer young, I could give him no more children and he felt it a duty, which he owed God, to take another and a younger woman that the measure of our glory might be full in the celestial kingdom hereafter. More, much more he said, but the words were empty air. I only felt the reality, the awful, naked, cruel reality. This then was the man for whose sake agony had been a joy, servitude a pleasure, and sacrifices as nothing. This, then, was my reward a—*it may be the reward of any faithful Mormon wife.* The reward which a hellish, diabolical creed makes passable. I did not cry out, I did not faint, I did not even weep in the extremity of my awful pain. I only felt the consciousness that by one swift stroke of the hand that should have shielded me, my life-long love was turned to bitter loathing; the fruit of a life's devotion had turned to ashes on my thirsting lips. MY TRUST IN A GOD WHO COULD THUS SCOURGE ME WAS SHAKEN, AND MY FAITH IN A CREED THAT DEMANDED IT WAS SMITTEN. I was passive under the blow, for struggle as I might it would avail me nothing. And then the wish was in his heart, since I could no longer serve him, I stand aside and give to a younger and perhaps fairer woman my place as sovereign wife and mother, and did not my own and his religion sanction his right to make this demand and teach me to obey it. I could have rebelled surely, but would only have brought discord and contention to the only dear ones left me now, my children. My burdens had been many, and this last one, though heavier than all, I would bear in silence for their sakes. For the completion of my misery I had not long to wait. The fair young wife was soon found and brought home, and for her so young and fair, deserving a better fate, I wept the tears I could not weep for myself. Bound like me by the fetters of an unmerciful creed she had usurped in good faith the place of a dethroned wife and mother.

"'HOW LONG, OH HOW LONG, IN THIS LAND OF BOASTED FREEDOM, SHALL SUCH THINGS BE POSSIBLE?' IS THE DUMB CRY WRUNG FROM MANY A TORTURED HEART IN UTAH? TOWARD THE NOBLE MEN AND WOMEN WHO, LIKE YOURSELVES, ARE MAKING EARNEST EFFORTS IN OUR BEHALF, THE HEARTS OF HUNDREDS OF MORMON WIVES GO OUT DAILY WITH A PRAYER OF GRATITUDE AND THANKSGIVING. THOUGH OUR LIPS SEEM DUMB WE GIVE YOU A SILENT GOD SPEED—SPEED, OH SPEED THE DAY WHEN OUR CHAINS ARE BROKEN AND WE ARE FREE. COME SOON AS IT MAY, FOR SUCH AS I IT WILL BE TOO LATE; BUT FOR OUR PURE UNSULLIED DAUGHTERS WE MAY YET HOPE DELIVERANCE IS POSSIBLE.

Very respectfully yours,
MORMON WOMAN AND WIFE OF A POLYGAMIST.
SALT LAKE CITY, Feb. 24, 1881."

[I have brought out these passages prominently in order to show English women, who form the largest number of victims, should any after this be tempted to go to Utah, what a God forsaken "Hell upon Earth it is;" and all will agree with me on reading the above pathetic story that the title of this book is not at all too strong.]

"To domineer and to control, Both o'er the body and the soul
Is the most perfect discipline, Of Church rule, and by right divine."
Hudibras.

"Judge Boreman says:—Polygamy or bigamy is a crime that is very prevalent throughout the Territory. Its polluting effects are seen on every side. The children of said marriages are generally growing up as wild animals, without training, instruction or parental care. It is, of course, utterly impossible, except in isolated cases, for one father to look after the training of children separated and in various families, and there is generally little or no effort made to look after them. The consequences are seen all over the Territory, that polygamy in every phase of its character is degrading and beastly. It drags men down to the level of the beast.

"Woman is placed in the same social position. She is looked upon as a drudge and slave, fit only to perform the hardest work and to gratify the slavish passions of those to whom she believes herself married.

"She never hears the endearing name of wife, but always hears the cheerless title of 'my woman.' She knows nothing of love and the charms of home are strangers to her. No section of the United States is filled with people so negligent as are the families in Utah; vice is very prevalent and general degradation everywhere marks the footsteps of this loathsome crime.

"Every community has numerous persons living in polygamy, and the leaders, nearly all guilty of this crime, persistently urge their deluded followers into committing the same degrading offence. Yet these very men will tell the world that they are law-abiding citizens! Such falsehoods are but too common, and men do not even hesitate to perjure themselves in regard to this offence."

"The condition of Josephine Taylor, who recently attempted to escape from the "Prophets" harem, is one of hopeless insanity. There seems to be no reason to question the cause of her demented condition. We spoke in the early history of her runaway escapade, of her unhappiness caused by a rigid observance of the tenets of which her father is the great exponent. It will be remembered that Josephine was at one time engaged to Thomas C. Griggs, one of the Clerks in the Co-op., but that the engagement was broken when she found he contemplated marrying another woman at the same time. Josephine is represented to have been a cultured and modest lady, but notwithstanding her faith in the dogmas of the Church she hesitated not to decide on the side of decency when this foul step to bigamy was proposed. Her love for Griggs was intense, and it was that love that drove her mad. She has at repeated times attempted to break away from her home. Her last endeavor was made on a recent evening, when, seizing a butcher knife, she rushed down the street swearing vengeance on the Co-op. clerk whom she said she would kill. Her condition is a splendid commentary on the beauties of polygamy.

"Griggs has married two wives, and if Tom Griggs insists, as he has hitherto done, that he never married No 2, he should be discharged from the Co-op. and busy himself testifying to the peculiarity of this people. Mrs. Griggs No. 2 will, however, call herself by Tom's last name while the little fellow will possibly take both his names. He will be handy too in case the bill passes Congress making children evidence of a polygamous marriage."

"John Cheshire, the polyg. is in a nice pickle. The old coon had to play it very fine to procure his polygamous wife, the courting being carried on very slyly. The legal wife was invited to spend an afternoon at the house at which Lizzie Turner was working, and was afterwards urged to remain at tea. She excused herself, saying she was compelled to visit her sister-in-law, after which she would return. She did so and found the old sinner of 60 years with his withered arms thrown around the blushing damsel of 19 years, and as might be supposed No. 1 was somewhat astonished. She remarked to her spouse that it was rather queer, the way he was holding Lizzie, and thereupon he arose and said he wished 'to introduce Mrs. Cheshire No. 2.' It was then the time No. 1 burst into tears, saying she would'nt have cared if he had married an older woman, but she didn't think the difference of ages warranted such a union. Afterwards when Lizzie went to her so-called husband's home, she was very summarily ejected by the indignant sons who said some rough things about the old man and called celestial marriage a name which 'will send them to hell across lots' as the Sainted Brigham used to remark. Lizzie left, but the old man felt left also, and between the action of his sons, the fear of the law and the publicity of the affair, he feels as though something was out of joint."

"The course of true love did not run smooth with a devoted couple on Sunday, and the truculent god Mars interfered with the rites of the unzoned goddess Venus, very much to the discomfiture of her votaries. A pious Saint living just outside the city, thought to secure his future exaltation by taking to himself another wife, and on the day above named, introduced his latest spouse to his household. Then arose the music. Wife No. 1 was seized with a sudden dislike for her rival in celestial altitude, and she went for the blushing damsel *vi et armis*. Benedict tried persuasion, but this had no soothing effect upon the irate female; he then tried a little burnt powder. Drawing his revolver he let fly at his rebellious wife (whom Jo. Smith's revelation says shall be destroyed,) and bored a hole through her arm. This silenced all opposition; the wounded woman sunk into a chair, faint and bleeding, and Wife No. 2 was inducted to the honors of matrimony with this example of her husband's force of character to cheer her on her way through life."

Extracts from Sermons.

The Tribune being a secular paper perhaps my Christian friends will prefer that I quote from a few sermons; therefore I introduce "Apostle" Kimball's sermon published in the Mormon Church Organ, *The Deseret News*, vol. 6. On page 291, it says:—

"I have no wife or child that has any right to rebel against me. If they violate my laws and rebel against me, they will get into trouble just as quickly as though they transgressed the counsels and teachings of Brother Brigham. Does it give a woman a right to sin against me because she is my wife? No; but it is her duty to do my will as I do the duty of my Father and my God. It is the duty of a woman to be obedient to her husband, and unless she is, I would not give a damn for all her queenly right and authority, nor for her either, if she will quarrel and lie about the work of God and the principles of plurality.

"A disregard of plain and correct teachings is the reason why so many are dead and damned and twice plucked up by the roots, and I would as soon baptize the devil as some of you." Kimball preached also as follows:—

"That woman who will sit in the corner and grunt, grunt, grunt, until she is all grunt together, and the bumps of grunt stick out in every direction, and cannot move her little finger to do one good action to build up God's kingdom, or assist her husband in doing it, will not be an heir to the inheritance.—*Journal of Discourses*, vol. 6, p. 325.

From "Apostle" Snow's sermon, *Deseret News*, vol. 1, p. 25, "You show me a man who is not selfish, you will show me no man at all; show me a woman who is not selfish, you will show me an idiot, and one who knows not the way to happiness or a crown of glory."

Says Brigham in one of his sermons:—"Whether the doctrine of polygamy is true or false is none of your business. We have as good a right to adopt tenets in our religion as the Church of England, or the Methodists, or Baptists, or any other denomination have to in theirs. Our doctrine is a Bible doctrine, a patriarchal doctrine, and is the doctrine of the gods of eternity, and of the heavens, and was revealed to our fathers on the earth, and will save the world at last, and bring us into Abraham's bosom, *if we ever get there*" (the italics are my own.)—*Journal of Discourses*, vol. 2, p. 187.

"If we ever get there," comports with the Mormon Prophet Smith's dying words, "God have mercy upon me, IF THERE IS ANY GOD." I will add, the Mormon Leaders are Atheists and Sceptics in every sense of the word, although many of the dupes are truly sincere and would die for the Mormon religion.

The Mormon Church Organ *The Deseret News*, vol. 6, p. 291, contains one of Brigham Young's sermons from which I extract the following:—" I would not have this people faultless. I have many a time in this stand dared the world to produce as mean devils as we can; we can beat them at anything. We have the greatest and smoothest liars in the world, the cunningest and most adroit theives, and any other shade of character that you can mention.

"We can pick out elders in Israel right here who can beat the world at gambling; who can handle the cards; can cut and shuffle them with the smartest rogue on the face of God's footstool. I can produce elders here who can shave their smartest shavers, and take their money from them. We can beat the world at any game.

"We can beat them because we have men here that live in the light of the Lord; that have the holy priesthood, and hold the keys of the kingdom of God. But you may go through all the sectarian world, and you cannot find a man capable of opening the door of the kingdom of God to admit others in. We can do that. We can pray the best, preach the best, and sing the best. We are the best looking and finest set of people on the face of the earth; and they may begin any game they please, and we are on hand, and can beat them at anything they have a mind to begin. They may make sharp their two-edged swords, and I will turn out the elders of Israel with greased feathers, and whip them to death. We are not to be beat. We expect to be a stumbling block to the whole world, and a rock of offence to them."

I extract from another of the same "Prophet's" sermons, published in the *Journal of Discourses*, vol. 6, p. 176:—"We have a goodly share of the genius, talent, and ability of the world; it is combined in the elders of this church and in their families. And if the Gentiles wish to see a few tricks, we have 'Mormons' that can perform them. We have the meanest devils on the earth in our midst, and we intend to keep them, for we have use for them; and if the Devil does not look sharp, we will cheat him out of them at the last.

"We are the smartest people in the world. But look out that the children of this world are not smarter than the children of light. I say that they shall not be; for we will beat them in every good thing, the Lord and the brethren being our helpers. The Lord bless you! Amen."

From the Mormon "Book of Revelations," section 22, par 4, we learn that :—"Now, I, the Lord, am not well pleased with the inhabitants of Zion, for there are idlers among them; and their children are also growing up in wickedness."

"There are many who swear occasionally; others get drunk, &c."— Brigham's Sermon, *Journal of Discourses*, vol. 6, p. 347.

"You design evils in your neighbourhoods, in your families, and in yourselves. The disposition to produce evil, to annoy, to disturb the peace of families, neighbours and society is produced by the power of the enemy over the flesh, through the fall."—Brigham's Sermon, *Jour. of Dis.* vol. 2 p. 3 30.

" We believe in dancing, it is useful to the limbs, the joints, and to the spirits as well."—President Young's Sermon, *Jour. of Dis.* vol. 6, p. 244.

" I had not a chance to dance when I was young, and never heard the enchanting tones of the violin, until I was 11 years old. I shall not subject my children to such a course of unnatural training, but they shall go to the dance read novels, and do anything else that will tend to expand their frames, add fire to their spirits, and make them feel free and untrammelled in body and mind. I mean to learn all that is in heaven, earth and hell." *Ibid* vol. 2. p. 94.

" We are of the House of Israel, of the royal seed, of the royal blood."—

" When the Lord pours out the Holy Ghost upon a Gentile he will have spasms, and you would think that he was going to have fits."

" Joseph Smith said that the Gentile blood was actually cleansed out of their veins, and the blood of Jacob made to circulate in them."—*Ibid*, p. 270.

" The ten tribes will also come, and they will be baptized and ordained under the hands of the Mormons, who bear the Holy Priesthood on the earth."—" Apostle " Woodruff, *Journal of Discourses*, vol. 2, p. 200.

" If brother Brigham was one particle better man than he is, he could not stay among us, he would have to leave us."—" Apostle " Smith, *Journal of Discourses*, vol. 2, p. 218.

" When I know that I am doing just as I am told by him who is placed to lead this people, I am then a happy man. I am filled with peace, joy, and pleasure."—" Apostle " Kimball, *Ibid*, p. 151.

" I look for the Lord to use His whip on the refractory son called " Uncle Sam," and make him dance nimbly to the tune of 'Oh! Oh!!' I expect John Bull will get the next whipping. I rejoice in the Lord my God, and feel happy in my spirit that the work of God is prospering by the progress of revolution, and the deeper corruption of the press and the people."

" I rejoice exceedingly that the work of God is progressing so rapidly upon the face of all the world. For war and bloodshed are just as necessary and just as much the work of God as repentance and baptism for the remission of sins." " Apostle " Grant's Sermon, *Journal of Discourses*, vol. 2, p. 148-9.

[This " Apostle " was also Speaker of the Mormon House of Parliament.]

" God is material; Christ is material; Angels are material; men are material; the universe is material. Nothing exists which is not material."—*Millenial Star*, vol. vi., p. 19.

" God cannot occupy two distinct places at once."—*Ibid*, p. 20.

" If God should reveal his will to Brigham concerning me, it would be, ' Let my servant Heber do all things whatsoever my servant Brigham shall require at his hands for this is the will of his Father in heaven.' If that is the will of God concerning me, concerning you it is the same.—" Apostle " Heber C. Kimball, *Jour. of Dis.* Vol. 2, p. 153.

" Now suppose my wives and my children would take the same course to please me, and be subject to me as I am to Brigham, would there be any sorrow, or confusion, or broils ? No, there would be no sorrow, there would be no blues in my family," *Ibid*, p. 153.

" I am never blue when I do Brigham's will; but when I do not do it, I grow blue. It always makes my family feel blue when they will not do as I wish them ; and I suppose it affects every family so in this town."

" I am going to deed all my property to the Church ; my wives and my children shall not have it to quarrel about, but I will deed it to the Church, and the Church shall dictate them from this time henceforth and forever."

" That is just as I feel; for if I put myself in the Church, and everything I have, and deed it all over to the Church, then I belong to the Church with all I possess." *Ibid*, p. 153.

" Well, then, put your inheritance into a situation that it will never be divided, and there will be no quarelling about it." *Ibid*, p. 154.

"What do you say to our being one, and clinging together? I speak to the brethren: I do not expect any woman to stick to me only my wives."

"If the women of every man stick to him, then we shall all be stuck together, and live together, and reign together, and get rich together, and increase together, and build up together, and be as one man in all things."

"There are some ladies who are not happy in their present situations; but that woman who cannot be happy with one man, cannot be happy with two."

"You know all women are good, or ought to be. They were made for angelic beings, and I would be glad to see them act more angelic in their behaviour."

"When you see a woman with ragged skirts, you may know she wears the unmentionables, for she is doing the man's business, and has not time to cut off the rags that are hanging around her. From this time henceforth you may know what woman wears her husband's pants. May the Lord bless you, Amen." *Ibid*, p. 154.

"A Mormon 'Apostle's' words are words of eternal life and salvation, just as much so as any written revelations contained in the Bible, Book of Mormon and Doctrines and Covenants." Brigham Young's Sermon, *Deseret News* extra.

From "Apostle" Hyde's Sermon, "If a man take unto himself many wives, it is all right with me, and with God." *Jour. of Dis*. Vol. 2, p. 208.

[Please remember that these "Apostles" are Members of Parliament.]

"If you outsiders marry a Mormon woman, with your eyes open to that fact, I cannot promise that your happiness with her will always be uninterrupted." *Ibid*, p. 208.

"There can be no fellowship between Mormon and Christian. They cannot exist under the same social system." *Ibid*, p. 207.

"On Sunday, brothers Kimball and Grant spoke very plainly and pointedly in relation to the intercourse of the Saints with the world, * * * Several felt insulted, and as the Indians say, 'thrown away' Brothers Grant and Kimball were only God's looking glasses." *Ibid*, p. 207. [Moral decency forbids my quoting all that these "Brothers" as "God's looking glasses" reflected, or held forth to the people.]

"When Devils are in the house and you don't like them, cast them out." Apostle Grant, *Ibid*, p. 277.

"The Latter-day Saints believe differently from other folks, for their works are different, and their testimony is different." *Ibid*, p. 278.

"Close houses are injurious to the health; if our houses were every one of them levelled to the ground, and we were obldiged to live in our wagons and tents, the people would be healthier from year to year than they are now.

"I really have some idea of adopting the plan. Though you know what they say about me in the east, should I take my 90 wives and their children, (this is 29 years ago) with carriages and wagons enough to convey them, it would make such a vacuum here, and so many others would wish to go, that there would be no Salt Lake City. I think I will take a few of them, but I dare not take the whole, for if I did, they would then know how many wives I have got, and that would not do." *Ibid*, p. 283.

"I am going to explore in the mountains, and I invite you to go. Take your wives, but not your babies, unless you take cradles along to keep them quiet." *Ibid*, p. 284.

Having given this much from these "Sacred Discourses" I quote from B. G. FERRIS, Esq., late Secretary of State for Utah Territory, p. 249.

"The children are subject to a frightful degree of sickness and mortality. This is the combined result of the gross sensuality of the parents, and want of care toward their offspring. These saintly pretenders take as little care of their wives as of their children; and of both, less than a careful farmer would of his cattle; and nowhere out of the 'Five Points' in New York City can a more filthy, miserable, neglected-looking, and disorderly rabble of children be found than in the streets of Salt Lake City.

"The pollution of the Latter-day Polygamist is thorough and complete, mind and body. There is no degree of profanity and blasphemy that he can not compass with the coolness of an every-day occupation. Every thing sacred which he breathes upon or touches, is profaned and polluted, from the throne of the Eternal to the family altar, around which are usually garnered all the hopes and joys of Christian minds. All his doctrines are based on literalism and materialism—all his joys are carnal and selfish.

"The following, from a letter of W. W. Phelps to the New York Herald is quite popular with the Saints:—

"I think your one-wife system will sing as small as our racing Gilpins, or 'dirty cotton court.' Of two evils, a Mormon chooses neither, but goes in for all good and more good: which, if, as Solomon said, a good wife is a good thing, then the more you have the more good you have; so that when the suffering female kind over the great globe are acquainted with the fact that 'the daughters of kings are among the Lord's honorable wives in heaven' (Psalm xlv.), 'and on the right hand the queen in gold of Ophir,' you will hear of more honorable women clinging to the Mormon holy priesthood than you ever thought of, or a narrow-contracted Christian clergy drove into corruption by night-closetings because their deeds are evil."

[Printer, put in some stars here, and skip the next eight lines. It will never do for the readers of this book.]

* * * * * * * * *

[This is 'Judge Phelps' the Endowment House Devil, In his 'Almanacana' he says:—"God was married, or how could he beget his son Jesus Christ lawfully, and do the works of *his* father?"]

The Secretary of State continues:—"Their system of plurality has obliterated nearly all sense of decency, and would seem to be fast leading to an intercourse open and promiscuous as the cattle in the fields. A man living in common with a dozen dirty Arabs, whether he calls them wives or concubines, cannot have a very nice sense of propriety. It is difficult to give a true account of the effects which have resulted from this cause, and, at the same time, preserve decency of language. It is related of one of the English Georges, that, when he became old and sapless, a plump maiden was selected for his seasons of repose, and made to act the part of a warming-pan to his majesty. The Saints are progressive. Three in one bed sleep warmer than two, when wood is scarce and a kingdom is to be built up. Last year they seriously discussed the subject of introducing a new order into the Church, by which the wives of absent missionaries might be sealed to Saints left at home, under the plea that the important business of peopling the celestial kingdoms ought not to be interrupted. Practically, this would make no great difference, as the proxies now readily make their way into these half-deserted tenements.

"Brigham Young stated in the pulpit that the time might come when, for the sake of keeping the lineage of the priesthood unbroken, marriages would be confined to the same families; as, for instance, the son of one mother would marry the daughter of another by the *same father*. This fact was spoken of by so many persons as to preclude all reasonable doubt of its truth. Why should not the blood of the priesthood, like that of the Incas, be kept *pure?*

"A case shows at least an entering wedge for the introduction of this improvement upon the system. One Watt came over from England with his half-sister, and on the way they concluded to enter into some of the sublime mysteries of Mormonism. When they arrived at Salt Lake City, they repaired to the "Governor's house" to be sealed. The lady was fairer than any at that time in Brigham's collection, and he told Watt it would not do; that the time had not yet arrived when persons so nearly related could be married; but that he would seal her to himself. This was done; but Brigham, for some reason, like Henry the Eighth with Catherine of Cleves, became, in a day or two, sick of the new Sultana; sent for Watt; told him he had reconsidered the matter, and concluded, on the whole, that the original proposition might be safely acted upon. Brigham was thereupon duly divorced, and Watt married to his half-sister." [Who presented him with a young Watt, months before the time prescribed by law. "Seal" means marry]. I pass over the incestuous suggestions.

To continue quoting from Ferris:—"The truth is, their doctrine of the anterior existence of the spirits of men, so strenuously taught and extensively believed, has had a strong effect in obliterating the sentiment of female chastity. If the bodies of men are tabernacles for pre-existing spirits to enter into, it can matter but little by whom they are begotton. It becomes a matter of mechanical employment; and no matter how often the workmen are changed, so long as the article is properly manufactured. The chaste union of two minds in the conjugal relationship becomes thus a thing entirely unknown.

"The high-priest dignitaries of the Church are exceedingly skillful in procuring young girls for wives. They inculate the idea that elderly members, who have been tried and found faithful, are surer instruments of salvation than the young, who may apostatize. A great many young women are fooled into this bubbling and seething caldron of prostitution. Woodruff, one of the twelve apostles, has a regular system of changing his harem. He takes in one or more young girls, and so manages, after he tires of them, that they are glad to ask for a divorce, after which he beats the bush for recruits. He has just taken a fresh one, about fourteen years old, and will probably get rid of her in the course of the ensuing summer. These maneuvers are practiced more or less by the whole gang; the girls discarded by one become sealed to others, and so travel the entire rounds; and when they accomplish the whole circuit, and are ready to start anew, they have a profoundly "realizing sense" of female modesty, to say nothing of some of its adjuncts.

"These things are producing results in the very vitals of the Mormon community as frightful as the barking monsters in the bowels of Milton's portress to the infernal regions:
'About her middle round
A cry of hell-hounds, never ceasing, barked
With wide Cerberean mouths full loud, and rung
A hideous peal.'

"Young men, in a majority of cases, find it impossible to obtain even one wife, and run into excesses rivalling some of the choicest purlieus of Eastern cities. When the door of licensed indulgences is so widely thrown open to the elders, it is scarcely to be supposed that the young will look on with indifference; nor can it be surprising that the affair of Absalom and his father's concubines should be considered and acted upon by the youthful Saint as a fair precedent.

"Various apostates have disclosed the fact that among the mysteries of Mormonism is a degree into which the most favored ones are initiated, of which the following account is given:

"When an apostle, high-priest or elder conceives an affection for a female, and has ascertained her views on the subject, he communicates confidentially to the prophet his love affair, and requests him to inquire of the Lord whether or not it would be right and proper for him to take unto himself this woman for his spiritual wife. It is no obstacle whatever to this spiritual marriage if one or both of the parties should happen to have a husband or wife already united to them according to the laws of the land.

"The prophet puts this singular question to the Lord, and if he receives an answer in the affirmative, which is always the case when the parties are in favor with the prophet, the parties assemble in the lodge-room, accompanied by a duly authorized administrator, and place themselves kneeling before the altar. The administrator commences the ceremony by saying,

"'You separately and jointly, in the name of Jesus Christ, the Son of God, do solemnly covenant and agree that you will not disclose any matter relating to the sacred act now in progress of consummation, whereby any Gentile shall come to the knowledge of the secret purposes of this order, or whereby the Saints may suffer persecution, your lives being the forfeit.'

"Then comes a mock ceremony of marriage, after which—the parties leave with a firm belief, at least on the part of the female, in the sacredness and validity of the ceremonial, and consider themselves as united in spiritual marriage, the duties and privileges of which are in no particular different from those of any other marriage covenant."

Then the late Secretary of Utah adds: "The reader will naturally ask if this can be true. A residence of less than six months will be very apt to remove any doubts he may entertain on the subject. If the husband of a female Saint happens to be a Gentile, it is a great point with the Mormons to have her sealed in this way without his knowledge. Her prostitution is easily effected, inasmuch as she is made to believe that it is necessary to her salvation, all Gentile marriages being void.

"It is a nest of adders, of which the sting can no longer remain unfelt. In Utah, the effect of the plurality system is most severely felt by the first or real wife. That it should have been tolerated at all is only to be accounted for by the deep fanaticism and lamentably lax morality existing at all periods among the Saints.

"A *wife*, in Utah, can not live out half her days. In families where polygamy has not been introduced, she suffers an agony of apprehension on the subject which can scarcely be conceived, much more described. There is a sad, complaining, suffering look, obvious to the most ordinary observer, which tells the story, if there were no other evidence on the subject.

"In every instance where it has been introduced, it has totally destroyed all union of affection and interest previously existing. The wife has no further motive to labor and economize for the family, because she finds one or more intruders who have the right to share in the benefits of her exertions; and the concubine, for a similar reason, feels no interest and makes no effort. The wife hates them for interfering with her comforts, and estranging the affections of her husband; they on the other hand, hate the wife and each other, and the children of each other. The husband hates the wife on whose affections he has trampled, and over whom he has tyrannized, and hates each concubine, of whom he tires when a fresh one is introduced; and the children hate each other as cordially as a band of half-starved young wolves. It is hate, and strife, and wretchedness through the whole family circle. Hecate herself, in her deepest malignity, could not have devised a more effectual scheme to destroy the happiness of mankind. The husband, under the double influence of domestic discord and gross indulgence, loses his energy, becomes discouraged, sinks into the bloated, vulgar debauchee, and illustrates that

'Our pleasant vices are made the whips to scourge us.'

"In many families where there are as yet no concubines, the wife is anxious to remove from this valley of Sodom, as well on her own account as to save her young daughters from becoming the inmates of a priestly harem; and as she has it in her power to obtain a divorce at any time, it may seem strange that she should remain the inmate of such a domestic hell. But a divorce would be of no practical benefit to her. She would be compelled to separate from her children; and, as she is powerless to perform an overland journey of over a thousand miles, to bring herself within the protection of a civilized government, she must, of course, remain, and seek a precarious livelihood, under the discouraging pressure of Church vengeance.

"Any number of cases illustrative of the degrading licentiousness of the system, and of the brutality and wretchedness which it produces, might be mentioned. In a conversation with one of the missionaries (and, withal, a man of more than ordinary shrewdness), I asked him what the effect of the system was upon the domestic relations. 'Why,' said he, 'you must be aware that human nature among the first wives is opposed to it. When a man's wife gets a little old, and he takes a fancy to a young one, why, you know, the old one will feel jealous that she is to give way to the other; but it is the order of the Church, and she must submit to it.' This was accompanied with a sly leer, such as would have done credit to a satyr.

"A man, by the name of Eldridge, was living with much apparent happiness with his wife at Nauvoo, at the time of the great break up there. Emma Smith, the prophet's widow, had seen enough of Mormonism, and, having secured some property out of the general wreck, resolved to remain in the States. When the Saints were on the point of removing, Emma Smith advised Mrs. Eldridge not to follow her husband to the valley of Great Salt Lake; told her he would certainly go into the plurality order, and then she would be treated with neglect; that was the case with them all. Mrs. E. replied that her husband had promised her that he would never go into it; that they were attached to each other; and that she had the utmost confidence in him. They went on together to Salt Lake, and, in 1851, the predictions of Mrs. Smith were verified Brigham Young, for some reason or other, desired to involve Eldridge in the meshes of spiritual wife-ism, and repeatedly importuned him on the subject. Eldridge told him he was living very happily with his wife, and that to bring another into the family would almost kill her. Young replied that, if his wife was opposed to the order of the Church, 'the quicker she was damned the better.' He also stated, among other things, that he was about to go off on an exploring tour in the Territory with a party (naming some of them); that he and the rest intended each to take along a new wife; that he (Eldridge) had better do so too, and they would have 'a nice time of it.' Eldridge finally yielded, and so worked upon his wife as to compel her to give her consent to his being sealed to a miserable drab selected for this occasion. From this period he became a perfect brute in the treatment of his wife; turned her from the best room in the house to make room for his concubine; and she, thoroughly crushed and despairing, realizes that her once peaceful and happy home has been changed into a domestic hell. This is a fair history of the fate of the first wife."

[Eldridge has wives "scattered all over the blooming shop" and is "a perfect brute." Once when selling pictures I called at the house of one of his female "sleeping partners." Another woman, also illigitimately related to Eldridge, was there, and as these slaves never have any money, they offered some eggs to pay for a picture called "The Resurrection of Christ." While they were collecting the eggs Eldridge came in and raved out, "I'll kick you and your bastard Christ pictures out of here if you ain't off at once." As I left I heard his female "white slaves" "catching it," and thought what a pity they cannot also leave. Eldridge is principal director in Uncle Sam's Bank, and runs the "Lord's Store" in Salt Lake City, and holds the "Melchizedek Priesthood."]

"Instances of brutal insensibility on the part of the men are common, and excite but little attention. A man connected with the stage, having a number of wives, came home one evening from rehearsing his part, and found one of them dead. This trifling circumstance, however, did not in the least interfere with his engagement at the theatre; he performed his part that evening; buried his deceased wife the next day; and kept on at the theatre as though nothing extraordinary had happened.

"It may excite surprise that so many females can be found who are willing to be made the ready instruments of debauchery; but they are generally young, exceedingly ignorant, and are made to believe that their salvation depends upon it, and it is regarded as no disgrace in the community in which they live. This community is so completely isolated as to form a world by itself, and its habits and morals are borrowed from the cock-pit and third tier of more civilized regions. The greatest opposition comes from the first wives: there are instances in which they advocate it; but many of these are divorcés from the States, and are somewhat familiar with having 'things in common.'

"Many of the older sealed ones are women who have been seduced to leave their husbands and families. These, of course, become thorough-paced strumpets, and, when too old for use, are noted devotees. A fair type of this class is a Mrs. Cobb, whose race would embellish the pages of Peregrine Pickle. This woman was living in Boston with her husband and family when Brigham Young visited that city as a missionary. He was at that time a good-looking man, and Madam Cobb made up her mind that to aid Brigham in building up a celestial kingdom was far preferable to the humdrum of her domestic duties. She accordingly raced off, taking one of her children (a young girl), was divorced from her husband, and afterward duly sealed to Brigham. She was the reigning Sultana for a time, and queened it with a high hand; but he finally tired of her, and she is now a full blown devotee; talks solemnly of being sealed to Joseph Smith and other dead prophets; and tries hard, by the extravagance of her nonsense, to make herself a mother in Israel. Her daughter, in the mean time, has grown up handsome in face, and accomplished in the peculiar graces which belong to female Mormondom. The mother and daughter deal frequently in crimination and recrimination with each other, calling things by their right names in choice Billingsgate; and the parent is in a fair way of draining to the bottom that cup of bitterness which she has prepared for her own lips." [The daughter is now a plural wife of one of Brigham's sons, while the mother is anxious to be sealed to Jesus Christ; she has often expressed this desire, and I have heard it has been granted.]

Sorry I cannot quote more of Mr. Secretary Ferris. Harper Brothers, New York, are the publishers of his book "Utah and the Mormons."

"In Utah it is an easy matter to obtain a divorce; all the legal wife has to do is to swear that she cannot live in the conjugal relation in peace and union, and a decree *nisi* is pronounced by the Mormon Judge. The second wife's marriage being illegal is the more easily dissolved. She can he separated without legal proceedings. The Priesthood can dissolve whatever bonds exists in her case. The plural wife goes to the Prophet, complains of the 'shocking neglect' of her husband, and how he prefers the society of his other wife, and that he had stayed two or three days more with his favourite than he had with her, and '*she* is not going to stand it.' The Prophet instructs his clerk to 'make out the papers.' The dissatisfied wife signs them, and her marriage is dissolved. The husband is notified that he is 'wanted at the office.' In most cases the unfortunate husband is glad to be released from the turmoils of Polygamy, and hastens to the office, signs the papers, pays a fee of ten dollars (£2) to the clerk, rejoices in the glory of being once more a free man—'a one-wifed bachelor.'"

A peep at one of these *singular* papers that divorce *plural* wives is always interesting; hence I give one from Mrs. Stenhouse's book, which is from the original copy:—

"This is to certify that in the beginning of 1869, when I gave a bill of divorce to Sarah Ann Lowery, I gave to her for the good of her four

children the following property, viz. :—a parcel of land about nine acres enclosed all around with a house of two rooms and one cow and heifer.
WM. C. RITTER."

The English reader may consider this an abundant provision for the discarded wife. But bear in mind in America land is cheap, 160 acres are given by the Government, all we have to do is to settle upon it and improve it. We can also purchase an additional 160 acres at 5s. per acre. So that our friend who was so lavish with his nine acres, was actually parting with what cost him about £1. True it was now "enclosed all around with a house of two rooms and one cow and heifer." But what is this "house of two rooms" like? These "Houses" are generally huts built of mud, dried in the sun; a few branches or slabs are thrown over the top for a roof, and covered also with mud; the mud floor becomes dry and hard and wears well, a rough batten door and small hole for window completes this palatial residence. The "Grass widow" will have to work hard to sustain herself and her four children.

An Englishwoman told me her husband had married a widow and her daughter, a girl of fourteen, and they all lived a life of wretchedness in a log cabin. Once, in a blinding snow storm, I sought shelter in the first hut I came to. The door was opened by a poor sickly looking man. Here in a small mud hut this man lived with his two wives and families. There were two beds on one side, the foot of one close to the foot of the other, while underneath were trundle beds for the children. The mud walls were not plastered, and the ceiling was composed of bushes and brambles which were covered on the outside with mud. It was "a shelter from the stormy blast." Each wife had a baby in her arms, while 8 more children were crying with hunger. When the storm abated I was glad to leave.

I once saw a log cabin about 18 feet by 16, which sheltered the husband and five wives, I failed to find out how many children they had, only that one wife had seven: if all were equally prolific, five times seven is thirty-five. One look into that hovel was sufficient, the stench prevented me from entering: I could just discover among the dirt and filth a bed in each corner, and then considering this is the Bedroom, Dining-room, Kitchen and Scullery for five wives and families, please forgive me for coming away without making further explorations. I once visited a poor old English dame who held tenaciously to moral decency. She was in trouble, and as I was an Englishman she claimed my advice. She had reared a large family in England, but the Missionary had come with bright inducements. In "Zion" they could dwell serenely under their own vine and fig tree, the deserts were to blossom as the rose, and so much of the glory and beauty of this "New Jerusalem" was depicted, that they became enchanted, and she and her husband "gathered to Zion," leaving their family all married in England. The old couple by working hard in their old age had managed to build a small log cabin, and now the old man was counselled to take a young wife and raise up a new posterity upon the earth. He had lost all his children; they were back in "Wicked Babylon," and having had "the Gospel" preached to them and refused it, were eternally lost. He had informed the old dame of his intention to obey counsel and bring home a young bride. This was what she told me. I looked around the hut and intimated there was no room. "That's what I said," remarked the poor old soul. "He then proposed" she continued, "to put up another bed at the foot of mine, but I said No! if another bed goes up, mine comes down!" I assured her she was perfectly right, advised her to stick to it, and stick she did. But—ah—But. She was very soon in her grave; and now the "happy" old man rocks the cradle with spectacles on, and rejoices in being able to raise up a "Righteous Seed."

The Hand Book Publishing Co., Salt Lake City, has just issued, price 25 cents (1/-) "Hand Book on Mormonism." It is a compilation of hard facts, by "Gentiles," who have lived long enough in "Zion" to know whereof they speak. On page 88 is the following:—

"Mrs. H—— came to Utah a devout Mormon. When her husband decided to take another wife, she accompanied him to the Endowment House, as the cruel law of 'celestial marriage' commands, but when Brigham Young asked the prescribed question:

"Do you give this woman to your husband, even as Sarah gave Hagar to Abraham?" she answered: 'Yes and No.'

"What do you mean by such an answer?" the Prophet demanded.

"I mean yes, if he cannot go into the presence of his God without this sacrifice on my part; but if I consult my own heart, *No*, No! a thousand times NO!"

"She says, 'On my way home from the Endowment House, I fainted three times; yet determined to do my whole duty. I welcomed the new bride to my house, as a sister—but oh! the martyrdom of the weeks that followed. At last, when on the verge of madness and suicide, I thought—'I will know whether the fault is in the system, or in my own rebellious heart; I will go to those who are wiser and better than I, and learn whether they have become reconciled to such a life. Accordingly, I paid a visit to two of the Prophet's plural wives, to whom we were always taught to apply for counsel.'

"One of them said: 'I have shed tears enough since I have been in polygamy to drown myself in twice over.' The other said: 'The plains, from the Missouri to this valley, are strewed with the bones of those whom this system has killed, and the cemetery on the hill is full of them.'

"Miserable comforters, truly. But I would make one more trial. I went to Brother C——'s. This was called a model polygamous family. The two wives were said to live together like the most affectionate sisters. I called on the first wife; told her how I felt, and asked: 'Sister C. is the fault in our religion, or my own wicked heart? Are you happy in polygamy?'

"She replied: 'I have never seen a happy day or hour since my husband's second marriage; I have never laid down on my bed at night without drenching my pillow with tears.'

"'But perhaps the second wife feels differently,' I said.

"'You can ask her. She is in the next room.'

"I did so, and this was her reply: 'For the sake of peace, I have given up everything. I have no longer a single right, either as woman or wife. If it had not been for my child, I would have ended my troubles by throwing myself into the river long before this.'

"No comfort or help here. I used to go down into my cellar to pray, and there, with my burning forehead pressed against the cold stones, I would plead that my rebellious will might be subdued; but the more I prayed the worse I felt; the more it seemed that if God had laid such an intolerable burden on woman, he must be a cruel tyrant instead of a kind Father. At last one day when I was praying, these words came to me, as distinctly as though a human voice had spoken them in my ear:

"'My child, it is man, not God, who has laid this cruel burden upon you.'

From that moment I was free. I no longer prayed to be reconciled to polygamy, but fought against it with all the strength of my soul.

Mrs. A. G. PADDOCK."

"Polygamy is taught as extending into the future life. Those sealed here are sealed for all eternity, and there will be an eternal increase of progeny.

"The Revelation of the Almighty from God to a man who holds the Priesthood and is enlightened by the Holy Spirit whom God designs to make a ruler and a governor in his eternal kingdom, is that he may have more wives, that when he goes to another sphere he may still continue to perpetuate his species, and of his kingdom there shall be no end. * * * * When the servants of God go to heaven, there is an eternal union, and they will multiply and replenish the world to which they are going."—Apostle Hyde's Sermon.

"The principle of increase is the grand moving principle and cause of the actions of men. The latter-day Saints are bound to put in practice those principles that are calculated to endure and tend to a continual increase in the world to come."—Brigham Young.

"Their theology teaches the legitimacy of marriage between brother and sister, and between parties of near relationship, in order that 'a pure family may be raised up.' Instances of a Saint marrying or 'being sealed' to a mother and to her daughters at the same time, are of frequent occurrence. Contracts are made with missionaries to find a wife or wives for parties here on condition of paying the expenses of the passage to this Territory. Young and innocent girls are thus purchased by old gray-headed polygamists and dragged into life as slavish in its character as was that system which always will be a foul blot upon our nation's history. It may well be repeated, and the declaration made emphatic, that polygamy means the enslavement and prostitution of woman; a venomous defiance of the authority of the United States Government, and the propagation of a horde of banditti in this Territory whose deeds will strike terror to every heart. The massacre at Mountain Meadows, the robber bands of Nauvoo, the outlawry of young Mormondom of to-day, away from the centers of civilization, are but the natural fruits of this terrible system, and only a forecast of the years to come, when those masses of ignorant, vicious, polygamous-bred 'hoodlums' of mixed parentage shall be thrown out like driftwood upon the sea of active life.

"80 per cent. of the plural marriages were necessiated by previous immorality. And yet notwithstanding this convenient cloak of wrong-doing, I have been informed by jurists who have resided in the Territory a long time, and who are well posted in the legal facts connected with this thing, that there is a fearful amount of illegitimacy. And I could name a small village where no ungodly Outsider is found to corrupt the morals of the young Saints, and yet there were over a dozen illegitimate births in one year among a population of 400 people. I have also been informed by persons whose truthfulness of statement cannot be impeached, and whose honesty of purpose cannot be doubted, that there is a fearful state of morals throughout the Territory, especially among the youth connected with polygamous families. That the young Saints are practically carrying out the theory of the Church on this subject without troubling themselves about the ecclesiastical ceremonies of the Endowment House."—*Ibid*, pp. 22.

"A BEAUTIFUL PICTURE.—Geo. C. Bates, well known in Salt Lake City, writes to the Denver *Tribune* that he was a resident of Utah for six years, three years of that time as United States Attorney, and three years as attorney for the Mormon Church. While acting in the latter capacity he was called south on church business, and gives the following account of his trip:—

"In January, 1873, I happened to visit the southern parts of the Territory on business for the church, and, stopping to change horses and dine, I saw around one table five polygamic wives of one old bishop, and in and around the ranch some thirty-six large boys and girls of all ages, from ten to sixteen and twenty years, and then and there learned that these young Mormons all slept in one large single room overhead in the winter, like so many pigs, and in the hot weather in summer they all hurdled together in the straw in the stable, living in promiscuous concubinage, and that several of the girls were bearing children to their brothers and cousins and uncles, as so many cows or ewes would do, and that this was a matter of daily happening, and was not discouraged, but was winked at, by the church, as a natural consequence of their religious teachings that every woman's future happiness was enhanced by the number of children she bore, no matter who might be their fathers."—HAND-BOOK ON MORMONISM, pp. 22.

I now quote from *Anti-Polygamy Standard*, vol. 2, No. 3, as follows:—

"Old Jim Butler, over 60 years of age, was sealed to his step-child, a little girl fifteen years old, at the Endowment House, Feb. 14th, 1876 (The Great Centennial Year of American Independence and Progress). Brigham performed the ceremony very much against the wishes of the child, who was compelled to comply with the bestial request upon pain of being turned into the streets destitute and homeless together with her mother. Both the mother and daughter, the pretended wives of this old heathen, live together with the old man in a little dirt hovel of one room.

"Old man Lareless, now seventy years of age, is using every means in his power to have his own grandchild, a girl sixteen years old, sealed to him."

MORMON SLAVES. (From *Salt Lake Tribune*.)

"A horrible story is told by a correspondent of the *Eureka Leader* of what he saw at Ogden, a railroad town in Utah, where a number of Sweedish immigrants were waiting to take the train to Brigham City: 'I was looking on with great curiosity, when I discovered a tow-headed, buxom girl weeping bitterly. Two or three old women were scolding at her and a withered old Mormon stood with his arm around her. He finally coaxed her off to his waggon, she screaming and crying that she would not marry him, and he never letting go of her until he sat her down upon the wagon tongue. A girl was following them. I halted her and asked her what was the trouble. She said that this girl was pledged to the old man and that he paid her passage out, and now she did not want to marry him, because he already had a wife and seven children. I asked if she would be forced to do so. The girl replied: 'Of course she will. They have pledged her to him.' Poor thing! the last that I saw of her she was struggling to get away from him, and the withered old fellow was holding on with both arms around her. It was sickening to think of such doings in a civilized land. Dark as that girls mind was, she had some grains of virtue and some delicate instincts. The despair pictured on her face showed that."

[This has been copied by the English press, and shows but one of the very many cases where white girls have been purchased as slaves for the Mormon Harems.

It is done in this way: Any old brute that wants to import a fresh young female slave, gives the missionary the money to pay the passage out of a "nice young girl" This Missionary comes into the factory towns of England and other places, procures the girls, pays the passage, ships them off, and sends the bill of lading to the old lechers, who await their arrival in Utah as seen in the foregoing articles.

Besides this, they have a Grand Lottery scheme called "The Perpetual Emigration Fund," "All prizes and no blanks." There are millions of money in this fund, which is used to import girls who cannot pay their fare to Utah. So soon as a man has paid in sufficient for one fare, he is entitled to draw "One Fair damsel." Two fares—Two fairs, and so on and so forth. While the Missionary is here ostensibly to "Preach the Gospel" but in reality to Nab girls for Utah's Harems. Now let the press of England re-publish the story and give my addition so that the girls may be cautioned.]

"A cargo commonly called emigrants, arrived in this city and were duly located in the stock yard at the Tithing office. Yesterday they branched off in all directions to view the beauties and attractions of Zion, and early in the morning a gentleman of the city had occasion to go into a saloon to get a glass of beer on his road home, and found the saloon literally packed with these new emigrants, both male and female who were punishing beer in a way entirely beyond the ability of the average Zionite. They were enjoying themselves hugely, and well they may while they have a little spare change, for when the priests get through fleecing them, they can look back on the little event with the satisfaction of knowing that all their hard earnings didn't go into the hands of the Latter-day robbers.

"IN one of the Mormon settlements of Utah, the Father of a girl 14 years of age has sold her to a polygamous bishop who has a harem of three concubines. And this is America in the Nineteenth Century.

"BISHOP JOHN HOPKIN, of one of Zion's stakes in Weber county, is over in Colorado selling Mormon serfs to the coal mining companies, who are discharging Americans to give places to these willing slaves of the rapacious priesthood.

"Two or three more happy homes started in Utah. Three hundred female converts to Mormonism left New York last week.

"Several car loads of fresh slaves for the Mormon Church are expected here on Thursday night. The women will be consigned to the harems while the men will be placed on farms to win bread for lazy priests.

"A letter from one of the Mormon settlements in Arizona, written to a brother Saint in Utah, says:—John W. Young has a Mormon contract on one of the railroads, and is bilking his brethren in a lively manner. He advertizes that he will pay them good wages, and now there are 200 idle Mormons who can't get work. The price he pays is one dollar per day, the victim boarding himself out of this amount, while the bilk contracts the slave to the railroad company at two dollars per day and found. When asked by the brethren why he don't pay and treat them better, he simply tells them : ' I'm not here for my health.'

"And this is the scoundrel who left Utah between two days to plant polygamy in Arizona, and when captured in Denver, a short time ago, cried out against Gentile persecution.

"The Church is making arrangements to drive a herd of the brethren into Colorado for the alleged purpose of working on the Rio Grande Railroad.

"The Church organ swears that the papers which assert Mormons are recruited from the slums of Europe, beat the brethren lying. A bold assertion, indeed. At any rate if they are not from the slums they are soon put there by the grasping priests after they arrive in Utah.

"As false prophets they grow rich, and yearly bring more wretched bigots here, while the poor people who pay the tithes have a hard struggle to live, and their children are growing up in ignorance ?

"Says the Mormon Church Organ :—' Zadkiel predicts a great deal of vice and immorality for Utah this year. Editors may sneer about the Utah state, but imperfect as it is now, it has within it the promise and potency of future development into a social order, that will command the admiration of all good people and the approbation and communion of the Eternal Powers.' For instance, take the case of Elder Pitkin, mentioned in *The Tribune*, a few days since. That commanded the approbation of every beast in Utah."

[Elder Pitkin is a "Melchizedek Priest," who prostituted his own daughter when she was but eight years old. I will spare the reader details. The child at the age of thirteen became a mother as the result of this incest. I could relate many similar cases which came under my own observation. I prefer, however, to quote other testimony, so incredible will these things appear to the uninitiated.] I continue to extract from the *Salt Lake Tribune* :—

"A girl, fifteen years of age, named Elizabeth Natrass, was brought before Judge Pyper charged with drunkenness and profanity. Her story to the Judge was simply horrible, and the language disgusting. She stated that some time ago her father had seduced her, and since then she had turned herself loose in all that was bad." * * * *

"The Mormon Church Organ reports a case of a woman kicking in West Jordan, in which the kicker, in the shape of a man, was fined 10 dollars. The Church paper praises the man and abuses the woman. thus illustrating how dearly the Latter-day frauds love the women."

"Susie Vance, one of Brigham's female Battle-axes, and by divine right to be some old polygamist's queen in the celestial world, but now unfortunately a soiled dove, was arrested last night for being drunk, and was lodged in jail. Her usual place of abode is at the Palace de Lunatic, where, let us hope her royal highness will return."

I leave this part to say a few words about the "Drunken Devils."

The Mormons claim to be a sober people, but what are the facts? "The Resources of Utah," published at Salt Lake City in 1873, says:—"There are five breweries in Salt Lake City. Shortly after this another very large brewery was built, and is now doing a tremendous business; while whiskey distillers are profusely abundant, and large quantities are imported from the States. One of "Zion's" Whiskey Firms, advertises in five languages occupying six columns—"The Saints gathered from All Nations" take to whiskey. But "John Bull Saints" like their beer as well, hence we find advertized in the Mormon papers that "Brother Margetts" makes "ENGLISH ALE A SPECIALTY," though he also deals in "Wines and Liquors." We are informed that at another "Saloon," "Choice Wines," Pure Liquors, ENGLISH ALE AND PORTER, Ice, Cold Beer, Superior Cigars, and 1,000 Fancy Drinks" can be had. Polygamists in trouble are told that another dealer has "snug apartments, shady and cool, where the thirsty can take a cold lunch. and quaff the flowing bowl in PEACE AND QUIETUDE"—quite a consideration for "Henpecked Saints." The Editor adds:—"Mr. S. is doing quite a snug business, and is therefore correspondingly 'apy.'" He is not the only one doing "a snug business" in that line. The fact is the troubles of polygamy drive both men and women to drink. I have known "Saints and Saintesses" sell their children's bread for drink, and thousands have told me they must have drink to drown their sorrows; but in this chapter I give, as far as possible, the words of others. Secretary Ferris on page 47, "Utah and the Mormons," says:— "The gross sensualities originating in Polygamy, coupled with parental neglect of offspring, occasion great mortality among children. To these may be added intemperance in drinking, very generally diffused, and which finds its gratification in a miserable article of whiskey and beer, manufactured in great quantities."

DR. MCKENZIE VISITED "ZION" TO START THE BLUE RIBBON MOVEMENT.

I now quote from *Salt Lake Tribune*, June 3, 1881:—

"Don't we Mormons have to suffer," said an old drunken Saintess, yesterday evening, when Dr. McKenzie picked her up out of the gutter and placed her in an express waggon and sent her home. She was one of five women belonging to the harem of an old polyg. on the East Bench of Zion.

"It is quite evident that some of the brethren have been pulling the wool over the eyes of Dr. McKenzie in regard to the temperate habits of the Mormons. By walking up Main street the Doctor will observe a sign "Holiness to the Lord, Zion's Co-operative Mercantile Institution, Wholesale Dealers and Rectifiers of Liquor." This institution under the all-seeing eye sells more whiskey than any house in Utah, and it all goes into the stomachs of the Saints. He can extend his walk to several saloons in Zion where Elders of the Church of Jesus Christ of Latter-day Saints in good standing deal out villainous whiskey to God's elect. Of course this is all done for Christ's sake.

"Some old hen writing in the (Mormon) *Procuress* winds her horn thus:—

"The 'Gentile' women of Utah have prepared a memorial to Congress, against the Mormon custom of plural marriage. But after all, what a sham morality is this cry against plurality of wives. In Utah, until the advent of the 'Gentile' population, there were no liquor saloons, no gambling hells, no houses of prostitution, no paupers and few criminals.

"It is a little difficult to fix the exact date when the Gentile population came to Utah, but before they came Brigham Young and the priesthood manufactured a most villainous brand of whiskey known as Valley Tan, and dispensed it to the Saints at high figures; before the Gentile population came here—as early as 1857—whole trains of emigrants were murdered, and every leading elder kept a private house of ill-fame. Brigham Young and the priests he has left here still owe a portion of the United States internal revenue tax on the crooked whiskey they made and sold to the people; only one of the murderers who took part in the wholesale human butcheries of early days has been punished, while some of the others are hid up in the mountains to escape justice, and the private houses of prostitution have multiplied ten fold, so that the inmates thereof, according to Emeline B. Wells, the editor of the paper we quote from, now number 50,000."

"Whereas these polygamous delegates charge that dram-selling, dram drinking, prostitution and kindred vices were unknown in Utah previous to the advent of the Gentiles; and

"*Resolved*, That it is a matter of public notoriety, that Brigham Young owned a large distillery, which not only supplied the Utah Saints but many outside the Territory with whiskey; that Zion's Co-operative Mercantile Institution deals largely in all manner of intoxicating drinks; that it is a well known historical fact that at a large meeting of the priesthood, presided over by Brigham Young himself, nearly every man present confessed himself guilty of adultery, outside of his polygamous relations, and that the Mormon preachers themselves publicly lament the great number of illegitimate births in purely Mormon settlements." Extract from THE ANTI-POLYGAMY MEMORIAL.

"Allread, that one-armed soldier now languishing in a Mormon jail at Manti, bears testimony to the truth of that resolution passed at the Rep. convention in Salt Lake. Allread was a saloon keeper who sold better whiskey than the Church of Jesus Christ of Latter-day Saints, and therefore gobbled the ducats of the boys. This was too much for the Lord's anointed scoundrels and they cast him into prison. Such reports, you know, dear brethren, hurt business and you must not rile the Saintly devils."

"Apostle Rich called to account our peculiar people for collecting at saloons and drinking with the ungodly outsiders; and then, when drunk, these Mormons sit down and yell, even singing those songs of Zion which are sung here in this sacred edifice. He had seen on the State road a dozen or so Mormon farmers too drunk to drive their horses, and in danger of getting hurt where not their horses so gentle. Nor was this all. Even our sisters drink. He happened to be in the Police Court one day when five Mormon women were brought up for drunkenness."

"EDS. TRIBUNE: Ask him how that difficulty ended which was brought about by that five gallon keg of whiskey that J. T. Barker brought from Evanston. Thomas, son of Apostle Rich, and others, after drinking and fighting all night, settled the matter in the morning of the 2d with a horse race, in which Thomas Rich broke his neck and died instantly. It was the most disgraceful scene I ever witnessed. ONE WHO WAS PRESENT."

"THE DESERET NEWS discussed the liqour question last evening and before getting through with her article she had emptied three bottles of beer and a pint flask of whiskey. The old girl lives her religion in true Mormon style. Let us look upon that Church sign. It reads, 'Holiness to the Lord, Zion's Co-operative Mercantile Institution, Wholesale Liquor Dealers.' Take in that sign, hide your red nose, or hold your rattling old tongue."

"There were several cases in the Police Court yesterday, including the drunks, and four fighters."

"I have seen windows in Main Street, Salt Lake City, ornamented with the inscription 'Holiness To The Lord,' surmounted with an All-seeing eye. In these windows, and directly beneath the inscription named, stood an array of bottles, labelled: 'Old Tom Gin,' 'Honey Dew Whiskey,' 'Put Up Expressly For Zion's Co-operative Mercantile Institution,' [often abreviated to 'Z.C.M.I.'" p. 308, *Fate of Madam l a Tour.*

I have seen Whiskey, Rum, and Brandy flowing in the gutters of Salt Lake City, and the "Siants" dipping the "Spirits" with buckets, and even filling the washtubs so that very soon the satiated sinners became in reality "Spiritual" Saints.

From the *Salt Lake Tribune* I extract from one of the many of Ginx's Letters to Brigham Young:—

"Brother Jim Jack is quite beyond my control again. He would leave the office early in the morning, and be gone nearly all day. But happening down on Whisky Street, immediately after he goes, I find that he makes a bee line for the nearest beer saloon. He will return in the afternoon, blind drunk. He spent the whole Sabbath at one of these Gentile brewers on the outskirts of the city. He is a complete beer bottle. I expect he will be full to-morrow. I pray God, my dear Brig, that you will feel easy about that crooked whisky matter. I need not remind you that our God has His hand over Israel, and that has He has been with you in all your ups and downs, and ins and outs for forty years, so He will abide with you in the future. Our prayer circles have had their effect, and God has restored you to health. I am, with fervent prayers, your brother in the holy covenant.

LION HOUSE, June 17, 1876. GINX."

"As early as 1869 there was 37 distilleries in Utah run by Mormons."—*Hand Book on Mormonism,* pp. 76.

"There are women among the Latter-day Saints who are loose in their conduct. There are families in this town as corrupt as hell." Apostle Hyde *Journal of Discourses,* vol. 2, p. 86.

"I can say 'Amen' to brother Hyde's last remarks, I know just as much about those matters as I want to know, and if I do not know more, it is because there is no more of it in the city. It is a hard matter for a man to hide himself from me in this Territory; the birds of the air they say carry the news, and if they do not, I have plenty of sources for information." Brigham Young *Jour. of Dis.* vol. 2, p. 90.

"Those who try to save their lives, will lose them, both temporally and spiritually." Brigham Young's Sermon, *J. of D.,* vol. 2, p. 254.

"Stay in the hell you are in, if you choose, or go to another if you can." *Ibid,* p. 255.

"Brother Brigham's word is sacred; and if you do not observe it, it will not be well, it will go hard with you if you disobey his advice. I have got my old gospel preparation (an old pistol) laid up drying, preparing himself for action, I do not fear anything on earth or in hell; if we do precisely as we are told. I never saw the time but I could whip out twenty of the best men on earth." Apostle Kimball, *J. of D.,* vol. 2, p. 107-8

"No matter whether we have been educated by the Jews, Gentiles, or Hottentots; whether we serve the true and living God, or a lifeless image, if we are honest before the God we serve." "Gentile signifies disobedient people." Brigham's Sermon, *J. of D.* vol. 2. p. 139.

"I cannot define any difference between temporal and spiritual labours." *Ibid*, p. 95.

"We wish to lay the corner stone of the Temple on the 6th day of April next, if the Lord will, and if the Lord will not." *Ibid*, p. 96.

"In the revelations of God there is a clear distinction made between the Sinner and the Ungodly. A person to be ungodly must have known godliness." Brigham Young *J. of D.*, vol. 2, p. 258.

"The Holy Priesthood is not on the earth, unless the Latter-day Saints have it. It is the Priesthood, again given to the children of men that raises the devil, and makes all hell angry; the devil's servants run to and fro and publish his lies about Christ and his church on the earth. The professors of Christianity, and the priests are not angry with us, but they are filled with wrath and indignation with themselves, and with the Almighty. Those sweet, loving, blessed Christians, the priest in the pulpit, and the deacon under it, and the sage followers of their own nonsense and the traditions of their fathers are the ones who are at war with the Eternal Priesthood of God.

"Who is it that stirs up the devil all the time? Those sanctified hypocrites, those old sectarians, who profess so much sanctity, and so much religion. They see that their old favourite dwelling is crumbling to the dust, never to be rebuilt again before Mormonism will triumph. That is what stirs up all the mischief." Brigham Young's Sermons, *Jour. of Dis.*, vol. 2 p. 180.

In the same sermon on page 182 occurs language that I must not reprint; even at my private lecture to men, where justice demands it. I always feel ashamed to read such "Sermons"; though they were preached before men women and children on the Sabbath, by "Apostles" and "Priests."

On page 253, he says:—We can make Utah Territory one of the greatest sinks of iniquity upon the face of the whole earth, and exceed the abominations of the ancient Sodomites.

"Apostle" Smith in one of his "Sermons" said:—"Our ways are not as the ways of the Lord, nor our thoughts as His." * * "What! got to have a woman sealed to me in order to be saved? Yes." *J. of D.* vol. 2, p. 215.

"If you have lost the Spirit, go and read the Book of Mormon, and the Book of Doctrine and Covenants and you will get it again." Apostle Kimball's Sermon, *Jour. of Dis.*, vol. 2, p. 234.

Speaking of the "Prophet," Kimball said:—"God has placed him as the President of this Church, as our leader, guide, and teacher, and we are bound not to come in contact with him—not to teach differently to what he does; that is, when we once ascertain fully his mind and views. I do not know that I have presented any views that are different from his: if I have, when he corrects me, I will remain silent upon the subject, if I do not understand it as he does. We should not teach anything, when we once ascertain his real mind, that will come in contact with his teaching." *Journal of Discourses*, vol. 2, p. 246.

"All that you have and are belong to God, and must be devoted to his Church. Not only your money, and goods and talents, but your wives and children should be at all times ready to be devoted to his servant."

"If President Young wants my wives I will give them to him without a grumble, and he can take them whenever he likes."

"When the family organization (Polygamy) was revealed from heaven, and the Prophet began on the right and on the left to add to his family, what a quaking there was in Israel. Says one brother to another 'the Prophet says all covenants are done away, and none are binding but the new covenants; now if the Prophet should come and say he wanted your wife, what would you say to that?' 'I would tell him to go to hell.' This was the spirit of many in the early days of this Church."

"What would a man of God say, who felt aright, when the Prophet asked him for his money? He would say 'Yes, and I wish I had more to help build up the Kingdom of God.' Or if he came and said, 'I want your wife?' 'O yes,' he would say, 'here she is, there are plenty more.'"

"If such a man of God should come to me and say, 'I want your gold and silver, or your wives.' I should say, 'Here they are, I wish I had more to give you, take all I have got.' A man who has got the spirit of God and the light of eternity in him, has no trouble about such matters." "Apostle" Grant's Sermon, *Journal of Discourses*, vol. 2, pp. 13 & 14.

The "High Priest" in "The Rocky Mountain Saints" p. 294 says:—

"Heber C. Kimball felt only too happy to follow in the wake of Grant; he used the most disgusting vituperatives, for which he was noted, and indulged in unheard-of accusations.

"He declared to the people that Brigham Young was his god, and their god, and the only god they would ever see 'Joseph Smith was God to the inhabitants of the earth when he was amongst us, and Brigham is god now.'

This strain was caught up and reiterated by many of the elders, from Orson Hyde, the president of the twelve apostles, down to the most ignorant teacher, and to question it openly was to be put under the ban."

"'Brother Brigham,' said I, 'are you my Saviour?' 'Most assuredly I am,' said he. 'You cannot enter the Celestial Kingdom, except by my consent. Do you doubt it?"—MRS. SMITH'S 15 YEARS AMONG THE MORMONS.

"How applicable to the latter-day Saints in Salt-Lake Valley, are the sayings of old: 'Their habitations is the munitious of rocks;' and they ask no odds of the world, but they are subject to God, who has redeemed this basin, and put Salt enough in it to save us; and we can make it rain when we please. The Bible says, 'Have salt in yourselves;' we have it here, and if there comes along a villain who is worthy of it, we can salt him up in Salt Lake too [Laughter]. Apostle Hyde, *Journal of Discourses*, vol. 2., pp. 70.

"By and bye we shall have all the women, and they (the Christian world) will have none." Apostle Hyde, *Journal of Discourses*, vol. 2, pp. 83.

"The following are one or two of about a dozen verses of Mormon "poetry," extremely popular among the "Saints"—

* * * * * * * *

"The time the prophet saw is on the wing,
When seven women to one man shall cling

"Not for the lack of clothing or of bread,
But for a husband—a man—a head!
To obviate reproach and share his name,
As to be single then will be a shame;

"For war will strew its victims o'er the plain,
And maddened men rush heedless to be slain;
A man shall be more precious in the land
Than golden wedges from the Ophir strand.

"If you perchance among the worthies stand,
And seven women claim your saving hand,
Do not reject the six and save the one,
And boast of magnanimity when done."

"Doggerel, no better than this, and much of it a great deal worse. might be heard in almost every meeting of the "Saints." [A lady's life in Polygamy, by Mrs. Stenhouse, P. 54.]

CHAPTER VII.

Chapter of Horrors—Danite Devils—Human Sacrifice—Mountain Meadow Massacre.

In this chapter I shall also let others tell the tale. I commence with Sermons by Brigham Young and his "Apostles." I quote from Brigham's Sermon "Love thy neighbour as thyself."

"When will we love our neighbours as ourselves? In the first place, Jesus saith that no man hateth his own flesh. It is admitted by all that every person loves himself. Now if we do rightly love ourselves we want to be saved and enjoy eternity and see no more sorrow nor death. This is the desire of every person who believes in God. Now take a person in this congregation who knows and understands the principles of eternal life, and suppose that he is overtaken in a gross fault, that he has committed a sin that he knows will deprive him of that exaltation which he desires, and that he cannot attain to it without the shedding of his blood, and also knows that by having his blood shed he will atone for that sin and be saved and exalted with the gods, is there a man or woman in this house but would say 'Shed my blood that I may be saved and exalted with the gods?'

"All mankind love themselves; and let those principles be known by an individual, and he would be glad to have his blood shed. This would be loving ourselves even unto an eternal exaltation. Will you love your brothers or sisters likewise when they have a sin that cannot be atoned for without the shedding of their blood? Will you love that man or woman well enough to shed their blood? THAT IS WHAT JESUS CHRIST MEANT. He never told a man or woman to love their enemies in their wickedness, never. He never meant any such thing; His language is left as it is for those to read who have the spirit to discern between truth and error; it was so left for those who can discern the things of God.

"I could refer you to plenty of instances where men have been righteously slain in order to atone for their sins. I have seen scores and hundreds of people for whom there would have been a chance if their lives had been taken and their blood spilled on the ground as a smoking incense to the Almighty, but who are now angels to the devil.

"I have known a great many men who have left this Church, for whom there is no chance whatever for exaltation, but if their blood had been spilled it would have been better for them.

"This is loving our neighbour as ourselves; if he needs help, HELP HIM; if he wants salvation and it is necessary to spill his blood on the earth in order that he may be saved, SPILL IT.

"Any of you who understand the principles of eternity, if you have sinned a sin requiring the shedding of blood, should not be satisfied or rest until your blood should be spilled, that you may gain that salvation you desire. THAT IS THE WAY TO LOVE MANKIND. Now brethren and sisters, will you live your religion? How many hundreds of times have I asked that question? Will the Latter-day Saints live their religion?"

Discourse in the Tabernacle, published in the "Journal of Discourses," Vol. IV., pp. 219, 220.

"Apostle" Grant, in his sermon upon the penalty for breaking the covenants of the Church, says:—

"Then what ought this meek people who keep the commandments of

God do unto them? 'Why,' says one, 'they ought TO PRAY TO THE LORD TO KILL THEM.' I want to know if you would wish the Lord TO COME DOWN AND DO ALL YOUR DIRTY WORK? Many of the Latter-day Saints will pray, and petition, and supplicate the Lord to do a thousand things they themselves would be ashamed to do. • • • •

"When a man prays for a thing, he ought to be willing to perform it himself.

"The Lord God commanded them not to pity the person whom they killed, but to execute the law of God upon persons worthy of death. This should be done by the entire congregation, showing no pity.

"What! do you believe that people would do right, and keep the law of God, by actually putting to death the transgressors? Putting to death the transgressors would exhibit the law of God, no matter by whom it was done. That is my opinion.

"You talk of the doings of different governments. What mode do they adopt to punish traitors? Do traitors forfeit their lives? Examine the doings of earthly governments on this point, and you will find the same practice universal. But people will look into books of theology, and argue that the people of God have a right to try people for fellowship, but they have no right to try them on property or life. That makes the devil laugh, saying: I have got them on a hook now; they can cut them off, and I will put eight or ten spirits worse than they are into their tabernacles, and send them back to mob them."

"If men turn traitors to God and His servants, their blood will surely be shed."—"Apostle" Kimball.

Brigham assured the Saints that these throat-cutting, blood-spilling doctrines were meritorious, glorious, and soul-saving. He says:—

"There are sins that men commit for which they cannot receive forgiveness in this world, or in that which is to come; and if they had their eyes open to their true condition, they would be perfectly willing to have their blood spilt upon the ground, that the smoke thereof might ascend to heaven as an offering for their sins, and the smoking incense would atone for their sins; whereas, if such is not the case, they will stick to them and remain upon them in the spirit-world.

"I do know that there are sins committed of such a nature that if the people did understand the doctrine of salvation, they would tremble because of their situation. And, furthermore, I know that there are transgressors who, if they knew themselves, and the only condition upon which they can obtain forgiveness, would beg of their brethren to shed their blood, that the smoke thereof might ascend to God as an offering to appease the wrath that is kindled against them, and that the law might have its course. I will say, further: I have had men come to me and offer their lives to atone for their sins.

"I know, when you hear my brethren telling about cutting people off from the earth, that you consider it is strong doctrine; but it is to save them, not to destroy them.

"As it was in ancient days, so it is in our day; and though the principles are taught publicly from this stand, still the people do not understand them; yet the law is precisely the same. There are sins that can be atoned for by an offering upon an altar as in ancient days; and there are sins that the blood of a lamb, of a calf, or of turtle doves cannot remit, but THEY MUST BE ATONED FOR BY THE BLOOD OF THE MAN. That is the reason why men talk to you as they do from this stand; they understand the doctrine, and throw out a few words about it. You have been taught that doctrine, but you do not understand it." The reader will see here how *apropos* is the following lines from *Hudibras*:—

"The only difference is, that then they slaughtered only beasts, now men."

"From "Apostle" Grants Sermon :—" There are men and women here who must have their blood shed or they cannot be saved. I advise you to go to the President immediately, and ask him to appoint a committee to attend to your case; and then let a place be selected, and let that committee shed your blood to atone for your sins.

"What disposition ought the people to make of covenant-breakers? Why, says one, forgive them. Very good, What did the Apostle say? He says they are worthy of death. I am inclined to believe his decision was a just one.

"Have not the people of God a right to carry out that part of the law as well as any other portion of it? It is their right to baptize a sinner to save him, it is also their right to kill a sinner to save him, when he commits those crimes that can only be atoned for by shedding his blood. We would not kill a man, of course, unless we killed him to save him. Do you think it would be any sin to kill me if I were to break my covenants? Let every man preach for himself, I am preaching my own faith to-day. Do you believe you would kill me if I broke the covenants of God and you had the spirit of God? Yes, and the more spirit of God I had the more I should strive to save your soul by spilling your blood when you had committed sin that could not be remitted by baptism. But, says one, will not Uncle Sam play the devil with you? Uncle Sam is a part of us and we are Uncle Sam, and it is us and Uncle Sam together. We have a right to worship God according to the dictates of our own conscience and have a right to carry out our religion, and there is nothing in the Constitution and laws of the United States to the contrary."

"We have been trying long enough with this people, and I go in for letting the sword of the Almighty to be unsheathed, not only in word, but in deed." [Please remember this man was an "Apostle," Mayor of Salt Lake City, and speaker to the "Lords House of Parliament."]

From the "Prophet" Brigham's Sermon :—"Justice will be laid to the line, and righteousness to the plummet; we shall take the old broadsword, and ask, 'Are you for God?' and if you are not heartily on the Lord's side, you will be hewn down."

"But now I say, in the name of the Lord, that if this people will faithfully live their religion, their sins will be forgiven them without taking life.

"Keep your tongues still, lest sudden destruction come upon you. I say rather than that the apostates should flourish here, I will unsheath my bowie-knife, and conquor or die. [Great commotion in the congregation, and a simultaneous burst of feeling, assenting to the declaration.] Now you nasty apostates, clear out, or 'judgment will be laid to the line, and righteousness to the plummet.' [Voices generally, 'Go it, go it!'] If you say it is all right, raise your hands. [All hands up.] Let us call upon the Lord to assist us in this and every other good work."

The foregoing are literal quotations from the *Deseret News*, "Journal of Discourses," vol. i., p. 82, and vol. iii. p. 226.

The "Hand Book on Mormonism," page 49, after quoting about the same as I have here, says :—

"The few selections taken from the so-called sermons of Brigham and others—many more can be produced—cause a shudder of horror to all who read them. But we know that the discourses, as delivered on the stand, were much more cruel, wicked, and blood thirsty than they appear in the printed works ; it was blood-curdling to hear them. The Mormon shorthand reporters, when transcribing the 'Sermons' for the printer, left out many blasphemous and bloody expressions, unfit for the public eye."

Among the Senate documents we find General Clark's dispatch to Governor Boggs, which says :—

"There is no crime, from treason down to petty larceny, but these people have been guilty of. They have committed treason, murder, arson, burglary, robbery, larceny, and perjury. They have societies formed under the most binding covenants and most horrid oaths to circumvent the laws, and put them at defiance; and to plunder and burn and murder, and divide the spoils for the use of the Church."

In "The Rocky Mountain Saints" is the affidavit of T. B. Marsh, an ex-Mormon, from which I extract the following :—

"They have among them a company, called the Danites, who have taken an oath to support the heads of the Church in all things that they say or do, whether right or wrong.

"The plan of the Prophet is to take the United States, and ultimately the whole world. The Prophet inculcates the notion, and it is believed by every true Mormon, that Smith's prophecies are superior to the laws of the land. I have heard the Prophet say that he would yet tread down his enemies, and walk over their dead bodies; that if he was not let alone he would be a second Mohammed to this generation, and that he would make it one gore of blood from the Rocky Mountains to the Atlantic Ocean; that like Mohammed, whose motto in treating for peace was the 'Alcoran or the Sword,' so should it be eventually with us, 'Joseph Smith or the Sword.'"

To successfully carry out their plans they organized an Army. John D. Lee in his confession says :—

"All the males over eighteen years of age were organized into a military body, and called 'The Host of Israel.' The first rank was a captain with ten men under him; next was a captain of fifty, that is he had five companies of ten; next, the captain of a hundred, or of ten captains and companies of ten. The entire membership of the Mormon Church was then organized in the same way. This was the first organization of the military force of the Church. It was so organized as revealed through the Lord's Prophet. God commanded Joseph Smith to place the Host of Israel in a situation for defence against the enemies of God and the Church of Jesus Christ of Latter Day Saints.

"Another organization was formed called the 'Danites.' The members of this order were placed under the most sacred obligations that language could invent. They were sworn to stand by and sustain each other. *Sustain, protect, defend,* and *obey* the leaders of the Church, under any and all *circumstances unto death*; and to disobey the orders of the leaders of the Church, or divulge the name of a Danite to an outsider, or to make public any of the secrets of the order of Danites, was to be punished with death. And I can say of a truth, many have paid the penalty for failing to keep their covenants. They had signs and tokens for use and protection. When the sign was given it must be responded to and obeyed, even at the risk or certainty of death. The Danite that would refuse to respect the token, and comply with all its requirements, was stamped with dishonor, infamy, shame, disgrace, and his fate for cowardice and treachery was death.

This sign or token of distress is made by placing the right hand on the right side of the face, with the points of the fingers upwards, shoving the hand upwards until the ear is snug up between the thumb and fore finger.

The "High Priest" Journalist in his Rocky Mountain Saints, says :—

"Dr. Avard organized the brethren into companies of tens and fifties, appointed Captains over each company, gave 'signs' and 'grips' by which they should know each other by day or by night, binding themselves by the most sacred oaths to preserve in secrecy their works of darkness," Then follows Dr. Avard's address to the Danite Captains :—

"My brethren, as you have been chosen to be our leading men, our captains to rule over this Kingdom of Jesus Christ, who have been organized after the ancient order, I have called upon you here to-day to teach you and instruct you in the things that pertain to your duty, and to show you what your privileges are. Take your respective companies and go out and take to yourself spoils of the ungodly Gentiles? For it is written, 'The riches of the Gentiles shall be consecrated to my people, the house of Israel;' and thus waste away the Gentiles by robbing and plundering them of their property; and in this way we will build up the kingdom of God, and roll forth the little stone that Daniel saw cut out of the mountain without hands until it shall fill the whole earth. For this is the very way that God destines to build up his Kingdom in the last days. If any of us should be recognized, who can harm us? For we will stand by each other and defend one another in all things. If our enimies swear against us, we can swear also. As 'the Lord' liveth I would swear a lie to clear any of you; and if this would not do, I would put them or him under the sand as Moses did the Egyptian, and in this way we will consecrate much unto 'the Lord,' and build up his Kingdom; and who can stand against us? And if any of us transgress we will deal with him amongst ourselves. And if any of this Danite Society reveals any of these things, I will put him *where the dogs cannot* bite him."

In Burton's "City of the Saints" I find the following :—

"The 'Danite band,' 'Destroying Angels'—Gentiles say Devils—'Sons of Dan, or Danites,' were organized for the purpose of dealing as avengers of blood with Gentiles; in fact, they formed a kind of 'Death Society,' Desperadoes, Thugs, Hashshashiyun—in plain English, assassins in the name of the Lord."

Elder Hyde, in his work on Mormonism says :—

"A 'Death Society' was organized and led by Captain 'Fearnaught' *alias* 'Apostle' Patten. Mich. iv. 13 furnished the first name; Arise and thresh, O daughter of Zion; for I will 'make thy horn iron and thy hoofs brass; and thou shalt beat in pieces many people; and I will consecrate their gain unto the Lord.' This accurately described their intentions, and they called themselves the 'Daughters of Zion.' Some ridiculed these bearded and bloody 'Daughters,' and the name did not sit easily. 'Destroying Angels' came next; the 'Big fan of the thresher that should thoroughly purge the floor.' Genesis xlix. 17 furnished the name finally assumed. 'Dan shall be a serpent by the way, an adder in the path that biteth the horse's heels so that his rider shall fall backward.' The 'Sons of Dan,' or Danites was adopted, and many times they have been adders in the path, and many a man has fallen backward and been seen no more."

Brigham Young in one of his Sermons said :—

"If men come here and do not behave themselves, they will not only find the Danites, whom they talk so much about, biting the horse's heels, but *the scoundrels will find something biting their heels.* In my plain remarks I merely call things by their own name." *Deseret News*, vol. 7., p. 143.

I trust enough is given to show the organization of this terrible band of cut-throats, and the kind of "Sermons" preached in "Zion." Now for some of their bloody work. Though I could fill this book with the most horrid tales which have been related to me, I prefer to use other testimony. I cannot however, refrain from mentioning a case of a neighbour of mine who is still a Bishop in the Mormon Church. He had two sons which grew "weak in the faith." They were both murdered by "Danites," and thrown over the garden wall with the remark to their mother who stood just inside :— "There learn how to train up your children properly."

The following extracts are from the Confessions of John D. Lee :—

"The Bishop notified Anderson that he must die by having his throat cut, so that the *running of his blood* would atone for his sins. Anderson being a firm believer in the doctrines and teachings of the Mormon Church, made no objections, but asked for half a day to prepare for death. His request was granted. His wife was ordered to prepare a suit of clean clothing in which to have her husband buried and was informed that he was to be killed for his sins, she being directed to tell those who enquired after her husband that he had gone to California.

"The Bishop, James Haslem, Daniel McFarland and John M. Higbee dug a grave in a field near the city, and that night about 12 o'clock, went to Anderson's house and ordered him to make ready to obey the Council. Anderson got up, dressed himself, bid his family good-bye, and without a word of remonstrance accompanied those that he believed were carrying out the will of the 'Almighty God.' They went to the place where the grave was prepared; Anderson knelt upon the side of the grave and prayed. The Bishop and his company then cut Anderson's throat from ear to ear and held him so that *his blood ran into the grave.*

"As soon as he was dead they dressed him in his clean clothes, threw him into the grave and buried him. They then carried his bloody clothing back and gave them to his wife to wash, when she was again instructed to say that her husband was in California. She obeyed their orders. The killing of Anderson was considered a religious duty and a just act. It was justified by all the people, for they were bound by the same covenants, and the least word of objection to thus treating the man who had broken his covenant would have brought the same fate upon the person who was so foolish as to raise his voice against any act committed by order of the Church authorities." Page 283, *Lee's Confession,* Published by Bryan, Brand and Co., St. Louis, U.S.A. W. H. Stelle and Co., New York.

"A quiet and orderly young man, a Gentile, was notified to let the girls alone. No Gentile was allowed to keep company with or visit any Mormon girl; but he still kept going to see some of them. The authorities decided to have the young man killed, so they called two of Bishop Dames' Destroying Angels, Carter and Gould, and told them to take that cursed young Gentile 'over the rim of the basin.' That was a term used when they killed a person.

"The destroying angels made some excuse to induce the young man to go with them on an excursion, and when they got close to Shirts' Mill, they killed him, and left his body in the bushes.

"The Indians found the body, and reported the facts to me. I was not at home that night, but Carter and Gould went to my house and staid there all night. They told Rachel (one of Lee's wives) they had been on a mission to take a young man, a Gentile, *over the rim of the basin,* and Carter showed her his sword, which was all bloody, and said he used that to help the Gentile over the *edge.* Rachel knew what they meant when they spoke of sending him ' over the rim of the basin.' It was a common thing to see parties going out with suspected Gentiles, to send them 'over the rim,' and the Gentiles *were always killed.*

"It was a common thing for small bands of people on their way from California to pass through by way of Cedar City on their journey. Many of these people were killed simply because they were Gentiles. The killing of Gentiles was considered a means of Grace and virtuous deed.

"Three men came to Cedar City one evening; they were poor, and much worn by their long journey. They were on their way to California. The Authorities ordered the brethren to devise a plan to put them out of the way, decently and in order. That the will of God, as made known through Bishops Haight and Klingensmith, might be done, these helpless men were coaxed to go to the distillery and take a drink. They went in company with J. M. Higbee, John Weston, James Haslem and Wm. C. Stewart, and I think another man, but if so, I have forgotten his name. The party drank considerable and when the emigrants got under the influence of the whisky, the brethren knocked the brains out of two of the men with the king-bolt of a wagon. The third man was very powerful and muscular; he fought valiantly for his life, but was overcome and killed. They were buried near the city.

"This deed was sustained by all the people there. The parties who did the killing were pointed out as true valiant men, zealous defenders of the faith and as fine examples for the young men to pattern after."

"John Weston took an Irishman, that had been stopping with him as his guest several days, on a hunt and when he got him in the forest, he cut the throat of the Irishman and left the body unburied. Weston received orders to kill the man because Bishop Haight considered him a spy."

"Bishop Klingensmith laid in ambush to kill Robert Keyes, because Keyes refused to give false testimony when requested to do so by the Bishop. When Keyes came within a few feet of the hiding place of the Bishop, this 'Holy' man raised his gun and took deliberate aim at Keyes heart."

"The authorities at Salt Lake City decided that Lieut. Tobin must be killed. Tobin had joined the Church there, and married a daughter of General Rich, one of the twelve Apostles. I think his wife was taken from him by order of the Church. He made several efforts to get out of the Territory. Finally he left Salt Lake intending to go to California, to escape the persecutions that were being forced upon him by the Church authorities. The 'Destroying Angels' were put on his trail, with orders to kill him without fail before they returned. Two desperate fanatics, Joel White and John Willis, were the 'Angels' selected, who knew nothing but to obey orders. These vile tools of the Church leaders were keeping their oaths of obedience to the Priesthood, and were as willing to shed blood at the command of the Prophet or any of the Apostles, as ever Inquisitor was to apply the rack to an offending heretic in the days of the Inquisition. In fact Mormonism is Jesuitism refined and perfected."

"White and Willis found Lieut. Tobin while he was sleeping, and going right up to him as he lay upon the ground, wrapt in his blanket, they shot him several times' they concluded to shoot him once more to make certain that he would not escape, so they put a pistol right up against his eye, and fired. The 'Angels' returned to Salt Lake City and reported that *their orders were obeyed.*"

"It was the usual course to send an 'Angel' after all who were charged or suspected of having violated their covenants. When a Danite or Destroying Angel was placed on a man's track, that man died, certain, unless some providential act saved him."

"William Laney, while on a mission to Tenessee, was saved by a family named Aden from a mob who threatened him with death because he was a Mormon preacher. When Fancher's train (The Emigrants killed at Mountain Meadows by the Mormons) reached Parowan, Laney met young Aden, and recognized him as the son of the man who had saved his life. Aden said he was hungry, that he and his comrades had been unable to purchase supplies from the Mormons since they left Salt Lake City, and that there seemed to be a conspiracy formed against that train by which the Mormons had agreed to starve the emigrants. Laney took young Aden to his house, gave him his supper, and let him sleep there that night. A few nights after that the Destroying Angels were ordered by Bishop Dame to kill Laney to save him from his sins, he having violated his endowment oath and furnished food to a man who had been declared an outlaw by the Mormon Church. The 'Angels' were commanded by Carter, a son-in-law of the Bishop. The Angels called Laney out of the house, saying the Bishop wished to see him. As Laney passed through the gate into the street, he was struck across the back of the head with a large club. His skull was fractured and for many months Laney lay at the point of death, and his mind still shows the effect of the injury, for his brain has never quite settled since. I have frequently talked with Laney about the matter, he knows that he will yet be killed if he make public the facts. Punishment by death was the penalty for refusing to obey the orders of the Priesthood.

"The sinful member was to be slain for the remission of his sins, it being taught by the leaders and believed by the people that the right thing to do with a sinner, was to take the life of the offending party, and thus save his never dying soul. This was called 'Blood Atonement.'"

"The Mormons nearly all believe in *blood atonement.* It was taught by the leaders and believed by the people that the Priesthood were inspired and could not give a wrong order. That the authority that ordered a murder committed, was the only responsible party, that the man who did the killing was only an *instrument* of the party commanding—just as much of an instrument as the knife that was used to cut the throat of the victim. This being the belief of *all good* Mormons, it is easily understood why the orders of the Priesthood were so blindly obeyed by the people. The Church authorities used the laws of the land, the laws of the Church, and 'Danite Angels' to enforce their orders, and rid the country of those who were distasteful to the leaders. And I say as a fact that there was *no escape* for any one that the leaders of the Church selected as a victim." From Lee's Confession, pp. 272 to 283.

"In Utah it has been the Custom with the Priesthood to make *eunuchs* of such men as were obnoxious to their leaders. This was done for a double purpose: first, it gave a perfect revenge, and next, it left the poor victim a living example to others of the dangers of disobeying counsel, and not living as ordered by the Priesthood.

"It was the favorite revenge of old, worn-out Priests, who wanted young women sealed to them, and found that the girl preferred some handsome young man. The old Priests generally got the girls, and many a young man was UNSEXED for refusing to give up his sweetheart at the request of an old and failing, but still sensual Apostle or member of the Priesthood.

"As an illustration I will refer to an instance that many a good Saint knows to be true, (including the Author of this Book.)

"Warren Snow was Bishop of the Church at Manti, San Pete County, Utah. He had several wives, but there was a fair, buxom young woman in the town that Snow wanted for a wife. He made love to her with all his powers, went to parties where she was, visited her at her home, and proposed to make her his wife. She thanked him for the honor offered, but told him she was then engaged to a young man, a member of the Church, and consequently could not marry the old priest. This was no sufficient reason to Snow He told her it was the will of God that she should marry him, and she must do so; that, in fact, a promise made to the young man was not binding, when she was informed that it was contrary to the wishes of the authorities.

"The girl continued obstinate. The 'teachers' of the town visited her and advised her to marry Bishop Snow. Her parents, under the orders of the Counsellors of the Bishop, also insisted that their daughter must marry the old man. She still refused. Then the authorities called on the young man and directed him to give up the young woman. This he steadfastly refused to do. He remained true to his intended, and said he would die before he would surrender his intended wife to the embraces of another.

"It was then determined that the rebellious young man must be forced by harsh treatment to respect the advice and orders of the Priesthood. His fate was left to Bishop Snow for his decision. He decided that the young man should be mutilated; Snow saying, 'When that is done, he will not be liable to want the girl badly, and she will listen to reason when she knows that her lover is no longer a *man.*

"It was then decided to call a meeting of the people who live true to counsel, which was to be held in the school-house in Manti, at which place the young man should be present, and dealt with according to Snow's will.

The meeting was called. The young man was there, and was again requested ordered and threatened, to get him to surrender the young woman to Snow, but true to his plighted troth, he refused to consent to give up the girl. The lights were then put out. An attack was made on the young man. He was severely beaten, and then tied with his back down on a bench, when Bishop Snow took a bowie-knife, and performed the operation in a most brutal manner, and than took the portion severed from his victim and hung it up in the school-house on a nail, so that it could be seen by all who visited the house afterwards.

"The party then left the young man weltering in his blood, and in a lifeless condition. During the night he succeeded in releasing himself from his confinement, and dragged himself to some hay-stacks, where he lay until the next day, when he was discovered by his friends. The young man regained his health, but has been an idiot or quiet lunatic ever since, and is well known by hundreds of both Mormons and Gentiles in Utah.

"After this outrage old Bishop Snow took occasion to get up a meeting at the school-house, so as to get the people of Manti, and the young woman that he wanted to marry, to attend the meeting. When all had assembled, the old man talked to the people about their duty to the Church, and their duty to obey counsel, and the dangers of refusal, and then publicly called attention to the mangled parts of the young man, that had been severed from his person, and stated that the deed had been done to teach the people that the counsel of the Priesthood must be obeyed. To make a long story short, I will say, the young woman was soon after forced into being sealed to Bishop Snow.

"This is only one instance of many that I might give to show the danger of refusing to obey counsel in Utah." *Lee's Confession*, p. 285-6.

From page 302, *The Rocky Mountain Saints*:—

"I was at a Sunday meeting in Provo, when the news of the San Pete castration was referred to by the presiding bishop—Blackburn. Some men in Provo had rebelled against authority, and Blackburn shouted in his Sunday meeting—a mixed congregation of all ages and both sexes—'I want the people of Provo to understand that the boys in Provo can use the knife as well as the boys in San Pete. Boys, get your knives ready, there is work for you! We must not be behind San Pete in *good works*.'

"This man, Blackburn, was continued in office at least a year after this, and was afterwards taken from his bishopric and sent on a mission to England.

"Many young women were forced to break off engagements with young men whom they loved, to gratify a bishop's preference, a missionary's feelings or a great elder's desires."

From Apostle Kimball's Sermon:—

"I would not be afraid to promise a man who is 60 years of age, if he will take the counsel of Brother Brigham and his brethren, he will renew his age. I have noticed that a man who has but one wife, and is inclined to that doctrine, soon begins to wither and dry up, while a man who goes into plurality looks fresh, young and sprightly. Why is this? Because God loves that man, and because he honors his work and word. Some of you may not believe this; but I not only believe it, but I also know it. For a man of God to be confined to one woman is small business, for it is as much as we can do to keep under the burdens we have to carry, and do not know what we should do if we only had one woman apiece."

From a "Sermon" delivered by Dr. Clinton, Justice of the Peace. Speaking of some men and women that he was not exactly pleased with and after using language unfit for publication, the Doctor said:—

"They ought to be shot with a double-barrelled shot gun. That is my doctrine; take a double-barrelled shot gun and follow them, and when you catch them, shoot them to pieces. I am the Justice of the Peace, I am the Coroner of the County, but I will never find' you, I will guarantee that."

Bishop E. Wooley followed the J. P., and said :—"I would do as the Doctor says, KILL THEM * * * Tear down their houses. THERE IS NO HELP FOR THEM * * * we will do as the Doctor said, and have a clean record." *Salt Lake Daily Review*, extra.

One of the "Apostles was to be privileged with the honour of 'pulling the nose of little Vic.!' (Queen Victoria)." *Rocky Mountain Saints*, p. 206.

27 years ago the American Government sent an Army to Utah to whip the Mormons into obedience of law and order. But the Mormons were victorious. There was a "high old time" in Utah. The Priest Journalist on page 372 *Rocky Mountain Saints* says :—"It was the gayest time ever known in Utah, dancing and theatrical amusements everywhere, while the songs of the Mormon camps, adapted to the popular negro melodies were heard in all their assemblies. The Sunday worship was enlivened with the jovial chorus of 'Dudah.' After partaking of the Lord's supper the following was sung,

'There's seven hundred wagons on the way, Du dah!
And their cattle are numerous, so they say, Du dah! du dah day!
Now, to let them perish would be a sin, Du dah!
So we'll take all they've got for bringing them in, Du dah! Du dah day!
   CHORUS.—Then let us be on hand, by Brigham Young to stand,
      And if our enemies do appear, we'll sweep them off the land.
'Old Sam has sent, I understand, Du dah!
A Missouri ass to rule our land, Du dah! Du dah day!
But if he comes, we'll have some fun, Du Dah!
To see him and his juries run, Du dah! Du dah day.
   CHORUS.—Then let us be on hand, &c.
'Old Squaw-killer Harney is on the way, Du dah!
The Mormon people for to slay, Du dah! Du dah day
Now if he comes the truth I'll tell, Du dah!
Our boys will drive him down to hell, Du dah! Du dah day!"
   CHORUS.—Then let us be on hand, &c.

"It is too lengthy to give entire—about 16 verses.—From such lyrical effusions as these, sung during 'divine worship' in the Tabernacle, the elevated tone of the sermons can be imagined."

"During this 'Mormon War,' the 'Saints,' who were 'spoiling for a fight,' burned two provision trains, one of 51 and the other of 23 waggons, and drove off their animals, causing great want in the Army. The American officer in command, having no use for 80 of the teamsters after the waggons were burnt, discharged them. They concluded to go to California. In passing through Salt Lake City, a Mormon armed guard was furnished to see them safe through. The following is a copy of the "orders" in regard to these teamsters:—*Life in Utah*, p. 194.

'SALT LAKE CITY, *April 9th*, 1858.

"The (Mormon) officer in command of escort is hereby ordered to see that every man is well prepared with ammunition and have it ready at the time you see those teamsters a hundred miles from the settlements. President Young advises that they should be all killed. Every precaution should be taken, and see that not one escapes. Secrecy is required.

"By order of General Daniel H. Wells.

"JAMES FERGUSON, *Assistant Adjutant General*."

Brigham had a Revelation how to emigrate the "Saints," in which the Saints were shown how to haul their baggage and food over the plains and mountains in hand carts. This went forth with the stamp of Divinity. "God had revealed it;" this was the "*Divine Plan*" of emigration. Think of it, Ladies, fancy pulling a cart with 200 lbs. of baggage over mountains and dales, 1,500 miles. On they trudge pulling the carts. When in the midst of the Rocky Mountains, tremendous snow storms came on. In the heavy snow its hard to pull the carts, "the Revelation" promised fine weather. Now their faith fails them; weary and hungry their souls faint within them. Their food, scant at best, nearly gone; they wade rivers and no dry clothing, no rest. What a Divine Plan! Several leading Mormons camped with them one night, made them kill their last calf and ate hearty of their scant provisions; in the morning these kind Mormon gentlemen drove their carriages through the river and waited on the opposite bank to see the women drag their carts through, then bade them good morning and sped on their way, leaving these poor dupes to get to Zion as best they could, finally reduced to starvation, and in the heavy drifting snow 250 souls perished. The reader can get full particulars of this horrid affair in *The Rocky Mountain Saints*, or at my lectures, where they will also see the pictures of the incidents related in my book besides several others, which space precludes my giving here. The following is from Mrs. Smith's "Fifteen Years among the Mormons," pp. 309 :—

"The widow of Hartley, 22 years old, is the most heart broken human being I ever saw. Dressed in deep black, the unrelieved picture of woe she presented, excited our curiosity and sympathy. Accompanied by my sister, I went to her, and after some delay and the assurance, that although we were Mormons, we were yet *women*, she told us her brief story, without a tear; yet with an expression of hopeless sorrow which I shall never forget. Oh! Mormonism is too hard—too cruel upon women. Can -will it be permitted for ever?

"It was not until I had suggested to her, that perhaps I had also a woe to unburden, as the result of my Mormon life, which might have some comparison to her own, that she commenced by saying :—

"'You may have suffered; and if you have been a Mormon wife, you must have known sorrow. But the cruelty of my own fate, I am sure, is without a parallel—even in this land of cruelty.

"'I married Jesse Hartly, knowing he was a 'Gentile,' but that made no difference with me, although I was a Mormon, because he was a noble man, and sought only the right. By being my husband, he was brought into closer contact with the members of the Church, and was thus soon enabled to learn many things about the Heads of the Church, that he did not approve, and of which I was ignorant, although I had been brought up among the Saints; and which, if known among the Gentiles, would have greatly damaged us. I do not understand all he discovered, or all he did; but they found he had written against the Church, and the Prophet required as an atonement for his sins that he should lay down his life. That he should be sacrificed in the Endowment House, where human sacrifices are made. They kill those there who have committed sins too great to be atoned for in any other way. The Prophet says, if they submit to this he can save them; otherwise they are lost. Oh! that is horrible. But my husband refused to be sacrificed, and so set out alone for the United States. I told him when he left me, and left his child, that he would be killed, and so he was. William Hickman and another Danite, shot him in the canyons. My child soon followed after its father, and I hope to die also; for why should I live? Here the murderers of my husband curse the earth, and roll in affluence unpunished.

"She had finished her sad story, and we were choking down our sobs of pity in silence, when she rose saying, 'I trust you will excuse me,' and went away, still wearing the same stony expression of agony, as when we first saw her. But this is but one case among a thousand others, that have never seen the light, and never will, until the dark history of the 'Danites,' or 'Destroying Angels,' is unveiled."

In a work by Mrs. A. G. Paddock, "*The Fate of Madame La Tour*," page 296, is the following :—

"During 1870 and 1871 the juries empannelled by the United States Marshall were composed altogether of Gentiles and seceders from the Mormon Church.

"During these years one hundred and twenty nine persons were indicted for the commission of murders, unspeakable mutilations, and other atrocious crimes.

These Juries not having been empannelled according to the laws of Utah, everyone of these indictments were set aside and the accused all set free.

"More polygamous marriages were contracted during 1880 than during any year since the settlement of the Territory."—*Ibid*, p. 324.

"An Englishwoman, who a few years ago abandoned her husband and children for the purpose of gathering with the Saints to Zion, has been divorced and re-married five times since she came to Utah. Another, after being divorced from five husbands, is now living in Polygamy with the sixth. A district judge reports the case of a Saintess, living near the place in which he holds court, who has been divorced *fourteen times.*—*Ibid*, p. 342.

I now extract from "The Prophets, or Mormonism Unveiled," by a lady who had a fearful experience in Zion. It is published by Wm. White Smith, 195, Chestnut Street, Philadelphia, U. S. On page 255, she says:—"This modern pandemonium, in which vice unchecked ran riot, would have rivalled Hades in its motley crew. It was a safe retreat for the forger and bogus coiner, house thief, and murderer. I should not dare to chronicle it had not others done so, as well as the passing papers of the day, and they have never been disproved."

This lady tells a fearful tale of a wife who killed the other wife of her husband. The story is too long to give entire, but from it I glean as follows :—

"A wife, who refused to consent to the plural marriage, cautioned her husband not to trifle with her feelings: that if the unnatural knot was tied death should speedily sever it. Notwithstanding this, one evening at supper time, the husband returned from the Endowment House with his new bride; the wife sternly commanded the intruder to leave the house at once, or submit to the consequence. This was all she said. The husband escorted his bride to her room and bade her prepare for supper. The bride, of course, must obey her husband and not his wife; and having arrayed herself gorgeously for the occasion, the husband conducted her to the table to partake of the evening repast with the family. The wife, always a woman of few words, seated herself at the table also, and remained silent. But 'still waters run deep,' and away down in the depths of that woman's heart were feelings unutterable. And while the husband and bride were exchanging loving glances and affectionate words, the wife and mother was deciding in her mind how best to end this fearful torture. A serious mental struggle ensued; finally the predominating thoughts were, 'Why should I make my children motherless? How can I destroy myself and leave my dear children to the care of this hated intruder? No, never! I cannot; I will not. But to live on in this state is impossible; to be constantly worried in mind over this will either dethrone reason or hurry me to a premature grave. This must not, shall not happen.' The idea now uppermost in her mind was 'slay the rival,' and thus put an end to all this vexation. This decided the matter. 'Death shall end what folly and crime began.' The supper ended, the husband and his bride retire. The husband partly turned and said, 'Good night!' to his wife. Imagine the feelings of that wife as she witnessed the disgusting and revolting scene. Her husband who swore at the marriage altar in England 'to forsake all others,' had now forsaken her to revel in the unlawful embraces of another; and in her own house, and before her very eyes, this wrong was being perpetrated. This was more than human nature could endure. She had already decided, now she felt an irresistible force urging her on to slay the guilty *pair*. But she reasoned, is *he* not the father of my children. She gave a deep sigh, then softly the words escaped her lips, 'with all his faults I love him still.' Then she hesitated for a moment, and concluded to spare *him*, but she would teach him that night that two wives could not live in that house. She thought of the dagger her husband had given her to protect herself in his absence. Now she would protect herself from this intruder in his presence with that very weapon. Grasping the dagger she silently approached the door of the bride-chamber and listened. Then peeping through the key hole she saw in that bright moonlight what she should never have seen.

"Her brain reeled, and sinking to the floor, she remained a long time in a dreamy, half-conscious state. The moon's bright beams had ascended still higher, and every object stood revealed in silvery light when she once more peeped into that room, and now they slept, and the sight of the peaceful slumber of her rival, reposing on that breast which should have been all her own, again aroused the demon in her heart; she tried the door: it was locked. She thought of the window, which was on the ground floor, and having no fastening, she could easily reach it from the garden. Proceeding thither she raised the sash, quietly crept in, bent over her rival, marked the smooth, beautiful brow, the finely chiselled features, and full voluptuous form, and contrasted them with her own faded beauty, once as lovely as that before her, but now with the roseate hues faded—faded in *his* service, and now trampled upon as valueless. She gloated over the sleeping victim, then the steel glittered once in the air, descended, and was raised reeking with the victim's life's blood! Again it descended, when the temporarily insane wife leaped through the window, fled to her room and caressed her sleeping babes! The terrible sequence of this horrible affair is too lengthy to give here, for I could go back to that bridechamber and detail the death of the bride who expired accusing her husband; how she was quietly buried in the garden with her mother who had silently yielded up her troubled soul on her murdered child's bosom. It was indeed a blessing for that broken hearted and widowed mother to die, within a few hours after her only child had ceased to live. And when afterward the husband found out the truth of the matter—it was as he had supposed—and now that the affair was hushed up, the husband and wife passed on in their career as if nothing had occurred, although her's was not the first blood that cried aloud to heaven for vengeance on betrayed and murdered innocence."

I could enumerate cases of this kind, and of others who have committed suicide. While I write this, scores of instances crowd into my mind. But I have made a mistake in contracting for a book of 200 pages. I should have had at least 800 pages more.

"A married woman, Mrs. L——, young, beautiful, and hitherto of unblemished reputation, fell a victim to the arts of the Prophet, and was to him as his plural wife. Her husband, a Gentile, knew nothing of it, and within a few months after he died; as it happened, many men died whose presence was not desired by the saints."—Madam La Tour, pp. 331.

In the same work chap. 18, Mrs. Paddock tells of two women brutally murdered, and adds:—" Julia H——, plural wife of a man who fills important offices in this city, was allowed the alternative of death by poison; but in the two cases named in this chapter, they were sacrificed with attendant barbarities which could not be paralleled outside the darkest abode of paganism."

I now quote from a petition from the women of Utah. "To the Senate and Representatives of the United States in Congress assembled."

"During all the years that their will has been law in Utah, no man's life no woman's honor has been safe, if either stood in the way of the despotic rulers of this people. Never in this world will the history of their dark and bloody deeds be fully written, for the victim and witnesses of many a tragedy are hidden in the grave.

"We adjure you in the name of the mothers who bore you, of the wives you love, of the sisters whose honor is dear to you, not to turn a deaf ear to the cry of those who ask protection from the tyranny of a system that, throughout its whole existence, has sought only to crush and degrade womanhood. Thousands of women in the Territory of Utah are to-day in a condition of abject slavery. Many of them would proclaim their wrongs to the world it they dared."

This petition is signed by 474 of the women of Utah. Mrs. Paddock in her book says;—"Many women to whom the memorial was presented said 'Every word in it is true, and we want to sign it, but we *dare not*."—Page 337. "Fate of Madam La Tour."

Did Congress Listen to this appeal? Yes! It "went in at one ear and out at the other," and though shortly afterward it did seem that justice in Utah was at last possible, Brigham Young was imprisoned by Judge McKean for the alarming space of 24 hours. Yet almost immediately afterward President Grant deposed the incorruptible Judge, whose only fault was the faithful and fearless performance of duty. Perhaps U. S. Grant will let me know why he did so, and I shall be pleased to insert his reason for so doing in future editions. At present I, and all those acquainted with the circumstances, are at a loss to understand why Judge McKean was removed from office.

From the Rocky Mountain Saints, page 462:—"In the controversy between Rigdon and the Twelve Apostles, at Smith's death, for the ruling supremacy of the Church, one Parrish said, 'he would follow the Twelve if they led him to hell.' Ten years later his zeal cooled, and he resolved to leave Utah.

"On the evening of the departure of the Parrish family, Potter and Durfee, two Danites, professed to aid them in leaving without observation, while in reality they were leading them to the place where they were to be killed. In the dark, Potter, who decoyed the elder Parrish, was accidentally shot and killed; old man Parrish was stabbed to death; his eldest son fell dead upon the road, and the younger son, though severely wounded, escaped and got back to town." [The Bishop, in command of this affair, still lives in Utah, the husband of numerous wives, six of whom are sisters; none of these guilty wretches were punished.]

"A month after the Parrish murders, Henry Jones and his mother were both killed. The mother was killed in the house, and the son, who tried to escape was pursued and killed. They are to come forth in the first resurrection, for they paid the atoning penalty, and are, therefore, entitled to the honours of the immortalized Saints.—*Ibid*, p. 469.

"A young man named Skeen was suspected of a disposition to apostatize. Thereupon he was arrested on a trumped up charge by Sheriff Ricks, who was also a Mormon High Priest. After Skeen lay down to sleep Ricks said to the guard, named Chambers, 'Whatever you see to night, your business is to keep still.' When the sleeper's breathing showed his slumber to be sound, Ricks placed his gun to the young man's breast and fired. The victim sprang up, ran to the door, fell, and in a few minutes expired. It was given out that he was killed in attempting to escape, but the testimony of Chambers, who saw the affair, was corroborated by several other men who swore that the gun had been held so close to Skeen's breast as to set his clothing on fire. Yet a Mormon jury pronounced Ricks, 'Not Guilty,' and his fellow-saints escorted him home with a band of music, flags flying, &c. I saw the procession and everybody understood the meaning." Fate of Madam La Tour, p. 347.

[I also "saw and understood." I have myself talked with Skeen's mother, and with Chambers about the affair. The burnt clothing shows that if young Skeen was "attempting to escape," he was running toward and not from the Sheriff who shot him. This is but one of the many cases where men have been so arrested and foully murdered.]

The murder of Yates, extracted from Bill Hickman's Book, p. 124:—"Yates had a fine gold watch and 900 dollars in gold. Joseph A. Young, a son of Brigham's, said his father wanted that man Yates killed. Col. Jones, Hosea Stout, and another, whose name I do not recollect, came to my camp fire and asked if Yates was asleep. I told them he was, upon which his brains were knocked out with an axe, a grave three feet deep was dug, the body put in and the dirt well packed on it, after which our camp fire was moved on to the grave. We were off before day light, and arrived at Salt Lake that day. My comrade and I went to Brigham's office. He asked what had become of Yates? I told him. He said that was right and a good thing. I pulled out the sack containing the money; the money was counted and we left."

From *The Rocky Mountain Saints*, p. 736, I extract from the speech of Governor J. B. Weller, of Utah, on the murder of Dr. Robinson:—"Dr. Robinson, aged 31 years, was an amiable, quiet Christian, universally loved and respected. Six months ago he married a young lady of one of our most estimable families. An armed force of the police, sent by the City authorities, destroyed his building and ejected him from his premises. Afterward, between 11 and 12 p.m. a man goes to the doctor's house, wakes him up, tells him that a brother of his (Jones) had broken his leg. The doctor hastily dressed and proceeds with this man upon what he regarded a mission of mercy. About 175 steps from his dwelling he was struck over the head with a sharp instrument, and then shot through the brain."

"Apostle" Snow, in a sermon distinguished by its profanity and brutal ferocity, which was not reported and can only be stated from memory:—"He plainly told the audience that whoever should be the executioner of divine justice and slay the apostate, their wives and children, would receive a bright crown of glory, and, what is more to be lamented, it was approvingly responded to by the audience. It was a sphere of murder, plain, palpable, frightful and sickening. The picture can never be effaced from the mind—a *preacher* in the pulpit ferociously enjoining the murder of men, women, and children for a difference of opinion, and thousands of faces intently gazing upon him with fanatical approbation. The regions of the damned could scarcely present a scene more truly diabolical.—Secretary Ferris, p. 332, *Utah and the Mormons*.

Utah is a rich mineral country, and many Gentiles came to "Zion" to open the mines and get rich. Apostle Woodruff preached for their benefit the following:—"Men that come here to seek for our gold and silver find that it is now too hot for them. The day has now come that they cannot bear the burning heat of Zion, and I am glad of it."—*Journal of Discourses*, vol. 6, p. 141.

Brigham talked a little plainer and said, "If any miserable scoundrels come here, cut their throats," and all the people said 'Amen!' *Ibid*, p. 253.

"So then these Saints of blessed memory, Cut throats in godly, pure sincerity."
Hudibras.

From "*Brigham's Destroying Angel*," or "*The Confession of Bill Hickman, Danite Chief of Utah*," page 205, I extract the following account of the "Aikin Massacre":—

"The party consisted of six men: John Aikin, William Aikin, —— Buck, a man known as 'Colonel,' and two others. They left Sacramento early in May, 1857. On reaching the Humboldt River they found a train of the Mormons from Carson, who were ordered home about that time. With them they completed the journey. John Pendleton, one of that Mormon party, in his testimony on the case says: 'A better lot of boys I never saw. They were kind, polite, and brave; always ready to do anything needed on the road.'

"The train travelled slowly, so the Aikin party left it a hundred miles out and came ahead, and on reaching Kaysville, twenty-five miles north of Salt Lake City, they were all arrested on the charge of being spies for the Government! A few days after Pendleton and party arrived and recognized their horses in the public *Corral*. On inquiry he was told the men had been arrested as spies, to which he replied, 'Spies, h—ll! Why, they've come with us all the way.' The party in charge answered that they 'did not care, they would keep them.' The Aikin party had stock, property, and money estimated at 25,000 dollars.

"They were then taken to the city and confined. They were told they should be 'sent out of the Territory by the Southern route.' Four of them started, leaving Buck and one of the unknown men in the city. The party had for an escort, O. P. Rockwell, John Lot, —— Miles, and one other. When they reached Nephi, one hundred miles south, Rockwell informed the Bishop, Bryant, that his orders were to 'have the men used up there.' Bishop Bryant called a council at once, and the following men were selected to assist: J. Bigler (now a Bishop), P. Pitchforth, his 'first councillor,' John Kink, and ——Pickton.

"The selected murderers, at 11 p.m., started from the Tithing House and got ahead of the Aikins', who did not start till daylight. The latter reached the Sevier River, when Rockwell informed them they could find no other camp that day; they halted, when the other party approached and asked to camp with them, for which permission was granted. The weary men removed their arms and heavy clothing, and were soon lost in sleep—that sleep which for two of them was to have no waking on earth. The party from Nephi attacked the sleeping men with clubs and the kingbolts of the waggons. Two died without a struggle. But John Aikin bounded to his feet, but slightly wounded, and sprang into the brush. A shot from the pistol of John Kink laid him senseless. 'Colonel' also reached the brush, receiving a shot in the shoulder from Port Rockwell, and believing the whole party had been attacked by banditti, he made his way back to Nephi. With almost superhuman strength he held out during the twenty-five miles, and the first bright rays of a Utah sun showed the man, who twenty-four hours before had left them handsome and vigorous in the pride of manhood, now ghastly pale and drenched with his own blood, staggering feebly along the streets of Nephi. He reached Bishop Foote's, and his story elicited a well-feigned horror.

"Meanwhile the murderers had gathered up the other three and thrown them into the river, supposing all to be dead. But John Aikin revived and crawled out on the same side, and hiding in the brush, heard these terrible words, 'Are the damned Gentiles all dead, Port?

'All but one—the son of a b—— ran.'

"Supposing himself to be meant, Aikin lay still till the Danites left, then without hat, coat, or boots, on a November night, the ground covered with snow, he set out for Nephi. Who can imagine the feelings of the man? Unlike 'Colonel' he knew too well who the murderers were, and believed himself the only survivor. To return to Nephi offered but slight hope, and incredible as it may appear he reached it next day. He sank helpless at the door of the first house he reached, but the words he heard infused new life into him. The woman said to him, 'Why another of you ones got away from the robbers, and is at Brother Foote's.' 'Thank God; it is my brother,' he said, and started on. The citizens tell with wonder that he ran the whole distance, his hair clotted with blood, reeling like a drunken man all the way. It was not his brother, but 'Colonel.' They fell upon each other's necks, clasped their blood-spattered arms around each other, and with mingled tears and sobs kissed and embraced as only men can who together have passed through death. A demon might have shed tears at the sight—but not a Mormon Bishop. The fierce tiger can be lured from his prey, the bear may become civilized, or the hyæna be tamed of his lust for human flesh—religious fanaticism alone can triumph over all tenderness, and make man tenfold more the child of hell than the worst passions of mere physical nature. Even while gazing upon this scene, the implacables were deciding upon their death.

"Bishop Bryant came, extracted the balls, dressed the wounds, and advised the men to return, as soon as they were able, to Salt Lake City. A son of Bishop Foote had proved their best friend, and Aikin requested him to take his account in writing of the affair. Aikin began to write it, but was unmanned. and begged young Foote to do it, which he did. That writing, the dying declaration of 'Colonel' and John Aiken, is *in existence to-day*.

"The murderers had returned, and a new plan was concocted. 'Colonel' had saved his pistol and Aikin his watch, a gold one, worth at least 250 dollars. When ready to leave they asked the bill, and were informed it was 30 dollars. They promised to send it from the City, and were told that 'would not do.' Aikin then said, 'Here is my watch and my partner's pistol—take your choice.' *Foote took the pistol.* When he handed it to him Aikin said, 'There, take my best friend. But God knows it will do us no good.' Then to his partner, with tears streaming from his eyes, 'Prepare for death, Colonel, we will never get out of this valley alive.'

They had got four miles on the road, when their driver, a Mormon named Wolff, stopped the wagon near an old cabin; informed them he must water his horses; unhitched them, and moved away. Two men then stepped from the cabin, and fired with double-barreled guns; Aiken and 'Colonel' were both shot through the head, and fell dead from the wagon. Their bodies were then loaded with stone and put in one of those 'bottomless springs'—so called—common in that part of Utah.

"Meanwhile Rockwell and party had reached the city, taken Buck and the other man, and started southward, plying them with liqour. It is probable that Buck only feigned drunkenness; but the other man was insensible by the time they reached the Point of the Mountain. There it was decided to 'use them up,' and they were attacked with slung-shots and billies. The other man was instantly killed. Buck leaped from the wagon, outran his pursuers, their shots missing him, swam the Jordan, and came down it on the west side. He reached the city and related all that had occurred, which created quite a stir. Hickman was then sent for to 'finish the job.' He shot Buck through the head, buried him in a ditch, went to Brigham Young and told him Buck was taken care of. Young said he was glad of it. Buck was the last one of the Aikin Party."

Hickman confesses to scores of murders which he committed in the name of the Lord, but I have no room to give them.

The late Governor of Utah, Stephen S. Harding, wrote a letter to the publisher of Bill Hickman's Book which appears on page 210, and from which I extract the following account of the "MORRISITE MASSACRE."

The substance of the story is as follows:—"Joseph Morris had been a faithful follower of Brigham Young, but concluded to turn prophet on his own account. He caused a schism in the Mormon Church, calling after him several bishops and elders, with the laymen, including five hundred rank and file. With him was one Joseph Banks, well educated. There was no great difference in the doctrines of Morris and Brigham, except in one particular:

Morris taught that he was the true prophet, 'anointed of the Lord,' and Brigham that *he* himself was 'God's Anointed.' Taking the testimony of both parties, it would be hard to settle the theological muddle, for both claimed to have the 'gift of tongues,' the power of healing, and laying on of hands,' of 'casting out devils,' and so on. It was but the old story over again;. There is not room in the Roman Empire for *two* Cæsars.'

"The Morrisites left the Mormon settlements and 'gathered in the name of the Lord' on the banks of Weber River, some forty miles north of the city. They took all their moveable property with them, including a large amount of grain. Some men they had sent to a distant mill with grain were arrested and kept prisoners. Fines were assessed against them, their cattle were seized on execution, and others stampeded and driven off. The last cow of many a poor man was taken, on which they largely depended, and the little children, not able to appreciate the faith of their parents, often went crying and supperless to bed.

"This deliberate cruelty of course created great excitement in the camp of the new prophet. As might have been expected, he stepped over the commands of Jesus, and went back to Moses for guidance; and, in retaliation, ordered a raid upon the Mormon stock, and that their owners should be captured and held as hostages. As this, to say the least, seems to have been the primitive way in which such matters were settled, all this would seem food for laughter, if the ending had not been so tragical.

"There was one easy way to settle it: to stop the wrongs continually inflicted upon these poor and deluded people. But the 'authorities' had other views. Twelve hundred miles separated Brigham's kingdom from the last belt of civilization, and he was 'monarch of all he surveyed.' It was somewhat necessary for him to follow legal forms, and writs of *habeas corpus* and warrants were issued by Judge Kinney (Chief Justice), and placed in the hands of (a Mormon) Sheriff Robert T. Burton. He called on the acting Governor, Secretary Frank Fuller, for an armed *posse*; his request was granted, and he left the city with five hundred armed men and five pieces of artillery. On the way he received volunteers to the number of nearly five hundred more.

"They marched to within half a mile of the Morrisite camp, which consisted of a few log houses, and several others made of willows, interlaced like basket-work, and plastered inside—no more fit for a place of defence than if they had been made of cobwebs. The *posse* took possession of the Morrisite herd, and killed such as they needed for beef, while the boys in charge of it were sent in by Burton with a paper containing a notice to the commander of the besieged, that if he did not surrender unconditionally within half an hour, firing would begin. Burton had placed his cannon in such a position as to rake the camp with a cross-fire.

"Morris had called his people to the Bowery, their place of worship, to decide what they should do. He told them the Lord would reveal their duty and the whole congregation raised a hymn of their own, hundreds of voices mingling with a wild charm, and producing a spirited effect upon the fanatical mind which can be imagined. Meantime Morris stood with imploring hands and eyes turned heavenward, and Banks stood by, believing the revelation would come in answer to their prayers. Morris encouraged his people, reminding them of the promises, 'They who wait on the Lord shall not perish,' 'One shall chase a thousand, and two put ten thousand to flight.'

"But no 'revelation' came, and as the last hallelujah died away, the sound of a cannon broke upon the melody, but the shot fell short of the camp. The next instant another cannon was fired, the shot struck the Bowery, two women fell dead, horribly mangled, and a girl of twelve years had her chin shot away. One of the women who fell had a child in her arms, which, strange to say, was not injured. Unhappily the poor girl did not die. I saw her years afterwards, the most ghastly human face my eyes ever beheld.

"The Morrisites had not more than ninety able-bodied men, all told, with over three hundred women and children. And now commenced assault and repulse, scouting and counterplotting, which continued all night and the next two days. Some ten persons were killed in the camp, of the new prophet. The third day, the besieged being exhausted, a white flag was raised as a signal of surrender. The order was given by Burton for the women and children to separate from the men, which was done, and the latter stacked their arms. Burton rode into camp with one of his officers beside him, and holding his revolver in his hand, he said 'show him to me.' Morris was pointed out, when Burton rode up and emptied one chamber of his revolver, the shot taking effect in the prophet's neck. He sank to the earth mortally wounded. Burton then shouted sneeringly, 'There's your prophet—what do you think of him now?' He then turned and discharged a second shot at Joseph Banks, who fell dead. A woman named Bowman ran up and exclaimed, 'Oh! you cruel murderer!' Burton fired his third shot, and she fell dead. Morris was meanwhile struggling in the agonies of death, when a Danish woman raised him in her arms, crying bitterly. Burton rode up to her and shot her through the heart, and the spirits of the victims mingled in one company to that bourne 'where the wicked cease from troubling, and the weary are for ever at rest.'

"The *posse* at the same time came into camp, and robbed the houses of all valuables—watches, jewelry and money—even tearing off the women's finger rings.

"The men were marched to the city, and the women taken to different Mormon settlements, after which they roamed about in utter destitution, 'scattered and peeled,' mere Pariahs of the plains, fleeing from the face of their 'brethren in the Lord,' and appealing to the Gentile traveller in the name of the merciful Jesus for the pittance of charity.

THE MOUNTAIN MEADOW MASSACRE.

In September, 1857, one hundred and twenty men, women and children were massacred by Mormons and Indians, at the Mountain Meadows in Utah. The victims under the command of Captain Fancher, were emigrants from Arkansas travelling to California in wagons. They were well fixed for the journey, good teams, plenty of stock and money to purchase supplies on the route. They had calculated purchasing flour and such things as they needed, at Salt Lake, but on arrival there, no one would sell them anything. Leaving Salt Lake they proceeded 300 miles on the southern route toward California when they came to Mountain Meadows. Here by a lovely spring, they concluded to camp awhile, and recruit their stock, now getting poor from want of good pasture, before crossing the dessert which lay before them. While encamped here, the Mormons rallied the Indians, painted and dressed themselves as Indians and surrounded the Emigrants on the morning of their intended departure. I will depict the scene as given me by a participant in that dreadful affair.

"The Mormons and Indians got quietly behind a hill which was within calling distance of the Emigrant camp. The Emigrants who were Christians, had commenced singing, after which one of their company prayed. The song and prayer over they hitch up, take a farewell drink from that beautiful spring and start on their journey. They had not proceeded far when a volley was fired at them by the Indians and mock Indian Mormons, killing 7 and wounding 16. Thinking it an Indian attack they hastily formed their wagons into a circle, called a corral, and defended themselves as best they could. Being well armed they kept the Mormons and Indians at bay. They fought all that day and night, and the next. On the third day of the battle, they were choking with thirst, weary for want of sleep and food. Without water, they can hold out but little longer, here are women parching, little children screaming for water. The fathers and brothers aroused by the cries of their loved ones for water, make desperate but fatal and unsuccessful efforts to get it; there was abundance in plain sight but so soon as a man showed outside the wagon fort he was mercilessly shot down. They dressed two little girls in white, and with white flags in their hands started them with a bucket to fetch water from the spring. Two well aimed shots from Mormon rifles ended the thirst and misery of those two dear little girls.

"On the fourth day the Mormons washed off their paint and dressed as white men, went to the Emigrant camp, offered to protect them and lead them safely back to the city. In this way they got them out and then murdered the whole lot, except a few children too young to tell the tale. As Bishop John D. Lee, who superintended the bloody deed, made a confession prior to his execution which has been published, I give the account of the council held to devise the treacherous plan of decoying the emigrants out, and their murder as he gave it. Lee was first tried in 1875, but the jury failed to agree. He was again tried in 1876. Meantime the Mormon leaders concluded to make Lee the scape-goat, and have him executed, consequently there was plenty of evidence and a jury to convict. Lee was executed at the Mountain Meadows, where the Massacre occurred, on the 25th March, 1877. I will first extract from the Publishers and Author's preface.

"The Mormon leaders were so greatly alarmed at the prospect of the publication of Lee's writings, and the consequent revelations of their secrets and crimes, that they sent their 'Blood Atoners' to threaten the life of Mr. Bishop, and, if possible, compel him to give up his manuscripts. The danger was so great that he was compelled to have his office guarded while engaged in copying the papers; and when they were ready to be forwarded to the publishers, the Wells, Fargo and Co., Express refused to receive them until they were furnished with an armed guard to protect them until they were beyond the reach of the Mormons. PUBLISHERS' PREFACE.

"John D. Lee was *one, and the only one of fifty-eight* Mormons who there carried out the orders of the Mormon Priesthood. * * *

"As one of the attorneys for John D. Lee I did all that I could to save his life. My associates were, and are, able men and fine lawyers, but fact and fate united to turn the verdict against us.

"After Brigham Young and his worshippers had deserted Lee, and marked him as the victim that should suffer to save the church from destruction, on account of the crimes it had ordered; after all chances of escape had vanished, and death was certain as the result of the life-long service he had rendered the church, the better nature of Lee overcame his superstition and fanaticism, and he gave to me the history of his life, and his confession of the facts in connection with the massacre, and wished me to have the same published. AUTHOR'S (W. W. BISHOP) PREFACE."

I now turn to Lee's Confession. Commencing on page 213, Lee says:—

"AS A DUTY to myself, my family, and mankind at large, I propose to give a full and true statement of all that I know of that unfortunate affair, which has cursed my existence for the last 19 years, and which is known as the MOUNTAIN MEADOWS MASSACRE.

"At the time, I and those with me, acted by virtue of positive orders from Bishop Haight and his associates, I was told by Haight that his orders to me were the result of full consultation with Bishop Dame and all in authority. It is a new thing to me, if the massacre was not decided on by the head men of the Church. The superiority that I claim for my statement is this:—

"ALL THAT I DO SAY IS TRUE AND NOTHING BUT THE TRUTH,

"I know that our total force was fifty-four white and over three hundred Indians. As soon as those persons gathered around the camp, Bishop Higbee reported as follows:—' It is the orders of the President that all the emigrants must be PUT OUT OF THE WAY,' that the emigrants had come through our country as the enemies of the Church of Jesus Christ of Latter-day Saints. * * * * * That none but friends were permitted to leave the Territory, and that, as these were our enemies, they must be killed. That the only safety for the people was the utter destruction of the whole rascally lot. * * * The men then in council knelt down in a prayer-circle and prayed, invoking the Spirit of God to direct them how to act in the matter. After prayer Higbee said, ' Here are the orders,' and handed me a paper from Bishop Haight.

"The substance of the orders were that the emigrants should be *decoyed* and all exterminated, so that no one should be left to tell the tale, and then the authorities could say it was done by the Indians. * * * I then left the council and went away to myself, and bowed in prayer before God. * * *

"When I got back, the council again prayed for aid. The council was called the City Counsellors, the Church or High Counsellors; and all in authority, together with the private citizens, then formed a circle, and kneeling down, so that elbows would touch each other, several of the brethren prayed for Divine instructions. After prayer, Bishop Higbee said: ' I have the evidence of God's approval of our mission. It is God's will that we carry out our instructions to the letter."

"* * * The meeting was then addressed by one in authority. He spoke in about this language: ' Brethren, we have been sent here to perform a duty. It is a duty that we owe to God, and to our church and people. The orders of those in authority are that all the emigrants *must* die. Our leaders speak with inspired tongues, and their orders come from the God of Heaven. We have no right to question what they have commanded us to do; it is our duty to obey. We must kill them all, and our orders are to get them out by treachery.'

"The emigrants were to be decoyed under a promise of protection. I was to demand that the children who were so young they could not talk should be put in a wagon. Then all the arms and amunition of the emigrants should be put in a wagon, and I was to agree that the Mormons would protect the emigrants and conduct them to the city in safety.

"The women were to march on foot and follow the wagons in single file. The men were to follow behind the women, they also to march in single file. Bishop Higbee was to stand with his company about 200 yards from the camp, and stand in double file, open order, with about 20 feet space between the files, so that the waggons could pass between them. The drivers were to keep right along. The women were to follow the waggons. The troops were to halt the men for a few minutes, until the women were some distance ahead, where the Indians were hid in ambush. Then the march was to be resumed, and the troops to form in single file, each soldier to walk by an emigrant, and on the right-hand side of his man, and carry his gun on the left arm, ready for instant use. The march was to continue until the wagons had passed beyond the ambush of the Indians, and until the women were right in the midst of the Indians. Higbee was then to give orders and words, ' *Do your duty !* ' At this the troops were to shoot down the men; the Indians were to kill the women and larger children, and the drivers of the waggons and I was to kill the wounded and sick men that were in the wagons. Two men were to be placed on horses near by, to overtake and kill any of the emigrants that might escape from the first assault. The Indians were to kill the women and large children, so that it would be certain that no Mormon would be guilty of shedding *innocent blood*—if it should happen that there was any innocent blood in the company that were to die. Our leading men all said that there was no innocent blood in the company.

"I, therefore, taking all things into consideration, and believing, as I then did, that my superiors were *inspired* men, who could not go wrong in any matter relating to the church, or the duty of its members, concluded to be obedient to the wishes of those in authority, I took up my cross and prepared to do my duty.

"Bateman took a white flag and started for the emigrant camp. When he got about half way, he was met by one of the emigrants. * * *

"I was then ordered by Bishop Higbee to go and negotiate the treaty and superintend the whole matter. He said, 'Brother Lee, we expect you to carry out all the instructions given by our council.' * * *

"Mc Murdy and Knight were ordered to drive their teams and follow me to haul off the children, arms, etc. I walked ahead of the wagons to the corral. I there met Mr. Hamilton on the outside of the camp. He loosened the chains from some of the wagons and moved one wagon out of the way, so that our teams could drive into their camp. The emigrants were strongly fortified; their wagons were chained together in a circle. In the centre was a rifle pit, large enough to contain the entire company. This had served to shield them from the constant fire poured into them from both sides of the valley, from a rocky range that served as a breastwork for their assailants. The valley at this point is not more than 500 yards wide, and the emigrants were near the centre. The Indians and Mormons had a splendid place for protection while they fired upon the emigrants. * * *

"As I entered, men, women and children gathered around me in wild consternation. I delivered my message and told the people that they must put their arms in the wagon, so as not to arouse the animosity of the Indians, I ordered the children and wounded and arms, to be put in the wagons, I hurried up the people and started the wagons off toward Cedar City. * * *

"The women and larger children walked ahead as directed, and the men followed them all in single file. The foremost man was fifty yards behind the hindmost woman.

"When they came up they cheered the armed Mormons, believing they were acting honestly. Higbee then gave the orders for his men to form in single file at the right of the emigrants. * * *

"It was my duty with the two drivers, to kill the sick and wounded who were in the wagons and to do so when we heard the guns fire. We were half a mile from Bishop Higbee and his men, when we heard the firing. As we heard the guns, I ordered a halt and we proceeded to do our part. * * *

"One little child six months old was carried in its fathers arms, and was killed by the same bullet that entered its father's breast; it was shot through the head, I saw it laying dead when I returned to the place of slaughter.

"Mc Murdy went to the wagon where the sick and wounded were, and raising his rifle to his shoulder said: "*O Lord, my God, receive their spirits, it is for Thy kingdom that I do this.*' He then shot a man who was laying with his head on another man's breast; the ball killed both men. * * *

"Knight shot a man in the head. A boy about 14 years old came running up to our wagons, and Knight struck him on the head with the butt end of his gun, and crushed his skull. * * *

"All that showed signs of life were at once shot through the head.

"Just after the wounded were all killed, I saw a girl, ten or eleven years old, running toward us from the main body of emigrants. An Indian shot her before she got within sixty yards of us. * * *

"While going back to the brethren I passed the bodies of several women. In one place I saw six or seven bodies near each other; they were stripped perfectly naked. I saw many bodies lying dead and naked on the field, near by where the women lay. I saw ten children; they had been killed close to each other; they were from ten to sixteen years of age. The bodies of the women and children were scattered along the ground for quite a distance before I came to where the men were killed. * * *

"When I reached the place where the dead men lay, I was told how the orders had been obeyed. Bishop Higbee said, 'The boys have acted admirably they took good aim, and all of the d—d Gentiles, but two or three fell at the *first fire.*' He said that three or four got away some distance, but the men on horses overtook them and cut their throats. * * *

"The bodies of men, women, and children had been stripped entirely naked, making the scene one of the most loathsome and ghastly that can be imagined.

"The brethren piled the dead bodies up in heaps, in little gullies, and threw dirt over them. The bodies were only lightly covered, for the ground was hard, and the brethren did not have tools to dig with. I suppose it is true the first rain washed the bodies all out again, but I never went back to examine. * * *

"The brethren were called up, and Higbee and Klingensmith, as well as myself, made speeches, and ordered the people to keep the matter a secret from the *entire* world. Not to tell their wives nor their most intimate friends, and we pledged ourselves to keep everything relating to the affair a secret during life. We also took the most binding oaths to stand by each other, and to always insist that the massacre was committed by Indians alone. This was the advice of Brigham Young, too, as I will show hereafter.

"It was voted unanimously that any man who should divulge, or tell who was present, or do anything that would lead to a discovery of the truth, should suffer death. The brethren all took a most solemn oath, binding themselves under the most dreadful and awful penalties to keep the whole matter secret, from every human being as long as they should live. No man was to know the facts. The brethren were sworn not to talk of it among themselves, and each swore to help kill all who proved traitors to the Church or people in this matter. * * *

"Bishop Dame then blest the brethren and we prepared to go to our homes. * * *

"According to the orders of Bishop Haight, I started for Salt Lake City to report the whole facts connected with the massacre to Brigham Young. I started about a week or ten days after the massacre, and was on the way about ten days. When I arrived in the City I went to the President's house and gave Brigham Young a full, detailed statement of the whole affair from first to last. I went over the whole affair and made as full a statement as it was possible for me to give. * * * He asked me many questions, and I told him every particular. * * * Brigham then said: 'Isaac (referring to Haight) has sent me word that, if they had killed every man, woman, and child in the outfit (there was 16 small children spared), there would not have been a drop of innocent blood shed by the brethren.'

"I gave him the names of every man that had been present at the massacre. I told him who killed various ones. In fact, I gave him *all the information there was to give.*

"When I finished talking about the matter, he said, 'Brother Lee, I am afraid of treachery among the brethren that were there. If any one tells this thing so that it will become public, it will work us great injury. I want you to understand now that you are *never* to tell this again, not even to Heber C. Kimball. *It must* be kept a secret among ourselves. When you get home I want you to sit down and write a long letter, and give me an account of the affair, charging it to the Indians. You sign the letter as Farmer to the Indians, and direct it to me as Indian Agent. I can then make use of such a letter to keep off all damaging inquiries.'

"He then told me to withdraw and call next day.

"I went to see him again in the morning. When I went in, he seemed quite cheerful. He said:—

"'I have made that matter a subject of prayer. *I went right to God with it*, and asked him to take the horrid vision from my sight, *if it was a righteous thing* that my people had done in killing those people at the Mountain Meadows. God answered me, and *at once the vision was removed*. I have evidence from God that he has overruled it all for good, and the action was a righteous one and well intended.

"'The brethren acted from pure motives. The only trouble is they acted a *little prematurely;* they were a *little* ahead of time. *I sustain you* and all of the brethren for what they did. All that I fear is treachery on the part of some one who took a part with you, but we will look to that.'

"I was again cautioned and commanded to keep the whole thing as a sacred secret, and again told to write the report as Indian Farmer, laying the blame on the Indians. That ended our interview, and I left him, and started for home."

Judge Heniingrey when before the Congressional Committee, having read to them what I have just given, says:—"This statement bears the impress of truth. It is the dying declaration of an old man of sixty-five, not only made in full view of eternity, but made with a determination that the world should know the truth, and told with an air of veracity, which is inherent in the statement itself, and inseparable from it.

"The same power I have thus set forth and described, is claimed for the Church and its Priesthood to-day. Of course, then, it follows that in all the minor details of society, social, religious and political, the Mormon people are under the absolute control of the Priesthood. And any disregard of their control and right to control the body, mind and soul of the abject Mormon subject, is punished by an ostracism more cruel in its hellish inventions of torment than any ever known to civilized man."

The Christian Herald, London, Nov. 21, 1883, gives an account of Miss Carter's Missionary work in Utah, in which she had a conversation with a man who confessed he had been one of the Mountain Meadow murderers. He confirms all the main features of the beforegoing statements, and especially mentions that he never closes his eyes but he sees the little girls dressed in white and sent out for water, falling dead there.

I have only to add that I have conversed with many of the participants in that awful human butchery. Many of these murderers have been in England as Missionaries. Some of them are here now. They preach with great zeal and convert thousands of Britishers to the Mormon faith, who emigrate to this "Hell upon Earth."

Imagine these assassins marrying English girls, and begetting children who must feel the curse of their fathers crime. What must be the feelings of Lee's numerous progeny, he having married many women between the massacre and his execution, and who, by his own confession had 64 children.

I now quote from page 289 of Lee's confession as follows:—

I took my wives in the following order:—First Agatha Ann Woolsey; second, Nancy Berry; third, Louisa Free (now one of the wives of Daniel H. Wells); fourth, Sarah C. Williams; fifth old Mrs. Woolsey (the mother of Agatha Ann and Rachel A. (I married her for her soul's sake, for her salvation in the eternal state); sixth Rachel A. Woolsey (I was married to her at the same time that I was to her mother); seventh Andora Woolsey (a sister to Rachel); eighth, Polly Ann Workman; ninth, Martha Berry; tenth, Delithea Morris. In 1847, Brigham Young married me to *three women in one night*, viz., eleventh, Nancy Armstrong (she was what we call a widow, she left her husband in Tennessee, to be with the Mormon people); twelfth, Polly V. Young; thirteenth, Louisa Young (these two were sisters), 14th, Emeline Vaughan; 15th, Mary Lear Groves; 16th, Mary Ann Williams. In 1858 Brigham Young gave me my 17th wife, Emma Batchelder. I was sealed to her while a member of the Legislature. Brigham Young said that Bishop Haight, who was also in the Legislature and I (both Mountain Meadow assassins) needed some young women to renew our vitality, so he gave us both a dashing young bride (one year after the massacre). In 1859 I was sealed to my 18th wife, Teressa Morse, by order of Brigham Young. The last wife I got was Ann Gordge ; Brigham gave her to me. This was my 19th, but, as I was married to old Mrs. Woolsey for her soul's sake, and she was near sixty years old when I married her, I never considered her really as a wife. Truly I treated her well and gave her all the rights of marriage. Still I never count her as one of my wives. That is the reason that I claim *only eighteen true wives.*

"By my eighteen real wives I have been the father of sixty-four children Ten of my children are dead and fifty-four are still living.

"This is all I care to say about the affairs of my family, I have but little more to say. I have selected Wm. W. Bishop, my attorney, to publish my confessions, so that the world may know just what I did, and why I acted as I have done. I have delivered to Mr. Bishop all the Manuscripts and private writings and wish him to have all that I may hereafter write."

CONCLUSION OF THE CONFESSION OF JOHN D. LEE.

"Written in prison at Fort Cameron, Utah Territory. Delivered to Hon. Sumner Howard (United States Attorney) by John D. Lee, on the field of execution (just before the sentence of death was carried into effect), and forwarded to Wm. W. Bishop by Hon. Sumner Howard, according to the last request of John D. Lee.

"Death to me has no terror. It is but a struggle, and all is over. I know that I have a reward in heaven, and my conscience does not accuse me. This to me is a great consolation. FAREWELL! JOHN D. LEE."

"On Friday, March 23rd, 1877, the guard having Lee in charge, reached Mountain Meadows, where it had been decided to carry the sentence into execution. Lee pointed out the various places of interest connected with the massacre, and recapitulated the horrors of that event.

"At 10.35, all the arrangements having been completed, Marshal Nelson read the order of the court, and said "Mr. Lee, if you have anything to say before the order of the court is carried into effect, you can do so."

THE LAST WORDS OF JOHN D. LEE.

"I have but little to say this morning. I am on the brink of eternity; I feel resigned to my fate, I have made out a manuscript which is to be published. I am not an infidel. I have not denied God and His mercies. I am a strong believer in those things. Most I regret is parting with my family. (Here he rested two or three seconds). These touch a tender chord within me. (Here his voice faltered) I declare my innocence of doing anything designedly wrong in all this affair. I would have given worlds if I could have averted that calamity.

"Not a particle of mercy have I asked of the court, the world, or officials to spare my life. I do not fear death. I shall never go to a worse place than I am now in. [NOTE, Lee's last words admit Utah to be a Hell upon Earth. There's no place worse than Hell].

"I am a true believer in the Gospel of Jesus Christ. I do not believe everything that is now being taught and practised by Brigham Young, I do not care who hears it. It is my last word—it is so. I believe he is leading the people astray, downward to destruction.

"Having said this I feel resigned, I ask the Lord my God, if my labors are done, to receive my spirit."

"Lee ceased speaking at 10.50, A.M. He was then informed that his hour had come and he must prepare for execution. Rev. G. Stokes a Methodist Minister, who accompanied Lee as his spiritual adviser, then knelt and prayed. The prisoner listened attentively.

"At the Conclusion of the prayer Lee said to Marshal Nelson, 'I ask one favour—spare my limbs and centre my heart.' He then shook hands with those around him. The marshal bound a handkerchief over the prisoner's eyes, but at his request his hands were allowed to remain free. The doomed man then strengthened himself up facing the firing party, as he sat on his coffin, clasped his hands over his head, and exclaimed:—

'Let them shoot the balls through my heart! don't let them mangle my body!' The Marshall assured him that the aim would be true, and then stepped back. As he did so, he gave the orders to the guards: READY! AIM! FIRE! A sharp report was heard, and Lee fell back on his coffin, dead. There was not a cry nor a moan nor a tremor of the body. The spirit of John D. Lee had crossed the dark river and was standing before the Judge of the quick and the dead.

"His soul had solved the awful mystery, and the CURSE that hovers over the Mountain Meadows had marked 'ONE' upon its list of Retribution.'

"A more dreary scene than the present appearance of Mountain Meadows cannot be imagined. The curse of God seems to have fallen upon it scorched and withered the luxuriant grass that covered it 20 years ago, and transformed the fertile valley into an arid and barren plain. Mormons assert that the ghosts of the murdered emigrants meet nightly at the scene of their slaughter and re-enact in pantomime the horrors of their massacre."—*Lee's Confession, pp.* 384-9.

Sometime after the massacre, a United States officer buried the bones of the victims, erected a monument of loose stones, and placed thereon this inscription:—

"HERE 120 MEN WOMEN AND CHILDREN WERE MASSACRED IN COLD BLOOD EARLY IN SEPTEMBER 1857. THEY WERE FROM ARKANSAS.

"VENGEANCE IS MINE, I WILL REPAY SAITH THE LORD."

I finish this Chapter of Horrors with an extract from *The Salt Lake Tribune*, of April 10, 1881:—

"A man ploughing a field between the Apostles, Cannons, and Jennings farms, southwest of the city a few days ago, turned up three skeletons of human beings, complete, and in a good state of preservation, showing that they had belonged to adults. When discovered they were piled out to one side and left lying there, such developments being too common in the pleasant valleys of Utah to excite much wonder. A gentleman brought a skull to this city and called with it at THE TRIBUNE office.

An examination reveals a distinct fracture across the top of the skull. The discoloration proves that the fracture must have been fatal to the possessor. A similar fracture exists on the left side, a portion of the bone above the eye being broken off and proving that a murderer and not the angel of death cut off the life of this one at least. What the other skulls might have revealed it is impossible to say as they were not seen by our informant. The condition of the one referred to indicates that the burial was made not a great many years ago as the bones present a remarkably smooth surface and the brilliant whiteness of mother of pearl. In the United States these remains would be the subject of an inquest, but in this promised land they are dismembered, dumped in a pile and left to bleach in the sun, which no doubt sees on each day the man or men who did the foul deed walking upon the streets of Zion.

"A gentleman, conversing with THE TRIBUNE, reporter about the find, said it was almost an everyday occurrence. 'There have been not less than five hundred murders committed in this valley alone (there are scores of valleys in Utah) and its history, if written, would be one of blood. It couldn't be written properly unless it was written in blood, and it would be too horrible to read and expect thereafter any peace of mind.'"

"When the history of the Mormon Church is faithfully written, it will chronicle such a black and hideous catalogue of crime committed in the name of God, as will forever put to blush the Spanish Inquisition, or the foulest atrocities that the heart of man, possessed of the fiend's misanthropy and religious fanaticism, has ever conceived. In proof of this, the Mountain Meadows Massacre; the conspiracy against the Morrisites; the murder of the Aiken party; the killing of Yates, and scores of other cold-blooded murders actually ordered by the leaders of the Mormons, incited thereto by their well-known and undisguised hostility to the human race, stand an eternal monument. It is a fact capable of proof, and generally admitted by the intelligent portion of the Mormon community themselves, that some of the apostles and bishops—the spiritual and temporal heads of the church—are tainted with the crime of murder, fraud, perjury, adultery, assault with intent to kill, and other heinous crimes and misdemeanors; to say nothing of the long list of unredressed wrongs, oppressions and treachery, not enumerated in the criminal laws, that have been practised upon their own unsuspecting victims in the Church, during the past twenty years, whose cries go up daily to high Heaven against them."—*Salt Lake Tribune.*

WHAT I SUFFERED—THROWN INTO DUNGEONS—MY GRAVE DUG—
HOW I ESCAPED AND GOT OUT OF HELL.

After quoting so much I deem it right to give a little of my own experience. Space prevents my giving in full the three "Patriarchal Blessings" I received so I give extracts as follows:—

"Salt Lake City, Utah, April, 13th, 1869.

"A blessing given by John Smith, Patriarch, upon the head of William Jarman, son of John and Ann Jarman, born in London, Middlesex, England, April, 1st, 1837.

"Brother William, I lay my hands upon thy head in the name of Jesus of Nazereth, to pronounce and seal a blessing upon thee. Therefore be at rest in thy mind and look forward to the future, that you may comprehend the blessings which are in store for the faithful. For thou art of the blood of Joseph and a descendant of Ephraim, and have a great work to perform in thy day. The Lord hath had his eye upon thee for years, and thou art numbered among the One Hundred and forty-four thousand saviours of men * * * Thou shalt confound the wisdom of the wicked, and set at naught the counsels of the unjust. Thou shalt converse with the noblemen of the earth and they shall wonder at thy wisdom; for thou shalt be filled with the spirit of the Lord above many of thy fellows. * * * Thou shalt also be blessed in thy Outgoings and in thy Incomings, Spiritually and Temporarilly, and also be prospered in the labor of thy hands, and thy name shall be perpetuated upon the earth, and handed down with thy posterity in honorable remembrance, and written in the Lamb's Book of Life, and Registered in the Chronicles of thy Fathers with thy Brethren. This blessing I seal upon thy head, and I seal thee up unto Eternal Life to come forth in the morning of the First Resurrection—Even so Amen. Recorded in Book A. page 903."

The Patriarch, John Young, Brigham's brother, gave me a blessing for two dollars, which is dirt cheap. It covers four pages of "Foolscap" closely written, in which I am confirmed "An Heir to the Holy Priesthood" as well as being "one of the 144,000 virgins without guile." I am also a Jew though born of Gentile parents, "Being a literal descendent of Ephraim," I am to "obtain a fullness of the Holy Priesthood in the own due time of the Lord." Also, "Wives and children and a numerous posterity on the earth, even upon Mount Zion." Then comes a sentence which makes me a good catch for an Insurance Company or Sick Benefit Society, it says:—" I seal upon your head the blessings of life and of health and prosperity and say you shall live on the earth till your hair becomes as white as the pure wool." I am to become "A Saviour upon Mount Zion; and clothed upon with Priestly Garments shall have power to officiate in the holy ordinances; be numbered among the great and the good, and receive an inheritance in the New Heavens and New Earth." After pronouncing blessings innumerable, this Patriarch winds up with " These blessings I seal upon you according to the holy order committed to the servants of the Lord to bind on earth and bind for heaven, and I do it by the power of the priesthood in the name of the Lord Jesus Christ. Even so, Amen."

The Patriarch C. W. Hyde "blessed" me real nice, one of his wives wrote it down and gave me a copy. He began with, "William, I place my hands upon thy head and seal upon you a Patriarchal Blessing, for the eye of the Lord has been upon thee from Everlasting to do a great and a mighty work in this Kingdom, and no weapon formed against thee shall prosper for the Lord has given his Angels charge over you that you may live long upon the earth to promote the glory and interest of the Kingdom of God on this Earth and thou shalt stand before Kings and rulers to proclaim this Gospel * * * Thou shalt have power to do any miracle that was ever done * * * Have power to open prisons. * * * Thou art of the house of Ephraim and a right to the fullness of the Priesthood with wives and a great Kingdom upon the Earth * * * you shall stand on the earth at the coming of the Messiah * * * Thou shalt lead many to Zion with the rich treasures to help rear the Temple * * * You shall redeem your father's household * * * These blessings I seal upon your head with Eternal lives with your father's household, forever and ever, Amen. Recorded in Book E. page 792,"

The price of these Patriarchal Blessings is Two Dollars per "Bless."

Notwithstanding the great and manifold "blessings," the Endowment House had so shaken my faith in Mormonism that I cared very little for my "High and Holy Calling." I became acquainted with a "Cockney" who felt about as I did, we both wished ourselves back in London. One day when calling on my Cockney friend, he introduced me to two of the "brethren" who had participated in the Mountain Meadow Massacre. I had heard of the affair as "an Indian Massacre," and was surprised to find that the Mormons were the principal actors in that fearful tragedy. When I learnt from these men the facts, I felt that to be associated with such a band of murderers would make me equally guilty. How could I uphold such deeds? I could never call these men "my brothers." I went at once to Brigham Young and demanded to have my name erased from their books, for I could no longer remain a Mormon, and told him the reason. On leaving Brigham he said to me "Oh ta, ta if you are going; You've got it bad, I see; your case shall be attended to."

Up to this time my life was burdensome, but now having asserted my rights and dared to be free, and having left the abominable Church, I felt more easier, I was indeed a converted man. I prepared to battle with the inevitable, for I knew the awful fate that awaits "Apostates." They do not always kill them, oftimes they are declared insane, and confined in a wretched Asylum. I am sorry I have not space to give the abundance of proof I have on this point. Even since I commenced writing this book, an American Lady has sent me a copy of her new book, entitled "Elder Northfield's

Home, or Sacrificed on the Mormon Altar, a story of the blighted curse of Polygamy." A New York paper says of it :—" It tells the story of an English girl who, becoming infatuated with a Mormon elder accompanies him to Utah. It will open the eyes of the mothers and fathers of the land to a curse which is darker than the shackles of slavery, more deadly than the plagues of Egypt." I have read the book with much interest. It tells how the girl was entrapped, her life in Utah Slavery, her attempted escape and capture; then placed in a lunatic asylum. It is a thrilling story; those of my readers who can afford one dollar (4/2) should send to Mrs. Jennie Bartlett, Monson, Mass. U.S.A., the Authoress, for a copy. It beats all the novels in the world, and clearly shows the Mormon Insanity dodge.

I naturally thought that as they knew of my asylum episode I should be pronounced insane, and speedily "die a raving maniac." Fearing they might place their "Danites" or "Destroying Angels" on my track, I made a friend of a "Chief Danite," who lived near me. I bought him. The price was high, but my readers will soon see that it was a good investment, for not long after my interview with Brigham, the Bishop waited on me, and gave me to understand that my blood must be shed to atone for my sins. I preferred to remain in my sins rather than have my throat cut, and told him so. I was not ready to acquiesce as he wished, and he went away "disgusted" with me.

A few days after my "Danite friend" came to me on the Q. T. He said, "For God's sake be careful; never show out after dark; when the chickens go to roost you go too." I told him that in London we seldom retired so early, I was afraid that going to bed so soon would prevent my sleeping, and make an awful long night of it. He smiled, promised to do me a good turn if he could, and we parted.

I kept a good look out, and so did the Mormon leaders, for one evening having met an old friend in the City, it was dark when I left him to go home. My house was in the suburbs, and I had some distance to go. When I got near home my Danite friend met me, pushed me back hurriedly and whispered, "Go back, your grave is dug in your garden; two men are waiting at your gate, and we have to kill you. Don't go home to-night; swear you ain't seen me, or you and I are both dead men."

Had I gone home the reader's eyes would not now be resting on these pages. Thousands that wished to inform the world, as I am now doing, are in their graves; as the Mormons say, "Dead men tell no tales."

The next morning I went to my "Hell upon Earth." Before going in, I found MY NEW DUG GRAVE in the garden. I looked down into *my* grave, a sight seldom witnessed by mortal eyes. The reader may have looked into the grave of a relative or friend, but into his own, never. I cannot describe my thoughts as I stood there by the side of my grave, which, but for the timely warning would now contain my body. There and then I swore that if spared to escape from that awful Sodom, I would spend the balance of my days in exposing the abominable evils of Mormonism.

"The spirit of the times can be gathered from the following beautiful expressions of President Young, his apostle son Brigham, and General D. H. Wells, then Mayor of the city, in a meeting of 1,500 men. Brigham Young, Jr., said: 'That fellow Sherman said the other night coming down the street that he felt rather timid about coming out after dark. I know the reason why he felt timid; he knows that he should be killed. That's what's the matter. Any man who violates his covenant should be killed!' President Young assented to this beautiful speech of his apostle by the nodding of his head, and when young Brigham had sat down the old man said: 'That man is an unprofitable servant that his master has to tell him to do everything. Brethren whatever your hand finds to do, do it with all your might.' Then Gen. D. H. Wells stood on his feet and said: 'The best thing that we can do for these men is to kill them." Extract from *Salt Lake Tribune*.

The usual plan of breaking up the Apostates' home was resorted to. The doctrine that no woman is saved but through her husband means that if the husband leaves the church the wife must leave him or she also is lost. My wife was, and still is, a Mormon fanatic. The Probate Judge and Great High Priest gave her a bill of divorce and most of my real estate. The second wife then wished to be legally married. This was done as I afterwards found to secure the balance of my property, as she could also get a divorce and property with it when married. Prior to the first wife's divorce, I had been *commanded* to put my stock of drapery into the Mormon Co-operative Store, just then started. This I refused to do; I had paid the tenth of it into the church as tithing. If a man or woman has but 10s. on arriving in "Zion," they must give 1/- to the church, and ever after the tenth of all their earnings. I give one verse from their "Sacred" Hymns in the *Mountain Warbler*, p. 67 :—

"TUNE—'*King of the Cannibal Islands*.'"

"Now, male and female, rich and poor, who wish to keep your standing sure,
That you salvation may secure. Come forward and pay up your tithing.
A tenth that is and nothing less, of all you do or may possess:
In flocks and herds, and their increase; in pigs and poultry, ducks and geese;
A tenth, indeed of all your toil, likewise the products of the soil;
And if you've any wine or oil, come forward, and pay up your tithing!"

CHORUS—
Then, if to prosper you desire, and wish to keep out of the fire,
Nay, if you to be Saints aspire, come forward and pay up your tithing.

I had "come forward," paid my tithing, and now they wanted the other nine-tenths. I failed to see the point. The first day I arrived in "Zion," the Bishop overhauled my fourteen boxes and bales of silks, velvets, linen, broadcloth, &c., and said, "The Church will open a store shortly, you can put these goods in and receive stock in the concern and a situation when we start. You see Brother Jennings, obtain a situation in his store so as to learn how business is done here." I got the situation and went to work. This was a trap as you will see. Mormons are so trickey, and suspecting everybody, they fix matters so that if a man dares assert his rights, or fails to "obey counsel" they have him, as in my case.

I showed Jennings my goods and tried to sell them to him, but he refused to purchase. The Church Store was duly opened, and as stated, I was "counselled" to put my stock into the concern; but I had been through the Endowment House, and wished to turn my goods into money and "Hook it." While planning a disposal of my goods, a policeman came with a warrant, arrested me on a charge of stealing these goods from Jennings and Co. Teasdale and Sadler, the partners of Jennings were there to swear to the goods and seize them. I was dragged off to a dungeon, while Teasdale and Sadler hauled my goods in wagons to their private office.

When brought into the Mormon court for examination, I sent for my attorney and the proceedings commenced. "Brothers" Jennings, Teasdale and Sadler swore to the goods, "BECAUSE THERE IS OUR PRIVATE MARK UPON THEM." When I saw the marks I felt overcome. There were the goods I had purchased in England with their private mark thereon. My attorney reserved his defence and asked for bail. This was put so high it was impossible for me to obtain it, and I was thrust back into the dungeon, here with a poor wretch who had not changed his linen for seven months. I had thousands of company, and oh, how they would bite this new comer!

The Mormon Grand Jury brought in a Bill of Indictment against me consisting of THIRTEEN different counts or charges, covering FORTY-TWO pages of Legal Cap. Lawyers think of it for a moment! I have the copy of that Indictment now before me, but its length precludes its insertion here.

Any lawyer can see it at my lectures, I hope to have copies printed and placed in the hands of every lawyer in England and America. It's a legal curiosity which charges me with stealing 15,767 dollars worth of my own goods. It is so framed that if I cleared one charge there were 12 charges more to clear, and if I managed to clear the first 12 charges, the thirteenth was fixed so as to make it impossible for me to clear it. Then I should have at least two years in Jail, and my property confiscated to the Mormon Church.

A few days before the trial, my attorney, who came to see me, was afraid I should be a corpse before the time set for my trial if I remained in that dungeon. He induced the prosecuting attorney to prevail upon the High Priest Judge to lower the bail. This was done, and I was liberated on bail.

To describe my trial which occupied two weeks, is impossible. I secured an extra attorney and did the best I could. We successfully proved that the goods were not marked when taken to the private office of Jennings and Co., that they remained in that office three days and nights, and when first seen after that they were marked. Besides on my way to Utah, when arriving at the Railway Terminus, my boxes were shunted on a plank from the car to the wagons, one of the boxes fell off and was smashed and its contents scattered. Those who gathered the things and helped pack them, swore that I had those very goods 500 miles back, and a month before I reached Salt Lake City. I cleared 12 charges, but the 13th charged that on the last day their Store was open prior to turning over the concern to the big Church Store, I stole from " Brothers " Jennings, Teasdale and Sadler 300 dollars in money These " Brothers " swore to it. Their Cashier and Book-keeper corroborated and produced the firms' books to show that on that day when every salesman was equally busy and returned over 300 dollars each to the Cashier, I who had been just as busy all day had only returned five dollars according to their books and oaths ; consequently I must have pocketed at least 300 dollars on that particular day.

When the Court adjourned for the night, I went to my attorneys' office, where I met Mr. Durkee the " Gentile " Governor of Utah. After stating the case to him I asked, " Can you do anything for me ? " He replied, " I do not see that I can. I am the Governor of the Territory, but Brigham Young is the Governor of the People. A Gentile Governor in Utah is the biggest farce on Earth." Mr. Durkee sent for other lawyers, who consulted with my attorneys in reference to the matter. These gentlemen said " though you have cleared the 12 charges, that 13th is a clincher put there on purpose to secure your conviction and your goods. You cannot go behind their books and prove them false ; look at the vast array of testimony on that point from the three members of the firm, their Book-keeper and also their Cashier. That is a thing we never attempt to do ; its useless and your conviction is sure."

Governor Durkee wrote out a free Pardon. I was now to become " A Pardoned Convict." Crushed, weary and heavy laden, I left to go home being still on bail. Pen cannot describe my feelings as I wended my way home in the dark. Suddenly I heard distinctly " Can't you see ? " Thinking it was someone in the garden I was passing, I took but little notice of it. I had not proceeded far when it seemed to be uttered immediately behind me this time—" Can't you see ? " I turned but saw no one, it was very dark. Thinking someone was near I called out " See what ! " the answer came " the date! the date ! 20th of February—The Last Day ! " All at once it came to my mind that I could remember a few who had dealt with me on that day, for every one who could, made purchases then, as the shops were all to be closed for one week. I thought of a man and his wife who had made extensive purchases that day. I went at once to their house. I asked " Do you remember buying some goods of me in Jennings' Store the last day it was opened ? "
" Oh yes," replied the wife, " I bought that 18 dollar shawl and—" " Excuse

me" I said "Do you remember how much your bill was?" The husband replied, "Yes, I have the account," producing which he said " 44 dollars and 50 cents." I asked "Do you know if the goods were paid for and how?" He replied " You gave me this bill," producing it, " and after I examined and found it correct you sent it with a 50 dollar bill to the Cashier, and five dollars and 50 cents change came back." I asked, " Do you know who the Cashier was and the cash-boy who took the money?" The man and his wife both declared they could swear that the Cashier was N. H. Felt, and the cash-boy his son, and they both saw the boy give the 50 dollar bill to his father and receive from him the change, which the boy brought to me. I thanked them and said that what they had told me must be sworn to in Court and that subpœnas would be presented them next morning. Here then I had evidence to prove those books wrong or the Cashier a thief. His books returned only five dollars as my total sales for the day, here was one sale of 44 and a half dollars, and the money seen to go into the Cashier's hands by two witnesses. I then went to others I thought of. The next man and wife could swear to over 70 dollars they saw the Cashier receive from me in about the same manner, and before the Court opened next morning I had many witnesses who could swear they saw me send to the Cashier that day over 300 dollars.

That "busted up" the 13th charge, and as nothing more remained against me, I saw Brigham's private reporter who had been present through the trial, rush out, and shortly return and hand a note to the Judge. When this High Priest Judge delivered his charge to the Jury of Priests, Elders and Teachers, he told them to acquit, and to pay no attention to the opinions he had hitherto expressed. He had considered me guilty and had so stated, but now at the close of the trial he had reason to change his mind. I was acquitted amid the hurrahs of the crowded court.

Though I had 13 witnesses whose testimony unrebutted was now on file and they ready again to offer the same evidence which must convict that Cashier, yet " Brother Jennings " never brought " Brother Felt " to trial. How's that? Echo answers in true Yankee style " How?" Then answers by asking " Was their books fixed for the occasion?" and then replies " They were ; " the same infernal agency that prompted the marking of my goods, fixed the books also.

This " Brother" Jennings is the " Hon." William Jennings, a member of the Legislature, a commander in the " Navoo Legion of cut throats " and Director of the " Deseret Bank," run by " Apostles and Priests, by inspiration and revelation," like the "Kirtland Bank" which "busted." Yet over the door of this " Revelation Bank " may be seen in large letters " U. S. (Uncle Sam's) Repository." This I fail to understand. When U. S. Grant visited Salt Lake City, he wined and dined with this " Hon." Wm. Jennings.

The Mormon Sheriff, R. T. Burton, the chief actor in the Morrisite Massacre, where women were murdered "for Christ's sake, " seized my goods ere they left the Court, to pay bills I never contracted.

"*The Utah Daily Reporter*," August 5th, 1869, says:—" The great larceny case against William Jarman, in the Probate Court, ended Saturday night at twelve o'clock in a verdict of 'NOT GUILTY.' This case has excited a great deal of comment throughout the City. It is the greatest case of larceny that has ever been tried in this Territory, involving property to a large amount, and many nice points of law. Mr. Jarman, it appears from the testimony in the case, arrived here last fall, bringing with him an assortment of merchandize and a large amount of money earned by him in England.

"He obtained a clerkship with William Jennings and Co., where he remained six months, when Jennings and Co. sold out to the Co-operative Association; Mr. Jarman became involved in a difficulty with the Church authorities and withdrew from fellowship.

"From this time the hand of persecution followed him with relentless energy, and finally culminated in a charge of grand larceny, preferred by Jennings and Co. The principal witnesses for the prosecution were Mr. Teasdale and Mr. Sadler, of the firm of Jennings and Co.; but their testimony was exceedingly contradictory, and the defence introduced witnesses to impeach and contradict their testimony. The defence introduced overwhelming testimony to disprove the charge and an acquittal was the result. From fifty to sixty witnesses were examined during the trial, which occupied twelve days, and the attornies for the accused consumed eleven hours in summing up the testimony before the jury. Z. Snow, Esq., appeared for the prosecution, and R. H. Robertson and H. W. Isaacson, Esqs., for the accused. The result is received with universal satisfaction by the people, who believed the charge unfounded from the beginning."

One night soon after the trial I was sent for to see a "Saint" on urgent business. It was 10 p.m. when we sat down to talk business. He touched upon all sorts of topics; when I broached business he said, "Don't hurry! won't you take something?" and fetching in whisky said, "Do take some:" it'll do you good!" I steadfastly declined; had I been a drinker and taken some then, it would have been my death, for stupified with drink, and that drugged, they could quietly put me with the others who tell no tales; but by keeping my brain clear I was always conscious, knew my danger, and kept on the look out. Who can blame me for abstaining from alchoholic drink?

The "Saint" kept discoursing upon all sorts of topics quite foreign to that I had come to talk about. I sat till 12 o'clock, then arose, said, "It's midnight, I'll see you to-morrow." He replied "I go off early, to be gone sometime; we will settle this matter now, sit down." I felt forced by an irrepressible power to hurry off. I got into the hall, found the door locked and key gone. I shouted "Open the door!" He asked "Are you armed" seeing me place my hands to my pistol pockets. I at once presented a pair of revolvers to his astonished gaze. The door was opened instanter. I got into the middle of the road, and fearing Danites might come up behind me I kept whirling around and presenting my pistols ready to fire, and thus I got home. (The sequel of this follows shortly.)

I was now given over to the tender mercies of Porter Rockwell, one of the great chiefs of these "Angels." I was unacquainted with this worthy until I began to notice him wherever I went. One day in the street I stopped to talk with my Cockney friend. Noticing this fellow watching me, I asked my friend who he was, told him I found him always following me. He replied, "That's old Port." I said "he looks more like old Rye Whisky." The Cockney gave his name and said "if he's following you he has his orders to kill you, and he'll do it dead sure, he has slain many a good man. There's only one way to get the blind side of him; he's mighty fond of whisky. If you can stuff him with that you're all right." I said "You leave me now, I'll fix him." My friend went one way and I started as if to pass "Port" and cross the street. Coming directly abreast of "Port" I stopped short and addressing him said "Excuse me sir, but can you tell me where the Patriarch John Smith lives?" "Oh yes! he said, down by Jordon Bridge." (The Patriarch lived within a stone's throw of where we stood.) "But," he continued "he ain't home, he won't be home till nine to-night." I thanked him very politely, and said "Well my friend, you've saved me a good jaunt, I feel it's my treat, do you ever indulge? won't you take something?" "Wal yes," said Port, "You're the best man I've seen to-day." And although the Scripture says "Woe unto him hat giveth his neighbour drink" "a drowning man will catch at a straw." I took him to a saloon, asked the landlord to show us to a private room as we had business to talk over. We were shown to a small room. "Friend what will you take, I asked?" He replied "My old stand-by, whisky, I suppose we can punish a pint can't we?" I said "I'll take Soda-water." Port ordered a pint of whisky. We sat down; here was the victim and his would-be murderer cosily seated in a snug little room. How to handle him properly, secure his friendship, and draw him out was the question. Our potations came and Port began to make himself at home and as the whisky got in, his wits got out. Presently Port emptied the pint, which was refilled. He became very talkative. I said "Excuse me sir, what is your name?" He answered, "Port Rockwell, they call me 'Old Port.'"

I made it a point to be very sociable, for I meant to get from him an account of some of the many murders he had committed, and his intentions toward myself. Finally I was successful; he said in answer to my question "I've had my orders to use you up, but you're a bully good fellow, don't you fear old Port, I'll not hurt a hair of your head. You know how to treat a man decent; you're all right." I saw that by a judicious use of whisky I had secured a friend, instead of becoming my "Destroying Angel," "Port," through a good supply of "Spirit" would be my "Guardian Angel."

He became quite confidential. In one of his moods he said "You got in a hell of a hurry that night when you fetched out yer shooting irons and got huffy." I asked him if he could explain that affair. "I guess I can," he answered "Between you and I, you're a lucky cuss; we attended to another poor devil that night who could'nt keep his mouth shut, like yourself; you're awful foolish let me tell you; howsoever, we did'nt catch on to him till midnight, and by the time we'd a fixed his wind-pipe so as he won't squeal again, kivered him up, and got to where we thought you was, you'd a got yer back up and gone." Port said this when the whisky had taken the place of his wits. I further drew from him that the "Saint" was to keep me there that night till the "Destroying Angels" came, that my grave was dug in the "Saint's" garden, and they intended to make "short work of it."

From that time I and Port were friends; and being in his charge I was perfectly safe. Port reported that I was a slippery customer, and difficult to catch. This much, past experience had proven. It cost me something to supply Port with whisky, but I trust my life may yet prove worth the outlay.

Things jogged along all right so long as I had money for whisky, but my second wife got a divorce and I was turned out in the streets homeless and penniless.

I sold my pistols to keep the whisky mill agoing. Port frequently posted me in regard to the various devices planned for my capture; though we were never seen together after the time mentioned, we had a way of communicating.

One night on my going as usual to our "Telegraph Office," as we called it, there was the cypher message "Meet Port midnight by old City wall, by Arsenal."

I met him and never shall forget his anxiety: I know that this man, guilty of "hundreds of murders" according to his own confessions to me, was true in his sympathy toward me and wished to aid me all in his power. He had then brought me a bundle of provisions, which he quickly handed me and hurriedly said "Here take that, fly to the mountains and hide at once, I have to leave this city by daylight. A far worse than I am is now on your track." He told me which way to go to escape him; for Port had given him instructions where to find me, or rather where not to find me, and had sent him off in another direction. Then giving me a gentle push said "Now be off and may God bless you."

It is really astonishing how these murderers can mix up the Divine Name in everything they do. I have seen men that I know are guilty of blood take the bread and break it at the Sacrament, and offer a prayer in the name of

Jesus Christ. It seems to me that all the blasphemy under the sun is centered in this so called "Zion"—this Hell upon Earth.

I am sorry space will not permit me to give more of my sufferings in this Hell upon Earth. I will briefly tell how I got away, and trust to my lectures for an opportunity to detail all I am prevented from giving here.

Though 500 American troops and gatling guns are now stationed at Camp Douglas, overlooking the City; a railway connecting it with the outside world; Gentiles there transacting business; and United States Courts in operation—yet the Mormons hold civil, ecclesiastical, and judicial power in Utah, and have things pretty much their own way.

General Garfield came to Salt Lake City, and through a friend of his I obtained an interview with him, which finally resulted in my escape. The reader may ask, why talk of an "escape" from Salt Lake, now that Railways, Troops, Gentiles, and U. S. Courts are there? I answer what good is either to one in the condition I was? The Railway is a ready money institution; no trust there. At cheapest rates it costs £15 to get back, and the generality of us not able to muster 15cents., or 15 pence. The first forty miles of railroad is built, controlled, and worked by Mormons. The journey from Salt Lake to New York at cheap rates takes about ten days, and food costs something when travelling. I ask how can the poor duped English girls, now living a life of sin and slavery in Utah, who scarcely ever get any money, raise the cash to go back? The Gentiles have enough to do to look after themselves. The troops are all very well in their place to overawe the Mormons, but they have nothing to do with the Civil Government. As to the United States' Courts, a more complete farce does not exist; for with Mormon Juries it is impossible to obtain a just verdict.

Look for a moment at the fact. The whole Territory is governed by the Mormon Power. There is the Mormon Parliament. The Lower and Upper House and its Cabinet. Then all the Officers of State are Church Officers. Mormon Mayors, Aldermen and Town Councillors in their various Cities— Mormon Police—in fact Mormon everything, with the exception of one Governor, and two or three judges who are like a figure 9 with the tail off.

Had the Mormons known that I was going away to expose their wickedness, think you for one moment they would have allowed me to escape? No, never! Suppose they knew it the night before I left; on going through the street a crowd of Mormons would be there through which I must pass. Superintending matters would be a policeman, who would grab me, while the "Saints" flock around, and one put, say a gold watch in my pocket, the owner of which would there and then charge me with highway robbery, and every Mormon priest swear to it. I am walked off to the City Hall, searched, the watch found on me, and I locked up. In the morning papers would appear as follows:—" Last night Wm. Jarman was arrestsd for stealing a gold watch from Mr. ——. On being searched the watch was found on him, and he was held for examination. During the night he attempted to escape and was shot by his keeper. He died instantly, the bullet piercing the heart." The keeper, coroner, and everyone who had to deal with the case being "Good Mormons" would be perfectly satisfied, and thus would end the career of Wm. Jarman. That's about how the business is managed now-a-days. But they did not know for after Brigham's death arrangements were being made for my going back into the Church, though I constantly put it off. I did business with Mormons, some very prominent ones. I had "an axe to grind"—(in English a game to play). There were matters I should never have found out had I not done so; yea, so late as 11 p.m. the night before I left, I had important business with the second man in the Kingdom, and everything considered O. K.

A good Brother holding the same "Priesthood" I had, helped me away; my luggage was shipped, and ticket bought by others, not me. My valuable books and papers were taken to New York by a gentleman and delivered to me there, and not till the morning after my first lecture in Brooklyn, where the associated press telegraphed it over the country, did the Mormons know where I was. When they saw the account in their papers they asked, "How did he get away?" I hope I have answered in a way to satisfy my readers. I know the "Saints" will not be satisfied until they know who assisted in spiriting away my books, papers, and myself, so that they could "Blood atone" them for their sins. But they will never know from me. "Port" died before I left Salt Lake, or I would not have said what I have. I could tell a hundred times as much as I have of such matters were it not that my friends who helped me are still living in "Zion," and for their sakes I keep it back feeling I have said quite enough to convince the world of the perfect horrors of this vile Mormonism, if not I am sure they would not believe the balance though an angel from Heaven proclaimed it. To my confidential friends now in "Zion," I say "Fear not! so far as I am concerned you are perfectly safe. When the Governments of America and England are ready for the question, I have ample proofs and evidence without breaking faith with you, and you are most of you old enough to die before these slow-coach Governments take any active steps in the matter." "Uncle Sam" has brought ONE out of the MANY human butchers to justice, and seems perfectly satisfied to let the others R. I. P.; and the murderers of wives, mothers, daughters, sisters, brothers, and fathers are allowed to occupy the best positions in the Territory. So much for the Great Boasted, "Free" Republic; and so much for "Christian" England in allowing her citizens to be thus deceived, enslaved, and slaughtered "for Christ's sake."

WHAT OTHERS SAY:—

A SERMON preached by the Rev. T. De WITT TALMAGE, D. D.

in the Tabernacle, Brooklyn, U.S., on the 26th of September, 1880.

'Then the Lord rained upon Sodom brimstone and fire from the Lord out of heaven.'—GENESIS xix. 24.

SODOM and Salt Lake City are synonymous. You can hardly think of the one without thinking of the other. Both in fertile valleys—valley of Siddim, valley of Utah. Both near a salt, offensive, fishless dead sea; for Dr. Robinson says there must have been a lake near by while yet ancient Sodom stood. Both the famous capitals of most accursed impurity. Both doomed.

In 1857, a company of emigrants started from Arkansas and Missouri for California. They were good, respectable, well-to-do people; but they had an idea that they might have larger comforts for their families on the other side of the mountains; so they undertook what always seems to be a terrible thing, travelling in the wagon emigrant train. They suffered everything on the way. By night the fires kept off the wolves, and by day there was fatigue and hunger, and heat, and gentle womanhood fainting with the long journey, and children crying for rest. There were one hundred and seventy in that company.

They must needs cross Utah Territory, and in Utah nearly all the emigrant trains were accustomed to take in new supplies of provisions; but Brigham Young heard that this emigrant train was coming, and he forbade, under pain of death, any Mormon in Utah giving any clothing, or food, or medicine, or kindness of any sort, to these emigrants. It was a revenge for the fact that a man in Arkansas had slain Elder Pratt, of the Mormon Church, because he (Elder Pratt) had stolen the wife of the man in Arkansas, and taken her to Utah and into Mormonism.

On and on went this emigrant train, suffering all indignity, until they came to a plain called Mountain Meadow. The Indians dashed down upon the emigrants, but the emigrants threw up a barricade, and in this temporary fortress drove back the red men most successfully. Then the Mormon militia dashed down upon these emigrants; but you know how men will fight when they fight for their wives and children, and so the Mormon militia were driven back.

Still it was only with great peril that any one could leave the temporary fortress, even to get water from the spring near by. There was great suffering from thirst, so one day they dispatched two little girls clad in white to bring water from the spring. They said, 'Most certainly the Mormon militia will not disturb them;' but no sooner had they appeared outside the barricade than they were shot dead by the stream.

Petitions for relief were signed by all the emigrants, and by Oddfellows and Freemasons, who made appeals to members of their particular order. Three brave men volunteered to carry that petition for relief to California. An aged Methodist minister of the group, in prayer, commended these men to God, and the emigrants all knelt in supplication; but hardly had these three brave men started on their journey than they were butchered.

Time passed on, and one day wagons were seen coming. 'Now,' thought the poor emigrants, 'we shall have relief,' and they could not restrain their glee at the thought of liberation. The wagons came up, and from them came a flag of truce, saying, 'If you emigrants will surrender, and put down your arms, you may walk out into perfect liberty, and you shall not be harmed.' Thinking the proposition a fair proposition, it was accepted, and they put down their arms, according to the arrangement, and then the men marched out first, then came the women, and then came the children. *After they were outside the barricade, the Mormon militia, with guns and knives and daggers, massacred all save a few little children, whom they thought to be too young to tell the story.* Aged and young husbands and wives, parents and children, left dead on the plain! Women belonging to the emigrant train, who were sick and unable to walk, were then taken out by the Mormons into the presence of their murdered families, stripped of their clothing, shot dead, and hurled upon the heap of corpses.

The wagons, the stock of the train, the dresses of the women and their jewellery, amounting in all to a property of 300,000 dollars, taken possession of by the Mormon Government. Years after, a Mormon woman, showing a silk dress that had been captured from the train—showing one of these silk dresses in Salt Lake City—one of the little girls that had been saved from the massacre recognised it. She said, 'Oh! that's my mother's. Where's mamma? Why don't mamma come? Mamma used to wear that!' and she burst into tears.

John D. Lee, the Mormon Bishop, was the presiding spirit in person of the massacre, and when, fifteen or eighteen years after, in the court-room, he gave testimony, he said he had orders to do that from head-quarters; and it appeared on the evidence that Brigham Young had given orders as to the disposition of the property of these murdered people, and had told the witnesses to hush up, and all Christendom to-day holds that man responsible for the tragedy. No wonder, when years after he visited the scene and found that the bones of the emigrants had been decently buried by the officers of the United States Government, and General Carlton had put up a head-board by the grave, with the epitaph, the inscription, 'Vengeance is mine, I will repay, saith the Lord'—no wonder that Brigham Young, seeing that inscription, ordered it to be torn down.

It is the presiding spirit of the Mountain Meadow massacre that I arraign to-day for trial before you, the jury of Americans. It still lives. It has its throne in Salt Lake City, and its foot on the heart of dishonoured women, and its breath is the pestilence of the nation. Gory, ghastly, hideous, infernal

Mormonism, stand up and look into the faces of the American jury that is to try you.

This summer, as well as on a previous occasion, I had the opportunity of inspecting this iniquity, and of asking many questions, and having them answered by Mormons and anti-Mormons. Many of the Gentiles of Salt Lake City called on me and asked me that when I got home I should present the case before the people on this coast. I solemnly promised them, and this morning I fulfil my promise. In regard to the alleged subsidence of Mormonism, I have to tell you that 750 Mormons had arrived in Salt Lake City or Utah, just before we went to Utah, and that there was another company still larger approaching the city, and that there were 10,000 added last year, and that there will be more than that added this year.

Three hundred missionaries, sent out to gather up victims, travel all over this land, and in Sweden, and Norway, and Russia, and *Germany, and England, and Wales, and Scotland.* (Germany has now prohibited Mormons from Proselyting in that country.) Many Scotch Presbyterians were recently brought there. These missionaries are compelled to go out, although their families may suffer the greatest penury, for this whole system is cruel and Herodic. These missionaries go to those who are in the struggle of life, and they hide all the hideous deformities of Mormonism, and tell these people, 'Now, if you will cross the ocean and go to Utah, you will have your expenses paid; and when you get there you will have gardens and farms of your own, and your hardships will be ended for ever.' No wonder some of these incautious people accept the invitation, and then fly from poverty to get into a most stupendous swindle. Oh! you ought to see the poor creatures carrying the tenth of their small income and the tenth of the small product of their farm or garden to the tithing-house of this insatiate institution. They are taxed until the blood comes. No escape but the grave. The co-operative societies and the co-operative stores of Utah are so many mills to grind out more money from the poor people to support a depraved priesthood.

I charge Mormonism with being one great and prolonged cruelty. Nobody denies the work of the destroying angels called Danites, whose chief business it was to hunt up antagonism to the Mormon Government and put it to death. It was for years the land of assassination and the field of blood. No one doubts the Hickman butcheries under Brigham Young. I saw a cellar where a mother and two sons had been put to death, the mother slain in the presence of the two sons, and the two sons butchered, because they had revealed the secrets of the Mormon Government. The whole world has heard the story of the destruction of the Aiken party. And these Mormons have a delicious vernacular by which they describe this putting to death. They say all these things with a smile and a jeer. 'Oh, they were put out of the way;' or, 'they met with a bad accident;' or, 'they were used up;' or, 'they were cut off just under their ears!'

Why have these atrocities stopped? Because a regiment of United States soldiers are on the hill overlooking the city, and with iron rake of destruction may rake that city if it attempts to repeat such atrocity. It is not because Mormonism is more merciful, but because it has not the courage.

I charge Mormonism with being a great blasphemy. Brigham Young in one of his sermons, declared that Christ himself was a practical polygamist; that Mary and Martha were his plural wives; that Mary Magdalen was another; and he said in the same sermon that the bridal feast in Cana of Galilee, where Christ turned water into wine, was the occasion of one of His own marriages! The whole tendency of the system is towards blasphemy. I was told over and over again that Brigham Young, with slight provocation, would swear like a fishwoman at Billingsgate.

I charge upon Mormonism that it is a disloyalty to the United States

Government. There is an oath taken in the endowment house at Salt Lake City, which subverts all other oaths. Perjury is no crime when enacted in behalf of Mormonism. Mormonism hates the Government of the United States with a perfect hatred. Fourth of July occasions and all patriotic demonstrations are an utter abhorrence to the Mormons, and the Gentile celebrators of the Fourth of July suffer every indignity. Mormonism would like to have the United States Government to perish to-day.

I charge upon Mormonism that it is an organized filth built on polygamy. There is a man in Salt Lake City who has three wives, and they are the mother, the grandmother, and the grand-daughter! I observed that there were additions built on the houses, and it was explained to me that, when a new wife is taken, then the house is enlarged, forgetting the fact that no house was ever large enough to hold two women married to the same man! Think of a system which applauds a man for such things. Think of a system which teaches that the more wives a man lives with at the same time on the earth, the higher his honour in heaven. Think of a system which commends a man for living in marriage at the same time with three sisters. Think of a system which wrecks the happiness of every woman that touches it, for, I do not care what they say, God never made a woman who can cheerfully divide a husband's love with another. Every honest wife knows she has a right to the entire throne of her husband's affection. They may smile to keep up appearances, but they have an agony of death, and the most pitiable thing in all the earth is an aged woman in Mormonism. The aged woman in other parts of the land we bow before; we take off our hat to her, we do her reverence. The softest chair in the house is grandmother's chair. She is the queen on Christmas and Thanksgiving days. The older she gets, and the more wrinkles on her face, and the more stooped her shoulder, the more we think of her; and when God takes her away to the eternal rest, it seems as if three-fourths of the house were torn down. But a woman getting aged in Mormonism, she is shoved back, and is paid less and less attention, and is of less and less account. Why? Another has taken the throne, and, after awhile, she will be dethroned, and another will come up, and another.

I tell you Mormonism is one great surge of licentiousness; it is the seraglio of the Republic, it is the concentrated corruption of this land, it is the brothel of the nation, it is hell enthroned.

This miserable corpse of Mormonism has been rotting in the sun, and rotting and rotting and rotting for forty years, and the United States Government has not had the courage to bury it. Moreover, *it is all the time gaining in influence.* Mormonism once meant Utah; now to a certain extent it means Idaho, Arizona, Nevada, Wyoming, New Mexico. Wider and wider and wider, and greater and greater and greater. It is going forth to debauch this nation. You have no idea of the influence it is having in American politics, or what it has already done at Washington. Mormonism receives 1,000,000 dollars every year through the tithing system, and has plenty of money with which to effect national legislation. The subject was brought before Congress and the matter referred to a Committee, and one of the members of the Committee said in derision, 'What do you make all this fuss about polygamy for? Those Mormons out there make a religion of having four or five wives, while some of us members of Congress practise the same iniquity without any religion!' A stout effort is being made to introduce Utah as a State of the Union, and if it be accomplished the United States Government puts its broad seal of approbation upon this stupendous indecency

'Now,' you say, 'what is best to be done?' Execute the law against polygamy. What right has the law to punish a man for bigamy, if one foot this side of Utah he have two wives, when one foot the other side the law lets him have twenty? What right has the law to smite libertinism in other parts of this country when there it licenses it? Are these Mormons the pets and the darlings of the nation, that they should have especial regulations? Do you believe that filthy pool of iniquity can stand in the midst of this continent and not have the whole air poisoned with the malaria? Mormonism is an insult to every home, to every church, to every father, every mother, every sister, and the curse of Almighty God will come down on this nation unless we extirpate it.

'What!' say you, 'would you interfere with a man's religion?' Oh! no. If these Mormons want to believe that Joseph Smith was God, or that Brigham Young is the second person of the Trinity, the law has no right to interfere with them. But Mormonism not only antagonises Christianity; it antagonises good morals, and the infidel and the Christian stand side by side in denouncing Mormonism as a foe to free institutions. Then, I say, away with it! Moral persuasion first, if possible; but moral persuasion will not accomplish it. They have declared, over and over again, that they will let their city go down under the bombshell before they will surrender polygamy, and I tell you that Mormonism will never be destroyed until it is destroyed by the guns of the United States Government.

It would not be war. I hate war. It would be national police duly executing the law against polygamy. Why did they not let General Johnson in 1857, with his 2,500 troops sent out under the order of President Buchanan, march right on until they did their work? President Buchanan never was charged with excessive courage, and he sent out Governor Powell, of Kentucky, and Major McCullough, of Tennessee, to offer pardon to all the Mormons who would put down their arms, and there has not been a President of the United States with enough moral courage since to clean out that national stable.

We all go to look at it. President Grant went to look at it. Secretary Schurz went to look at it. Secretary Thompson went to look at it. President Hayes went to look at it. Everybody goes to look at it. We cross the continent, and it is one of the arts of Mormonism to be very gracious to public men. The Mormons struggle as to who shall have the privilege of entertainment. I never addressed a more genial audience in my life than last August in the Mormon opera-house, a great many Mormons present. They bow you into the city, and they bow you out of the city, and none of us dare touch them. We all want to be Congressmen, or President of the United States, or Minister to England, and if we oppose Mormonism it will oppose our political interests. And so, if I were an aspirant for any political office, this sermon might perhaps be very impolitic.

If there be any truth in the transmigration of souls, I hope that the soul of Andrew Jackson will get into the body of some of our Presidents, and make proclamation that within thirty days all these Mormons must decide upon one wife, or go to jail, or quit the country. Then have Congress make provisions for the carrying out of this order. If the Mormons submit to the law, all right. If not, then send out troops of the United States Government, and let them make the Mormon Tabernacle their head-quarters, and with cannon of the biggest bore thunder into them the seventh commandment. Arbitration by all means; but if that will not do, then peaceful proclamation. If that will not do, then howitzer, and bombshell, and bullets, and cannon-ball.

If a gang of thieves should squat on a territory and make thievery a religion, how long would the United States Government stand that? Yet a community founded on theft would not be so bad as a community founded on the grave of desolated, destroyed, embruted womanhood.

I call the attention of the American Congress to this evil. The hour has come. Let some Senator of the United States at the next meeting of Congress, or some member of the House of Representatives, with eloquent tongue and persistent purpose, and good morals of his own, lift the anti-Mormon standard, and then unroll the tragedy and outrages of that appalling system before the Government and before the people, and that man will gather around him all the sympathies of all the families, and all the Churches, and all the reformers, and all the high-toned men and women of America. The thing has got to be done. It is only a question of when. Let this man of whom I speak in the name of God go forth and do his duty, and he will at the same time make his political fortune. Come, now, instead of exhuming the wrapped-up and entombed mummy of negro slavery, and tossing it about in these Presidential elections, have one live question—Mormonism, the white slavery of to-day, and have it decided at the ballot-box whether that institution shall go forth with its pestiferous influence, or whether, under the law of our civilization and the stroke of the law, it shall perish.

'But,' says some one, 'that would be a very expensive crusade.' It would not cost the United States Government one farthing. Confiscate so much of the Mormon domain as is necesaary to pay for the extermination, and take some of those vast sums of money that are being poured into the lap of that old mother of harlots, and pay it out as honest taxes to support the United States Government. Utah is rich enough to pay for all the costly and expensive surgery of taking out this dripping cancer of Mormonism. Let the pulpits and the platforms and the printing-press agitate, and agitate, and agitate until Congress and the White House shall hear rumbling all around the sky the storm of popular indignation against this gigantic, organized, and national crime.

I make no war against Mormonism as a religion. I war against Mormonism as an immorality, as a defiance of civil law, as an institution anti-American. When Brigham Young's men, with bowie-knives, broke up Judge Drummond's court in 1856, and compelled him to adjourn it *sine die*, and when Mormonism poised loose rocks on the top of cliffs, where you may see them to this day, expecting to throw them over on the United States troops as they passed under, Mormonism showed what she thought of our Government.

Now as I have empannelled you as a jury to sit in trial of this giant of lust and disloyalty, and the evidence has been presented before you, are you ready for the verdict before you leave the jury-box? Guilty or not guilty? 'Guilty,' says one. 'Guilty,' say all.

Then what shall the sentence be? It must not be a small incarceration, it must not be a slight censure. While we have only pity for the victims of this abomination, and we pray God He will speedily deliver them, for this institution of Mormonism, as such, only extinction and death. But where shall be the execution, and when shall the execution take place? What scaffolding will be strong enough to hold such a monster of iniquity? One end of the scaffolding must be planted on the Rocky Mountains and the other on the Sierra Nevadas. But what Friday of what gloomy week, of what gloomy month, of what gloomy year would be gloomy enough for the execution of this beastly outlaw? What grave deep enough for this stout, thousand-armed, thousand-footed, thousand-headed, thousand-horned, thousand-fanged corpse? What epitaph for that grave unless it be this:—

Here lies Mormonism, the outlaw, the libertine, and the murderer, the hero of Mountain Meadow massacre. Born February 22, 1827. Died 1882, at the hand of the law and under the instruction of the Almighty. 'Then the Lord rained upon Sodom brimstone and fire from the Lord out of Heaven.'

Oh! good people of the United States, whether I address you face to face or through the printing-press, which every Monday morning in most of our cities gives me an audience—for which I am very thankful—whatever way I reach your ear or your eye, I have to tell you that, unless we destroy Mormonism, Mormonism will destroy us. If God be good and pure and just He will not let this nation go unwhipped much longer if we allow that iniquity to go unchallenged. Every day as a nation we consent to Mormonism we are defying the hail, and the lightning, and the trumpet, and the drought, and the mildew, and the epidemic, and the plague, and the hurricane, and the earthquake of an incensed God.

My plea this morning is in behalf of fifteen thousand Gentiles, who in Utah are suffering persecution for their principles, or speechless because they do not want their commercial interests sacrificed.

I plead for thousands of foreigners who, deceived and betrayed from their own country, have been introduced into Mormonism, and, thousands of miles away from their native country, can make no resistance, but must live and die in dumb despair.

I plead for womanhood in Utah—womanhood under foot, womanhood in the sewer, womanhood crushed until it cannot weep, womanhood looking out of the barred windows of a perdition of anguish towards what seems an unpitying heaven, crying, 'O Lord! how long, O Lord!'—womanhood in the pandemonium of a polygamous home—womanhood with the garlands of hope and affection and honour torn with the swine's snout of incestuous abomination—womanhood that, if it had a chance, or had had a chance in the past, would have been as pure and good as that which presides at your table to-day, or which long ago bent in benediction over your peaceful cradle before you began the struggle with the world.

O! men with wives and daughters and mothers; O! brothers with sisters, do not your ears tingle, and does not your blood run cold at this story of Mormonism? And are you not determined at the ballot-box, and with pen and tongue, and in every possible way, to war against it? O! you wives, who will to-night kneel before God, thanking Him for the home in which you are the undisputed queen—O! mothers with daughters coming up honoured and defended, no rough hand to touch them from cradle to grave, will you not in your prayers to-day sympathise with your sisters who are dying the slow death of Mormonism? O! ye aged couples, who have been in each other's company for thirty, or forty, or fifty years, climbing the hill of life together, and now going down on the other side the hill in the light of the setting sun; but all the way up and all the way down supreme in each other's affections; united in holy marriage so long ago that all the witnesses but God are dead; your sympathies strengthened by the birth-hour, when one life was spared and another added, and by the grave over which both your hearts broke at once; her face, with all the wrinkles, more attractive now to you than when rosy with youth, because it is written all over with precious memories; side by side, so long, so long, so long, that when God takes one of you He will soon take the other—O! ye aged couple, remember this day, in prayer before God, those to whom old age brings neglect and dethronement of affection. And may the God who setteth the solitary in families bless all our homes. The best cornerstone for the republic is the hearthstone. May God keep it inviolate! (Amen.')

JUDGE CRADLEBAUGH'S SPEECH IN CONGRESS.

Mr. Cradlebaugh.—Mr. Speaker, having resided for some time among the Mormons, become acquainted with their ecclesiastical policy, their habits, and their crimes, I feel that I would not be discharging my duty if I failed to impart such information as I have acquired in regard to this people in our midst who are building up, consolidating, and daringly carrying out a system subversive of the Constitution and laws, and fatal to morals and true religion.

* * * * *

Mormonism is one of the monstrosities of the age in which we live. It seems to have been left for the model Republic of the world, for the ninteenth century, when the light of knowledge is more generally diffused tnan ever before, when in art, science and philosophy we have surpassed all that ages of the past can show, to produce an idle, worthless vagabond of an impostor, who heralds forth a creed repulsive to every refined mind, opposed to every generous impulse of the human heart, and a faith which commands a violation of the rights of hospitality, sanctifies falsehood, enforces the systematic degradation of women, not only permits, but orders, the commission of the vilest lusts, in the name of Almighty God himself, and teaches that it is a sacred duty to commit the crimes of theft and murder. It is surprising that such faith, taught, too, in the coarsest and most vulgar way should meet with any success. Yet in less than a third of a century it girdles the globe. Its missionaries are planted in every place. You find them all over Europe, thick through England and Wales, traversing Asia and Africa, and braving the billows of the southern oceans to seek proselytes. And, as if to crown its achievements, it establishes itself in the heart of one of the greatest and most powerful governments of the world, establishes therein a theocratic government overriding all other government, putting the laws at defiance, and now seeks to consummate and perpetuate itself by acquiring a State sovereignty and by being placed on an equality with the other States of the Union.

Mormonism is in part a conglomeration of illy cemented creeds from other religions, and in part founded upon the eccentric production of one Spaulding, who, having failed as a preacher and shopkeeper, undertook to write a historical novel. He had a smattering of biblical knowledge, and chose for his subject "the history of the lost tribes of Israel." The whole was supposed to be communicated by the Indians, and the last of the series was named Mormon, representing that he had buried the book. It was a dull, tedious, interminable volume, marked by ignorance and folly. The work was so flat, stupid and insipid that no publisher could be induced to bring it before the world. Poor Spaulding at length went to his grave, and the manuscript remained a neglected roll in the possession of his widow.

Then arose Joe Smith, more ready to live by his wits than by the labor of his hands. Smith had early in life, manifested a turn for pious frauds. He had figured in several wrestling matches with the devil, and had been conspicuous in giving in eventful experiences in religion at certain revivals. He announced that he had dug up the book of Mormon which taught the true religion; this was none other than poor Spaulding's manuscript which he had purloined from the widow. In his hands the manuscript became the basis of Mormonism. Joe became a prophet; the founder of a religious sect; the president of a swindling bank; the builder of the city of Nauvoo; mayor of the city; general of the armies of Israel; candidate for President of the United States, and finally a martyr, as the Saints choose to call him. But the truth is that his villainies, together with the villainies of his followers, brought down upon him the just vengeance of the people of Illinois and Missouri, and his career was brought to an end by his being shot while confined in jail in Carthage. It was unfortunate that such was his end, for his followers raised the old cry of martyrdom and persecution, and, as always proved, "the blood of the martyr was the seed of the church."

Mormonism repudiates the cellibacy imposed by the Catholic religion upon its priesthood, and takes in its stead the voluptuous impositions of the Mohammedan Church. It preaches openly that the more wives and children its men have in this world, the purer, more influential and conspicuous will they be in the next; that wives, children, and property will not only be restored, but doubled in the resurrection. It adopts the use of prayers and baptism for the dead, as a part of its creed. Mormons claim to be favored with marvellous gifts—the power of speaking in tongues, of casting out devils, of curing the sick, and of healing the lame and the halt. They claim that they have a living prophet, seer, and revelator, who holds the keys of the Kingdom of Heaven, and through whose intercession alone access can be had. They recognize the Bible, but they interpret for themselves, and hold that it is subject to be changed by new revelation, which, they say supercedes old revelation. One of their doctrines is that of continued progression to ultimate perfection. They say God was but a man, who went out developing and increasing until he reached his present high capacity; and they teach that Mormons will be equal to him; in a word, that good Mormons will become gods. They teach the shedding of blood for remission of sins, or, in other words, that if a Mormon apostatizes his throat shall be cut, and his blood poured out upon the ground for the remission of his sin. They also practice other revolting doctrines, such as are only carried out in polygamous countries, which is evidenced by a number of mutilated persons in their midst. They hold that the prophet's revelations are binding upon their consciences, and that they are bound to obey him in all things. They say that the earth and the fullness thereof is the Lord's; that they are God's chosen people on earth; that their mission on earth is to take charge of God's property, and, as faithful stewards, that it is their duty to obtain it, and are taught that, in obtaining it, they must not get in debt to the Lord's enemies for it; in other words, they teach that it is a duty to rob and steal from Gentiles. They have christened themselves "The Church of Jesus Christ of Latter-day Saints." They claim that Mormonism is to go on spreading until it overthrows all the nations of the earth, and, if necessary for its accomplishment, its success shall be consummated by the [sword; that Jackson county, Missouri, is to be the seat of empire of the Mormon Church; that hence the Mormons are to be finally gathered, and that from that Zion shall proceed a power that will dethrone kings, subvert dynasties, and subjugate all the nations of the earth.

I have said that their doctrines were repulsive to every refined mind. Every other false faith which has reigned its evil time upon this goodly world of ours has had some kindly and redeeming features. Even the semi-theocracy of the Aztecs, as Prescott tells you, disfigured as it was by horrid and bloody rites, was not without them. Buddhism and Brahmanism, with all their misshapen fables, still inculcated, in no small degree, a pure code of morals. Nor is the like assertion untrue of Mohammedanism. It was reserved for Mormonism, far off in this bosom of our beloved land, to rear its head, naked in all its hideous deformity, and unblushingly, yes, defiantly, proclaim a creed without the least redeeming feature, and of such character that the Thugism of India cannot match it.

So at variance is the practice of polygamy with all the instincts of humanity, that it has to be passed upon the people with the greatest assiduity as a part of their religious duty. It is astonishing with what pertinacity through all their "sermons and discourses" it is justified and insisted on. Threats, entreaties, persuasions, and commands, are continually brought in play to enforce its cheerful observance. So revolting is it to the women, that to aid in its enforcement they are brutalized, their modesty destroyed by low, vile, vulgar expressions, such as I could not repeat, and would not ask the clerk to read in your hearing.

But their teachings, officially reported by themselves, give you a better idea of their estimation of woman than anything I could say.

Such, then, is Mormonism in regard to all that beautifies life in the conjugal relation; such are their sentiments and commands pronounced under the assumed authority of God upon the female sex. When President Kimball calls his numerous wives his "cows" he but reflects the Mormon idea of women in the social scale.

The view is sickening. I turn with loathing and disgust from their legalized status of systematic debauchery and lust. Before it the entire nature recoils. No wonder that it requires the whole enginery of the Mormon church threats, and intimidations to compel the women to submit to it. I pity that man or woman who can for one moment look upon this organized, systematic, enforced degradation and prostition with any other feeling than that of abhorence and disgust. In matters of affection woman is a monopolist—she wants the whole heart, or she wants none. But in Utah she is compelled to take the part only of the smallest of hearts—a Mormon's heart—little attention and no devotion.

MORMON MISSIONARIES.

Those guilty of Murder are sent out as Missionaries, and should they leave the Church while on a Mission, and attempt to expose Mormonism, extradition would fetch the murderers back to expiate their crimes. It is a very noted and well known fact in "Zion" that criminals guilty of their various crimes are sent to England and other countries on a mission for three years; in other words, transported. They are not allowed expenses, but must travel "Without purse or scrip!" that is "Bum their way." They raise the cash to pay their fare here by selling whatever they may possess. If they fall short, a ball or some entertainment is given and the proceeds go towards paying the "needy brothers" expenses.

Better let convicts from Dartmoor preach the Gospel, than convicts from Utah. The corrupt Mormon Church sends their vile representatives here as tramps without visible means of support, to impose upon and deceive the British public, their principal aim being to entrap girls and drag them away to their filthy harems in Utah. Of course a few "Brethren" are needed also as well as a host of "sisters," for Zion's old sinners are dying off, and male recruits come in handy to help "build up the kingdom;" but young females are in constant demand.

The Mormon missionary however is not over particular. If he can seduce a young married wife, that is considered a good prize, or if a mother of several daughters can be induced to leave her "old man" and "gather to Zion" with her daughters, that is looked upon as "a good haul." The Mormon Elder, who generally represents himself as "a single man," and "disengaged" often seduces a wife by the promise of marrying her himself when they get to "Zion." Of course they marry *pro tem* at once, and when the "dear lady" gets to Utah and finds "her lover" already has a dozen wives or more, it is too late to repent. I have met in Utah very many wives who have thus been seduced and decoyed away from good husbands. Since I have been home I have met many of these deserted husbands who have enquired of me about their runaway wives. I have only room to mention one case, so I will take one right here in Exeter. When the bills announcing my first Lecture and Exhibition in England was posted on the walls I stood examining one. A well dressed gentleman was also looking at it; presently he said to me "That must be an interesting entertainment, I certainly shall go." Something I said made him surmise that I was the man referred to in the bill and he was anxious to know if it was so. I never shall forget that man when I informed him of the fact. He came to my house and there, bitterly weeping, told me the same old story. The Mormon Missionary had seduced his wife. She had stolen away with his daughters and they were now in Utah.

In the *Anti-Polygamy Standard* Vol. 2, No. 4, is a letter from Mrs. J. Hawkini. She says:—"I have lectured in Liverpool, Manchester, and London. More than fifty women have enquired if I knew their husbands in Utah. I cannot describe the great amout of misery that has been caused here by Mormonism, so many children left without a father's care, and without a mother's too, for many women have left their husbands and large families of children for the sake of this Latter-day fraud." She gives cases which I am sorry I have not room to give. I wish all my readers could get these *Standards* and read for themselves.

"For 'tis more easy to betray than ruin any other way."—*Hudibras*.

How long, Oh how long! will our Government allow this thing to continue.

In the *Millennial Star*, No. 53, Vol. xlv., published at 42, Islington, Liverpool, which contains a scurrilous article concerning myself, and which was presented to me by a Mormon at Plymouth, I find a list of Missionaries who have acted as "Editors of the Star," I cannot notice them all, but make the following extracts :—"The Star was first issued in Manchester with Parley P. Pratt as editor, in May 1840."—

"Parley P. Pratt, an "apostle," while in Manchester, England, enticed a young woman named Walker to his embraces, and though not married to her there, she was all to him that a wife implied in all its relationship. If he did not break the law against bigamy, it is well known that he did against fornication, both English and Divine. Dare any of the Mormons deny it ?"—*Salt Lake Tribune*.

This Pratt tried wife stealing in America, and was killed by the husband.

"Parley P. Pratt seduced, ran away with, and married the wife of Hector McLean of Arkansas, who like a true man took Pratt's life.—*Utah Reporter*.

The *Star* then mentions "Apostle" Woodruff. I refer my readers to what Secretary Ferris says of Woodruff on page 117 of this book.

Then comes "Apostle" Hyde, this man's Harem in Utah may be imagined when the reader considers the extracts from his sermons given in this book. He was not only fond of women but devoted to whisky.

Next we have "Apostle" (now Prophet) Taylor. This is the man that denied Polygamy in France, married a young lady in New York and ran off with two sisters from England and married both of them, notwithstanding he had five wives in "Zion" at the time. I refer to chapter four if you wish to know more of this "Boss Devil."

The next I notice is "Apostle Orson Pratt." This Polygamist, like all the others, left all his wives in Utah when he came to England on a Mission, and did what the most of them do when here select a lamb or two of the flock for themselves. I quote from the *Salt-Lake Tribune*:—

"Orson Pratt, while in England, took Eliza Crookes to wife, lived with her there as such, and brought her to this country to be neglected and die an untimely death in Tooele. He well knew that he despised and broke the laws of that country. Dare any Mormon deny the fact ?"

Now comes "Elder Calkins." I shall allow the *Salt-Lake Tribune* to tell you about him:—

"Elder Calkins, who presided over the Mormon European Mission during the time "this people" were in rebellion against our Government, asked Brigham Young for the privilege of taking a new wife in England, and received full consent and blessing; he took as a triplicate spouse the person of Miss Perkes. The legal Mrs. Calkins, whom he left in this city, had permission to visit her native State, in consequence of ill-health, while her lord was in England, and after he had taken the Miss Perkes. Pleading change of climate, she prevailed on Calkins to allow her to visit England, and did so with the proviso that she should only be known as his sister. He had the honour of having his two 'wives' live with him under the same roof, the one a living lie, on the soil of old England, where the law makes such a condition criminal. Dare the Mormons deny these facts ?"

There are so many of these scamps I must shorten my remarks. I notice Elder N. V. Jones who shot a poor man that came begging to his door.

Also Apostle Cannon, who denied his wives in Congress, and urged a man to commit murder.

The following is from *The Springfield Republican*, April 22, 1882.

"The New York Tribune publishes a sworn statement by Adolph Razin, formerly a Mormon living in Utah, who says that Apostle Cannon, urged him (Razin) to murder Alman W. Babbit, then secretary of the Territory of Utah. Cannon told him that, according to the doctrine of blood atonement practised by the church, Babbit must be killed for offences against the church and that he (Razin) as Babbit's best friend and a 'Levite' in the church must shed his blood. Babbit at that time contemplated a journey to Washington, and Cannon urged Razin to accompany him for the purpose of finding an opportunity to murder him. Razin indignantly refused to commit the murder. Babbit was assassinated, however, as he (Razin) believes at the instigation of Cannon and in accordance with the Mormon doctrine of blood atonement. The Tribune publishes several affidavits to show that Razin is a man of veracity and good repute."

I have Razin's affidavit. Daniel H. Wells, "The one-eyed Pirate," and the "Messiah" of the Endowment House, has also been here, and "young Briggy, Prince of Utah." Elder N. H. Felt, the Cashier who either stole 300 dollars from Jennings or fixed the books to secure my imprisonment has also been here converting the English to Mormonism, "Elder Graham" the "Star Actor" of Utah, left the stage there and came here to preach "The Gospel." Elder D. McKensie the noted Counterfieter and Convict has also enlightened the British people in regard to matters and things relating to the "Latter-day Saints." One Bishop O. F. Whitney is named in this precious "Star," I suppose it means the drunken sot known in Salt Lake City as "Ort Whitney." I know of no other O. Whitney good enough to come to England as a Missionary. I trust this will suffice to show the kind of men who come here as Missionaries. How well we may say of the Mormon missionary—

"And thus they cloak their naked villiany, and seem a Saint when most they play the Devil."—*Shakespeare.*

I leave this bright Millennial Star for awhile and quote from American Papers.

"CHEYENNE, Wyo, April 20, 1881. 54 Mormon Missionaries passed over the Union Pacific road to day, on their way to Wales on a proselyting expedition. All were inferior and coarse-looking men, and most of them have from two to five wives at home. They will work in the mining and iron district in Wales."—*Boston Evening Traveller.*

"The way to make a Welshman thirst for bliss, and say his prayers daily on his kness, is to pursuade him that most certain 'tis the moon is made of nothing but green cheese; and he'll desire of God no greater boon, but a place in heaven to feed upon the moon."—John Taylor.

"Utah is sending out an unusually large number of 'Shepherds' this season to gather in the lambs. The Government which stands by, and, either through cowardice or from policy, fails to take the villians by the throat is a party to the iniquity. The most approved 'deadlock' that could be invented would be the Nation's great hand clutching the throat of the Utah iniquity." *Chicago Inter-Ocean.*

Extract from the *Rochester (U. S.) Herald*:—"Its system of propogandism in Europe is pursued with more than usual earnestness since Brigham Young's death. Thousands of female dupes, are annually brought over to the Salt Lake Zion."

From the La Cross (Wisconsin U. S.) *Republican and Leader*:—

"Mormon agents are in Europe inaugurating a boom for polygamy. A great number of immigrants are arriving and being conducted to 'Zion' by the enthusiastic followers of the faith. The exact number that comes destined for Utah is not known, but it is known to be large. The number of women is greatly in excess of that of men."

"This church of Latter-day Lepers sends its procurers abroad under the protection of our flag, and fills its harems with victims duped with the promise of freedom—the most flagrant crime perpetrated to day in the name of liberty. *New York Herald."*

"The arrival at New York of 800 Mormon immigrants on one day last week naturally called public attention to the problem which this inchoate rebellion in the territories will sooner or later present to the government of the United States for settlement. It has often been suggested that, if nothing can be done to exterminate, or even check, polygamy within our borders, these defiant law-breakers ought to be prevented from sending abroad their panderers under the protection of our flag. But beyond a circular letter from Secretary Evarts, requesting our representatives to notify all whom it might concern that polygamy is a crime under our statutes, punishable by severe penalties, nothing has ever been done. Of course a circular letter could make little headway against shrewd and active Mormon missionaries, backed up as they are by a large propagandial fund in the Bank of England.

Especially is this likely to be true when these emissaries are able to say that the law is a dead letter, and to point to thousands of persons living undisturbed with 'plural wives.'"—*Boston (U. S.) Herald*, July 11, 1881.

"Another squad of Mormon tramps left the city yesterday to rope the ignorant classes into the Latter-day Fraud."—*Salt Lake Tribune*, June 1 1881

"EDS. TRIBUNE: In 1879 three lying Mormon elders decoyed my sister Mary Ann Lunnon born in Nov. 1865, (and not yet 15,) into the Mormon faith, while in New Zealand, against her father's consent, and with the assistance of a few sisters of the Mormon faith, they succeeded in getting her on a steamer in Lyttelton in March, 1880, notwithstanding her father and friends were doing all they could to prevent her, and also had the police trying to prevent her. She stowed herself on the steamer and came to Utah, arriving here about nine weeks ago. She is on the road to shame and disgrace through the horrid doctrines of the Mormon Church. Being her only natural guardian in America, I have applied to the United States District Attorney to aid me, but have failed. She is now staying with one of John W. Young's wives. She was enticed by the Mormon priests against the instructions of the circular issued by Secretary Evarts. She may become the inmate of a Mormon harem, a fate almost as bad as eternal damnation.

SALT LAKE, June 24, 1880."   JOHN T. LUNNON.

Speaking of the Aikin murders, *The Salt Lake Tribune* says:

"Old residents have been talking of that dark crime until Bro. Bishop Murdock's name has become familiar with its horrid details. Now he goes on a mission! What a powerful religious agent he will be with his hands dipped in blood."

"Contracts are made with missionaries to find a wife or wives for parties in Utah, on condition of paying the expenses of the passage. Young and innocent girls are thus purchased by old gray-headed polygamists and dragged into a life as slavish in its character as was that system which always will be a blot upon our Nation's history. Polygamy means the enslavement and prostitution of women."—*Hand Book on Mormonism*, p. 43.

Secretary Ferris on page 284 "Utah and the Mormons," says:—

"The Mormon missionaries make especial efforts to gain female converts esteeming success in this work paramount even to the acquisition of wealthy disciples. When, however, they manage to obtain a lodgment in a family where girls and money both abound, they regard themselves in pursuit of a prize for which they will put forth their best exertions. Such a family transferred to Salt Lake City is an object of great consideration. The wealth of the father speedily finds its way into the coffers of the Church, and the daughters are in due time distributed among the high-priests, or have the proud distinction of starting new harems. Men who have become miserable sots, and otherwise burdensome, are sent off, in the hope that they will die or reform. Two were appointed to the mission in China, one of whom was a wretched inebriate. These men went to California, on their way to their post, in the same train with us. At the sink of Mary's River, near the commencement of the forty-mile desert, was one of those troublesome liquor stations which cluster the route, and at this place both of these messengers of mercy became beastly drunk; and one of them, being quarrelsome in his cups, got into a fight, and carried the unequivocal marks of the encounter in his face for some days."

On page 245, speaking of the Mormon Missionary, Mr. Ferris says:—
"He exhibits to the world a present, active religious zeal, and compasses sea and land to make proselytes to his faith; but his mission is that of the swindler and the cheat: he goes with a lie in his mouth, and labors only to enlarge his own borders, and build up and strengthen his own dominions, and pander to his own pleasures. He belongs to the external and the ultimate: he is all rind—all kernel—all husk. He delights in literal constructions."

On page 18 and 19 of the Hand Book on Mormonism is the following:—
"At each semi-annual conference, missionaries are appointed to go to the outside world. They go at their own expense, and are required to stay until recalled by the Priesthood. At the least calculation, there are 300 such missionaries constantly in the field, seeking those whom they may catch in their Mormon net. These missionaries are well posted in the chicanery of the Mormon doctrine. They go to the lower classes of society, to those who are suffering the evils of poverty and represent to them that Utah is the poor man's paradise—God's chosen place where He has commanded all His people to gather. Where the land is free to every Mormon, the gift of the Church! Where all the Saints live in blessed accord! Where there is no poverty, but where all, rich and poor, old and young, live in blissful enjoyment, and each one calls his neighbor brother.

"If the emigrant is too poor to pay his own passage, aid to reach Utah is furnished from the emigration fund. And soon he starts for the Eldorado. He lands at Castle Garden, N. Y., with hundreds of others, under the leadership of some Mormon elder. He is taught that all Americans who are not Latter-day Saints are ungodly Gentiles, whom he should avoid as dangerous persons. He is made to believe that every blessing he now or ever will receive is the gift of God through the Mormon Church. And a refusal to render prompt obedience to the priesthood will bring upon him the most dire calamities. But when he reaches Utah, he finds he has been deceived, that things are altogether different from what was represented. I am told by those who are well-informed in this matter that at least two-thirds of the emigrants are so disappointed that if they could return to their native lands and place themselves as they were before embracing Mormonism, they would gladly do it. But, alas! the Church has no emigration fund *from* Utah. Like the fable of the lion's den and the animals, the tracks go inward but not outward.

"The emigrant is now in the net. Having come to Utah as a matter of policy, he next considers what is the best thing to do. He has been terribly deceived. He has lost the little faith he may have had in the truth of Mormonism; but what to do becomes the practical question with him. He cannot return to the land whence he came. He is, therefore, compelled to remain in Utah. But he soon finds that the power of the Mormon priesthood is an absolute despotism.

"It may be said that I draw on my imagination in this picture. But there are thousands in the Territory who know that the half is not told. Again and again have I had this tale of deception poured into my ear by the deluded ones who have thus been influenced by those who enjoyed their hospitality, and in whose word they had implicit confidence, to leave the home of their childhood and loved friends, with the hope of bettering their condition."

From *The Salt Lake Tribune* I extract the following in regard to the President of the British Mission:—"A Revelation given through GINX to JOHN HENRY, the Bishop of the 17th ward,"—

",Verily, verily, I say unto you, my servant John Henry Smith have I caused to be ordained to a bishopric in my Church, because he is lineally descended of Aaron, and with him I am well pleased. But he hath not yet hearkened to all my words, wherefore I command him to take unto wife, in obedience to my celestial law, one of the daughters of Zion, even the daughter Josephine of my servant Nick, who is Groesbeck of the Wasatch. And I command my maid servant Josephine, who is also called Pet, to cleave unto her John Henry when she shall become his second wife, that I may bestow upon them the blessing I have promised. Even so, Amen.

"I sent a copy of this revelation to our beloved Prophet, that it might be filed away in the archives of the church, and incorporated in the next edition of the Doctrine and Covenants.

"John and Pet are getting ready to go to St. George to be sealed. Bedding and everything of that sort, is being hustled together for them.

LION HOUSE, March 3, 1877.   GINX."

As I hope to meet John Henry Smith when I lecture in Liverpool shortly I prefer to say more then. He certainly will come to my lectures, for I always state in my circulars the following:

☞ *I challenge those Mormon Missionaries who are now in England to refute my Accusations.*

Not one of them has come forward to meet me as yet, I sincerely wish they would. What are they afraid of? I am not a "Danite." The fact is they cannot, dare not meet me, so they have taken their usual course, Defamation of character. They wish the public to believe that I am a "vile fellow" not worthy of credence, so that I may not get audiences. Why vilify? If my statements in regard to them are false, they could easily prove it. But they well know that what I say is true and that I dare not tell it all, for it is too indecent.

THE REMEDY.

As with slavery, the American Government will seek to remedy the Mormon evil by pacific measures and dally with the question until compelled to settle it by force of arms. The sooner an army is sent to Utah to compel obedience to the law the better. For during the delay the Mormon power is increasing. They have already made fast friends of the Indians, and well armed them. They are busy in the Southern States making converts to Mormonism, for whipped on the slave question, the South have little or no love for the U. S. Government, and the Mormons are successfully winning the disaffected Southerners and firing their hearts with the hope that the South, Mormons and Indians combined will sever the union of States, firmly establish the Southern Confederacy, and concentrate a great Mormon and Indian power in the West. I know this to be the Mormon programme, and all they ask is to be let alone till they have time to perfect their plans.

If the American Government wish to avert a bloody struggle they must at once stop Mormon intrigue in the South; place the Indians under complete control, and imprison every Mormon convert that arrives at Castle Garden or any other part of the United States. For foreigners are brought to Utah on purpose to build up the Mormon power and to fight against the Government and people of the United States, and for immoral purposes.

Let Congress pass a law disfranchising all who wear the "Endowment Garment" and have taken the Endowment House Oaths; by those oaths they have virtually disfranchised themselves. All who remain faithful to these oaths must be disloyal to every other Government but that of the Mormon Church.

Then let the Government send plenty of troops to preserve order, and aid in establishing proper schools, free from Mormon dictation. Discharge all Mormon Postmasters and Postmistress so that the people can communicate with their friends without fear of their letters being over-hauled or stopped, and let all the offices of the Territory be held by Non-Mormons.

I would also advise the Government to aid the "Josephites" or true law-abiding Mormons all in its power, to disseminate their principles of law and order among the Utah Fanatics, for there are thousands that will never be satisfied with anything but Mormonism, hence they should be supplied with the best there is. This is the best Remedy I can suggest short of a war of extermination.

A fund should also be raised to assist those who wish to leave the Territory.

No Mormon should be allowed a seat in Congress, for he is there only in the interest of Mormonism.

Take from the Mormon Church the power to perform the marriage ceremony, and have all marriages solemnized by Non-Mormon Judges, or ministers of other denominations. For though I use the words "*Mormon Church*," I do not consider Mormonism a Religion. I have seen enough of it to convince me that it is an Infernal Despotism, which seeks only political power and agrandisement under the cloak of religion. I challenge the whole of the so-called "Church of Jesus Christ of Latter-day Saints" to produce one Christian man or woman among the lot. Among the dupes there are sincere Mormons, but no Christians. A Christian could not remain among them, and thousands who were devout Christians when they joined the Mormons, are to day thorough infidels. We may as well try to find Christians among Mohammedans as among Mormons.

EXTRACT FROM THE PREFACE OF "TELL IT ALL," BY MRS. STENHOUSE.

"Our day has seen a glorious breaking of fetters. The slave-pens of the South have become a nightmare of the past; the auction-block and whipping-post have given place to the church and school-house; and the songs of emancipated millions are heard through our land.

"Shall we not then hope that the hour is come to loose the bonds of a cruel (Mormon) slavery whose chains have cut into the very hearts of thousands of our sisters—a slavery which debases and degrades womanhood, motherhood, and the family?

"Let every happy wife and mother give her sympathy, prayers, and efforts to free her sisters from this degrading bondage. There is a power in combined enlightened sentiment and sympathy before which every form of injustice and cruelty *must* finally go down.

"May He who came to break every yoke hasten this deliverance.
"HARRIET BEECHER STOWE."

W. Hepworth Dixon says:—"In the New Jerusalem you can buy drink at every corner, and find companions of your revels as easily as at St. Giles' in London, or Five Points in New York."—Extract from "*Right Across*," pg.

Father Maloney, a Catholic Priest, went to the Mormon Tabernacle one Sunday afternoon. In a letter to the *Tribune*, he says "The obscenity of language was such that a gentleman of the first social standing in society had to apologize to his lady for taking her to the Tabernacle."

The Western Times of January 14th, re-published from the *Bath Journal* extracts from the sermon of Elder Ross, at that time on a mission to this country. The following is an extract from *The Western Times*:—

"After a few introductory remarks claiming for Mormon missionaries like himself, the direct and positive sanction of the Almighty to proclaim the truth to the world, he said he had come to enlighten the people of England on the subject of marriage. To this end my friends, said he, let us see what the Scriptures say. Now the first marriage I ever heard of, and I don't suppose you heard of any before, was the marriage of Adam and Eve. And what, my friends, do we read of them? Why it is written that the Lord caused Adam to fall into a deep sleep, and while he was asleep, the Lord took from his side a rib, with which he made the woman. And now listen to this, *the Lord brought the woman unto him*. Thus we see my friends, that the marriage was of the Lord's doing; and, according to the Scripture all marriages ought to be like it. [According to the doctrine subsequently supported by the speaker, God should have made Adam not one wife from a rib; but a wife from every rib]. As regarded Abraham, Isaac and Jacob, he continued, they all had more than one wife. Abraham had not only a wife, but he had a handmaiden, Hagar, of whom was born a son, Ishmael. Now Ishmael in our day would be called a bastard; but the lord blessed him as much as he did Isaac, and said his seed should be as the sands of the sea in number. He next came to Jacob, and he had two wives, for he served Lama seven years for Rachael, and he was then deceived by him, for Lama gave him Leah instead so that he served seven years more for Rachael. And, let them remember this, these two wives were so good, and saw so evidently the necessity of God's will being fulfilled, that each of them gave to Jacob a handmaiden, now these men were approved of by the Almighty and so were their actions. Then, they all knew what was written of David—that he was a man after God's own heart, and he had seven wives. Yet when Saul transgressed against the Lord, all the property belonging to Saul was given to David, and amongst it his seven wives, so that David then had fourteen wives; and he was a man after God's own heart. See you that, my friends, exclaimed the preacher with emphasis; and it was particularly noted that the women, old and young, strangely enough, at such points as these, invariably cried "Amen!" Then there was Solomon, he had 700 wives, and not only 700 wives, but 300 concubines—and he was the wisest man that ever lived. So the Scriptnres say; mind my friends 'tisn't I that says it, 'tis the Bible. Now then, look at another point, the Lord's prophecy to Abraham was, that his seed should be as the sands of the sea in number. Now, let any one take one cubic foot of sand and count the number of grains, and he would find that there were more grains of sand than there were people on the whole face of God's earth at the present time. But let them take one foot of sand and compare it with all the sand of the sea. How would that be then? Take that, and see if by monogamy the Lord's prophecy could ever be fulfilled! Therefore, argued he, that not only was polygamy according to God's will; but that procreation would go on, not only in this world, but for ever and ever. Was it not written in the word, that he that findeth a wife findeth a good thing. He thought they had found it so. But if he that found one wife found a good thing; surely he that found many wives must find a better! To show you that our plan of polygamy is better than monogamy (he continued) we have only to look round about and see what is going on. Why, in this enlightened country, as you call it, one fifty of the population is composed of old maids and prostitutes—half old maids and half prostitutes.

Now, every one knows that prostitutes can't fulfil the prophecy of the Lord, and the old maids are not allowed to do it. If they were to try, no one would speak to them and they would be shut out of society. (A complete rumble of "Amens" were heard to follow this sentence.) He continued—he could show them that a great deal of mischief arose from this principle of monogamy in other ways. For instance, many of them calling themselves Christians sent out missionaries to convert the heathens, and hoped by preaching and praying to do so. But what was the result, they couldn't get converts, because of this principle of monogamy. He could give them an instance. A missionary of the Sandwich Islands, had a chief come to him who wanted to be baptized. The missionary said to him, you have got more than one wife. Yes, replied the chief, I've got seven. Well, I can't baptise you then, said the missionary, because the Christian religion only allows one wife at a time. The chief went away, but in a month came again, and asked to be baptised. I told you, said the missionary, I could not baptise you if you had more than one wife, and you have got seven. No I am't got but one now, said the chief. Not but one? asked the missionary, what have you done with the other six? Ate 'um up; ate 'um up, said the chief. Now did'nt that show the mischief monogamy did.

But they would be saying that he had been talking all about the Old Testament, and thought perhaps he could'nt find proof in the New Testament for these things; but he would show them that he could. And, first, it would astonish some of them perhaps when he told them that his firm belief was, and he would prove it, (awful blasphemy) that Jesus Christ was a married man! And not only that he had one wife, but many? for was it not written in the prophecy concerning him that King's daughters should be his companions, and what did it mean when it said women should be companions to a man? Why that they should be his wives to be sure? Moreover, he could prove this again. Was not Jesus Christ called the Everlasting Father in Scripture. Now, he would put it to them, how could he be a father unless he had a wife and children! That affair was settled then.

Now, he dare say, they thought there must be a good deal of cavilling and quarreling where polygamy was practised; but he could tell them that at Salt Lake they were the happiest people on the face of God's earth. He did not mean to say that there never was a dispute, for he would be plain and honest with them, for they (the Mormonites) never spoke but the truth. But disputes did arise occasionally. He remembered a case of two Irishmen. One, named McLeon, was sent on a mission from the Salt Lake, and during his absence another Irishman took advantage of one of his wives. When he came back two women went up to him and said McLeon, so and so, has been too great with your wife. McLeon, as soon as he heard this, went to the other and as soon as he saw him he drew his revolver and shot him through the heart. Then he went to the Elders and told them what he had done, and they all with one accord cried "Amen." And so would I cry amen, exclaimed the speaker, and were a man to do so with a wife of mine, nothing but want of power should prevent me serving him in the same way. That is the way to keep people honest.

After some further remarks in the same style, the speaker concluded by thanking his audience for their attention, and hoping they had been gratified and enlightened on so important a subject. We regret to add that the very general "Amens" which followed, seemed to show that the audience were quite willing to add polygamy to the dark pile of human mockeries already heaped together by the designing leaders of this fanatical sect.

In giving thus far, the substance of our correspondent's report, we have been actuated only by a sense of duty to Society. The crime of polygamy assented to by a pretendedly religious auditory, without a dissentient voice, is a dreadful and an insidious moral evil that ought to be known. No freedom of conscience can sanction an offence against the laws of the land. In a land where polygamy is prohibited no man has a right to preach it.

It will be seen from Dr. Talmage's sermon that he does not take a sentimental view of the question—he believes in drastic measures, and that speedily, for it is obvious that the so-called religious element has no place in the question: the whole system has been proved to be the most gigantic swindle of modern times, and for blasphemy and brutality has no parallel in history. I therefore unhesitatingly say that if there is no corruption in Washington, there will be no more degradation of women in Utah. Public opinion, therefore, must agitate this question. The law, sentimental nonsense aside, is sufficient to reach the evil, and it must never be forgotten that the civil code is sovereign, at any rate in European nations, and the American Government must be stimulated to do its duty. So far as England is concerned, my book and my lectures will prevent the emigration of any more deluded Britishers to Utah—those who go after this will be only the insane and vicious.

Will Americans, who boast of the greatest civilization in the world, permit any longer to prevail in their territory in this nineteenth century such laws as those of Romulus, who made it lawful for husbands to repudiate their wives and sometimes murder them? Like the Romans of old, the Mormons are.

"Wont their pompous pedigree to trace
From Gods—to hide the meanness of their race."

A Heaven on earth they hope to gain, But we do know full well,
Could they their glorious ends attain; This kingdom must be Hell!
Mercurius Pragmaticus, No 2, April 11, 1648.

Rev. Dr. Talmage says:—"I commend Mr. Jarman's important story of Mormon crimes and his own sufferings. He profoundly interested the audience which packed Brooklyn Tabernacle, and many were unable to obtain entrance."

Rev. J. A. Corey, of Maine, says:—"Jarman on American Mahommedanism and White Slavery, cannot fail to startle and interest all. He gave six lectures in our Church."

Rev. R. W. Harlow, Highlandville, Mass., says:—"Mr. Jarman gave six very interesting lectures in our Church, which was densely packed, and the views shown were first-class in every particular."

Rev. O. W. Adams, Cambridge, says:—"Mr. Jarman's lectures are the best ever heard. All should hear the startling facts he reveals. His views are very fine."

Mr. Jarman is a man of ability and draws crowded houses.—*Quincey Patriot.*

The Baptist Church last week, and Music Hall this, were packed. Mr. Jarman is a most graphic and stirring speaker. They are the best lectures and pictures ever given in America.—*Providence Journal.*

Thousands of men and treasure were on hand to rescue Gordon, and no man deserved more of his country. Shall thousands of our countrymen and women live in worse than bondage, when only Christian and philanthropic help is needed on their behalf?

Price of this book in England, 1s.; *in America,* 35 *cents. Booksellers and News Agents write for the most liberal terms to the only Publisher—* W. Jarman, Excelsior Villa, Elmside Park, Mount Pleasant, Exeter, Devon.

APPENDIX A.

The *Journal of Discourses* is published by direct authority of the Mormon Church, as shown by the certificate of Brigham Young and his two Counsellors, at the beginning of volume one, which is too lengthy to give here. The volumes I mostly quote from contain the following Title Page and Preface :—

"JOURNAL OF DISCOURSES delivered by PRESIDENT BRIGHAM YOUNG, HIS TWO COUNSELLORS, THE TWELVE APOSTLES, and others. Reported by G. D. Watt, J. V. Long, and others, and humbly dedicated to the Latter-day Saints in all the world. Liverpool: Edited and Published by Asa Calkin, 42, Islington. London: Latter-day Saints' Book Depot, 35, Jewin Street, City,"

PREFACE.

"The *Journal of Discourses* will become a *complete* journal of all the Sermons delivered by the First Presidency and the Twelve; the choicest Sermons of the Prophet Brigham, and also many choice gems from others of the leading Shepherds of Israel—Gems of Inspiration.

"The *Journal of Discourses* needs no recommendation to make it interesting to every Saint who loves to drink of the streams that flow from the fountain of Eternal Truth. It is made up of the choicest fruit that can be culled from the tree of knowledge, suited to the tastes of all who can appreciate such delicious food. It contains the principles of the Gospel of Salvation to this generation. By the rules and precepts found in it, he that reads with the light of the Holy Spirit may measure himself and the progress he has made in the way of Eternal Life. Like a mirror it will reflect upon the souls of the meek and humble the beams of light which emanate from the presence of the Father. Hypocrites, and workers of iniquity, will find in it the most cutting rebukes, that, when uttered, tingled the ears of those who heard, and caused the wicked to feel the canker worm of conscious guilt, which will gnaw upon their vitals until the day shall come when they have paid the penalty of transgression, and are permitted to reap the blessing of repentance.

As the Kingdom advances, and the Saints emerge from the receding shadows of sectarianism and the prejudices of early education, the revelations of the Lord, through his servants, abound with increasing intelligence, and are more cogent and powerful in administering rebuke to the wicked, comfort and consolation to the Saints, and reveal more distinctly the way-marks which point the way to exaltation and eternal lives.

There is a feast of fat things continually spread in Zion for the faithful, and the longing appetite for celestial food need never go unsatisfied. Some discourses in this Volume mark distinct eras in the progress of the work. Among these we will only notice the discourses on the principles of Consecration, and those in which President Young has administered severe but well-merited rebuke to the General Government of the United States and its corrupt officials, and indicated the future course and policy of Utah.

According to the measure of light in which a man lives, the past serves as an index to the future. The marks which recent events have left on the dial plate of time, indicate a rapid increase in the brilliancy of the light which shines from Zion, and that the voice of "The Lion of Lord" will increase the terror of the wicked, and send trembling and dismay into the camps of the enemy. Let him that would be saved *watch and pray*, and read with an understanding heart the words that flow from the lips of Prophets and Apostles, and, when he has read, *practise the principles they teach*.

APPENDIX B.

The following is the Title page and Preface to "The Mountain Warbler:"—

THE MOUNTAIN WARBLER,

BEING A COLLECTION OF

ORIGINAL SONGS AND RECITATIONS,

BY WILLIAM WILLES,

WITH SELECTIONS FROM OTHER WRITERS,

FOR THE USE OF CHOIRS, SABBATH SCHOOLS AND FAMILIES.

PRINTED AT THE DESERET NEWS BOOK AND JOB ESTABLISHMENT,

SALT LAKE CITY, 1872.

The frequently expressed desire of many friends to publish this work, with the encouraging fact that the authorities of the Church have sanctioned it, are the chief incentives I have for venturing on the undertaking.

My sincere thanks are tendered my poetic friends for the privilege of inserting their popular productions.

I dedicate the work to the service of my Heavenly Father's cause on earth, and to the Superintendents, Teachers and Pupils of the Sabbath and Day Schools, and the Choirs of Deseret.

WILLIAM WILLES.

Salt Lake City, March, 1872.

The following are extracts from a few of the hymns published in the above book:—

TUNE—"*The King of the Cannibal Islands.*"

Come, Mormons, all attention pay, while I attempt to sing my say;
I've Chosen for my text to day, come forward and pay up your tithing.
These may not be the very words which ancient holy writ records;
But Malachi, I think affords a verse with which the sense accords,
It seems that he had cause to scold the Saints or Israelites of old;
In fact, they needed to be told come forward and pay up your tithing.

Just as it was in olden times, with ancient Saints in other climes;
The call is now, bring out your dimes, come forward and pay up your tithing.
Our prophet says, "when elders preach, the law of tithing they should teach,
Pay up themselves, and then beseech all those that come within their reach;"
This makes me now appeal to you, to follow counsel: right pursue;
And whilst all evil you eschew, come forward and pay up your tithing.

(The last verse and chorus of this is on page 160 of this book.)

TUNE—"*King of the Cannibal Islands.*"

Oh dear, I'm sad, I've got the blues, I've lately heard some dreadful news,
I really tremble in my shoes, 'tis all about the Mormons!
For sure they are the strangest set, that ever in this world were met,
They live in a place called Deseret, in the midst of the Rocky Mountains.

In all the nations of the world, these Mormons have their flag unfurled,
And sent their missionaries round to spread their awful doctrines.
It matters not which way we turn, nothing but Mormons we discern,
I wonder how there came to be ' So many beastly Mormons.'

These Mormons marry many wives, and every man among them strives
To raise the greatest crowd of boys, to thrash the wicked Gentiles.
And men and women all agree to Brigham they'll obedient be,
And at his little finger's crook, they'll bring outsiders all to book.

So, now I think you'll all agree, it is a shocking thing to see
So many people led astray by their "beastly abominations."
I wish that Uncle Sam would send the troops—and make these Mormons quickly bend
To Christian institutions; for if he don't we're all undone,
As sure as light is in the sun ; the Mormons they will take away
Our glorious state and nation.

(For the balance and chorus see page 35.)

TUNE—"*Bonny Breast Knots.*"

What peace and joy pervades the soul, and sweet sensations thro' me roll,
And love and peace my heart console, since first I met the Mormons.
They sing the folly of the wise, sectarian precepts they despise;
A heaven far beyond the skies, is never sought by Mormons.

CHORUS :—Hey, the merry, O, the busy, hey the sturdy Mormons;
I never knew what joy was, till I became a Mormon.

At night the Mormons do convene, to chat awhile and sing a hymn;
And one, perchance, repeat a rhyme he made about the Mormons.
The Mormon fathers love to see their Mormon families all agree;
The prattling infant on the knee cries "Daddy, I'm a Mormon."

As youth in Israel once decried to wed with those that heaven denied,
So youth among us now have cried "we'll marry none but Mormons."
High be our heaven, the Mormons cry, our place of birth and where we die;
Celestialize and purify this earth for perfect Mormons.

TUNE—"*So early in the morning.*"

There is a people in the West, the world call Mormonites in jest,
The only people who can say, we have the truth, and own its sway.
Away in Utah's valleys, away in Utah's valleys,
Away in Utah's valleys, the chambers of the Lord.

The truth in many lands is known, in power the Lord rolls forth the stone,
Which, from the mountains has gone forth, and will in time fill all the earth.
Go forth from Utah's valleys, &c.
Go forth, &c., the chambers of the Lord.

And all ye Saints where'er you be, from bondage try to be set free,
Escape unto fair Zion's land, and thus fulfil the Lord's command,
And help to build up Zion, &c.
And help, &c., before the Lord appear.

TUNE—"*The days that we went Gipsying.*"

The Mormon Creed I'll now explain, which you may quickly learn,
'Tis "mind your own business," and that's no small concern.
For all the people in the world that I have ever known,
Are apt to mind their neighbours, and oft forget their own.

CHORUS :—So let us mind the Mormon creed, and then we all shall thrive,
Shall hide a multitude of sins, and save our souls alive.

The Mormons oft forget their creed, altho' it is so plain,
And meddle where they have no need, and cause much grief and pain.
Whereas, if they would only heed the Spirit's warning voice,
They'd find that this is just the creed that's worthy of their choice.

TUNE—"*Disappointed Milkman.*"

I'm a merry-hearted Mormon, by the truth I'm set free,
And I wish all the world were as happy as me;
I've started for salvation and hope I shall win,
So with this explanation my song will begin.
CHORUS:—For the Gospel is restored to the earth once again,
    And the way of salvation to man is made plain.

Sometimes when a calm doth come over the deep,
Our nets we spread out, and the fish they will leap,
And into the great net the fish they will throng,
So we pull them on board and bring them along.

We get garfish and blackfish, and minnows and whales,
And sharks in abundance, and good fish ne'er fails;
There are flying-fish and star-fish and suckers and trout,
And all sorts of fish from the net we take out.

We've cat-fish and dog-fish and lobsters and crabs,
And cuttle-fish and devil-fish and thorn-backs and dabs;
Many scorpions and pollywogs and crocodiles grim,
With shoals of big sea-hogs fill the net to the brim.

And now I say to you fish who in the net have been caught,
I hope you are the true fish that can never be bought;
Else old Satan will buy you and you'll slip through the sieve,
And go to destruction as sure as you live.

TUNE:—"*Aunt Sally.*"

They cry "deluded Mormons" in all the world around,
And the reason why they do is very far from sound;
It's only just a cry that is echoed from tongue to tongue,
Of these awful wicked Mormons, and their leader, Brigham Young.
CHORUS:—True Saints rally, around the standard come,
    Away in Utah's valleys, our lovely mountain home.

The world is tied in bundles before the burning day,
The stone it swiftly trundles, and does its power display.
The Mormons they are growing in everything that's good,
And Babylon is going down as they did in Noah's flood.

There's nothing can destroy us if we are firm and true,
Tho' wicked men among us, the Lord will trot them through,
He will not leave a grease-spot to mark the place they trod,
But hurl them to destruction beneath the Iron Rod.

THE DEVILS' HYMN.

One spot on the earth is free to Mormon virtue,
And may it gain a wider reign, As sin melts away;
Where happy men and women too, With what the Gentiles never knew,
Can know just what to do, Oh, come, come to-day.

All over the globe, good deeds will never hurt you,
But, make you great in Church and State, Where truth bears the sway.
Like as it were at Noah's Flood, The prophet's voice and martyr'd blood,
By Saints are understood, Oh, come, come to-day.

The great day has come with Saints and angels smiling,
With prophets true and light anew, To point out the way;
In thrilling tones of harmony, We'll manifest our constancy,
In God, truth, and liberty, Oh, come, come to-day.
[The Endowment House Devil.]   W. W. PHELPS.

TUNE.—"*Red, White, and Red.*"

In the vales of the mountains The Saints in the West;
Have reared up a kingdom Where safely they rest;
But the wicked feel envy And strife in their heart,
They wish to divide us And rend us apart.

CHORUS:—Hurrah, hurrah, we've nothing to dread,
      Three cheers for the Quorum by whom we are led.

Ever since the true prophet Came forth to the world,
The shafts of the wicked Have at us been hurled;
But the more they oppose us, The more do we grow;
And the blessings of Heaven To us ever flow.

The destruction which now Threatens every land,
Might all be averted, Could they understand.
The man who is placed As Vicegerent of God,
And all would be saved From the uplifted rod.

The school of experience, The dearest of all,
Will bring to the nations A terrible fall.
They all are refusing The offers of peace,
They surely must perish, And Zion increase.

APPENDIX C.

Extract from page 2 of *The Seer* the "*First Epistle of* ORSON PRATT *to the Saints scattered throughout the United States and British Provinces—Greeting:*—" DEAR BRETHREN: Having been appointed by the First Presidency, and that the Saints may more fully learn the nature of my mission among them, I will insert the following LETTER OF APPOINTMENT:—" This certifies that Professor Orson Pratt, one of the Apostles of the Church of Jesus Christ of Latter-Day Saints, is appointed by us to preside over the affairs of the Church throughout the United States and the British Provinces; and also, to write and Publish Periodicals, Pamphlets, Books, &c., illustrative of the principles and doctrines of the Church, and to do all other things necessary for the advancement of the work of the Lord among all nations. ELDER PRATT is authorized and required to receive and collect tithing of the Saints through all his field of labors: and we request the Elders and other officers and members of the Church to give diligent heed to his counsels as the words of life and salvation, and assist him to funds to enable him to travel, print, establish book agencies, and perform all other duties of his calling, and the blessings of our Father in Heaven shall rest upon them. BRO. PRATT is one of the Perpetual Emigrating Fund Company, and is hereby appointed and authorized to act as Travelling Agent, and he is instructed to collect, and disburse and aid to promote the emigration of poor Saints to the valleys of the mountains.

"BRO. ORSON PRATT is too well and favorably known to need any testimonial further than his own presence and acquaintance to secure the esteem and confidence of all among whom his lot may be cast. His acquirements and attainments are of the highest order, and possessing, as he eminently does, every requisite of an honorable and high-minded gentleman, we take great pleasure in recommending him to the kindness and consideration of all good men.
BRIGHAM YOUNG,
HEBER C. KIMBALL,
WILLARD RICHARDS,
Presidency of said Church.

"The principal features of my mission are contained in the foregoing letter:—'Awake then, O awake! flee to the mountains for refuge! for a day of trouble is at hand—a day of fierce battle and war—a day of mourning and lamentation for widows and orphans whose husbands and fathers shall fall in battle; it shall be the day of the Lord's controversy for His people * * *

"The time is drawing nigh for these things to be fulfilled; for this nation have rejected the Book of Mormon; they have rejected the Church of Christ which the Lord in mercy established in their midst. * * *

"The Saints are respectfully invited to subscribe for *The Seer*, that through its pages they may learn more perfectly their duties, and have a knowledge of the times, and seasons, and purposes of the Most High in regard to the generation in which they live * * * that they may be well instructed in all the great principles of eternal salvation, that through their faithfulness to the same they may enter into the fulness of celestial glory. With the most anxious desire for your welfare, I subscribe myself your humble servant and brother in the bonds of the Gospel Covenant. ORSON PRATT.

Washington, December 20th, 1852.

APPENDIX D.

Affidavit of Mrs. Mary Ettie V. Smith, relating to certain matters in the Territory of Utah.

"State of New York, ⎫
 Livingstone County. ⎭ *ss.*

"Mary Ettie V. Smith, late of Great Salt Lake City, in the Territory of Utah; and now of Stuben county, in the State of New York, being duly sworn deposes and says: That she has been a resident of said Territory for about five years; and has been a member of the community of Mormons for 15 years: That she is at present 28 years of age; that she was a believer in good faith in Mormonism, until she discovered, after going to Utah, the principal business of the Prophet Brigham Young, and the other heads of the Mormon Church to be the commission of crimes of the most atrocious character; among which may be included robbery, murder and treason to the General Government, and a large number of lesser crimes: and that she was held a prisoner there for a long time, against her wish and consent, after she had expressed a desire to return to the U. S.; and that a large number of persons, particularly women, have been, and are, as she verily believes, so held and restrained, and debarred of the exercise of their personal liberty; and that many of these persons, were they to be assured of the protection of the Government, could and would give such evidence before a legal tribunal, as would, if such tribunal were unawed, and uncontrolled by the Mormons or their influence, lead to the conviction of Brigham Young, and many, and probably most of the heads of the Church, of such crimes as are punishable by death.

"And this deponent further says that as an illustration of the above, she will state, that in the year 1853, she was present when Brigham Young, General Wells, and John and Wiley Norton, discussed and adopted a plan for the murder of Wallace Alonzo Clarke Bowman, an American citizen, at the time engaged in the Mexican trade, and in the quiet and legal pursuit of his lawful business: and that said Bowman was so murdered by direction of said Brigham Young; and after the manner determined upon as aforesaid. That she saw and recognized his body after his death; and that she cut a lock of said Bowman's hair after his death, and gave the same to Dr. Hurt, at the time Indian agent of the Territory.

"That John Norton and James Furguson, now believed to be living at Salt Lake, told this deponent in the presence of various other persons, to wit: Jane Furguson, (wife No. 2 of said Furguson) and others, that they, the said Norton and Furguson shot the said Bowman, in Salt Creek canon: that a large amount of property was taken from said Bowman, by the said Mormons: and that at this time, said Brigham Young, was governor of the said Territory of Utah.

"That the facts above stated, with reference to the imprisonment, robbery and final murder of said Bowman, can be proved by a large number of reliable witnesses now in Utah; and one besides herself now in the state of New York. That the account given of the same in her Narrative, now about to be published, is substantially true: and that among many others, the following persons would swear to these facts, if properly approached, and well assured of protection against the assassination of the 'Danites,' to wit: ———: ——— and ——— ——— the two wives of ——— ——— and the mother of ———; (———) and ——— ———, wife of ——— ———; ——— ——— wife No. 2 of ——— ———; ——— ———, and his wife, ——— ———; and others; all living in Great Salt Lake City.

"This Deponent further says, that she was present at another time, in the year 1851; when the said Brigham Young, governor of the Territory of Utah, 'counselled' and directed the robbery of a Dr. Roberts; and that afterwards she was present, when the said Dr. Roberts was robbed, at night, on the public highway, in pursuance of the said instructions of the said Prophet and Gov. Young; that said robbery was committed by Captain James Brown, now living at Ogden city, in said Territory, and Hiram Clauson, of Great Salt Lake City; and in presence of Ellen, the wife of said Clauson, and in presence of this deponent; and that she has good reason to fear the said Roberts was afterwards murdered by said Brown and Clauson: that she can furnish proof of many similar crimes; an account of which she deems it unnecessary to give in detail at this time; and further this deponent saith not."

(Signed)
MARY ETTIE V. SMITH.

Subscribed and sworn this 21st day of August, 1857, before me.
CHARLES R. KERN,
Justice of the Peace.

APPENDIX E.

REVELATION GIVEN TO JOSEPH SMITH, NAUVOO, JULY 12th, 1843.

Verily, thus saith the Lord unto you, my servant Joseph, that inasmuch as you have inquired of my hand to know and understand wherein I, the Lord, justified my servants Abraham, Isaac, and Jacob; as also Moses, David, and Solomon, my servants, as touching the principle and doctrine of their having many wives and concubines: Behold! and lo, I am the Lord thy God, and will answer thee as touching this matter: therefore prepare thy heart to receive and obey the instructions which I am about to give unto you; for all those who have this law revealed unto them must obey the same; for behold! I reveal unto you a new and an everlasting covenant, and if ye abide not that covenant, then are ye damned; for no one can reject this covenant and be permitted to enter into my glory; for all who will have a blessing at my hands shall abide the law which was appointed for that blessing, and the conditions thereof, as was instituted from before the foundations of the world; and as pertaining to the new and everlasting covenant, it was instituted for the fulness of my glory; and he that receiveth a fulness thereof, must and shall abide the law, or he shall be damned, saith the Lord God.

And verily I say unto you, that the conditions of this law are these: All covenants, contracts, bonds, obligations; oaths, vows, performances, connections, associations, or expectations, that are not made, and entered into, and sealed, by the Holy Spirit of promise, of him who is anointed, both as well for time and for all eternity, and that, too, most holy, by revelation and commandment, through the medium of mine anointed, whom I have appointed on the earth to hold this power (and I have appointed unto my servant Joseph to hold this power in the last days, and there is never but one on the earth at a time on whom this power and the keys of this priesthood are conferred), are of no efficacy, virtue, or force in and after the resurrection from the dead; for all contracts that are not made unto this end, have an end when men are dead.

Behold! mine house is a house of order, saith the Lord God, and not a house of confusion. Will I accept of an offering, saith the Lord, that is not made in my name? Or will I receive at your hands that which I have not appointed? And will I appoint unto you, saith the Lord, except it be by law, even as I and my Father ordained unto you, before the world was? I am the Lord thy God, and I give unto you this commandment, that no man shall come unto the Father but by me, or by my word, which is my law, saith the Lord; and everything that is in the world, whether it be ordained of men, by, thrones, or principalities, or powers, or things of name, whatsoever they may be, that are not by me, or by my word, saith the Lord, shall be thrown down, and shall not remain after men are dead, neither in nor after the resurrection, saith the Lord your God; for whatsoever things remaineth are by me, and whatsoever things are not by me, shall be shaken and destroyed.

Therefore, if a man marry him a wife in the world, and he marry her not by me, nor by my word, and he covenant with her so long as he is in the world, and she with him their covenant and marriage is not of force when they are dead, and when they are out of the world; therefore they are not bound by any law when they are out of the world; therefore, when they are out of the world, they neither marry nor are given in marriage, but are appointed angels in heaven, which angels are ministering servants, to minister for those who are worthy of a far more, and an exceeding, and an eternal weight of glory; for these angels did not abide my law, therefore they can not be enlarged, but remain separately, and singly, without exaltation, in their saved condition, to all eternity, and from henceforth are not gods, but are angels of God forever and ever.

And again, verily I say unto you, if a man marry a wife, and make a covenant with her for time and for all eternity, if that covenant is not by me or by my word, which is my law, and is not sealed by the Holy Spirit of promise, through him whom I have anointed and appointed unto this power, then it is not valid, neither of force when they are out of the world, because they are not joined by me, saith the Lord, neither by my word; when they are out of the world, it can not be received there, because the angels and the gods are appointed there, by whom they can not pass; they can not, therefore, inherit my glory, for my house is a house of order, saith the Lord God.

And again, verily I say unto you, if a man marry a wife by my word, which is my law, and by the new and everlasting covenant, and it is sealed unto them by the Holy Spirit of promise, by him who is anointed, unto whom I have appointed this power and the keys of this priesthood, and it shall be said unto them, Ye shall come forth in the first resurrection; and shall inherit thrones, kingdoms, principalities, and powers, dominions, heights and depths, then shall it be written in the Lamb's Book of Life that he shall commit no murder whereby to shed innocent blood, and if ye abide in my covenant and commit no murder whereby to shed innocent blood, it shall be done unto them in all things whatsoever my servant hath put upon them in time and through all eternity; and shall be of full force when they are out of the world, and they shall pass by the angels and the gods, which are set there, to their exaltation and glory in all things, as hath been sealed upon their heads, which glory shall be a fullness and a continuation of the seeds forever and ever.

Then shall they be gods, because they have no end; because they have all power, and the angels are subject unto them

Verily, verily, I say unto you, except ye abide my law of Polygamy ye can not attain to this glory; for strait is the gate, and narrow the way, that leadeth unto the exaltation and continuation of the lives, and few there be that find it, because ye receive me not in the world, neither do ye know me. But if ye receive me in the world, then shall ye know me, and shall receive your exaltation, that where I am, ye shall be also. This is eternal lives, to know the only wise and true God, and Jesus Christ whom he hath sent. I am he. Receive ye, therefore. my law. Broad is the gate, and wide the way that leadeth to the death, and many there are that go in thereat, because they receive me not, neither do they abide in my law.

Verily, verily, I say unto you, if a man marry a wife according to my word, and they are sealed by the Holy Spirit of promise according to mine appointment, and he or she shall commit any sin or transgression of the new and everlasting covenant whatever, and all manner of blasphemies, and if they commit no murder wherein they shed innocent blood, yet they shall come forth in the first resurrection, and enter into their exaltation; but they shall be destroyed in the flesh, and shall be delivered unto the buffetings of Satan, unto the day of redemption, saith the Lord God.

The blasphemy against the Holy Ghost, which shall not be forgiven in the world nor out of the world, is in that ye commit murder, wherein ye shed innocent blood, and assent unto my death, after ye have received my new and everlasting covenant, saith the Lord God; and he that abideth not this law can in no wise enter into my glory, but shall be damned, saith the Lord.

I am the Lord thy God, and will give unto thee the law of my holy priesthood, as was ordained by me and my Father before the world was. Abraham received all things, whatsoever he received, by revelation and commandment, by my word, saith the Lord, and hath entered into his exaltation, and sitteth upon his throne.

Abraham received promises concerning his seed, and of the fruit of his loins—from whose loins ye are, viz., my servant Joseph—which were to continue so long as they were in the world; and as touching Abraham and his seed out of the world, they should continue; both in the world and out of the world should they continue as innumerable as the stars; or, if ye were to count the sand upon the sea-shore, ye could not number them. This promise is yours also, because ye are of Abraham, and the promise was made unto Abraham, and by this law are the continuation of the works of my Father, wherein he glorifieth himself. Go ye, therefore, and do the works of Abraham; enter ye into my law (of Polygamy) and ye shall be saved. But if ye enter not into my law, ye can not receive the promises of my Father, which he made unto Abraham.

God commanded Abraham, and Sarah gave Hagar to Abraham to wife. And why did she do it? Because this was the law, and from Hagar sprang many people. This, therefore, was fulfilling, among other things, the promises. Was Abraham,, therefore, under condemnation? Verily, I say unto you, Nay; for the Lord commanded it. Abraham was commanded to offer his son Isaac; nevertheless, it was written, Thou shalt not kill. Abraham, however, did not refuse, and it was accounted unto him for righteousness.

Abraham received concubines, and they bare him children, and it was accounted unto him for righteousness, because they were given unto him, and he abode in my law: as Isaac also, and Jacob, did none other things than that which they were commanded; and because they did none other things than that which they were commanded, they have entered into their exaltation, according to the promises, and sit upon thrones; and are not angels, but are gods. David also received many wives and concubines, as also Solomon, and Moses my servant, as also many others of my servants, from the beginning of creation until this time, and in nothing did they sin, save in those things which they received not of me.

David's wives and concubines were given unto him of me by the hand of Nathan my servant, and others of the prophets who had the keys of this power; and in none of these things did he sin against me, save in the case of Uriah and his wife; and, therefore, he hath fallen from his exaltation, and received his portion; and he shall not inherit them out of the world, for I gave them unto another, saith the Lord.

I am the Lord thy God, and I gave unto thee, my servant Joseph, an appointment, and restore all things; ask what ye will, and it shall be given unto you, according to my word; and as ye have asked concerning adultery, verily, verily, I say unto you, if a man receiveth a wife in the new and everlasting covenant, and if she be with another man, and I have not appointed unto her by the Holy Anointing, she hath committed adultery, and shall be destroyed. If she be not in the new and everlasting covenant, and she be with another man, she has committed adultery; and if her husband be with another woman, and he was under a vow, he hath broken his vow, and hath committed adultery; and if she hath not committed adultery, but is innocent, and hath not broken her vow, and she knoweth it, and I reveal it unto you, my servant Joseph, then shall you have power, by the power of my holy priesthood, to take her, and give her unto him that hath not committed adultery, but hath been faithful; for he shall be made ruler over many; for I have conferred upon you the keys and power of the priesthood, wherein I restore all things, and make known unto you all things in due time.

And verily, verily, I say unto you, that whatsoever you seal on earth shall be sealed in heaven; and whatsoever you bind on earth, in my name and by my word, saith the Lord, it shall be eternally bound in the heavens; and whosoever sins you remit on earth, shall be remitted eternally in the heavens; and whosoever sins you retain on earth, shall be retained in heaven.

And again, verily, I say whomsoever you bless, I will bless; and whomsoever you curse, I will curse, saith the Lord; for I, the Lord, am thy God.

And again, verily, I say unto you, my servant Joseph, that whatsoever you give on earth, and to whomsoever you give any one on earth, by my word and according to my law, it shall be visited with blessings and not cursings, and with my power, saith the Lord, and shall be without condemnation on earth and in heaven, for I am the Lord thy God, and will be with thee even unto the end of the world, and through all eternity; for verily I seal upon you your exaltation, and prepare a throne for you in the kingdom of my Father, with Abraham your father. Behold! I have seen your sacrifices, and will forgive all your sins; I have seen your sacrifices, in obedience to that which I have told you; go, therefore, and I make a way for your escape, as I accepted the offering of Abraham, of his son Isaac.

Verily, I say unto you, a commandment I give unto mine handmaid, Emma Smith, your wife, whom I have given unto you, that she stay herself, and partake not of that which I commanded you to offer unto her; for I did it, saith the Lord, to prove you all, as I did Abraham, and that I might require an offering at your hand by covenant and sacrifice; and let mine handmaid, Emma Smith, receive all those that have been given unto my servant Joseph, and who are virtuous and pure before me; and those who are not pure, and have said they were pure, shall be destroyed, saith the Lord God; for I am the Lord thy God, and ye shall obey my voice; and I give unto my servant Joseph that he shall be made ruler over many things, for he hath been faithful over a few things, and from henceforth I will strengthen him.

And I command mine handmaid, Emma Smith, to abide and cleave unto my servant Joseph, and to none else. But if she will not abide this commandment, she shall be destroyed, saith the Lord, for I am the Lord thy God, and will destroy her if she abide not in my law; but if she will not abide this commandment, then shall my servant Joseph do all things for her, as he hath said; and I will bless him, and multiply him, and give unto him an hundred-fold in this world, of fathers and mothers, brothers and sisters, houses and lands, wives and children, and crowns of eternal lives in the eternal worlds. And again, verily, I say, let mine handmaid forgive my servant Joseph his trespasses, and then shall she be forgiven her trespasses, wherein she hath trespassed against me; and I, the Lord thy God, will bless her, and multiply her, and make her heart to rejoice.

And again, I say, let not my servant Joseph put his property out of his hands, lest an enemy come and destroy him—for Satan seeketh to destroy—for I am the Lord thy God, and he is my servant; and behold! and lo, I am with him, as I was with Abraham thy father, even unto his exaltation and glory.

Now, as touching the law of the priesthood, there are many things pertaining thereunto. Verily, if a man be called of my Father, as was Aaron, by mine own voice, and by the voice of him that sent me, and I have endowed him with the keys of the power of this priesthood, if he do any thing in my name, and according to my law, and by my word, he will not commit sin, and I will justify him. Let no one, therefore, set on my servant Joseph, for I will justify him; for he shall do the sacrifice which I require at his hands, for his transgressions, saith the Lord your God.

And again, as pertaining to the law of the priesthood: if any man espouse a virgin and desire to espouse another, and the first give her consent, and if he espouse the second and they are virgins, and have vowed to no other man then is he justified; he can not commit adultery, for they are given unto him; for he can not commit adultery with that that belongeth unto him; and if he have ten virgins given unto him by this law, he can not commit adultery, for they belong to him, and they are given unto him; therefore is he justified. But if one or either of the ten virgins, after she is espoused, shall be with another man, she has committed adultery, and shall be destroyed; for they are given unto him to multiply and replenish the earth, according to my commandment, and to fulfil the promise which was given by my Father before the foundation of the world, and for their exaltation in the eternal worlds, that they may bear the souls of men; for herein is the work of my Father continued, that he may be glorified.

And again, verily, verily, I say unto you, if any man have a wife who holds the keys of this power, and he teaches unto her the law of my priesthood as pertaining to these things, then shall she believe and administer unto him, or she shall be destroyed, saith the Lord your God; for I will destroy her; for I will magnify my name upon all those who receive and abide in my law. Therefore it shall be lawful in me, if she receive not this law, for him to receive all things whatsoever I, the Lord his God, will give unto him, because she did not believe and administer unto him according to my word; and she then becomes the transgressor, and he is exempt from the law of Sarah, who administered unto Abraham according to the law, when I commanded Abraham to take Hagar to wife. And now, as pertaining to this law, verily, verily, I say unto you, I will reveal more unto you hereafter, therefore let this suffice for the present. Behold! I am Alpha and Omega. AMEN.

www.ingramcontent.com/pod-product-compliance
Lightning Source LLC
Chambersburg PA
CBHW020239170426
43202CB00008B/153